Cisco Unity Fundamentals

Brian Morgan, CCIE No. 4865

Moises Gonzalez

Cisco Press

800 East 96th Street
Indianapolis, IN 46240 USA

Cisco Unity Fundamentals

Brian Morgan, CCIE No. 4865 and Moises Gonzalez

Copyright © 2005 Cisco Systems, Inc.

Published by:

Cisco Press
800 East 96th Street
Indianapolis, IN 46240 USA

Printed in the United States of America 2 3 4 5 6 7 8 9 0

Second Printing February 2006

Library of Congress Cataloging-in-Publication Number: 2002104804

ISBN: 1-58705-098-6

Warning and Disclaimer

This book is designed to provide information about the fundamental aspects of Cisco Unity messaging services. Every effort has been made to make this book as complete and as accurate as possible, but no warranty or fitness is implied.

The information is provided on an "as is" basis. The authors, Cisco Press, and Cisco Systems, Inc. shall have neither liability nor responsibility to any person or entity with respect to any loss or damages arising from the information contained in this book or from the use of the discs or programs that may accompany it.

The opinions expressed in this book belong to the author and are not necessarily those of Cisco Systems, Inc.

Trademark Acknowledgments

All terms mentioned in this book that are known to be trademarks or service marks have been appropriately capitalized. Cisco Press or Cisco Systems, Inc., cannot attest to the accuracy of this information. Use of a term in this book should not be regarded as affecting the validity of any trademark or service mark.

Corporate and Government Sales

Cisco Press offers excellent discounts on this book when ordered in quantity for bulk purchases or special sales.

For more information please contact:
U.S. Corporate and Government Sales
1-800-382-3419, corpsales@pearsontechgroup.com

For sales outside the U.S. please contact:
International Sales, international@pearsoned.com

Feedback Information

At Cisco Press, our goal is to create in-depth technical books of the highest quality and value. Each book is crafted with care and precision, undergoing rigorous development that involves the unique expertise of members from the professional technical community.

Readers' feedback is a natural continuation of this process. If you have any comments regarding how we could improve the quality of this book, or otherwise alter it to better suit your needs, you can contact us through e-mail at feedback@ciscopress.com. Please make sure to include the book title and ISBN in your message.

We greatly appreciate your assistance.

Publisher	John Wait
Editor-in-Chief	John Kane
Executive Editor	Jim Schachterle
Cisco Marketing Program Manager	Nannette M. Noble
Cisco Representative	Anthony Wolfenden
Production Manager	Patrick Kanouse
Development Editor	Dan Young
Project Editor	Marc Fowler
Copy Editor	Bill McManus
Technical Editors	Jeremy Cioara, Michael Ciarfello, Jim Rzegocki, and Martin Walshaw
Team Coordinator	Tammi Barnett
Book and Cover Designer	Louisa Adair
Production, Composition, and Indexing	Argosy Publishing

CISCO SYSTEMS

Corporate Headquarters	**European Headquarters**	**Americas Headquarters**	**Asia Pacific Headquarters**
Cisco Systems, Inc.	Cisco Systems International BV	Cisco Systems, Inc.	Cisco Systems, Inc.
170 West Tasman Drive	Haarlerbergpark	170 West Tasman Drive	Capital Tower
San Jose, CA 95134-1706	Haarlerbergweg 13-19	San Jose, CA 95134-1706	168 Robinson Road
USA	1101 CH Amsterdam	USA	#22-01 to #29-01
www.cisco.com	The Netherlands	www.cisco.com	Singapore 068912
Tel: 408 526-4000	www-europe.cisco.com	Tel: 408 526-7660	www.cisco.com
800 553-NETS (6387)	Tel: 31 0 20 357 1000	Fax: 408 527-0883	Tel: +65 6317 7777
Fax: 408 526-4100	Fax: 31 0 20 357 1100		Fax: +65 6317 7799

Cisco Systems has more than 200 offices in the following countries and regions. Addresses, phone numbers, and fax numbers are listed on the
Cisco.com Web site at www.cisco.com/go/offices.

Argentina • Australia • Austria • Belgium • Brazil • Bulgaria • Canada • Chile • China PRC • Colombia • Costa Rica • Croatia • Czech Republic Denmark • Dubai, UAE • Finland • France • Germany • Greece • Hong Kong SAR • Hungary • India • Indonesia • Ireland • Israel • Italy Japan • Korea • Luxembourg • Malaysia • Mexico • The Netherlands • New Zealand • Norway • Peru • Philippines • Poland • Portugal Puerto Rico • Romania • Russia • Saudi Arabia • Scotland • Singapore • Slovakia • Slovenia • South Africa • Spain • Sweden Switzerland • Taiwan • Thailand • Turkey • Ukraine • United Kingdom • United States • Venezuela • Vietnam • Zimbabwe

About the Authors

Brian Morgan, CCIE No. 4865, is a certified Cisco Systems instructor as well as a CCSI certified to teach ICND, BSCI, CUSE, CUSA, CVOICE, BCRAN, CBCR, CIT CATM, and various customized CCIE Bootcamp courses.

He's been active in the networking industry for more than 14 years. Prior to teaching, Brian spent a number of years with IBM in Network Services where he attained MCNE and MCSE certifications. He was involved with a number of larger LAN/WAN installations for many of IBM's Fortune 500 clients.

Brian is currently working with Paranet Solutions, a renowned nationwide professional services firm.

Brian is the proud father of fraternal twin girls (Amanda and Emma) and husband to Beth. His hobbies include spending time with his family and friends as well as scuba diving and writing the occasional book.

Moises Gonzalez is a Cisco AVVID test engineer for the Cisco System IP Communications Business Unit, where he focuses on testing Cisco CallManager with Cisco Unity and other voice-mail systems. Since joining Cisco, Moises has written comprehensive technical documentation for Cisco Systems. He has more than 10 years of networking and telecommunications experience. Prior to joining Cisco Systems, Moises tested and provided third-level support for the Unity product as well as other products. Moises has also been an instructor for CTI-based solutions. He has an MCSE, CNE, Unity Engineer certifications, and has passed the Cisco IP Telephony (CIPT) exam.

About the Technical Reviewers

Jeremy Cioara, CCIE No. 11,727 is a Cisco network instructor at Interface Technical Training (www.interfacett.com), where he teaches courses on IP Telephony, CCNP, and CCIE lab preparation. He has focused on network technologies for more than a decade. During this time, he has achieved many certifications including CCIE, MCSE, and CNE. Some of his field work includes network design and consulting at MicroAge, Qwest, and Health Dialog. He is currently focusing on technical instruction and authoring on topics including Cisco IP telephony, routing, and switching.

Mike Ciarfello is a senior consultant for an upstate New York Cisco GOLD certified Partner network consulting and integration firm. Throughout his more than 8 years of industry experience, Mike has been through the gauntlet of the computer industry, starting with PC and application support, then moving into the network operating systems arena, in which he obtained his Novell Master CNE. He then transitioned into the LAN and WAN arena, obtaining CCNA, CCDA, CCDP, CCNP, and CCIE written certifications or tests. Mike currently specializes in voice over IP and IP Telephony solutions and is holding or pursuing certifications from multiple vendors. Mike also has a very broad array of clients ranging from small to medium businesses to Fortune 500 companies, including various national and international enterprise clients, telecommunications providers, and Internet-backbone providers.

Jim Rzegocki is the training manager for the Cisco Enterprise Communications Software Business Unit (ECSBU), the group within Cisco that makes Cisco Unity. He is responsible for developing training materials and certification exams for Cisco Unity, as well as providing classes and training material for Cisco Personal Assistant. Jim also works closely with ECSBU trainers to provide customized, focused classes on Cisco Unity on a worldwide basis for Cisco employees, partners, and end users.

Jim has been at Cisco for 3 years and has worked for more than 16 years developing training materials for computer hardware and software companies. He has been a professional educator for 29 years with certification to teach in three states.

Martin Walshaw, CCIE No. 5629,CISSP, CCNP, CCDP, CCSP is a Systems Engineer working for Cisco Systems in the Enterprise Line of Business in South Africa. His areas of specialty include Convergence, Security & Content Delivery Networking, which keeps him busy both night and day. During the last 15 years or so Martin has dabbled in many aspects of the IT Industry, ranging from Programming in RPG III and Cobol to PC Sales. When Martin is not working, he likes to spend all of his available time with his patient wife Val, and his sons Joshua and Callum. Without their patience, understanding and support projects such as this would not be possible.

Acknowledgments

Brian Morgan:

I would like to give special recognition to Amy Moss. Her understanding and patient assistance throughout this project is nothing short of miraculous.

Thanks to Moises Gonzalez for picking up the project and making it what it is. He put in a great deal of effort above and beyond the call.

A big "thank you" goes out to the production team for this book. Jim Schachterle, Christopher Cleveland, and Dan Young have been incredibly professional (not to mention patient) and a pleasure to work with. I couldn't have asked for a finer team. It was great to be reunited with Chris and Dan for this project.

I'd like to acknowledge the work of the technical edit team of Jeremy Cioara, Michael Ciarfello, Jim Rzegocki, and Martin Walshaw.

Although mentioned in the dedication, I think I'd be remiss in failing to acknowledge the support and encouragement provided by my wife, Beth, throughout the duration of the project.

Moises Gonzalez:

I would like to acknowledge the following people: Michael Kale, Michael McCann, Bill Baldwin, Chris McAlpin, Jeff Lindborg, Marquis Harper, Jennifer Baldwin, Steve Oliver, Betty Mai, Dennis Kurian, Jack Lungrattanasang, and T.J. Garner for their technical expertise; Cliff Chew, Nancy Griffin, and Becky Rodriguez for their support; and Anne Smith and Dan Young for guiding me through the development of this book.

Both authors would like to acknowledge the following contributors to documents that were important to the quality of this book: John Albee, Peter Bosco, and Jim Rzegocki.

Dedications

Brian Morgan:

This book is dedicated to Beth, Emma, and Amanda. Thank you for making me complete and putting up with the time-lines and deadlines associated with the creation of this book.

Moises Gonzalez:

This book is dedicated to my family and friends. My mother for teaching me to be strong, to always try harder, and for always giving me her encouragement. My dad for his dedication to his family and for giving me the discipline to accomplish my dreams. Blas (Eddie), Juliza, Evelyn, and Ninive for setting a good example as brothers and sisters. Travis and Juan who have shown me what friends really are with their support. A special dedication to my sister Ninive, for her support, motivation, friendship, and encouragement to continue finding new challenges.

Contents at a Glance

Table of Contents

Icons Used in This Book

You will see that through out this book various icons are used to show Cisco-specific and general networking devices, peripherals and other items. The following legend explain what these icons represent.

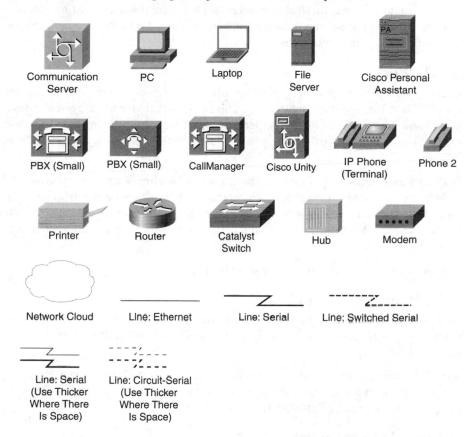

Command Syntax Conventions

The conventions used to present command syntax in this book are the same conventions used in the IOS Command Reference. The Command Reference describes these conventions as follows:

- **Boldface** indicates commands and keywords that are entered literally as shown. In actual configuration examples and output (not general command syntax), boldface indicates commands that are manually input by the user (such as a **show** command).

- *Italics* indicate arguments for which you supply actual values.

- Vertical bars (I) separate alternative, mutually exclusive elements.

- Square brackets [ ] indicate optional elements.

- Braces { } indicate a required choice.

- Braces within brackets [{ }] indicate a required choice within an optional element.

Introduction

The goal of any book, this one included, is to provide a transport mechanism for the transfer of knowledge. The knowledge and information presented herein is meant not only to provide a basis for learning the Cisco Unity system but also to provide a somewhat comprehensive technical reference for future needs of Cisco Unity administrators. The lack of a comprehensive hardcopy resource for Cisco Unity systems provided a catalyst for the creation of this particular book.

Goals and Methods

The most important and somewhat obvious goal of this book is to provide you with a resource for learning how to administer a Cisco Unity system environment. This book will provide key areas and notes of interest. Also included are some things learned through experiences in a Cisco Unity environment. The authors hope that the information provided herein will enable you to implement the Cisco Unity system with a minimum of trouble.

One key methodology used in this book is to help you discover which important topics you need to review in more depth, to help you fully understand and remember those details, and to help you prove to yourself that you have retained your knowledge of those topics. So, this book does not simply assume that you will memorize the information that is presented; instead it helps you to truly learn and understand the topics, by providing the following:

- Explanations and information to fill in your knowledge gaps

Who Should Read This Book?

This book is designed to be a resource that covers information presented in the Cisco Unity System Administration (CUSA) and Cisco Unity System Engineering (CUSE) courses. However, this book is meant to be a technical resource as well.

Cisco Unity installers, administrators, and engineers are the primary intended audience. However, the information is presented in a manner that makes it well suited to anyone who simply desires knowledge of the functions and features offered by Cisco Unity.

How This Book Is Organized

Although this book could be read cover to cover, it is designed to be flexible and allow you to easily move among chapters and sections of chapters to cover just the material that you need more work with. Chapters 1 through 11 are the core chapters and can be covered in any order. If you do intend to read them all, the order in the book is an excellent sequence to use. Each section includes introductory text regarding the information to follow as well as requisite knowledge recommended to fully benefit from the information to be presented.

The core chapters, Chapters 1 through 11, cover the following topics:

Chapter 1, "Cisco Unified Communications System Fundamentals," provides an overview of Cisco Unity call flow, Cisco Unity integration, and Cisco Unity features, as well as information regarding the features included in the Cisco Personal Assistant.

Chapter 2, "Using Your Cisco Unified Communications System," introduces the basic administration tasks and tools in Cisco Unity, along with a more in-depth discussion of the Cisco Personal Assistant.

Chapter 3, "Setting Up Cisco Unified Communications," covers the Cisco Unity Administrator, the primary tool that is used in the administration of the Cisco Unity environment. Also covered are the basics of a Cisco Unity system.

Chapter 4, "Unified Communications Subscribers," discusses the setup and configuration of Cisco Unity subscribers from both a global and an individual perspective. This discussion covers account policy, subscriber templates, and other key functions.

Chapter 5, "Cisco Unified Communications System Customization," discusses additional customization of the Cisco Unity subscriber experience through the creation and modification of call handlers and call routing tables.

Chapter 6, "Cisco Unified Communications System Maintenance," delves into a number of the tools that are available for Cisco Unity administration and maintenance. These tools allow for efficient monitoring of the health of the Cisco Unity system and explores reporting functions for the Cisco Unity environment.

Chapter 7, "Understanding Cisco Unified Communications System Hardware," describes the Cisco Systems platform overlays for supported Cisco Unity hardware. Each platform meets particular specifications that are dictated by Cisco.

Chapter 8, "Cisco Unified Communications System Software," explains the architecture of the Cisco Unity system when it is used with Microsoft Exchange or Lotus Domino. This includes a discussion of the Cisco Unity software installation for both new installations and upgrades.

Chapter 9, "Cisco Unified Communications Integrations," discusses the concept of a Cisco Unity integration, including definition of the needs of integrations with PBX or Cisco CallManager switches. Also discussed are details associated with various integration scenarios.

Chapter 10, "Unified Communications Networking," discusses the concept of networking with Cisco Unity systems. Digital, SMTP, VPIM, AMIS, and Bridge networking functions are discussed in this chapter.

Chapter 11, "Unified Communications Backup and Utilities," deals with the ongoing needs of backing up a system. It also covers a number of extremely valuable tools that you can use in the day-to-day operations of the environment.

Appendix A, "Chapter Review Questions," includes the answers and explanations to the review questions presented at the end of each chapter.

Cisco Unity Administration

Upon completing this chapter, you will be able to perform the following tasks:

- Describe how calls are routed between Cisco servers and telephone switching equipment

- Describe the flow of information between Cisco Unity servers and telephone switching equipment

- Describe the features available in Cisco Unity 4.0

- Describe the features available in Cisco Personal Assistant (PA) 1.4

CHAPTER 1

Cisco Unified Communications System Fundamentals

This chapter introduces the Cisco unified communications system. To administer Cisco Unity and Cisco PA efficiently and effectively, it is important to have an understanding of the environment they inhabit and operate within. Understanding how calls route through the systems and what you can do with them as they travel is crucial to your ability to administer a Cisco unified communications system.

Understanding Cisco Unity's Call Flow Essentials

Understanding how calls flow through the unified communications systems is very important for system administrators of PA and the voice-messaging system Cisco Unity. As you become more familiar with how calls flow through the system, you will be able to change the flow as needed and troubleshoot problems more efficiently.

Outside Caller Call Flow

In Cisco Unity, an outside caller is someone who Cisco Unity cannot identify as a Cisco Unity subscriber. Generally, this is a person who is calling in from the outside who wants to reach an individual at a place of business. When a subscriber is busy or away from their phone, Cisco Unity can answer the call and take a message for them. The subscriber can later hear their message either over the phone or by using IBM Lotus Notes, Microsoft Outlook, or Cisco Unity Inbox (depending on the configuration setup of the Cisco Unity system). In addition, if Cisco Unity subscribers call in from a phone other than their defined office extension, Cisco Unity treats those calls as outside callers until they sign in and identify themselves.

Figure 1-1 illustrates how a call from an outside caller might flow through the system, the corresponding steps of which are described next:

Figure 1-1   *Cisco Unity Outside Caller Call Flow*

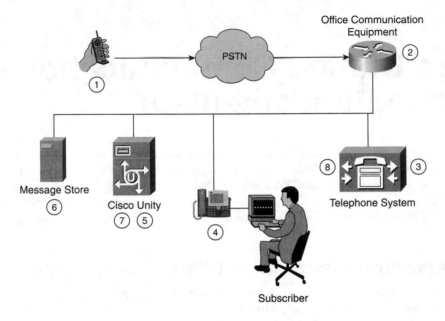

Step 1   The outside caller dials a phone number from his mobile phone. The phone number dialed is a Direct Inward Dialing (DID) number that belongs to a Cisco Unity subscriber.

Step 2   The Public System Telephone Network (PSTN) routes the caller to the office communications equipment.

Step 3   The DID number is programmed to ring a phone extension. Based on DID information provided by the PSTN, the business telephone system sends the incoming call to the telephone that it is programmed to connect to that DID number.

Step 4   The telephone rings four times, but the subscriber does not answer the phone because he is busy working on a presentation. The telephone system has been programmed to forward any unanswered calls to voice mail after four rings. The telephone system forwards the outside caller to the voice-mail system.

Step 5   Cisco Unity receives the call and the extension of the subscriber to take a message for. Cisco Unity has a list of subscriber extensions and the e-mail aliases to send messages to. Cisco Unity records a message from the caller, addresses it to the subscriber's alias, and then sends it to the message store server.

Step 6   The message store server receives the message and stores the message for the subscriber.

Step 7   While Cisco Unity is monitoring events in the message store, it notices a new voice-mail message for the subscriber and sends the message waiting indicator (MWI) ON code to the telephone system for the subscriber's extension.

Step 8   The telephone system lights the lamp at the subscriber's telephone set. The telephone now displays an MWI to alert the subscriber of a new message.

NOTE   If a previous message had been sent to this subscriber, the MWI would have been activated at that time. Therefore, the lamp or indicator remains activated.

Subscriber Call Flow

A Cisco Unity subscriber is a person who has a user account on the Cisco Unity system. Each subscriber account has a Profile page that stores specific information about that subscriber, such as the extension, security code, recorded name, and the e-mail alias to send messages to.

Figure 1-2 illustrates the call flow of a subscriber who is retrieving a message from Cisco Unity, the corresponding steps of which are described next:

Figure 1-2   *Cisco Unity Subscriber Call Flow*

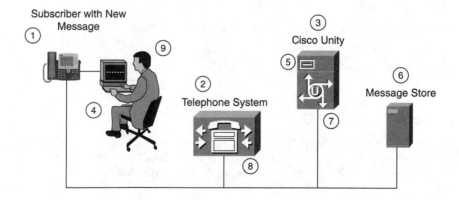

Step 1   The subscriber notices the MWI on her telephone and calls the voice-mail system to retrieve messages.

Step 2   The telephone system directs the call and the caller information (the telephone extension) to the Cisco Unity system.

Step 3   Cisco Unity receives the call and the extension of the telephone from the telephone system. Cisco Unity recognizes the extension from its list of subscribers, and accesses the subscriber's e-mail message store to retrieve the voice message. Cisco Unity asks the subscriber to enter her password. After entering the password, Cisco Unity offers to play the message for the subscriber.

Step 4   The subscriber chooses to listen to the message. Cisco Unity plays it and then offers a menu of actions to take with the message, such as save as new, delete, or forward. The subscriber presses the digit 3 to delete the message. While the subscriber is listening to the message, Cisco Unity sends an MWI OFF code. If the subscriber hangs up while the message is being played or does not press 3, then the MWI turns back on.

Step 5   Cisco Unity verbally confirms to the subscriber that the message is deleted and sends the subscriber's delete message command to the message store server.

Step 6   The message store deletes the message. (The message is either deleted or moved to the deleted items folder, depending on the settings in the subscriber's account.)

Step 7   Cisco Unity sends the MWI OFF code to the telephone system.

Step 8   The telephone system receives the MWI OFF code and turns off the MWI on the phone.

Step 9   The MWI of the telephone is off.

Cisco PA Outside Caller Call Flow

Cisco PA is a system that provides a way to connect calls to the particular telephone number at which you can be reached at a given time. When callers try to contact you through Cisco PA, you can set it up with different instructions on where you would like to be reached depending on the calling number and time.

Figure 1-3 illustrates how a call from an outside caller might flow through a system that is using Cisco PA, the corresponding steps of which are described next:

Figure 1-3   *Cisco PA Outside Caller Call Flow*

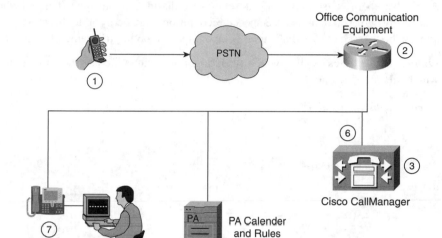

Step 1   The outside caller dials a phone number from his cell phone. The phone number dialed is a DID number that belongs to a Cisco PA subscriber.

Step 2   The PSTN routes the caller to the office communications equipment. (Cisco PA integrates only with Cisco CallManager.)

Step 3   Cisco CallManager has been set up to route the DID call to Cisco PA's media ports.

Step 4   Cisco PA receives the call and the DID information.

Step 5   Cisco PA checks the subscriber's transfer rules and the current date and time so it can correctly process the call based on previous instructions the subscriber has given Cisco PA. At that time, the rules indicate the subscriber wants all calls sent to the desk phone.

Step 6   Cisco PA sends an initiate-transfer sequence to Cisco CallManager, along with the extension to which the call should be transferred.

Step 7   The subscriber receives the call at his desk.

Cisco PA Subscriber Call Flow

As a subscriber to Cisco PA, you can set up specific rules to manage when and where the calls you receive go. You can also use speech recognition with a corporate directory (or personal address book) to have PA dial a telephone number by saying the name of the user.

Figure 1-4 illustrates a call flow of a subscriber interacting with PA, the corresponding steps of which are described next:

Figure 1-4 *Cisco PA Subscriber Call Flow*

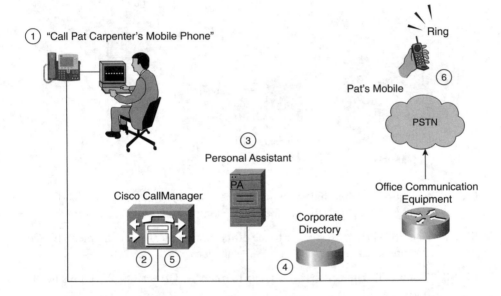

Step 1 The subscriber wants to call Pat Carpenter on Pat's mobile number. The subscriber picks up the handset and dials the extension of Cisco PA.

Step 2 Cisco CallManager makes the connection between the subscriber's phone and an available media port (called a computer telephony integration [CTI] route point in Cisco CallManager) on Cisco PA.

Step 3 PA requires the subscriber to log on. After the subscriber is logged on, Cisco PA asks the subscriber what to do. In response to this question, the subscriber says "Call Pat Carpenter's mobile phone."

Step 4 Cisco PA performs the speech recognition and looks for a match in the corporate directory, where it finds an entry for Pat's mobile phone. Cisco PA then sends the transfer-initiate sequence to Cisco CallManager and the telephone number to connect the call.

Step 5   Cisco CallManager receives the request and the phone number. It makes a connection to the appropriate office communications equipment and sends Pat's mobile number to the PSTN.

Step 6   Pat's mobile phone rings, and Pat answers the phone.

Understanding Unified Communications Integrations

This section describes a Cisco Unity integration, the features it provides, and the basic Cisco Unity integration methods. This section also describes a Cisco PA/Cisco CallManager integration.

It is very important that system administrators of both Cisco Unity and Cisco PA understand how the unified communications servers exchange information with telephone switching equipment. Once you know how Cisco Unity integrates with this equipment, you can troubleshoot problems with it as necessary.

Communications Integration

A communications integration is defined by when a telephone system and the voice-messaging system have a connection between each other, which allows them to send information to each other in a predetermined format. This connection can be a physical one or over a network connection, depending on the systems. In a business environment, when you add a telephone to the telephone system, you need to enter specific information for that new phone, such as the extension that callers dial to reach that phone, the numbers that the user at that extension may dial, forwarding information used when the user is busy or does not answer, and other data. This information is used by the telephone system so that when you call a person, their phone rings and they can answer the call.

The voice-messaging system also uses this information. When you are on the phone and someone calls you, the phone system sends the call to the forwarding destination. In this case, it is the voice-messaging system. When the telephone system sends the call to the voice-messaging system, it also sends information about the person who is calling and the reason the call is being forwarded. After the voice-messaging system receives the call and the information, it can react to the call in the correct way. In this way, when someone calls you at your desk, the call routes to your phone. If you are unavailable, the call then goes to voice mail, giving the caller the opportunity to leave you a message. After the caller leaves a message, the voice-messaging system sends information to the telephone system, telling it to light the lamp on the desk phone.

Figure 1-5 illustrates the type of data sent between the phone system and Cisco Unity.

Figure 1-5 *Information Sent Between a Phone System and Cisco Unity*

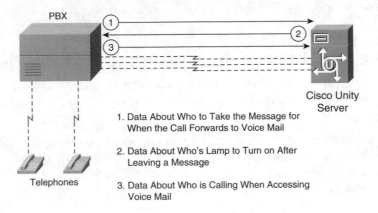

1. Data About Who to Take the Message for When the Call Forwards to Voice Mail

2. Data About Who's Lamp to Turn on After Leaving a Message

3. Data About Who is Calling When Accessing Voice Mail

Integration Attributes

A Cisco Unity voice-processing system connects to a telephone system, also known as a private branch exchange (PBX), to provide automated attendant, audiotext, and voice-mail service to subscribers. The way in which the systems cooperate and share information determines the level of service that subscribers receive. A telephone system must provide the three following telephone system features for Cisco Unity to qualify the phone system as an integration:

- **Automatic call forward to a personal greeting**—Any incoming calls routed to an unanswered or busy extension are automatically forwarded to the subscriber's mailbox in the voice-mail system so that callers can leave a message. This corresponds to arrow 1 in Figure 1-5 and Figure 1-6.

- **Easy message access**—The voice-processing system recognizes subscribers when they dial in, saving them from having to enter their personal ID. With this feature, subscribers should set a password on their voice mailbox. This corresponds to arrow 2 in Figure 1-5 and Figure 1-6.

- **MWIs**—MWIs alert end users that they have a new message in their voice mailbox. Indicators can be a light on the phone (blinking or steadily lit), a word on the liquid crystal display (LCD) panel of a phone, a message-waiting ring on the phone, or a stutter dial tone. This corresponds to arrow 3 in Figure 1-6.

Figure 1-6 illustrates the attributes of an integration between Cisco Unity and a telephone switch.

Figure 1-6   *Attributes of an Integration*

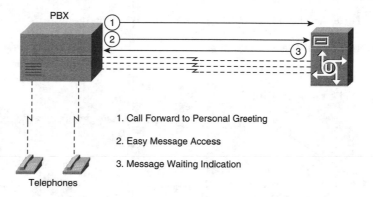

1. Call Forward to Personal Greeting

2. Easy Message Access

3. Message Waiting Indication

For more information on the integration between a telephone system and the Cisco Unity system, see Chapter 9, "Cisco Unified Communications Integrations."

Telephone System Integrations with Cisco Unity

The type of integration the telephone system supports determines how the delivery of information between Cisco Unity and the telephone system takes places. The five integration types supported by Cisco Unity 4.0 are as follows:

- Cisco CallManager
- Dual-tone multifrequency (DTMF)
- Simplified Message Desk Interface (SMDI)
- PBXLink
- Session Initiation Protocol (SIP)

Each integration is an agreement about the communication protocol and messaging channel to be used. Chapter 9 covers more information regarding how each integration functions, and it also lists the telephone systems that are supported with Cisco Unity.

The information shared between the telephone system and Cisco Unity is the common information that was discussed earlier, in the "Communications Integration" section of this chapter.

Cisco CallManager and Cisco PA Integration

Cisco PA integrates with Cisco CallManager through media points. Cisco CallManager passes calls to Cisco PA through the use of CTI route points. You must build these structures at the Cisco CallManager console.

Figure 1-7 illustrates a Cisco PA/Cisco CallManager integration.

Figure 1-7   *Cisco PA/Cisco CallManager Integration*

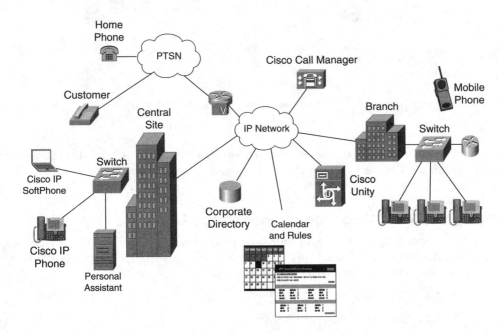

When Cisco CallManager receives a call intended for a PA-enabled extension, it first routes the call to Cisco PA. Cisco PA performs a lookup for the user from the corporate directory. The directory must be Lightweight Directory Access Protocol (LDAP)-compliant (Microsoft Exchange 2000 Active Directory or Exchange 5.5 Directory Service).

If the user has routing rules or call forwarding configured, Cisco PA then routes the caller to the appropriate destination through Cisco CallManager.

The destination of the routed call could be a mobile phone, home phone, or any other phone that you can dial from the Cisco CallManager, such as a Cisco IP SoftPhone, Cisco IP Phone, and even Cisco Unity voice mail.

NOTE   The Cisco IP SoftPhone is a communications application for your laptop PC.

Understanding Cisco Unity Features

Cisco Unity administrators must be acquainted with the system features so that they can implement as much of the system's capacity as is required and possible. In addition, it is important that they know the difference between the standard and optional features. When implementing optional features at the level required by corporate messaging needs, the administrator can then choose the correct licensing to purchase.

Using Cisco Unity Standard Features

The standard features in Cisco Unity discussed in this section include (* = new feature in Cisco Unity 4.0):

- Voice mail
- Automated attendant
- Audiotext application
- System Administration web page
- Cisco Personal Communications Assistant (Cisco PCA)*
- Cisco Unity Assistant (CUA)
- RSA (Rivest, Shamir, and Adelman) enhanced phone security
- Cisco Unity Greeting Administrator (CUGA)*
- FlexLM software security*
- Live Reply*
- Flex Stack*
- 12- to 24-hour clock support*
- Cisco Unity System Preparation Assistant (CUSPA)*
- Cisco Unity Installation and Configuration Assistant (CUICA)*
- DVD installation*
- Multiple directory handlers*
- SIP support*
- Additional Europe, Middle East, and Africa (EMEA) voice board support
- Digital networking

Voice Mail

Voice mail allows outside callers and internal users (called subscribers) to leave detailed, private messages 24 hours a day, seven days a week. An outside caller records the message with their own voice, which eliminates misunderstood and inaccurate written messages and captures the tone of the caller's voice. Subscribers gain access and listen to their messages from any touch-tone phone. It allows subscribers to listen to their messages, send voice messages to other subscribers, and customize settings such as their personal greetings.

Voice mail saves time by allowing a caller to leave a message immediately, even if the person the caller is trying to reach is away or on the telephone. Voice mail allows a company to better manage its communications and its employees' time.

Automated Attendant

You can set up the automated attendant feature with Cisco Unity, which can make the answering and handling of calls in an organization much easier. Cisco Unity's automated attendant greets and guides callers through the system in a friendly and timely fashion. By doing this, it makes the messaging process as effortless as possible. Cisco Unity gives the caller the option to press a touch-tone key at any time during the voice-mail conversation to speak to an operator.

If the system is using the automated attendant feature and an external caller enters a subscriber's extension number from the opening greeting, the extension can be set up in Cisco Unity to ring that phone's extension. If the subscriber picks up the handset, the call connects. If there is no answer or if the extension is busy, the call routes to the subscriber's voice mailbox, where the caller receives the subscriber's personal greeting.

If a caller does not know the extension, the caller may be able to search the directory of subscribers (referred to as the Alpha Directory in Figure 1-8). If the system finds only one match, Cisco Unity connects the caller directly to the extension. If it finds more than one match, the caller can then choose the appropriate extension from the list given by Cisco Unity's automated attendant.

Figure 1-8 illustrates the call flow options of a caller using the Cisco automated attendant.

Figure 1-8   *Cisco Automated Attendant*

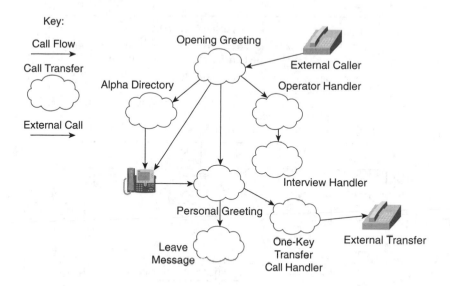

Audiotext Application

Call handlers are the building blocks of the Cisco Unity system. A call handler is a set of call-processing instructions that tells the system what to do when a call reaches that particular system ID. All the entities on a Cisco Unity system, whether they are subscribers, the operator, the opening greeting, or some other user-defined box, are call handlers. Some of them are special cases, so they look different from a standard call handler. However, they are the same.

You can use call handlers to set up specialized call routing, create one-key dialing menus, or provide announcements of prerecorded information. Your call handlers can be as simple or as complex as you wish. One of the simplest applications is the delivery of prerecorded information (called an audiotext application).

When you use the automated attendant to answer incoming calls, you're really using a call handler. The Opening Greeting call handler, to which callers first dial in, can be very simple, or it can take advantage of some powerful features, such as one-key dialing. You can provide a menu of choices for incoming calls with one-key dialing. Callers press one touch-tone key to route their call to the department or service they want. In the background, the one-key dialing menu routes the call to a system ID, whether it is to another menu (another call handler), an extension, or any other system ID. One-key dialing is a shortcut to any listed system ID.

Figure 1-9 illustrates an example of an audiotext application tree.

Figure 1-9 *Audiotext Application*

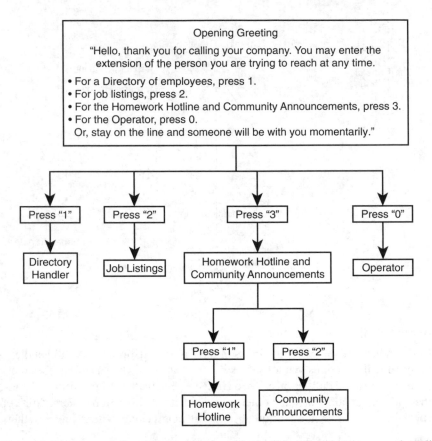

Figure 1-9 is an example of an opening greeting call handler that uses one-key dialing to offer a menu of choices.

In this example, pressing the touch-tone 1 routes the caller to the spell-by-name Cisco Unity directory (also known as the directory handler). Pressing the touch-tone 2 routes the caller to a call handler that is set up to play a list of job opportunities. Pressing the touch-tone 3 routes the caller to a call handler that is set up to offer a second layer of menu choices for the Homework Hotline and Community Announcements. There are two choices within that call handler in this example. When someone wants to check the Homework Hotline, they press the touch-tone 3, while the opening greeting is playing. Then, in the next call handler, they hear the second menu of choices, and they can press the indicated touch-tone button that routes them to the Homework Hotline list.

For more information about call handlers, refer to the *Cisco Unity System Administration Guide,* which you can find at Cisco.com by performing a search of the title.

System Administration Web Page

The Cisco Unity System Administration web page, shown in Figure 1-10, is a web-based console that provides a single point of administration. It is designed to be easy to use and simplifies some of the functions of Microsoft Windows 2000 and Exchange. This includes the creation of users in Active Directory and Exchange for subscribers. It does not require giving up Exchange administrative rights to administrators. The easily accessible console has an HTML interface using Microsoft Internet Information Server (IIS) to serve up Active Server Pages (ASPs).

Figure 1-10 *System Administration Web Page*

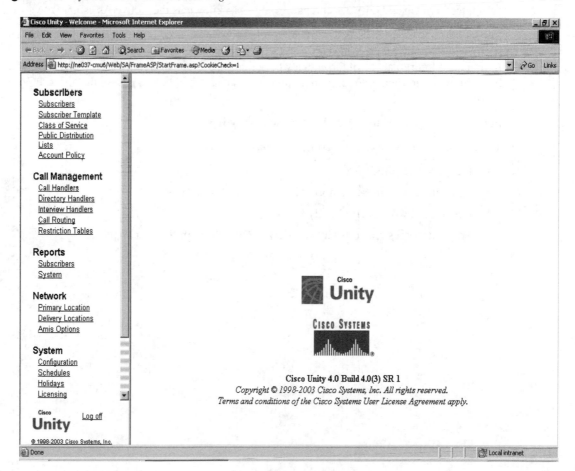

ASPs are dynamic HTML structures. This allows Cisco Unity to hold a wide variety of data in many of the screens. For instance, the Subscriber pages can hold data on any of the subscribers (up to 7500 on the largest servers) on the system.

Cisco PCA

Cisco PCA is a feature that is enabled or disabled by modifying the class of service (COS) of a subscriber. This is a browser interface that has two components: the Cisco Unity Inbox and the CUA.

The Cisco Unity Inbox gives subscribers the option to listen to, compose, reply to, forward, and delete messages through a website. For Cisco Unity 3.1 and earlier, this was known as the Visual Messaging Interface (VMI). The CUA gives subscribers the option to customize their personal settings, such as recorded greetings and message delivery options, from their computers. On Cisco Unity 3.1 and earlier, this was known as the Active Assistant (AA).

The interface to Cisco PCA is a web browser that allows a Cisco Unity subscriber to collect and send voice-mail messages without using the telephone. The subscriber can use Microsoft Internet Explorer to access it through a web session. You can configure Cisco Unity to send an SMTP type of notification to an e-mail alias with an attached link to access the Cisco PCA Inbox.

Figure 1-11 illustrates the Cisco PCA, Cisco Unity Inbox.

The advantages of using the Cisco Unity Inbox includes:

- It is groupware independent.
- You can receive message notification via SMTP to groupware.
- It leverages what users already know.
- Voice messages are accessible on desktop PCs through Internet Explorer.

Figure 1-11 *Cisco PCA—Cisco Unity Inbox*

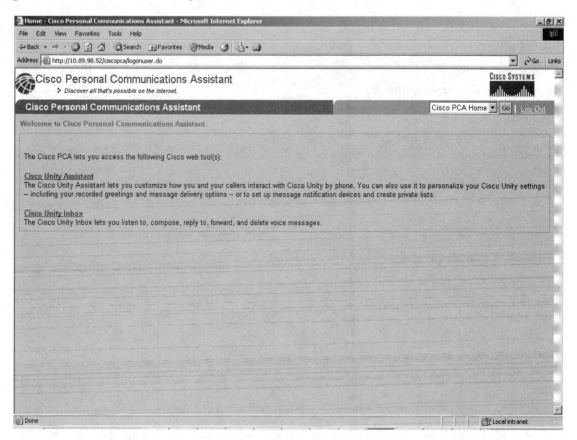

CUA

The CUA is the second component of the Cisco PCA. Most voice-mail systems allow users to change the settings of their voice-mail account via a conversation that is available only over the telephone. Cisco Unity offers a fully functional telephone conversation for all users, but it also offers the CUA.

A subscriber can do most of the day-to-day maintenance of their account via a web browser. You enable a subscriber to use the CUA by modifying their COS on the Licensed Features page. Once the CUA is enabled, a subscriber can record their own greetings either over the telephone or by using a microphone on a multimedia PC; change their call-transfer and screening options; change a wide variety of message settings concerning notification, playback, and addressing; and change a variety of personal settings, including their recorded name, telephone password, and directory listing. The ability to change some of these settings is dependent on settings that can be made on a number of Cisco Unity administration pages.

Figure 1-12 illustrates the Cisco PCA, CUA.

Figure 1-12 *Cisco PCA—CUA*

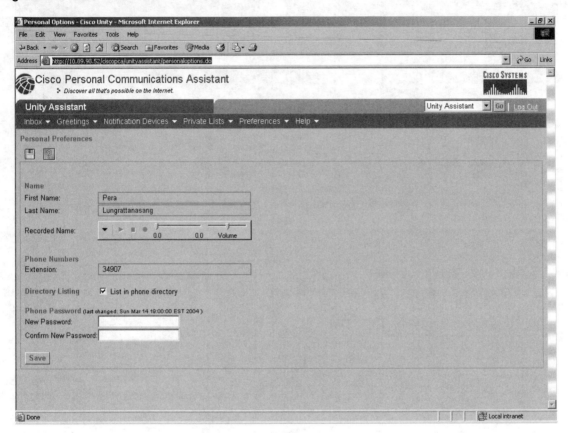

The advantages of using the CUA include:

- It is easy to use.

- It leverages what users already know.

- It leverages the power of the desktop client.

- Subscribers have another option with which to make changes to their personal settings for voice mail.

RSA Security or Enhanced Phone Security

Cisco Unity subscribers can be set up to use a secure login mechanism called the two-factor user authentication. The type of enhanced phone security is provided when working with the RSA SecurID system and Cisco Unity. The RSA SecurID system has two main components:

- RSA SecurID Authenticators
- The RSA Access Control Entry (ACE)/Server

The RSA SecurID Authenticators system and the RSA ACE/Agent assigns each authorized Cisco Unity subscriber an RSA SecurID authenticator. The authenticator generates and displays a new, unpredictable number every 60 seconds. This number, also known as a secure ID or token code, is unique to the subscriber. RSA offers authenticators as hardware, software, and smart cards. Each Cisco Unity subscriber who has an authenticator must have a user account on the ACE/Server.

You use the RSA Database administrator program on the ACE/Server to create and maintain the user accounts. A user account contains the RSA alias and PIN, and information about the user authenticator. By using the information in a user account, the ACE/Server generates the same secure ID as the user authenticator.

In the Cisco Unity Administrator, you assign subscribers to a Class of Service (COS), which has the enhanced phone security enabled. By default, Cisco Unity uses a subscriber Exchange alias as the subscriber RSA alias. When logging on to Cisco Unity over the phone, subscribers enter an ID as usual. Then, instead of a password, subscribers enter a passcode, which is a number that combines the subscriber PIN and the secure ID displayed on the subscriber authenticator. The first time that a subscriber logs on, they need to create a PIN, unless they are already assigned one. In these cases, a subscriber needs to enter only a secure ID, instead of a passcode. Then the subscriber conversation walks the user through the process of creating a PIN.

Cisco Unity uses the ID to look up the user RSA alias, and then sends the RSA alias and passcode to the ACE/Agent installed on the Cisco Unity server. The ACE/Agent encrypts the RSA alias and passcode and sends it to the ACE/Server. The ACE/Server looks up the user account, and then validates the passcode by using the information stored in the account. The ACE/Server returns a code to the ACE/Agent, which in turn passes it along to Cisco Unity.

The ACE/Server return codes are as follows:

- **Passcode accepted**—The Cisco Unity system allows a subscriber access to their messages.
- **Access denied**—The Cisco Unity system prompts the subscriber to enter the passcode again. You may see this return code if the ACE/Server is unavailable.
- **Secure ID expired**—The secure ID of the subscriber has expired and Cisco Unity prompts them to enter the next secure ID shown on the authenticator.
- **New PIN needed**—A new PIN is needed and Cisco Unity prompts the subscriber to enter a new PIN.

CUGA

CUGA is a new feature in Cisco Unity 4.0. It allows any subscriber who is the owner of a call handler, or a member of a distribution list that is assigned as the owner of the call handler, to rerecord that call handler greeting over the phone using the telephone user interface (TUI), without using the System Administrator console. The new conversation component (called the Greetings Administrator) allows you to do this. The Cisco Unity System Administrator sets up a way for subscribers to access the Greetings Administrator conversation. Prior to Cisco Unity 4.0, an administrator needed to log on to the System Administration web page to modify call handler greetings.

With Cisco Unity 4.0, the administrator must define how secure they want to make Greetings Administration access. You can set this with a simple one-key dialing entry from any call handler greeting or a call routing rule configured to use Dialed Number Identification Service (DNIS). The owner of the call handler needs the following information to use the Cisco Unity Greetings Administrator:

- The phone number or call handler caller input to dial for access to the CUGA
- The ID of the call handler owner
- The password of the call handler owner
- The extension of the call handler

Once a subscriber has this information, they can access the Greetings Administration conversation. This is a simple conversation that allows a caller to use touch-tone to control greetings and use the handset of the phone to perform items such as record and play back the greetings, enable or disable the alternate greetings, and determine which greeting is currently active for a call handler.

The RSA SecurID system is not available for subscribers who use the Cisco Unity Greetings Administrator to change call handler greetings using the TUI.

FlexLM

FlexLM is the new licensing-control method used by Cisco Unity 4.0. Before version 4.0, Cisco Unity used a security dongle that attached to the server via either a parallel or USB port. Cisco Unity now uses a software file licensing mechanism that removes the need for the external device. When you purchase Cisco Unity, the software license file is the control component that ensures you have all the features and capacity you paid for, while controlling your ability to make duplicate copies of Cisco Unity.

Each Cisco Unity server requires a separate and unique license file. The file is obtained from Cisco and added to the Cisco Unity system as part of the install process. You can change it at any time as part of an update/upgrade process. If the network interface card (NIC) fails on your Cisco Unity 4.0 server and needs replacement, you need to contact Cisco Systems to obtain a new license file. You can do this by contacting the Cisco licensing team at licensing@cisco.com and providing them with the original MAC address (physical address) of the NIC and the address of the new NIC. The e-mail should include an explanation of why you are switching the NIC. The licensing team will deactivate the license associated with the old NIC and issue you another license file for the new one.

Live Reply

Live Reply is a new feature in Cisco Unity 4.0 that enables Cisco Unity to immediately transfer a user to the subscriber who left a message they are listening to. Live Reply is a COS-controlled feature. When enabled, subscribers who are listening to messages by phone can act on a subscriber message by pressing 4-4 to have Cisco Unity call the subscriber immediately. If you are using the Optional Conversation 1, press 8-8 for this feature. Live Reply is disabled by default.

Cisco Unity dials the extension of the subscriber who left the message only when:

- The subscriber who left the message is homed on the same Cisco Unity server as the subscriber who is attempting to reply.

- The Transfer Incoming Calls to Subscriber's Phone setting for the subscriber who left the message is set to ring an extension or another number. (The Transfer Incoming Calls to Subscriber's Phone field is on the **Subscribers > Call Transfer** page on the Cisco Unity System Administration web page.)

Live Reply does not work if the message was left from an outside caller or a nonsubscriber. In addition, it does not work for Internet, Bridge, or AMIS subscribers. These are used for users that do not have mailboxes in the local message store. They are discussed in detail in Chapter 10, "Unified Communications Networking."

When Live Reply is enabled, it is not mentioned in the main Cisco phone menus. Consider telling subscribers that it is available. It is, however, referenced in the Help menu for the Cisco Unity phone conversation, the *Cisco Unity User Guide*, and the *Cisco Unity at a Glance* card.

Flex Stack

Flex Stack is a new feature that allows subscribers using the TUI to have their messages played back to them according to message type (voice, fax, e-mail), priority, or the order in which the messages were recorded (last-in, first-out [LIFO] or first-in, first-out [FIFO]). This feature can be set at a per-user level, so each subscriber can choose in what order they want their messages played back to them during the TUI message playback session. The Cisco Unity system administrator can set this up for each user, or subscribers can set the Flex Stack order themselves with Cisco PCA, depending on the COS they belong to.

12- to 24-Hour Support

Based on the needs of a given subscriber in a given application, the Cisco Unity system administrator can set up a subscriber account to use a 12-hour a.m./p.m. time format or a 24-hour military time format. Cisco Unity uses that time format when a subscriber who is using the TUI is checking messages, when Cisco Unity states someone left a message, or when the subscriber is setting up a message-delivery schedule. If using the 12-Hour clock setting, subscribers hear 1:00 p.m. when listening to a time stamp for a message left at 1:00 p.m. If using the 24-Hour clock setting, subscribers hear 1300 when listening to a time stamp for a message left at 1:00 p.m.

CUSPA

CUSPA is a new Cisco Unity 4.0 tool developed to help simplify the process of making a server ready for Cisco Unity software installation. CUSPA checks the server for all Microsoft Windows components and applications that are needed by Cisco Unity and provides semiautomated installation for what is missing.

CUSPA is discussed in more detail in Chapter 8, "Cisco Unified Communications System Software."

CUICA

The CUICA is a launch pad for the various wizards that you must use to complete Cisco Unity software installation and configuration. These wizards include: Cisco Unity Permissions Wizard, Cisco Unity Setup Program, Cisco Unity Install License File Wizard, Cisco Unity Service Configuration Wizard, Cisco Unity Message Store Configuration Wizard, and Cisco Unity Telephony Integration Manager. The CUICA interface enforces dependencies by guiding the installer through the wizards in this order. The interface also provides the installer with updated status as each wizard is successfully completed. This is run after CUSPA.

CUICA is discussed in more detail in Chapter 8.

DVD Installation

Cisco Unity comes with ten CD-ROMs for all of its software. You can now order the software either on one DVD or ten CD-ROMs. Because the computer industry is moving toward making DVD drives the standard on all PC platforms, Cisco Systems offers the option to its customers to take advantage of the computer resources available. Presented with the choice to insert one DVD or to put in ten CD-ROMs sequentially, the simpler, streamlined method seems destined to be the favorite. CD-ROM sets of Cisco Unity are still available to accommodate those servers that do not have a DVD drive installed.

NOTE	You need Microsoft Windows 2000 Server software if you did not order the part number that includes Windows 2000.

Multiple Directory Handlers

The multiple directory handler feature provides a way to quickly and effectively perform directory searches for systems that have a large number of subscribers. You can use this feature for call routing where Cisco Unity provides centralized call processing in branch office deployments or headquarters.

On a new installation, Cisco Unity 4.0 comes with one default directory handler. A subscriber is listed in it as long as the subscriber's profile has three components:

- A correctly spelled text name
- The recorded name of the subscriber
- The List in Phone Directory box checked

All subscribers who meet those requirements are listed in the default directory handler. Prior to Cisco Unity 4.0, only one spell-by-name directory handler was available. In Cisco Unity 4.0, you can build as many directory handlers as you need. You can choose the subscribers that will be available in each directory handler based on local Cisco Unity server, location, COS membership, distribution list membership, or dialing domain membership. This enables you to provide segmented directories for departments, branch offices, outside sales people, or whatever other classification makes sense in a corporate setting.

SIP Support

SIP is the Internet Engineering Task Force's (IETF) standard for multimedia calls over IP. SIP is a peer-to-peer, ASCII-based protocol that uses requests and responses to establish, maintain, and terminate calls (or sessions) between two or more endpoints. Cisco Unity accepts calls from a proxy server and direct invites from a SIP-enabled endpoint (for example, a SIP IP phone). Cisco Unity relies on a proxy server or call agent to authenticate calls. SIP uses a request/response method to establish communications between various components in the network and to ultimately establish a conference (call or session) between two or more endpoints. A single call may involve several clients and servers. A unique phone or extension number identifies users in a SIP network.

The unique SIP address uses the format sip:*userID@domain*, which is similar to an e-mail address. The user ID can be either a username or an E.164 address. When a user initiates a call, a SIP request typically goes to a SIP server (either a proxy server or a redirect server). The request includes the caller's address (From) and the address of the called party (To).

When someone initiates a call, a SIP request is normally sent to a SIP server. This can either be a proxy or redirect server. The request includes the calling party's address (who it is coming from) and the called party's address (who the call is going to).

SIP messages are in text format, which uses the ISO 10646 in UTF-8 encoding. SIP messages also contain a start line, which specifies the method and protocol, several header fields that state call properties and service information, and an optional message body that contains a session description.

Cisco Unity supports the following SIP functions:

- User Agent Client (UAC)
- User Agent Server (UAS)
- Proxy Server (only third-party servers)

For more information on SIP support with Cisco Unity, go to Cisco.com and perform a search for "SIP Compliance for Cisco Unity."

EMEA Voice Board Support

Cisco Unity supports several new voice boards: the D/120JCT-LS and D/120JCT-Euro revision-two cards and the D/41JCT-LS and D/41JCT-Euro cards.

To make Cisco Unity 4.0 integrate with more European circuit-switched telephone systems, these new voice boards have been added to the list of supported voice boards. Different voice boards are necessary because varying voltages and wiring patterns are used in different parts of the world. The *Cisco Unity Installation Guide* provides an appendix on voice boards that gives technical and setup information. This guide can be found at Cisco.com by performing a search of the guide's name.

Digital Networking

In Cisco Unity, *networking* is the general term for messaging between a Cisco Unity server and other messaging systems (including another Cisco Unity server). There are several forms of networking, which are all dependent on the kind of servers involved as targets for messages. Digital networking is available as a standard feature; all other forms are optional. If an organization has multiple Cisco Unity servers and they all have access to the same global directory, then digital networking allows messages to pass between servers easily. If there is a networked telephone switch also attached to these servers, it would be possible for outside callers to search the directory of any Cisco Unity server they call in to, select a subscriber on any other Cisco Unity server, and leave a message to the subscribers.

Digital networking is explained in more detail in Chapter 10.

Using Cisco Unity Optional Features

The optional features in Cisco Unity that are discussed in this section include the following:

- Unified Messaging (UM)
- Integrated Faxing—integrate with popular third-party fax servers (Exchange only)
- Text-to-speech feature
- Localized versions

Unified Messaging

Cisco Unity delivers UM via ViewMail for Outlook (VMO) and Domino Unified Communications Services (DUCS). This give users better access to, and management of, all of a subscriber's messages—e-mail, voice mail, and fax. VMO integrates with Microsoft desktop clients such as Outlook 98, 2000, and XP. DUCS is an IBM Lotus–developed client software package that enables UM features to function on the Lotus Notes client.

Cisco Unity provides an intuitive GUI that is accessible from any networked PC. With just a click of the mouse, subscribers can access e-mail, voice mail, and fax messages, and reply to, forward, or save them in public or personal folders within Exchange/Outlook. The icons accompanying those messages make it easy to distinguish between e-mail, voice, and fax communications, saved and new messages, and the priority (normal, urgent, and private) with which you receive messages. You can view your faxes on screen and print them from any networked PC, or forward them to any fax machine from a touch-tone telephone. Subscribers can download all types of messages and work with them off line, and apply Inbox Assistant rules to streamline communications management.

In addition, UM enables you to listen to your e-mail over the phone with an optional text-to-speech (TTS) engine. When integrated with a supported third-party fax server, you can also forward fax messages to a location where you may be staying. Cisco Unity unites traditionally independent communications methods so that employees can work more efficiently.

Integrated Faxing

One of the other features of Cisco Unity is Integrated Faxing when using Cisco Unity UM with Exchange. With one of the approved fax server/software solutions, you can configure Cisco Unity to call you, send a numeric page, or send a text page to alert you of a new fax. When you are using the TUI, Cisco Unity can be set up to state how many new faxes you have and offer to send them to a fax machine telephone number you specify. You can forward a fax message to another subscriber or reply with a voice message if the fax message was from another subscriber. Subscribers can also send their e-mail messages to a fax machine. The third-party fax solutions that are qualified for Fax Integration with Cisco Unity are the following:

- Biscom FAXCOM for Microsoft Exchange, Version 6.19 or later
- Captaris RightFax Version 6 or later
- Esker FaxGate Version 7 or later
- Fenestrae FAXination Version 4 or later
- Interstar LightningFAX Version 5.5 or later
- Omtool Fax Sr. Version 3 or later
- Optus FACSys Version 4.5 or later
- TOPCALL, all versions

For more information on Cisco Unity fax integration, go to Cisco.com and perform a search for Article ID: 4628, "Cisco Unity Supported Third-Party Fax Integrations."

Text-to-Speech Feature

The TTS feature enables you to hear your e-mails over the telephone. Cisco Unity reads the text portion of an e-mail message to you and provides other information such as the name of the sender (if the sender is a subscriber) and the time and date that the message was sent. This is a COS option that the system administrator can set up. The text-to-speech feature is available for up to 36 sessions, based on the platform you use. Cisco Unity supports the RealSpeak engine only. In addition, Cisco Unity no longer supports the TTS3000 speech engine with Cisco Unity 4.0. The RealSpeak engine is now available in many languages; its speech is regarded as among the best, if not the best, in the speech-synthesis field. The TTS engine can be installed for several languages. You can install up to nine TTS languages with Cisco Unity 4.0.

Localized Versions

The Cisco Unity system architects designed the localized components so that Cisco Unity can easily localize into whatever languages the market demands. Cisco Unity is available in English with several different prompt sets, depending on the locale of the server. It is also available in fully localized versions for French, German, and Japanese. In a fully localized version, all prompts, administrative interfaces, TTS engines, and documentation are in the native language, with prompts spoken by a native language speaker. Partially localized versions are available in Dutch, Norwegian, two varieties of Spanish (Columbian Spanish and European Spanish), two varieties of Chinese (Chinese Mandarin and Taiwan Mandarin), Italian, Brazilian Portuguese, Swedish, Danish, and Korean. Partially localized versions always have the prompts, recorded by a native language speaker, and often have TTS engines in the native language. The administrative interfaces and documentation of partially localized versions are in the English language.

The number of languages that you can load and use for phone and GUI languages depends on how many languages you are licensed for. For example, if a company has two language licenses, but four languages are installed, Cisco Unity allows only two languages to be loaded and used at any particular time. You do have the option to choose which languages to select at any given time. Figure 1-13 illustrates the Cisco Unity 4.0 localized components.

Figure 1-13 *Cisco Unity 4.0 Localized Components*

Language	System Prompts	Help Files	ViewMail for Outlook/ Cisco PCA	Text to Speech	Documentation	Locale (LCID) Code
Australian English (ENA)	ENA	ENU	ENU	Use ENU or ENG	ENU	3081
Brazilian Portuguese (PTB)	PTB	ENU	PTB			
Chinese Cantonese ZHH (Hong Kong) (ZHH))	ZHH	ENU	ENU		N/A / N/A	ENU / ENU
Chinese (Mainland) CHS Mandarin (CHS)	CHS	ENU	CHS	CHS	ENU	2052 / 9226
Colombian Spanish (ESO)	ESO	ENU	ESO	ESP	ENU	1029
Czech (CSY)	CSY	ENU	ENU	N/A	ENU	1030
Danish (DAN)	DAN	ENU	DAN	DAN	ENU	1043
Dutch (NLD)	NLD	ENU	ENU	NLD	ENU	2070
European Portuguese (PTG)	PTG	ENU	ENU	N/A	ENU	1034
European Spanish (ESP)	ESP	ENU	ESP	ESP	ENU	1036
French (FRA)	FRA	FRA	FRA	FRA	FRA	1031
German (DEU)	DEU	DEU	DEU	DEU	DEU	1040
Italian (ITA)	ITA	ENU	ITA	ITA	ENU	1041
Japanese (JPN)	JPN	JPN	JPN	JPN	JPN	1042
Korean (KOR)	KOR	ENU	KOR	N/A	ENU	5129
New Zealand English (ENZ)	ENZ	ENU	ENU	Use ENU or ENG	ENU	
Norwegian (NOR)	NOR	ENU	ENU	NOR	ENU	1044
Swedish (SVE)	SVE	ENU	ENU	SVE	ENU	1053
Taiwan Mandarin (CHT)	CHT	ENU	CHT	CHS	ENU	1028
TTY English (ENX)	ENX	ENU	ENU	Not supported	ENU	33810
UK English (ENG)	ENG	ENU	ENU	ENU	ENU	2057
U.S. English (ENU)	ENU	ENU	ENU	ENU	ENU	1033

NOTE   The following are some considerations related to the languages supported for Cisco Unity. Chinese and Japanese text to speech requires special settings. You can find more information about this on the Cisco Unity System Administration Guide. Also, although the user Help and user documentation is translated into French and German, the Cisco Unity Administrator Help is not available in these languages.

Using Cisco Unity Optional Networking Features

The main goal of networking in Cisco Unity is to deliver messages from a Cisco Unity server to a target messaging server and from the target to a Cisco Unity server. This can be either between Cisco Unity servers or from a Cisco Unity server to a third-party messaging system. The experience that a user has is very simple: they leave a message for someone who is a subscriber on the system, and the subscriber receives it. The user does not need to know what type of server the subscriber resides on or the communications protocols and software setup that are required to transfer the message. This is all transparent to the user.

The optional networking features in Cisco Unity that are discussed in this section include the following:

- Networking with the Audio Messaging Interchange Specification, analog (AMIS-a) protocol
- Voice Profile for Internet Messaging (VPIM) protocol
- Bridge networking (Octel analog)

AMIS-a Networking

Cisco Unity can be set up to use AMIS when the target messaging server is another voice-mail server that supports the AMIS-a specification. This provides an analog method for transferring voice messages between different voice-messaging systems.

AMIS-a support is available when integrating with Microsoft Exchange. You can use AMIS networking to assist customers in transitioning their legacy voice-mail systems to an IP telephony solution. The industry-standard protocol provides a way for disparate voice-mail systems to exchange messages. The protocol uses DTMF to address and control format, and analog voice to transfer messages. The originating system sets up the call, establishes a connection over the telephone network, and then sends data frames as DTMF tones and voice data as audio to the destination system. The destination system sends response frames as DTMF tones. For each subscriber that is located on another voice-mail system, you add an AMIS subscriber to Cisco Unity. These subscribers are accessible through the Cisco Unity directory.

An AMIS subscriber has similar attributes to an Exchange custom recipient. AMIS subscribers do not impact Exchange licensing counts because its message store resides on the other voice-mail system. If you have several Cisco Unity servers that are using the same directory and are networked together, only one Cisco Unity server requires licensing for AMIS networking.

The following are supported AMIS-compliant voice-messaging systems with Cisco Unity 4.0(x):

- Active Voice Repartee
- Avaya Interchange with AMIS-analog Networking Gateway
- Avaya INTUITY AUDIX

- Avaya Octel 100 Messaging
- Avaya Octel 250/350
- Centigram Voice Mail
- Nortel Networks Meridian Mail
- Siemens PhoneMail

AMIS networking is explained in more detail in Chapter 10.

Voice Profile for Internet Messaging

VPIM networking in Cisco Unity for Exchange allows different voice-messaging systems to exchange voice, fax, and text messages over the Internet or any TCP/IP network. VPIM is a digital standard that is based on the SMTP and Multipurpose Internet Mail Extension (MIME) protocols. Messaging servers digitally transfer voice, text, and fax messages between each other. VPIM networking may allow organizations to save long-distance charges on messages between target servers because those messages are traveling over a TCP/IP network rather than over more costly PSTN lines. As with AMIS networking, if you have several Cisco Unity servers that are using the same directory and are networked together, only one Cisco Unity server requires licensing for VPIM networking.

Supported VPIM-compliant voice-messaging systems with Cisco Unity 4.0(x) include:

- Mitel/Baypoint NuPoint Messenger (formerly known as Centigram Series 6)
- Nortel CallPilot
- Nortel Meridian Mail with Meridian Mail Net Gateway
- Avaya Interchange (supported only with Cisco Unity 4.0(x) in the voice-messaging configuration)

VPIM networking is explained in more detail in Chapter 10.

Bridge Networking

Cisco Unity uses a Cisco Unity Bridge server to communicate with remote Avaya Octel messaging systems. The Cisco Unity Bridge server is like a networking gateway that resides between Cisco Unity and an Octel system or Avaya Interchange on an Octel analog network. Cisco Unity sends VPIM messages to a Bridge server via IP. The Bridge server in turn, communicates to the OctelNet nodes using the Octel analog networking protocol. The Bridge server does this via analog lines connected to a Brooktrout TR114 four-port card installed and configured inside the Bridge server. The Bridge must be installed on its own dedicated server and it can communicate with up to 998 Octel servers. You can configure up to 24 analog ports per Bridge server. The messages are delivered in real time via these analog ports to the target OctelNet nodes, so delivery of 100 hours' worth of messages takes 100 hours of port transmission time.

Using Cisco PA Standard Features

The Cisco PA features discussed in this section include the following:

- Follow Me
- Name dialing using a personal address book or corporate directory
- Name synchronization with a personal address book and Exchange contacts list
- Mail browser
- Web-based user administration
- Web-based system administration
- Rules-based routing
- Speech recognition

Follow Me

The Follow Me feature is a special rule type that uses speech recognition to immediately redirect all callers to an alternate destination (telephone), over a specified period of time. For example, a user could route calls to a hotel room telephone during a business trip. You can also activate predefined rules from any phone.

Name Dialing

Name dialing is a powerful PA voice-recognition tool that allows PA users to simply say the name of the person to whom they want PA to transfer them. You can also set up name dialing for outside callers to be able to say a person's name and have PA transfer them to that person. For example, if you say "Call Mike Davis," PA searches the corporate directory and personal address book to see if it can find a match and place the call for you. You can also limit PA's search to just your personal address book when you dial by name, which improves the accuracy of the dialing by searching fewer names.

Name Synchronization

Name synchronization allows users to synchronize their personal address book with their Exchange contacts list. Just as with a personal address book, the contacts list may contain business associates or friends of the user who are not normally listed in the corporate directory. If you synchronize your Exchange contacts with your personal address books, the contacts become part of the personal address book and Cisco PA can then access them for verbal dialing through speech recognition or rules-based routing. The personal address book entries can also become part of your Exchange contacts list.

Mail Browser

Cisco PA also allows access to Cisco Unity through verbal commands. By using the voice-recognition feature, a user is able to access Cisco Unity, listen to, send, skip over, save, or delete messages. PA can also recognize commands given through your touch-tone keypad. After PA is set up, you can start using this feature by simply dialing into PA and saying "voice mail."

Web-Based User Administration

Cisco PA web-based administration comes in two forms: the user and the administrator's interfaces. Figure 1-14 illustrates the Cisco PA User Web Administration Console.

Figure 1-14 *Cisco PA 1.4 User Administration, Welcome Page*

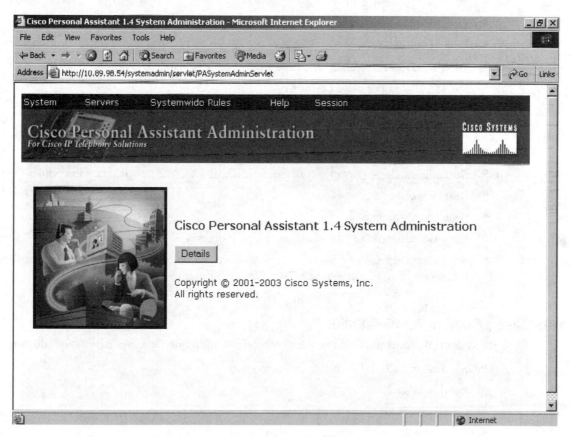

A PA-enabled user can perform the following:

- Create and modify destinations (phone numbers and e-mail-based paging addresses where a user wants to be reached)
- Create and modify destination groups for you can be reached in multiple numbers
- Create and modify callers in the Cisco PA address book
- Create and modify groups of callers
- Create and modify rules and rule sets
- Activate rule sets
- Create and modify dial rules
- Test call-forwarding rules
- Test dial rules
- Turn on/off call forwarding all (CFA) and screening capabilities
- Turn on/off authentication when calling from a personal destination
- Set a Cisco Unity mailbox number
- Create nicknames to simplify name dialing
- Select a time zone
- Set name-dialing preference for speech recognition
- Set name-dialing preference for automatic additions to the personal address book
- Reset spoken name
- Select a call-pickup timeout
- View the name of the user who is currently logged in
- Select language/locale for GUI and speech-recognition engine (North American English, British English, French, French Canadian, or German)

Web-Based System Administration

PA system administrators can use the web administration interface to perform the following:

- Set a central Cisco PA system call-in number
- Load-balance calls
- Configure Cisco PA redundant servers
- Configure Cisco PA to access an LDAP directory
- Configure Cisco PA to access Microsoft Exchange 5.5, Exchange 2000, and Exchange 2003
- Configure one or more languages/locales

- Provide information, warning, and error messages
- Provide system and error reporting
- Manage the Cisco PA system control center

Figure 1-15 illustrates the Cisco PA 1.4 System Administration, Server Configuration page.

Figure 1-15 *Cisco PA 1.4 System Administration Page*

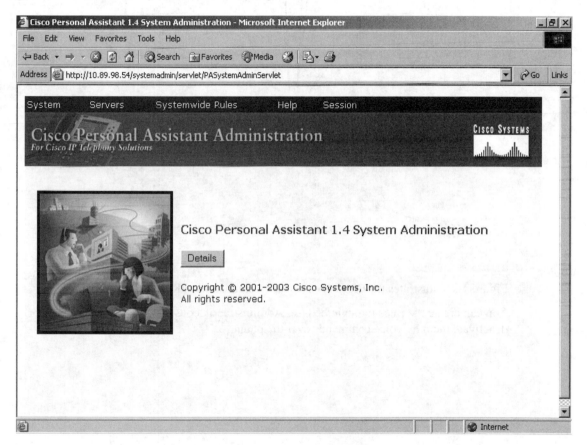

Rules-Based Routing

The Cisco PA rules-based routing is a powerful tool that allows users to redirect calls to their phone based on certain rules. The rules can be set by a schedule (time of day, day of week, or range of dates), and/or calls from certain individuals or a group of individuals. PA can redirect calls to mobile phones, home phones, or voice mail, or it can even try more than one destination.

Figure 1-16 illustrates Cisco PA call-routing examples.

Figure 1-16 *Cisco PA 1.4 Call-Routing Examples*

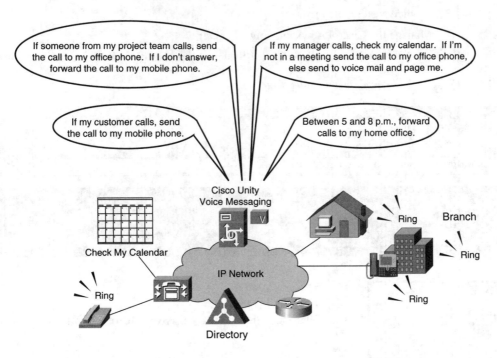

Figure 1-17 illustrates the Cisco PA 1.4 User Administration Rule-Sets page.

You can create the rules through the User Administration console, and you can activate or deactivate them by voice commands over the phone.

Figure 1-17 *Cisco PA 1.4 User Administration, Rule-Sets Page*

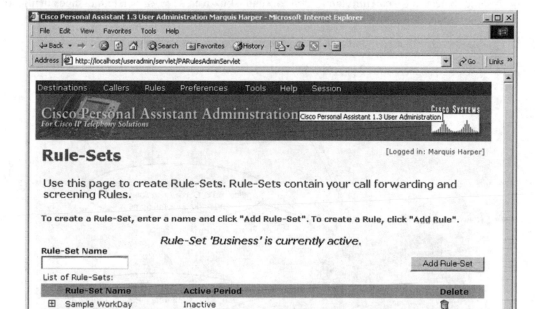

Speech Recognition

The speech-recognition feature allows callers to speak commands to Cisco PA. This includes dialing a person by telling Cisco PA, for example, to "call Mary Lane"; activating or deactivating a predefined Rule-Set; accessing, listening to, and deleting Cisco Unity voice or e-mail messages; and even sending an e-mail page to a colleague.

Cisco PA also allows a user to work within Cisco Unity through verbal commands. The user is able to access Cisco Unity and listen to, send, skip over, save, or delete messages using voice commands.

Figure 1-18 illustrates Cisco PA 1.4 speech-recognition examples.

Figure 1-18 *Cisco PA 1.4 Speech-Recognition Examples*

Using Cisco PA Optional Features

Cisco PA optional features discussed in this section include the following:

- Localizations
- IP Phone Productivity Services: CalendarView and MailView

Localizations

Cisco PA is now available in a localized format for the following languages:

- French (full)
- German (full)
- French Canadian (TUI and ASR only)
- British English (TUI and ASR only)

With a full localized version, the TUI (also known as the conversation), automatic speech recognition (ASR), and the web-based administrative interfaces are all available in the targeted language. This is the case with English, French, and German. The French-Canadian and British English localizations provide the TUI and ASR.

IP Phone Productivity Services

IP Phone Productivity Services brings the power of Cisco PA to Cisco 7940, 7960, and 7970 IP display phones. The CalendarView feature allows users to view their appointment calendar by day or by week. They can respond to meeting requests or change their responses. As a reminder, IP Phone Productivity Services can provide notification of upcoming appointments by phone display or pager. It also allows you to log in to any 7940/7960/7970 Cisco IP Phone in a Cisco CallManager cluster for access, including any desk, coworker's office, conference room, or lobby phone.

The MailView feature allows users to access their voice-mail and e-mail messages in their Cisco Unity mailbox without dialing the voice-mail server. They can listen to their voice-mail messages and then reply to, forward, or delete them. They also can read, forward, or delete their e-mail messages and see whether the message is read or unread.

Also available with IP Phone Productivity Services is the ability to synchronize the personal address book with the Microsoft Exchange contact list through the IP phone display. You may also activate or deactivate Rule-Sets, or confirm a certain Rule-Set is active.

Figure 1-19 illustrates the Cisco PA 1.4 IP Phone Productivity Services available on 7940 and 7960 Cisco IP display phones.

Figure 1-19 *Cisco PA 1.4 IP Phone Productivity Services*

Chapter Summary

In this chapter, you learned about how calls are routed between Cisco servers and telephone switching equipment; the flow of information between Cisco servers and telephone switching equipment; the features available in Cisco Unity 4.0; and the features available in Cisco PA 1.4. Specifically, you have learned how to do the following:

- How an outside caller interacts with Cisco Unity and PA
- How a subscriber interacts with Cisco Unity and PA
- Describe a Cisco Unity communications integration
- Describe the features that constitute a Cisco Unity integration
- Describe the different methods of integrating Cisco Unity with a telephone system
- Describe the integration of Cisco PA and Cisco CallManager
- Cisco Unity and PA standard features
- The new Cisco Unity 4.0 features
- Cisco Unity and PA optional features

For additional information, refer to these resources:

- *Cisco Unity System Administration Guide*
- *Cisco Personal Assistant Administration Guide*
- Various Cisco Unity Telephone Switch Integration Guides available at Cisco.com
- *Cisco Unity Design Guide*
- Cisco Unity white papers available at Cisco.com
- *Cisco Personal Assistant Installation and Administration Guide*
- Cisco Personal Assistant—Enhance Productivity by Streamlining Communications data sheet

Chapter Review Questions

Use this section to test yourself on how well you learned the concepts discussed in this chapter. You can find the answers to the review questions for this chapter in Appendix A.

1 Name three of the standard features new to Cisco Unity 4.0.

2 Name an optional networking feature that is new in Unity 4.0.

3 What new feature enables Cisco Unity to transfer a user immediately to the subscriber who left a message that the user is currently listening to?

4 True/False: Cisco Unity 4.0 now supports multiple directory handlers.

5 Which IETF standard does Cisco Unity now support in version 4.0?

6 What client software package allows Unified Messaging on Lotus Notes client desktops with Cisco Unity?

7 Name three of the qualified third-party fax solutions for Cisco Unity Integrated Faxing.

8 What text-to-speech engine does Cisco Unity 4.0 support?

9 What new networking feature in Cisco Unity 4.0 uses a standard that is based on the SMTP and MIME protocols?

10 When using Cisco PA, what feature enables you to be transferred to a person by saying that person's name?

11 What Cisco PA feature can provide users with notification of upcoming appointments on the phone display?

Upon completing this chapter, you will be able to perform the following tasks:

- Use the Cisco Unity features and functions to route calls and present subscriber options for voice message retrieval

- Use Cisco Personal Communications Assistant (Cisco PCA) to expand the already diverse features available in Cisco Unity

- Use Cisco Personal Assistant (PA) to provide speech-enabled access to Cisco Unity voice messages, corporate directories, conference calling features, and contact lists from any telephone

CHAPTER 2

Using Your Cisco Unified Communications System

This chapter discusses the basics of the Cisco Unity system operation. The basis of the Cisco Unity system is, of course, managing calls. However, that is where its overall similarity with traditional voice-messaging systems ends. The manner in which the Cisco Unity system handles calls is of particular importance. Use of the Cisco Unity system Telephone User Interface (TUI) is discussed in this chapter as an additional introduction to the system.

The Cisco Unity system offers a diverse feature-set to its users. This diversity includes the capability to receive voice messages in a Microsoft Outlook or Lotus Notes e-mail client through the use of ViewMail for Outlook (VMO) or Domino Unifiec Communications Services (DUCS). Also of interest in this chapter is a discussion of Cisco PCA.

Cisco PA, not to be confused with Cisco PCA, allows a subscriber to customize the method by which calls are handled. Rule-sets are used in Cisco PA to specify how personal calls should be treated when certain conditions are met and these rule-sets can be configured through a web interface.

Using Cisco Unity

When you administer a Cisco Unity or PA system, you need to provide services directly to end users of the system. To accomplish this, you must thoroughly understand the array of available features and functions and how to properly deploy those features and functions. You also need to gain comprehensive knowledge of various modes and facets of system-to-user and user-to-system interaction. This first-hand knowledge of the technologies that are being used will help you to support the system.

Knowing the extent of the form and function of a Cisco Unity or PA installation is important because it helps you to reduce troubleshooting and the mean time to repair (MTTR) in an outage or other user-support situation.

To benefit fully from this section, it is recommended that you have the following prerequisite skills and knowledge. (If you need a quick review, see the designated chapter, where you can find more information on the topic.)

- Knowledge of how calls are handled in a Cisco Unity system (See Chapter 5, "Unified Communications System Customization")

- Knowledge of the interaction between Cisco Unity and Microsoft Exchange/Active Directory and/or Lotus Domino (see Chapter 8, "Cisco Unified Communications System Software")

Managing Calls

When an inbound call arrives, it is processed by a telephone system like Cisco CallManager. You can have a Cisco CallManager interact with the Cisco Unity system and pass along any pertinent information that can be provided. This may include caller ID, name of the caller, or other information. The information passed is dependent on Cisco CallManager and its configuration. Once the Cisco Unity system receives the call, numerous possibilities can be explored in handling the call.

Upon seeing that the call is not sourced from a configured Cisco Unity subscriber, the Standard Opening Greeting is played to the caller. In cases where a subscriber-to-subscriber call is being made, the caller simply hears the subscriber conversation as configured by the individual.

Understanding the TUI

When the Cisco Unity System receives a call from an outside caller, the caller hears the Cisco Unity conversation, a prerecorded set of instructions and options that is made available to callers and subscribers to meet the needs of each. The Cisco Unity conversation enables the caller to access the Cisco Unity Automated Attendant, conduct subscriber searches using directory assistance, use call-routing options, and play audiotext messages. Subscribers hear the subscriber conversation, which enables them to enroll as new subscribers, send or receive messages, record greetings, and change personal settings.

For subscribers, there are two types of conversations, the standard conversation and the optional conversation. The standard conversation is the default subscriber conversation. The optional conversation allows subscribers to hear message-retrieval menus that closely resemble traditional voice-messaging choices with which they may be familiar. The optional conversation needs to be activated to use it.

As a best practice, you should always configure an option to "0-out" during the personal greeting or while in the Auto Attendant to get a human operator. There are a number of options that can be configured using one-key dialing beyond the simple operator functionality.

If the caller does not make any selections on the keypad, they are automatically routed to the operator as if they had pressed 0 in the Auto Attendant. This also serves to aid any callers who are using pulse-dial telephones.

By choosing to use the Automated Attendant feature, the caller may enter a subscriber extension. The Cisco Unity system forwards the call according to the configuration of the subscriber Profile. Of course, if that subscriber does not answer, the call can be routed back to the Cisco Unity system, and then to appropriate call handlers for additional forwarding to voice mailboxes, cell phones, pagers, and any number of other configurable options.

In situations where a caller does not know the direct subscriber extension, a search function can be executed to parse the directory of subscribers based on extension or name. When the caller finds a single match, the call is forwarded to the subscriber's voice mail or directly to the extension. The automatic forward feature on a single match is a configurable feature. Optionally, you can present the caller with the chance to verify the subscriber name before the call is forwarded. In the case of multiple matches, the caller is presented with a choice of the matches to choose from before the call is forwarded. This is known as a Directory Handler and will be discussed in the "Setting Up Cisco Unity" section of Chapter 3, "Cisco Unified Communications General Setup."

In cases where a subscriber is dialing into the system, the TUI presents the same basic options; however, the subscriber is able to access personal settings and, of course, messages. The TUI settings available to the suscriber are as follows:

Greetings:

- Record a personal greeting
- Enable or disable greeting

Call Transfers:

- Transfer calls to an extension or send to the greeting
- Change extension

Message Notification:

- Enable or disable a notification device, and change its number

Message Playback:

- Select full or brief Cisco Unity conversation menus

Message Addressing:

- Switch between addressing to other subscribers by name or by extension (by pressing ##)*

Personal Settings:

- Record a name
- Specify fax delivery number
- Change directory listing status
- Change password

Private Lists:

- Add and delete members

Defining Subscribers

A Cisco Unity subscriber is simply defined as a person for whom a Cisco Unity account is created. This can include a number of available options, but at the most basic level, the subscriber is a voice-mail user.

When a call comes into the Cisco Unity system, the system verifies the calling and called number information. In doing so, it scans the Cisco Unity system directory, seeking a match based on the source extension of the call. If the system finds a match, it prompts the subscriber for the password. Essentially, the system recongnizes that someone is attempting to retrieve messages or access the system for other available features. If the system does not find a match, it plays the Opening Greeting by default.

If a call is forwarded to the Cisco Unity system, Cisco Unity looks at the called party number received by Cisco CallManager or some other telephone system to search its directory for an extension match. If the Cisco Unity system finds a match, it plays the Standard Greeting of the called extension. If no match is found, the Opening Greeting is played, unless otherwise configured by the system administrator.

When a subscriber accesses the system for the first time and presses * and then enters their extension number, they are typically presented with a special first-time subscriber conversation that is meant to enroll them in the system. The system prompts the subscriber to record a voice name and a personal standard greeting. It then provides the opportunity to set a password.

When a subscriber is first created in the Cisco Unity system, their Microsoft Windows default password is set to 12345678 and the phone (voice mail) password is set to 12345; these defaults can be changed by using the appropriate subscriber template for creating additional subscribers.

Each subscriber must set their own personal password, as mandated by the subscriber template in effect at login. The administrator has the option of configuring the subscriber template to not require a password. The password is not stored in clear text anywhere in the system. If a subscriber forgets their password, an administrator can, using the Cisco Unity System Administrator, delete the existing password and assign a new, temporary password, which the user should change at first login. Otherwise, the only information available to the administrator is that the subscriber box does indeed have a password set and when it was last changed. Passwords on subscriber mailboxes are optional, but are highly recommended.

The normal subscriber conversation proceeds through a series of four major actions each time a subscriber calls into the system. For each of the actions, subscribers may use full or brief menus for the actions after login. The choice of full or brief menu structure, once made, affects the entire subscriber mailbox. The subscriber can take the following actions:

1   **Check new messages**—Upon receipt of a new voice message, the system lights the message waiting indicator (MWI) on the subscriber's phone. The messages are sorted in the mailbox in the configured order. The order can be changed by the subscriber. Depending on the choices made by the administrator when adding subscribers, Cisco Unity can tell how many new and saved messages are in the stack, who the sender is, how long the message is, and what number message this is in the total stack. The following list shows the standard conversation for the retrieval of messages when using a telephone:

   a. Press 1 for new messages:
      — Press 1 for voice messages
      — Press 2 for e-mails
      — Press 3 for faxes
      — Press 4 for receipts
      — Press # for all messages

   b. Press 3 and then 1 to review saved messages:
      — Press 1 for voice messages
      — Press 2 for e-mails
      — Press 3 for faxes
      — Press 4 for receipts
      — Press # for all messages

   c. Here are the options during a message:
      — Press 1 to restart a message
      — Press 2 to save a message
      — Press 3 to delete a message
      — Press 4 to slow playback a message
      — Press 5 to change the volume of a message (available on some systems)
      — Press 6 to fast playback a message
      — Press 7 to rewind a message
      — Press 8 to pause/resume a message
      — Press 9 to fast-forward a message

— Press # to fast-forward to end a message

— Press # # to save a message as is

d. After-message options:

— Press 1 to replay a message

— Press 2 to save a message

— Press 3 to delete a message

— Press 4 to reply to a message

— Press 4 then 2 to reply to all a message

— Press 4 then 4 to call the subscriber (available on some systems)

— Press 5 to forward a message

— Press 6 to save a message as new

— Press 7 to rewind a message

— Press 8 to deliver an e-mail or fax to a fax machine (available on some systems)

— Press 9 to play the properties of a message

— Press # to save a message as is

2 **Send a message**—Subscribers can quickly and easily send messages to other subscribers or distribution lists, such as all sales representatives. This can be done by entering extensions or by using the subscriber directory. Subscribers have the option to pause while recording a message or start over from the beginning of the message.

After addressing and recording a message, the subscriber has the following standard options:

a. Press # to send a message now

b. Press 1 for other message options

i. Press 1 to change the address

— Press 1 to add a name

— Press 2 to hear the current selected names

— Press 3 to remove a name that was selected

ii. Press 2 to change a recording

— Press 1 to hear a recording

— Press 2 to save a recording

— Press 3 to rerecord a recording

— Press 4 to add to a recording

iii.Press 3 to set a message for special delivery

— Press 1 to set a message as urgent

— Press 2 to flag a message for return receipt

— Press 3 to set a message as private

— Press 4 to set a message for future delivery

iv. Press 4 to review a message

v. Press # to send a message

3 **Review old messages**—The options available here are the same as those listed under Step 1, "Check new messages." Once a message has been heard in its entirety, it is changed in status to an old message. The old message is moved to the old-message stack and the MWIs are extinguished.

NOTE The MWI is extinguished only if the last unheard message or new message is heard in its entirety. The system keeps old messages until a subscriber, or an administrator with sufficient authority, deletes them. Deleted messages are deleted by default; however, an administrator can configure deleted messages to be moved to a Deleted folder in case the messages need to be restored at a later time. This is done in the class of service (CoS) configuration on the Cisco Unity System Adminstrator. Subscribers can review any of their old messages on the system. During that review they may redirect a message to another subscriber.

4 **Change setup options**—Subscribers have the option to change setup options over the phone, including greetings, transfer and delivery options, and personal options, such as their password, recorded name, spelled name, and directory listing.

When you are logging in, you can press 4 to access the setup options. Here are then the options:

a. Press 1 for greetings and call transfer settings

i. Press 1 to change greetings

— Press 1 to record this greeting

— Press 2 to turn on/off alternate greeting

— Press 3 to edit other greetings

— Press 4 to hear all greetings

ii. Press 2 Message options

— Press 1 to switch between transferring calls to an extension or a phone number

    b. Press '2' Message settings

        i. Press 1 to change the message notification

        — Press 1 for pager settings

        — Press 2 for Home phone settings

        — Press 3 for Work phone settings

        — Press 4 for Spare phone settings

        ii. Press 2 to change fax delivery settings

        — Press 1 to keep the current number

        — Press 2 to enter a new number

        iii. Press 3 to change the style of your menu

        — Press 1 to select either a full or brief menu

        iv. Press 4 to edit your private lists

        — Press 1 to hear your list

        — Press 2 to change names on list

    c. Press 3 for your personal settings

        i. Press 1 to change your password

        ii. Press 2 to change your recorded name

        iii. Press 3 to change your directory listing

        — Press 1 to change the listing status

In addition, at any time during the conversation (whether you are checking a message or setting up options), the subscriber can press 0 for help or * to cancel or move back one level in the menu structure.

Table 2-1 illustrates the configurable standard conversation options available in the Cisco Unity System Administrator. These options are found on the SA **Subscribers > Subscriber Template > Conversation** page.

Table 2-1   *Standard Conversation Options*

Field	Considerations
Menu Style	Choose one of these options:
	Full Menus—Subscribers hear comprehensive instructions; select for a new subscriber.
	Brief Menus—Subscribers hear abbreviated versions of the full menus; select for a more experienced subscriber.
Volume Level	Select the volume level at which the subscriber hears the Cisco Unity conversation. Subscribers can also adjust the volume temporarily from their phones.

Table 2-1   *Standard Conversation Options (Continued)*

Field	Considerations
Language	Select the language in which the subscriber conversation plays instructions to the subscriber. This setting also controls the language used for text-to-speech (TTS) e-mail. **NOTE** To use TTS e-mail, your organization must have purchased TTS e-mail licenses and installed the appropriate TTS languages. TTS e-mail is controlled by COS.
Time Format	Select the time format used for the message time stamps that subscribers hear when they listen to their messages over the phone: **System Default**—Subscribers hear message time stamps in the time format specified in the Use 24-Hour Time Format for Conversation and Schedules field on the **System > Configuration > Settings** page. **12-Hour Clock**—Subscribers hear 1:00 p.m. when listening to the time stamp for a message left at 1:00 p.m. **24-Hour Clock**—Subscribers hear 13:00 when listening to the time stamp for a message left at 1:00 p.m. Subscribers can set their own time format preferences in Unity with Cisco Cisco PCA.
When Exiting the Conversation, Send Subscriber To	Select the destination to which Cisco Unity sends the subscriber when exiting the conversation: **Call Handler**—Sends the call to the call handler that you select. **Directory Handler**—Sends the call to directory assistance. **Greetings Administrator**—Sends the call to a conversation for changing call handler greetings over the phone. **Hang Up**—Disconnects the call. Use carefully; unexpected hang-ups can appear rude to callers. **Interview Handler**—Sends the call to the interview handler that you select. **Sign-In**—Sends the call to the subscriber login conversation. **Subscriber**—Sends the call to the subscriber that you select.

continues

Table 2-1 *Standard Conversation Options (Continued)*

Field	Considerations
Identify a Subscriber By	Select how subscribers address messages to other subscribers. Subscribers can address messages over the phone by entering a subscriber's extension, first name, or last name. Addressing by name requires lettered keypads on subscriber phones.
	In the subscriber conversation, subscribers can switch between addressing by name and addressing by extension by pressing the # key twice. Note that when the Enable Spelled Name Search check box is unchecked on the **System > Configuration > Settings** page, subscribers can address messages over the phone only by entering subscriber extensions.
Subscriber Recorded Name	Check this check box to have Cisco Unity play the recorded name of the subscriber when the subscriber accesses Cisco Unity by phone.
	Uncheck the check box to have Cisco Unity go directly to the message count.
Message Count Totals	Check this check box to have Cisco Unity announce the total number of unopened messages. The number includes voice, e-mail, fax, and return receipt messages.
Voice Message Count	Check this check box to have Cisco Unity announce the number of voice messages that have not been heard.
E-Mail Message Count	Check this check box to have Cisco Unity announce the number of unopened e-mail messages.
Fax Count	Check this check box to have Cisco Unity announce the number of unopened fax messages.
Saved Message Count	Check this check box to have Cisco Unity announce the total number of messages that have been opened but not deleted. The number includes voice, e-mail, fax, and return receipt messages.
Message Type menu	Check this check box so that Cisco Unity plays the following menu when subscribers log on to Cisco Unity over the phone:
	Press 1 to hear voice messages
	Press 2 to hear e-mails
	Press 3 to hear faxes
	Press 4 to hear receipts
	Press # to hear all messages
	Note that although the e-mail and fax options are available in the Message Type menu, Cisco Unity plays e-mails and faxes only when the subscriber is assigned to a COS that has the TTS and FaxMail features enabled.
	Subscribers can also enable the Message Type menu by using Cisco PCA.

Table 2-1   *Standard Conversation Options (Continued)*

Field	Considerations
Sort by Message Type	Select a message type, and then click the Move Up and Move Down buttons to reorder the list of message types. Cisco Unity plays messages in the order that you specify here. Subscribers can also specify the order in which Cisco Unity plays new and saved messages by using Cisco PCA.
Then by	Click Newest First or Oldest First to specify the message order for new and saved messages.
Sender's Name	Check this check box to have Cisco Unity announce the name of the sender, if the message is from an identified subscriber.
Message Number	Check this check box to have Cisco Unity announce the sequential number of a message ("Message one is.."). Use with the Message Count Totals check box to help the subscriber keep track of the number of unheard messages.
Time the Message Was Sent	Check this check box to have Cisco Unity announce the date and time a message was sent, before playing the message.
Time the Message Was Sent	Check this check box to have Cisco Unity announce the date and time a message was sent, after playing the message.

Using ViewMail for Microsoft Outlook

VMO is a desktop subscriber interface for unified messaging installations. VMO is a licensed software package that works with the Cisco Unity system. VMO is simply another Outlook form that is installed on the subscriber's workstation from the Cisco Unity CD-ROM.

Figure 2-1 illustrates a voice-mail message opened using VMO.

Figure 2-1   *VMO Interface*

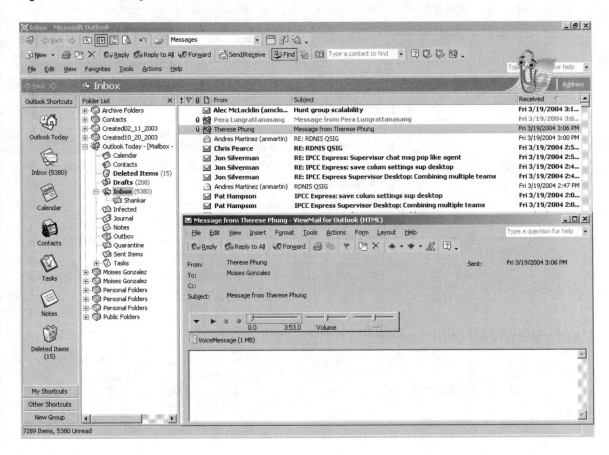

The VMO interface adds the capability to manipulate a voice mailbox from the subscriber messaging client. Normal tasks associated with voice mail and voice messages, including listening to, sending, replying to, or forwarding voice messages, can be performed from the client.

The Media Master control when using Microsoft Outlook supports the creation and editing of subscriber recordings via the multimedia devices on the workstation or the phone. The ViewMail for Outlook form can be used with Microsoft Outlook 98, Outlook 2000, and Outlook XP. As of this writing, ViewMail cannot be used with Microsoft Outlook Web Access because it does not support the use of Microsoft Outlook forms.

NOTE   The Cisco Unity system may require that subscribers enter their credentials when they use the phone as a playback or recording device in VMO, such as when subscriber computers are in a different domain than that of the Cisco Unity system.

The form presents the voice message to the user who is using the Media Master Control, an intuitive play/pause/record set of controls. In addition, the first control on the Media Master is the Options menu, where users set their playback and recording devices and can copy and paste voice messages onto their desktop, for example. The Media Master control when using MS Outlook is an eXtensible Markup Language (XML) control that is used in every place in the Cisco Unity system interface where sound needs to be played or recorded. It is the same in the SA, the Cisco Unity Assistant (CUA), and the Cisco Unity Inbox.

If the subscriber has not installed VMO, the voice messages are simply e-mailed as .wav file attachments. VMO also provides the capability to hear the messages through PC speakers. If the message was left by another subscriber, it is possible to reply to the message simply by clicking the VMO Reply button. The Media Master Control when using MS Outlook allows a message to be recorded and sent. The Cisco Unity system processes the message just as if it had been left via a telephone handset and activates the MWI of the destination subscriber. If a user uses the Outlook Web Client, the file appears as a .wav attachment. This is especially useful for traveling or remote users. As an added feature, the text of the message can be included in the e-mail along with the voice-message attachment.

Using DUCS for Lotus Notes

DUCS for Cisco Unity is a desktop interface that allows unified messaging features for an IBM Lotus Notes user. IBM Lotus has constructed a software suite of applications called Domino Unified Communications Services (DUCS). DUCS for Cisco Unity is an application that is included with the purchase of the DUCS software suite. E-mail and voice-mail capabilities are provided in one software application. The DUCS for Cisco Unity software is installed on the client workstation by the administrator or the end user.

The software is essentially a Lotus Notes Mail template built and supported by IBM Lotus and, as mentioned, obtained from IBM or an IBM reseller through the purchase of the DUCS software suite. Subscribers are able to listen to, send, reply to, or forward voice mails. The client software supports the capability for subscribers to record through their multimedia device or through their phone.

Customizing VMO

VMO interaction is customizable in a number of differing ways. These alterations can affect sounds played when message events occur, allow for auto-playback of messages (if the check box to play automatically is checked, which by default it is not), or allow messages to be saved to a messaging client. There is also a check box that allows the option to save only the message header in the Sent Items folder.

The sound that notifies the subscriber of new voice messages arriving in the Inbox can be customized by importing a custom .wav file. This enables the subscriber to add a more personal touch to the delivery of voice-mail messages to their desktop. However, this option is available only if the subscriber's computer has multimedia speakers.

Another setting that can be altered is the one dealing with message playback. Setting up the automatic voice message playback feature causes voice messages to begin playing as soon as they are opened. With automatic playback disabled, the Media Master control bar is used to play voice messages.

If your Outlook Inbox is set to save copies of sent messages in the Sent Items folder, a copy of each voice message that you send using VMO is also saved. Over time, this can cause hard disk constraint issues. Therefore, the option to disable the saving of sent messages has been provided in the VMO client.

At times, there will be deployments and installations to sites that are using lower bandwidth links. In these circumstances where throughput is limited, it is possible, though not the default action, to configure messages to download to the local workstation prior to playback.

Understanding Cisco PCA

Cisco PCA serves as a centralized point of access to subscriber web-based applications. The Cisco PCA portal includes the Cisco Unity Inbox (formerly known in Cisco Unity version 3.1 and earlier as the Visual Messaging Interface, or VMI) and the Cisco Unity Assistant (formerly known in verions of Cisco Unity 3.1 and earlier as Active Assistant, or AA). Cisco PCA is available to subscribers through a URL. Subscribers need not have any particular COS rights to access it, but they do need appropriate COS rights to the Cisco Unity Inbox and the CUA. Cisco PCA is automatically installed during the Cisco Unity system installation. This easy-to-use web interface gives subscribers desktop access to manage their voice-mail account.

To fully benefit from this section, it is recommended that you have the following prerequisite skills and knowledge (refer to Chapter 1, "Cisco Unified Communications System Fundamentals," for a quick review of either topic):

- Knowledge of Cisco Unity standard and optional features
- Knowledge of Cisco Personal Assistant standard and optional features

To access the interface, point the Microsoft Internet Explorer browser to http://UnityServerName/ciscopca.

NOTE   The address http://UnityServerName/ciscopca URL is case sensitive!

From this interface, subscribers can change their greetings, passwords, message notification devices, and schedules, create private lists, enable or disable call screening, and change their call transfer. The CUA is considered appropriate for "power" voice-mail users. Some administrators are uncomfortable allowing subscribers to change their greetings and program message notification for other devices. With some training, almost any subscriber will find that the CUA is a powerful tool to use to manage their voice-messaging account.

Understanding the Cisco Unity Assistant

The Cisco Unity Assistant (CUA) allows subscribers to access their voice-mail messages via Internet Explorer.

By using the CUA, a subscriber can change a number of options, including the following:

Greetings:

- Record a personal greeting
- Enable or disable a greeting
- Switch between the system prompt and personal greeting

Call Transfers:

- Transfer calls to an extension or send to the greeting
- Change extension

Call Holding and Screening:

- Select the action that Cisco Unity performs for unidentified callers when the subscriber phone is busy, including placing the caller on hold, prompting the caller to hold or leave a message, and sending the caller directly to the greeting
- Select the action that Cisco Unity performs when the subscriber answers calls from unidentified callers, including telling the subscriber who the call is for, announcing that Cisco Unity is transferring the call, prompting the subscriber to accept or refuse a call, and prompting the caller to say their name

Message Notification:

- Enable or disable a notification device, and change its number
- Specify dialing options
- Select the types of messages and message urgency for which Cisco Unity calls a device
- Set up a notification schedule, and specify what happens when a device does not answer, is busy, or fails

Message Playback:

- Select full or brief Cisco Unity conversation menus
- Select the action that Cisco Unity performs when the subscriber calls Cisco Unity, including greeting the subscriber by name and announcing the number of new messages by type
- Select the action that Cisco Unity performs when messages are played, including announcing the name and number of the sender who left a message, whether the time stamp is played before or after the message, and the volume level at which messages are played

Message Addressing:

- Switch between addressing messages to other subscribers by name, or by extension
- Specify the order in which to address messages by name (last name followed by first name, or vice versa)

Caller Options:

- Allow callers to edit messages
- Allow callers to mark messages urgent

Personal Settings:

- Record a name
- Specify a fax delivery number
- Change directory listing status
- Change password
- Select the language used for the subscriber phone conversation

Private Lists:

- Enter a display name
- Record a name
- Add and delete members

Understanding Cisco PA Call Flow

When a Cisco PA–enabled subscriber number receives an outside call from the Public Switched Telephone Network (PSTN), PA retrieves subscriber information from the Lightweight Directory Access Protocol (LDAP) directory. Cisco PA works only in conjunction with a Cisco CallManager system. Subscribers can configure individual rules for calls that are destined for their own phone number(s). If rules have been configured, those rules are executed to route the call as specified. Calls can also be set up with the "follow me" feature where no rules lookup occurs and all calls are immediately sent to an alternate location or device. Rules-based call routing can be handled according to caller ID, date and time of day, or the user's meeting status based on the user's calendar.

Cisco PA has the capability to forward and screen incoming calls according to subscriber-configured rules set up in the PA web interface. The PA administrator should provide end users the URL for the PA server. Upon initial use of the PA web interface, a welcome screen is presented. On this page, the default language is configured. This specifies the language in which system prompts are heard. Subsequent visits result in the presentation of the Rule-Sets page to configure call-forwarding preferences.

The web interface offers numerous features. However, the focus at this time is on two of the more important features, Destinations and Callers, which are accessible through links at the top of the web interface page. Figure 2-2 shows the Cisco PA web interface, particularly the Rule-Sets page.

Clicking the Destinations link allows the user to define the desired destination of calls made, by name and number. The Callers link allows the user to define entries in their personal address book. These links serve to direct calls to a specific PA user. Once defined, Rule-Sets can be put in place to actually initiate the call forwarding to the desired PA user.

Figure 2-2 *Cisco PA Administration Rule-Sets Page*

Understanding Cisco PA Speech Recognition

Cisco PA contains options to support speech-recognition capabilities. This allows a subscriber to use voice dialing when calling individuals listed in the corporate directory or a personal address book, set up conference calling, activate or deactivate Rule-Sets, or use their voice-mail account.

When calling into PA, the subscriber is prompted to enter a PIN. This PIN is established in the Cisco CallManager (CCM) system. PA may not always prompt for the PIN. The deciding factors of whether or not the subscriber is prompted for the PIN depends on the source of the calling number and the function PA is attempting to execute. The PA must recognize the calling number. Otherwise, the PIN is required by the system to permit the subscriber to use any PA functions. Also, any time rules are altered or executed, the Follow Me feature is enabled or disabled or other call-forwarding functions are altered, the PIN will be required by the system.

Once logged in, the subscriber hears all prompts in their configured language. If no language was configured, PA uses the default language established by the system administrator. Speech-enabled directory dialing allows calls to be placed through PA by speaking a subscriber's name or phone number aloud.

Using PA-Driven Voice Mail

Cisco PA's voice-recognition features allow the subscriber to access Cisco Unity voice-mail messages through spoken commands. PA also interprets touch-tone commands. When the subscriber dials into PA for voice-mail access, PA first plays a welcome message and prompts for the desired action. The subscriber simply speaks the desired command, such as "Check messages". The system prompts the subscriber for the PIN. The PIN used for PA and the subscriber password to access Cisco Unity are not the same. They are stored in different locations, one in PA or CCM, the other in Cisco Unity. If PA cannot verify the entered PIN, the subscriber is transferred to the Cisco Unity voice-mail system and prompted to enter the password established with it.

While listening to messages, the subscriber may use voice commands to complete tasks, such as list or read messages, skip messages, delete messages, and call back the sender of a message (if listed in the corporate directory). The voice-mail session is ended by the voice command "Good bye."

Chapter Summary

In this chapter, you learned about the Cisco Unity features and functions to route calls. Specifically, you learned how to do the following:

- Determine the means by which calls are handled for individual subscribers.

- Use tools to aide in the delivery, sending, and manipulation of messages such as VMO and PA to further complement the user-friendliness of the system overall.

- Use speech-recognition capabilities to allow subscribers to speak commands to place calls to contacts in the corporate directory or personal address book.

- Configure call handling for individual subscribers, including forwarding of calls, handling of messages, and other traditional voice-messaging capabilities

- Use the Cisco PA web interface to create and activate Rule-Sets for the subscriber based on time of day, date, location, and other pertinent variables

For additional information on the preceding topics, refer to these resources:

- "White Paper: Client Access in a Voice Messaging-Only Deployment (Cisco Unity Version 4.0)." This white paper is available on Cisco.com. Select **Products and Services > Voice and Telephony > Cisco Unity > Product Literature > White Papers**.

- *Cisco Unity User Guide.* This is available for both Microsoft Exchange and Lotus Domino installations; make sure that you choose the correct version. Go to Cisco.com and select **Products and Services > Voice and Telephony > Cisco Unity > Technical Documentation > User Guides** to choose the appropriate guide.

Chapter Review Questions

Use this section to test yourself on how well you learned the concepts discussed in this chapter. You can find the answers to the review questions for this chapter in Appendix A.

1. Explain briefly the process that occurs when a Cisco Unity subscriber logs in to the system for the first time.

2. List four typical voice-mail subscriber options when using the TUI.

3. List at least two items that can be customized in the VMO settings.

4. When a user is prompted for a PIN by Cisco PA, what is the result when the PIN cannot be verified due to an incorrect entry?

5. Which interface allows a subscriber to configure Rule-Sets to enable call forwarding based on personal preferences for PA?

6. Each subscriber must set a password as mandated by the subscriber template in effect at login. If a subscriber loses or forgets the password set, what course of action should be taken?

7. Describe the circumstance that will cause the MWI on the subscriber phone to be turned off.

8. To configure call hold and screening features, which utility, discussed in this chapter, should be used?

9. For Cisco PA to be fully used by a subscriber, it must be able to retrieve subscriber information from an LDAP directory. Under what circumstance does this feature properly function?

10. Cisco PA's voice-recognition capabilities allow voice message access using voice commands. List at least two tasks that are possible using voice commands.

Upon completing this chapter, you will be able to perform the following tasks:

- Use the Cisco Unity System Administrator to perform supervisory tasks, such as create subscriber accounts, set system schedules, specify settings for individual subscribers or groups of subscribers through the use of subscriber templates, and implement a call management plan

- Use configuration tools to manage settings, directory objects, system schedules, and licensing and subscriber authentication

CHAPTER 3

Setting Up Cisco Unified Communications

To manage a Cisco Unity system and administer it efficiently, you need to understand the product and its features. As with many other software functions, Cisco Unity has settings and configuration options that are both global and record-specific. This chapter is dedicated to the introduction of basic system administration, including layout, security, and help functions. Basic rules of voice processing, as well as some additional tools, are discussed to give you a better understanding of the information presented.

Among the topics discussed in this chapter is the basic use of the Cisco Unity System Administrator web tool to administer the system. Nearly every facet pertaining to the configuration of Cisco Unity is web-based in nature.

Following an introduction of the Cisco Unity System Administrator is a discussion of Cisco Unity setup to give you a basic idea of what tasks are involved in getting a new installation up and running.

Using the Cisco Unity System Administrator

The Cisco Unity System Administrator is the tool that you will use to perform the majority of administrative tasks, so you need to become familiar with this tool to effectively administrator and set up a Cisco Unity system.

Before you begin to read about how to use this tool, to fully benefit from this section, it is recommended that you have the following prerequisite skills and knowledge. (If you need a quick review, see the designated chapter, where you can find more information on the topic.)

- A working knowledge of the Cisco Unity telephone user interface (TUI) and subscriber tools for managing voice messages and settings (see Chapter 2, "Using Your Cisco Unified Communications System")

- A solid understanding of Cisco Unity basic features and functions (see Chapter 1, "Cisco Unified Communications System Fundamentals")

The Cisco Unity System Administrator is accessible by using Microsoft Internet Explorer 6.0 or later and is optimized to be viewed at 1024 × 768 resolution using 256 colors (but not below 800 × 600, because it is not accessible at 640 × 480). It is broken into three differing frames:

- **Navigation bar**—The navigation bar on the left holds all the links to the different areas of administration and it's organized by section.

- **Title strip**—The title strip gives the title of the page; that is the name of the subscriber or call handler. It also contains the command icons to view, add, and delete, and the name of the record being accessed.

- **Page body**—The page body gives all the current information and settings. Whereas the address of the console is dependent on your naming conventions, the default address of the Cisco Unity System Administrator is http://<Cisco Unity server Name>/Saweb.

Figure 3-1 shows a logical view of the entire page, including the navigation bar, title bar, and page body.

Figure 3-1   *Cisco Unity System Administrator Page Layout*

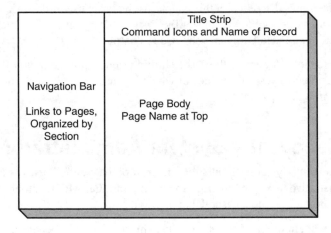

Defining the Navigation Bar

The navigation bar is one of the primary tools used on the main page of the Cisco Unity System Administrator. This bar exists on the left margin of the Cisco Unity System Administrator main page so that it is easily accessible by the Cisco Unity System administrator.

Two levels of navigation are available in the Cisco Unity System Administrator. The first level of the navigation bar shows individual data categories and furnishes web links to each group of pages within each of the categories.

The second level furnishes web links to each page within a selected group. After you select a page, you can access individual records on that page by clicking the Find icon.

The navigation bar consists of six major portions (see Figure 3-2):

- **Subscribers**—This is where you can create, delete, or modify subscriber specific settings. This section includes links to the subscriber, subscriber template, class of service (COS) settings, public distribution lists, and account policy pages.

- **Call Management**—This is where you set how a call is handled by Cisco Unity. This section includes links to the call handlers, directory handlers, interview handlers, call routing, and restriction tables pages.

- **Reports**—This is where you can generate reports for either subscribers or system information. This section includes links to subscribers and system reports pages.

- **Network**—If you are linking Cisco Unity with another voice messaging system, this section will show the different options available for networking. The networking options you are licensed for will appear here. This section includes links to both primary and delivery location pages. If the system is licensed for AMIS or bridge networking, you see those options here also.

- **System**—This section includes links to configuration, schedules, holidays, licensing, authentication integrations, and ports pages.

- **Unity Servers**—Includes links that provide a list of all the Cisco Unity servers that are digitally networked together.

You will need to be completely familiar with the links on the navigation bar, which should come naturally to you over a short period of active administration.

Figure 3-2 *Cisco Unity System Administrator Navigation Bar*

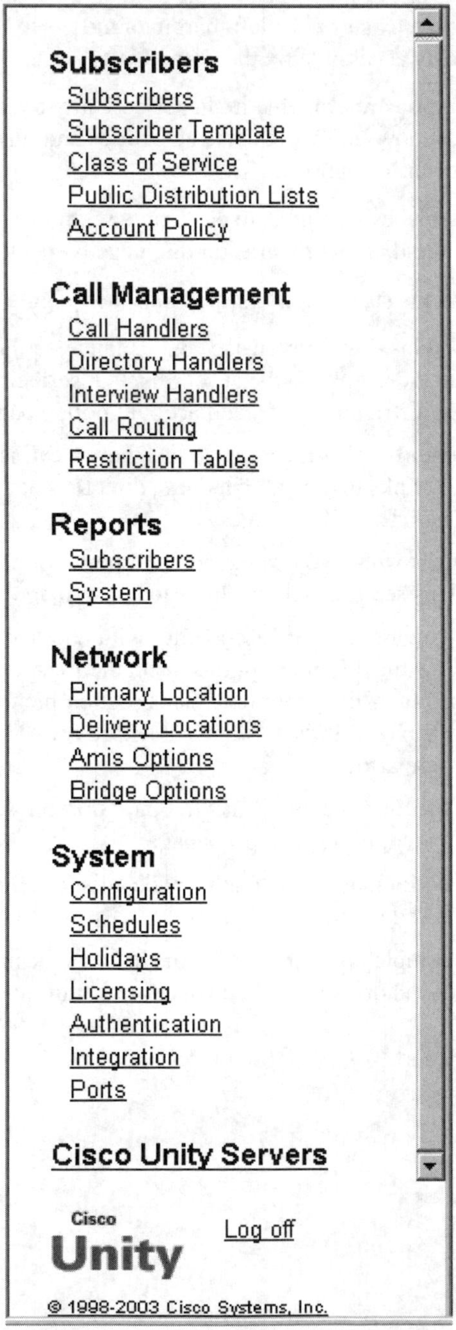

Defining the Title Strip

The title strip is relatively self-explanatory. It serves to display the name of the record or of the group of settings that appears on the page. The title strip also features command icons that initiate actions, such as saving and finding records. At any given time, the icons are presented in color. If a grayscale icon appears, it indicates that the option associated with that icon is unavailable on that particular page. These icons include:

- **Save**—Saves entered data. This option is grayed out until changes have been recorded in the record. If a different major link is clicked after making changes to the entries but not saving the changes, the system prompts the administrator to save the changes, do not save, or cancel.

- **Find**—Opens the Find window to allow for a search of available records for the displayed category.

- **Add**—Opens an Add window to allow the addition of new records.

- **Delete**—Deletes the displayed record after prompting for confirmation of the deletion.

- **Run**—Generates a report (only available on Reports pages).

- **Online Documentation**—Provides access to the Help index and provides access to information for field-by-field documentation for each page.

- **Field Help**—Displays question marks next to fields and buttons for which Help is available.

Defining the Page Body

The page body of the Cisco Unity System Administrator is relatively self-explanatory. When you click a link, the corresponding page fills this space and you can make configuration entries. When you select the links displayed, this is where you will see actual information for each page that is entered into the Cisco Unity system. The page name is highlighted at the top of the page.

Protecting System Administration

As with any high- or unrestricted-access account, it is imperative that you protect the system administrator account. A Cisco Unity system has numerous security features to provide some level of protection. Among the features offered by the system is a choice between two authentication methods, the Anonymous method and the Integrated Windows method (formerly Windows NT Challenge/Response authentication). The Microsoft website contains general information about both authentication types, including strengths and weaknesses of each.

Table 3-1 provides an overview of the authentication methods by describing some of the advantages and disadvantages of each.

Table 3-1 *Authentication Methods*

Authentication Type	Advantages	Disadvantages
Integrated Windows authentication	User credentials are not sent across the network. Microsoft Internet Explorer and Microsoft Windows use a challenge/response mechanism to authenticate the user.	Windows cannot validate the identity of a user when the user is logged on to an untrusted domain and, therefore, denies the user access to the Cisco Unity System Administrator.
	Integrated Windows authentication is the default in Microsoft Internet Information Server (IIS); therefore, no additional setup is required.	When subscribers log on to the Cisco Unity System Administrator from another domain, they are prompted to re-enter their credentials every time that they want to use the phone as a recording and playback device for the Media Master.
Anonymous authentication	When subscribers log on to the Cisco Unity System Administrator from another domain, they can enter the applicable credentials on the Cisco Unity Log On page for the domain that the Cisco Unity server is in.	When a subscriber enters credentials on the Cisco Unity Log On page, the credentials are sent across the network in clear text. To solve this problem, configure Cisco Unity to use Secure Sockets Layer (SSL).
	When subscribers log on to the Cisco Unity System Administrator from another domain, they are not prompted to re-enter their credentials each time that they want to use the phone as a recording and playback device for the Media Master.	Because Integrated Windows authentication is the IIS default, an administrator must configure the system to use Anonymous authentication.

By default, IIS is configured to use Integrated Windows authentication to authenticate the username and password. During the Cisco Unity installation process, the installer has the option to configure IIS so that the Cisco Unity System Administrator uses Anonymous authentication instead.

It is important to keep in mind that, until an administrative subscriber account is created, the Windows credentials associated with the default administrator account must be used to log on to the Cisco Unity System Administrator tool.

System Administrator permissions are based on a subscriber's COS. Through COS, additional administrative tasks and capabilities can be delegated to individual subscribers. All Cisco Unity administrators must also be Cisco Unity subscribers. Figure 3-3 shows the Cisco Unity System Administrator Subscribers page.

Figure 3-3   *Cisco Unity System Administrator Subscribers Page*

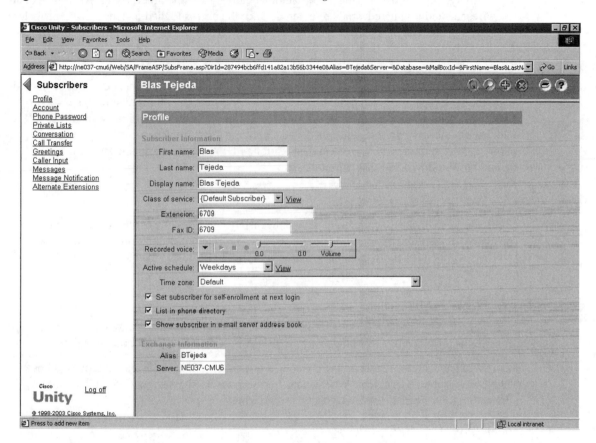

The manner in which the authentication is performed has an effect on the behavior of the system. The administrator account, however, remains unchanged. It is possible to maintain only the initial (default) administrator account. Typically, for customization, and even for tracking and change control, separate accounts are created for each administrative user in the domain.

It is, however, possible to track administrator actions. Actions such as entry creation, updates, deletions, and so on of Cisco Unity entities can be tracked by the Cisco Unity system.

Internet Explorer uses the Microsoft Windows 2000 Challenge and Response for System Administrator (SA) access. Netscape Navigator is not supported for SA access because there is no mechanism for challenge/response processes. SA permissions are based on a subscriber's COS. Through COS, you can delegate the system administration tasks, or a portion of them, to other subscribers. A Cisco Unity administrator must also be a Cisco Unity subscriber.

To further augment security, IIS in Windows 2000 can be configured to govern the length of time that the browser can be left idle/unattended before Cisco Unity automatically logs off the administrator. This is configured by altering the Session Timeout limit in IIS. After 20 minutes of inactivity, the subscriber is logged off automatically by the idle timer; the browser must then be refreshed and login credentials re-entered. Once the user is logged off, the system provides a link to log on again.

NOTE   The Cisco Unity system limits to five the number of administrator accounts that can be logged in to the system at any given time. Each administrative user should make sure to use the Log Off link to close the System Administrator after they have completed their administrative tasks. Otherwise, the workstation should be locked any time the administrator is away. When the administrator returns, Anonymous authentication prompts for the username and password once again, but Windows Authentication does not.

Regardless of which authentication method the installer chooses, the authentication method can be altered at any time by an administrator. Before any changes of this sort are made, however, all Cisco Unity administrators in the organization should agree that the change should be made.

Using Onscreen Help

Throughout the Cisco Unity system, including the System Administrator, an onscreen help function is provided to assist new or less-experienced Cisco Unity administrators.

Two help icons are available on the console: a question mark icon (?) and an icon of a book. The ? icon is a field help icon, whereas the book icon is used to access Cisco Unity online documentation. Figure 3-4 illustrates these two icons.

Figure 3-4   *Field Help and Online Documentation Help Icons*

Figure 3-5 shows the result of clicking the online documentation icon. Note that a new window has opened with information specific to the selected field.

Figure 3-5   *Onscreen Help Using the Book Icon*

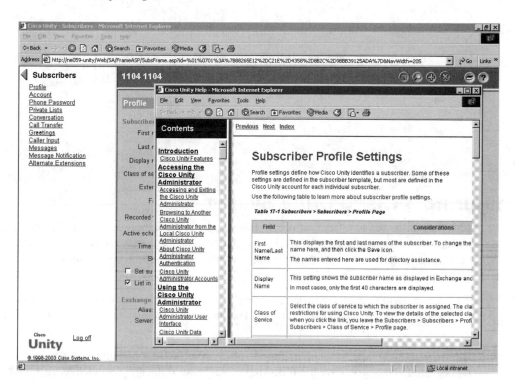

Using Cisco Unity Media Master

To enable you to record and play back voice, Cisco Unity uses the same interface consistently throughout the product. The drop-down menu allows you to choose the phone or the PC speakers and microphone to record and play back voice. It is also possible to copy and paste voice files (.wav only). The Options selection is where you specify what telephone extension Cisco Unity dials to reach a subscriber, and the name of the Cisco Unity server that will dial the extension.

The Media Master control bar appears on each Cisco Unity System Administrator page on which recordings can be made. It allows recordings to be created and played, either with a phone or with a computer microphone and speakers, by clicking the Media Master controls. Figure 3-6 shows the Media Master control bar.

Figure 3-6 *Media Master Control Bar*

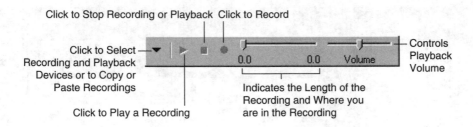

Configuring a Cisco Unity System

This section serves as a Cisco Unity system setup and configuration guide. The actual architecture and processes involved in installation of the software are covered in the "Understanding Cisco Unity for Exchange Architecture" section of Chapter 8, "Cisco Unified Communications System Software."

The ever-growing dependence on telephony and associated technologies has made voice mail an imperative tool in any business model. That in mind, it is important to understand how to set up a Cisco Unity system properly.

Before you study how to set up a Cisco Unity system, to fully benefit from this section, it is recommended that you have the following prerequisite skills and knowledge. (If you need a quick review, see the designated chapter, where you can find more information on the topic.)

- A basic understanding of the features and functions available to subscribers and administrators (see Chapter 1)
- A strong understanding of the functionality of the Cisco Personal Communications Assistant (PCA) (see Chapter 2)

Obviously, any software package must be properly installed and configured on supported platforms before it may become a useful addition to any environment, and Cisco Unity is no different. Numerous general settings must be configured on every Cisco Unity system before any subscribers can be added. Learning how to set up a Cisco Unity system efficiently and effectively is an important task for an administrator.

NOTE   If the Cisco Unity system will use the failover feature, begin the installation on the primary server. The task list alerts you when to install the secondary server. Both Cisco Unity servers must have the same configuration.

Creating a Cisco Unity Task List

This section discusses the basic steps of getting through a new installation of the Cisco Unity software.

When you are installing a system that will become a critical piece of the overall network infrastructure, you must exercise proper due diligence. Before you perform the installation, you must assemble various pieces of information, software packages, and a proper hardware platform on which to install the system. You must decide how and where this particular Cisco Unity system will fit into the network. Figure 3-7 provides a snapshot of the steps necessary to ensure a successful rollout.

Figure 3-7 *Cisco Unity Setup Task List*

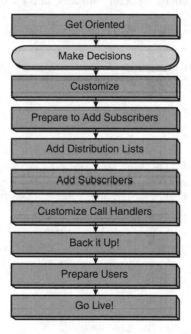

After the Microsoft Windows 2000 and Microsoft Exchange or Lotus Domino installations are complete, the Cisco Unity installation, itself, can proceed. The first few steps in the task list are some of the most vital.

- **Get oriented:** In the orientation phase, you make crucial decisions regarding placement and server roles. These decisions dictate how and where the server will interact with the network as a whole. Improper placement or underestimation of the load and demand that will be placed on the server has the potential to easily create problems. All of these considerations should be taken into account before you place any Cisco Unity server platform, to ensure that you purchase the proper hardware and licensing.

- **Make decisions:** Once you have defined the roles and responsibilities for the Cisco Unity system, you should consider the subscriber population of the system. Some questions that need to be answered ahead of time include: How many subscribers? What kinds of subscriber templates and distribution lists will be necessary? What features should be made available to subscribers, such as one-key dialing, voice-command capabilities, and so on?

- **Customize, prepare to add subscribers, and add distribution lists:** With subscriber needs in place, it is time to consider call routing. How calls are routed will have profound effects on the usability of the Cisco Unity system. Will the default directory and call handlers adequately meet the needs of all subscribers, or will some customization be necessary and, if so, to what degree?

- **Add subscriber, customize call handlers, make a backup, prepare users, and go live:** Once the process is complete and the system is ready for subscribers, you should perform a full backup of the server. This is imperative in case a restoration of the base system becomes necessary. With the backup complete, you can create subscribers. Preparing users with the proper training to use the system should then follow and then taking the system into production.

Understanding Configuration Settings

To open the Configuration Settings page, select **System > Configuration > Settings** in the Cisco Unity System Administrator. This page contains significant information about the system. These settings are typically adjusted as part of the "customize" phase (refer to Figure 3-7). As such, the values must be supplied, or left at default settings, on any system you set up. The Settings page is composed of system-wide settings, such as the default schedule, time format, search and security option, and cleanup intervals for diagnostic and log files. The Software Versions page provides information regarding what software is running, and all the associated Cisco Unity services and their version numbers. This information is useful when you need to contact the Cisco Technical Assistance Center (TAC).

Replicating Cisco Unity Directory Objects

Cisco Unity allows you to replicate to the Cisco Unity database Cisco Unity directory objects, which include mail users, locations, and distribution lists. The replication settings allow you to replicate objects on a specific schedule. There is, however, a Replicate feature that allows forced replication on demand.

Be careful about what you replicate, because replicating all Cisco Unity directory objects may significantly impact system performance. Also, consider replicating all objects during off hours.

Table 3-2 provides field names and descriptions for the options on the Configuration Settings page.

Table 3-2   *Configuration Settings Page*

Field	Description
Default Schedule	Select the default schedule, which is used for all Cisco Unity operations unless specifically changed for a call handler, subscriber account, or call-routing table.
	Default: Weekdays (the only other option is All Hours–All Days).
Use 24-Hour Time Format for Conversation and Schedules Conversation	Check this check box to use a 24-hour time format for all Cisco Unity operations; otherwise, a 12-hour format is used.
	Default: unchecked.
Enter Spelled Name Search	Check this check box to allow subscribers to address messages to other subscribers by spelling a subscriber's first or last name over the phone. When checked, subscribers in the process of editing private lists can search for other subscribers by spelling the subscriber's name via the phone.
	When unchecked, subscribers can search for subscribers over the phone only by entering subscriber extensions. If checked, it does not prevent searching the subscriber database by entering a subscriber extension.
	Default: checked.
RSA Two Factor	Check this check box to enable enhanced phone security, which uses RSA two-factor user authentication. To use enhanced phone security, an ACE/Server must be installed and configured for your system. Additionally, a new COS must be created or an existing COS modified for the subscribers who are using enhanced phone security.
	Default: unchecked.
	NOTE RSA and ACE/Server subject matter is not covered in this book.

continues

Table 3-2 *Configuration Settings Page (Continued)*

Field	Description
Subscribers Are Identified as Message Senders Only if They Log On	Check this check box to disable identified subscriber messaging system-wide.
	When identified subscriber messaging is enabled, Cisco Unity automatically identifies a message left during an internal call as originating from the extension from which the call was made.
	Regardless of enabled or disabled status, if a subscriber logs on before leaving a message from an internal location other than the extension assigned to the subscriber, such as from a conference room, Cisco Unity identifies the call as originating from the extension of the logged-on subscriber rather than the extension from which the call is placed.
	This field is applicable only when the phone system provides caller and called party information to Cisco Unity. A system-wide setting is not configurable for an individual subscriber or subscriber template.
	Default: unchecked.
Cisco Personal Communications Assistant (PCA)	The URL for Cisco PCA should be entered here so that it is automatically included as a link in the body of the e-mail message that is sent to the subscriber.
Cleanup Interval for Logger Data Files in Days	Indicate how often data files should be deleted.
	Default: 7 days.
Cleanup Interval for Logger Diagnostic Files in Days	Indicate how often diagnostic files should be deleted.
	Default: 7 days.
Cleanup Interval for Report Files in Days	Indicate how often report files should be deleted.
	Default: 7 days.
Replicate Cisco Unity Directory Objects	Choose Changed Objects to manually synchronize changes from Active Directory or Exchange 5.5 Directory into the Cisco Unity SQL database.
	Choose All Objects only if Cisco Unity has been down for a considerable length of time.
Cisco Unity Computer Settings	*Display only.* This setting shows the name of the Cisco Unity server and the Windows Domain name.
Fax Settings	This setting shows the name of the fax domain.

Table 3-2   *Configuration Settings Page (Continued)*

Field	Description
Disk Usage	*Display only.* This setting shows, in megabytes, the total, used, and free disk space on the Cisco Unity server.
Recording Settings	The **System > Configuration > Recordings** page contains settings for recording time limits and for silence thresholds (the amount of silence before Cisco Unity assumes the caller is no longer on the line) before, during, and after recordings.
Contacts	The **System > Configuration > Contacts** page is where you enter the names and phone numbers of the people responsible for maintaining or administering the Cisco Unity server. This information might be useful to a technician who is accessing Cisco Unity from offsite.
Phone Languages	Phone languages are the languages in which Cisco Unity can play system prompts to subscribers and callers. The default phone language and other system-wide phone language settings are specified. Also specified are the default text-to-speech (TTS) language, which is the language that subscribers hear when their e-mail is read to them over the phone. Note that to use TTS languages, an organization must have TTS e-mail and the appropriate languages installed.
Graphical User Interface (GUI) Languages	The settings on this page determine the languages in which the Cisco Unity System Administrator pages can be displayed. A default GUI language and other system-wide GUI language settings can be specified.

It is useful to understand the settings and capabilities of the Cisco Unity System. Proper configuration of the Recordings, Contacts, Phone Languages, and GUI Language settings is necessary to ensure proper operation of the system.

Recording Settings

The Recordings page contains settings for recording time limits and for silence thresholds (the amount of silence before Cisco Unity assumes the caller is no longer on the line) before, during, and after recordings.

To encode information, such as sound or video, as data, it is necessary to use a compression/decompression algorithm (codec). Codecs vary in form, function, efficiency, and quality. Cisco Unity is no exception to the rule when it comes to encoding and storing voice messages, greetings, and so on. Cisco Unity supports the following audio codecs:

- G.711 Mu-law (default)
- G.711 A-law
- G.729a
- Intel Dialogic OKI ADPCM 8 kHz
- Intel Dialogic OKI ADPCM 6 kHz
- GSM 6.10
- G.726 (Cisco Unity Version 4.01 or later)

For information on choosing and implementing audio codecs, refer to "White Paper: Audio Codecs and Cisco Unity," which is available at Cisco.com (click **Products & Solutions > Voice & IP Communications > Voice Software > Cisco Unity > White Papers**).

WARNING   If a Cisco Unity system is configured with a failover system, recordings settings are not replicated between the primary and secondary servers. The values must be changed manually on both servers.

Table 3-3 includes additional information about the recordings settings in the configuration section of the System Administrator.

Table 3-3   *System > Configuration > Recordings Page*

Field	Considerations
Allowed Time for Recording in Milliseconds	Select the number of milliseconds for the DTMF clip length. This setting indicates how much to truncate the end of a recording when a message is terminated with a touch-tone. Default: 170 milliseconds.
Allowed Time for Short Recording in Seconds	Select the number of seconds that Cisco Unity uses as a cutoff for short and long recordings. Recordings shorter than this number are considered short recordings; recordings longer than this number are considered long recordings. Default: 10 seconds.

Table 3-3   *System > Configuration > Recordings Page (Continued)*

Field	Considerations
Allow How Much Silence Before Time Out in Seconds	Select the number of seconds after which Cisco Unity will end the message, greeting, or recorded name if the subscriber or caller has not begun speaking. A value lower than 2 or 3 seconds may not give the subscriber or caller enough time to begin speaking. Default: 5 seconds.
Discard Any Recording Less Than in Seconds	Select the minimum length of recordings, in seconds, for messages or greetings. Note that this setting is not applied to recorded names. Default: 1 second.
Short Recording (Short Recording Trail Limit or Less)	Select the number of seconds of silence that Cisco Unity uses to detect the end of a short recording. When Cisco Unity detects a pause equal to the number of seconds specified, it assumes that the speaker has finished recording the message, greeting, or recorded name. Callers are more likely to pause longer during long messages. That in mind, it may be prudent to set a smaller pause length for short recordings than for long recordings. Cisco Unity uses the Allowed Time for Short Recording in Seconds setting to determine whether a recording is short or long. Default: 2 seconds.
Long Recording (Over Short Recording Trail Limit)	Select the number of seconds of silence that Cisco Unity uses to detect the end of a long recording. When Cisco Unity detects a pause equal to the number of seconds specified, it assumes that the speaker has finished recording the message, greeting, or recorded name. Callers are more likely to pause longer during long messages. That in mind, it may be prudent to set a greater pause length for long recordings than for short recordings. Cisco Unity uses the Allowed Time for Short Recording in Seconds setting to determine whether a recording is short or long. Default: 3 seconds.

Contacts

The **System > Configuration > Contacts** page is where the names and phone numbers of those people responsible for maintaining or administering the Cisco Unity server should be entered. This information will be useful should it be necessary to access the Cisco Unity system from offsite.

Phone Languages Settings

Phone languages are the languages in which Cisco Unity can play system prompts to subscribers and callers. You can specify a default phone language, along with other system-wide phone language settings. In addition, you can configure the default TTS language, which is the language that subscribers hear when their e-mail is read to them over the phone. Note that to use TTS languages, your organization must have TTS e-mail and the appropriate languages installed.

If you prefer, you can customize the language settings for specific Cisco Unity components, such as subscriber accounts, routing rules, call handlers, interview handlers, and the directory handler.

Use Table 3-4 to learn more about phone languages settings.

Table 3-4 *System > Configuration > Phone Languages Page*

Field	Considerations
License Counts – Total	*Display only.* This setting shows the total number of phone language licenses for the installation. This determines how many phone languages can be loaded at one time. Note that the number of phone language licenses does not limit the number of phone languages actually installed on the Cisco Unity server.
License Counts – Loaded	*Display only.* This setting shows the number of languages in the Loaded list.
License Counts – Unused	*Display only.* This setting shows the number of unused phone language licenses. Note that this number might not be the same as the number of languages in the Available list.
Available	This list displays the languages that have been installed on the Cisco Unity server but that are not currently loaded. When a language is loaded, by moving it from the Available list to the Loaded list, the Loaded and Unused License Counts fields are adjusted accordingly. Languages can be moved to the Loaded list only if the Unused License Counts field is greater than zero.
Loaded	This list displays the languages that can be selected for use by the subscriber conversation and various Cisco Unity components, such as call handlers. When a language is unloaded, by moving it from the Loaded list to the Available list, the Loaded and Unused License Counts fields are adjusted accordingly. Any call handlers or other Cisco Unity components that were using the unloaded language are reset to use the default phone language.

Table 3-4   *System > Configuration > Phone Languages Page (Continued)*

Field	Considerations
Default Phone Language	Select the default language in which system prompts are played to subscribers and callers. Only the languages shown in the Loaded list can be chosen as the default language.
Default Text-to-Speech Language	Select the default language that subscribers hear when having their e-mail read to them over the phone. This is typically the same language selected in the Default Phone Language field, with the following exceptions: If Australian or New Zealand English is selected as the phone language, select either United States English or UK English as the default TTS language. There is no appropriate TTS language available for Brazilian Portuguese or Korean.

GUI Languages Settings

The settings on the GUI Languages page determine the languages in which the Cisco Unity System Administrator pages can be displayed. The default GUI language and other system-wide GUI language settings can be specified.

To change the GUI language used in the Cisco Unity System Administrator or Cisco PCA, select a language in the browser. (Subscribers use the Cisco PCA website to access the Cisco Unity Assistant and the Cisco Unity Inbox.)

For the Cisco Unity System Administrator, the language selected in the browser must be one of the languages in the Loaded list on the GUI Languages page. If the language selected in the browser is not among the loaded languages, Cisco Unity uses the default GUI language. For Cisco PCA, the language selected in the browser must be one of the languages that Cisco PCA offers.

WARNING   If you have a Cisco Unity failover system, recordings settings are not replicated between the primary and secondary servers. You must change values manually on both servers.

Managing Calls Using System Schedules

The System Schedules page can be found by clicking on the **System > Schedules** links in the Cisco Unity System Administrator. Schedules are one of the variables that Cisco Unity uses to manage calls. The standard and closed subscriber and call handler greetings play according to the days and times specified in a schedule.

Cisco Unity offers two predefined schedules in the Settings page: All Hours–All Days, and Weekdays, both of which can be modified. Any defined schedule, be it default or defined, may be used as the default schedule for Cisco Unity. The default schedule is set to Open from 8 a.m. local time to 5 p.m. local time and the Observe holidays option is checked. This default schedule is used for all call handlers, subscriber templates, and call routing tables. The Cisco Unity system may use up to 64 different schedules.

Every call handler in the system uses a schedule to determine which greeting it plays. The Standard greeting is played during the time set as Open (for example, "Thank you for calling XYZ Corp. If you know your party's extension, enter it at any time or press '0' for an operator."); the Closed greeting plays during all other times (for example, "Thank you for calling XYZ Corp. Our offices are now closed. Please call back during our normal business hours 8 a.m. to 5:00 p.m., Monday through Friday.") This schedule is typically configured by the administrator and based upon business hours and holidays. A holiday schedule is configured and activated using an Observe holidays check box. During that time, Cisco Unity will play the Closed greeting during all hours for the specified holiday(s).

Using Holiday Settings

When a holiday setting is in effect, Cisco Unity plays closed greetings and observes closed transfer rules. You can configure several years of holidays in advance. Those holidays can be copied from one year to the next, adjusting dates as necessary. Because many holidays occur on different dates each year, confirm that the holiday schedule remains accurate annually.

Licensing

Software licensing has long been a controversial issue. Cisco Unity is similar to the vast majority of software packages on the market in that it does require licenses to install the software legally.

Cisco Unity itself is not the only licensed portion of the overall product. Cisco Unity provides the base functionality. There are add-on software products that also must be properly licensed. Functions, such as the Cisco Unity Inbox subscribers and Audio Message Interface Standard (AMIS) networking, are licensed, whereas other functions, such as ViewMail and Cisco PCA, are not licensed.

All the licensing issues can be complex to track. Thereof, Cisco Unity provides a licensing tool that tracks the number of used and unused Cisco Unity subscribers, vendor-managed inventory subscribers, and secondary server licenses available to a particular server. This provides a single point of reference to be used in keeping track of license counts for various features offered by the system. Prior to version 4.x, Cisco Unity servers required a hardware key to activate the system. The hardware key is simply a small USB device or a parallel port device roughly the size of a key chain. With the use of the FlexLM licensing product, this key is no longer necessary because all licensing information is held in a system file on the hard drive. This file contains all the information about ports, features, number of users, and so on that are enabled on this Cisco Unity system.

License files are required to install or to upgrade Cisco Unity software and to change licensed features. To obtain the license files that provide the settings purchased by the customer, the Cisco Unity software must be registered on Cisco.com.

Shortly after registration, Cisco e-mails the license files. The e-mail from Cisco contains instructions on how to save and store the files. The Cisco Unity Installation Guide provides specific instructions later in the installation process on the use of the license files during the installation or upgrade.

The following information is required during software registration:

- **Media Access Control**—The MAC address (physical address) for the network interface card (NIC) in the Cisco Unity computer. If the Cisco Unity server uses dual NICs as a fault-tolerant team, a virtual MAC must be identified by the administrator and assigned by the device driver (for the team rather than either physical MAC address) when the license is ordered. The license file will be registered to the specified virtual MAC address and the active NIC used. The virtual MAC is assigned in the NIC configuration under the network properties on the server.

- **Product Authorization Key**—The PAK is listed in the Cisco Unity Software Keys booklet that is shipped with the software CD-ROMs. Lotus Domino integration packages may not include a license book. In that case, the PAK is imprinted on the CD-ROM sleeve.

Registered users of Cisco.com can browse to the following URL to begin the registration process:

http://www.cisco.com/cgi-bin/Software/FormManager/formgenerator.pl

Nonregistered users can browse to the following URL to begin the registration process:

http://www.cisco.com/pcgi-bin/Software/FormManager/formgenerator.pl

In either case, the license information should be e-mailed back to the e-mail address of record in the registration within 24 hours. If it does not come back in a timely manner, it is recommended that you contact TAC to investigate the matter.

It is worth the time invested to check out these URLs when setting up a Cisco Unity system for the first time. It allows verification of correct license features, add-ons, and number of licenses.

Setting Up Authentication

Authentication settings dictate the logon and lockout policy, which applies when subscribers access Cisco Unity by using Cisco PCA. If the Cisco Unity System Administrator uses the Anonymous authentication method, the policy that you specify here also applies when subscribers use the Cisco Unity System Administrator to access Cisco Unity. The basics of the available authentication options were discussed earlier in this chapter, in the section "Protecting System Administration." This section discusses the Cisco PCA that is used by individual subscribers (nonadministrators).

It is important to consider that when subscribers log on to Cisco PCA, their credentials are sent across the network to Cisco Unity in clear text. The same is true if the Cisco Unity System Administrator uses the Anonymous authentication method. For increased security, it is therefore recommended that Cisco Unity be configured to use the SSL protocol. As a best practice, it is also recommended that Cisco Unity administrators not use the same subscriber account to log on to the Cisco Unity System Administrator as they use to log on to Cisco PCA.

Changes to authentication settings affect all Cisco Unity subscribers. These settings cannot be changed for individual subscriber accounts, though they can be individually locked out to prevent subscribers from using Cisco PCA or the Cisco Unity System Administrator to access Cisco Unity.

Note that the authentication settings represent a different logon and lockout policy from the one that applies when subscribers access Cisco Unity by phone. Table 3-5 describes the authentication settings.

Table 3-5　*Authentication Settings*

Field	Considerations
Remember Logons for __ Days	If desired, check this box and enter the number of days that Cisco Unity will store logon information. When this box is checked, logons are stored and encrypted as cookies on the subscriber computer.
	When Cisco Unity remembers logon information, subscribers do not have to enter it to log on to Cisco PCA. Instead, the logon credentials for a subscriber are automatically populated in the Log On page.
	If IIS is configured so that the Cisco Unity System Administrator uses the Anonymous authentication method, this setting also applies to subscribers logging on to the Cisco Unity System Administrator.
	Default: blank.

Table 3-5   *Authentication Settings (Continued)*

Field	Considerations
Remember Passwords for __ Days	If desired, check this box and enter the number of days that Cisco Unity will store password information. When this box is checked, passwords are stored and encrypted as cookies on the subscriber computer.
	When Cisco Unity remembers subscriber passwords, subscribers do not have to enter their password to log on to Cisco PCA. Instead, a subscriber password is automatically populated in the Log On page.
	If IIS is configured so that the Cisco Unity System Administrator uses the Anonymous authentication method, this setting also applies to subscribers logging on to the Cisco Unity System Administrator.
	Default: blank.
Session Key Duration	This field indicates the length of time that the browser can be left unattended before Cisco Unity automatically logs the subscriber off.
	The value in IIS dictates the browser session duration, but this field can be used to change the value for the Session Timeout field in IIS. When the value for the Session Timeout field is changed directly in IIS, however, the changes you make are not reflected here.
	Regardless of whether the session duration is updated here or directly in IIS, the new timeout value applies to the next new browser session.
	If IIS is configured so that the Cisco Unity System Administrator uses the Anonymous authentication method, this setting also applies to subscribers logging on to the Cisco Unity System Administrator.
	Default: 20 minutes.
Disallow Blank Passwords	Check this box so that subscribers are prohibited from logging on to Cisco PCA without entering a password in the Log On page, even if the Windows account policy allows blank passwords.
	If IIS is configured so that the Cisco Unity System Administrator uses the Anonymous authentication method, this setting also applies to subscribers logging on to the Cisco Unity System Administrator.

continues

Table 3-5 *Authentication Settings (Continued)*

Field	Considerations
Lock Out Accounts	Check this box to specify an account lockout policy for the subscribers using Cisco PCA.
	When this box is checked, enter the appropriate values in the following fields:
	Accounts Are Locked Out For __ Minutes
	Accounts Will Lock Out After __ Logon Attempts
	Reset Account Lockout Counters After __ Minutes
	If IIS is configured so that the Cisco Unity System Administrator uses the Anonymous authentication method, this setting also applies to subscribers logging on to the Cisco Unity System Administrator.
	Default: checked.
Accounts Are Locked Out For __ Minutes	Enter the number of minutes that Cisco Unity will prevent subscribers from accessing Cisco Unity by using Cisco PCA.
	If IIS is configured so that the Cisco Unity System Administrator uses the Anonymous authentication method, this setting also applies to subscribers logging on to the Cisco Unity System Administrator.
	This option is unavailable when the Lock Out Accounts box is unchecked.
	Default: 30 minutes.
Accounts Will Lock Out After __ Logon Attempts	Enter the number of failed logon attempts after which subscribers cannot access Cisco Unity by using Cisco PCA.
	If IIS is configured so that the Cisco Unity System Administrator uses the Anonymous authentication method, this setting also applies to subscribers logging on to the Cisco Unity System Administrator.
	This option is unavailable when the Lock Out Accounts box is unchecked.
	Default: 5 attempts.

Table 3-5   *Authentication Settings (Continued)*

Field	Considerations
Reset Account Lockout Counters After __ Minutes	Enter the number of minutes after which Cisco Unity will clear the count of failed logon attempts to Cisco PCA, unless the failed logon limit is already reached and the account is locked. A Cisco Unity administrator may unlock any account at any time.
	If IIS is configured so that the Cisco Unity System Administrator uses the Anonymous authentication method, this setting also applies to subscribers logging on to the Cisco Unity System Administrator.
	This option is unavailable when the Lock Out Accounts box is unchecked.
	Default: 30 minutes.

Integrating Cisco CallManager

The integration settings are specified during installation in the Cisco Unity Telephony Integration Manager (UTIM), which configures Cisco Unity to work with the specified phone system. Once the integration is set up, there should be no need to change the integration settings, but they can be reviewed on the Integration page or revised in UTIM.

NOTE   If a Cisco Unity failover system is used, changes to the integration settings must be made in UTIM on each server individually. Integration settings are not replicated between the primary and secondary servers.

Table 3-6 details the settings available for Cisco CallManager integration. All the fields are display only.

Table 3-6   *Cisco CallManager Integration*

Field	Displays
Integration Name	The name of the Cisco CallManager integration entered in UTIM.
Manufacturer	The phone system manufacturer selected in UTIM.
Model	The phone system model selected in UTIM.
Software Version	The phone system software version selected in UTIM.

continues

Table 3-6   *Cisco CallManager Integration (Continued)*

Field	Displays
Trunk Access Code *(for dual phone system integrations only)*	The number that Cisco Unity dials to transfer a call from one phone system to the other. This code was entered in UTIM.
Cluster Name	The name of the Cisco CallManager cluster entered in UTIM.
Internet Protocol (IP) Address/Name	The IP address of the publisher (primary) Cisco CallManager server. This address was entered in UTIM.
IP Port	The TCP port used by the Cisco CallManager servers. This port was entered in UTIM. Typically this is set to Port 2000.
Real-Time Protocol (RTP)/IP Port Base	The first (or base) port number for RTP used by the Cisco CallManager servers. This first port number was entered in UTIM.
Reconnect	Whether Cisco Unity automatically reconnects to the publisher (primary) Cisco CallManager server after failover has been corrected. The setting True indicates that automatic reconnection is enabled. This value was set in UTIM.
IP Addresses	The IP addresses of the subscriber (secondary) Cisco CallManager servers. These addresses were entered in UTIM. The term 'subscriber' used here refers to the Cisco CallManager secondary servers.
MWI On Extension	The extension that Cisco CallManager uses to turn message waiting indicators (MWIs) on. This extension was entered in UTIM.
MWI Off Extension	The extension that Cisco CallManager uses to turn MWIs off. This extension was entered in UTIM.
Resynchronize At	The time each day that Cisco Unity resynchronizes MWIs for every subscriber account. This time was entered in UTIM. Resynchronization occurs only when it is enabled in UTIM.

Changing the Opening Greeting

The choice of whether to use the Automated Attendant or a live operator is one to be made by individual companies or entities. If a live operator is not made available for every incoming call, Cisco Unity can provide an unattended switchboard function in its Automated Attendant feature. The opening greeting, found under the Call Handlers page, is the one that all external callers hear. Once on the Call Handlers page, the Opening Greeting is found via a search using the Search icon. In essence, this is the operator. This greeting guides callers through the options available to them when they attempt to contact individual subscribers. It should be thorough in its options and concise in its wording.

The Opening Greeting is a call handler. The responsibility of this call handler is to answer all calls forwarded to the Cisco Unity system when using Automated Attendant. The settings that are necessary for the Automated Attendant feature to work, mapping inbound trunk calls to be forwarded to Cisco Unity, are set at the phone system. If you decide to use the opening greeting, you'll probably prefer to rerecord the default Cisco Unity greeting because it is somewhat generic in its offerings. Cisco Unity greetings and messages may be recorded in two ways:

- **Via multimedia device**—The Media Master can use a multimedia-recording device. It may be used from any desktop PC that has access to the Cisco Unity System Administrator pages. Recording greetings is available when you see the recording tool bar.

- **Via telephone**—The Media Master has a drop-down menu that allows you to choose which device to use. The Phone Record and Playback setting must be set with an extension to call. The Cisco Unity system will dial that extension and be ready to record or play back greetings when it is answered. When using the telephone option, the Cisco Unity system uses the last port configured for TRaP.

The following is a sample opening greeting that represents an Automated Attendant message for a fictional corporation, XYZ Corp.:

"Thank you for calling the XYZ Corp. If you know your party's extension, please dial it at any time. For a directory of extensions, press 555. Otherwise, please press 0 or hold. An operator will be with you shortly."

The Opening Greeting may also involve more elaborate settings, such as one-key routing. Options available using one-key dialing in this way are endless and make for a more complete caller experience. From the caller's point of view, the fewer keys to push the better the experience. For example:

"Press 1 for Sales, Press 2 for Service..."

Ideally, there should be an option for the caller to press 0 at any time to get to a live operator. Of course, the presentation of the "zero-out" option is at the discretion of the administrator(s).

Configuring the Directory Handler

The directory handler is a special predefined call handler with default settings. The settings included for the directory handler include an optional extension, search options, match list options, and caller input options.

The system directory setup provides the opportunity to specify how the system acts when a caller searches for a particular subscriber. Each subscriber may be enabled to add or delete themselves in the system directory through their system setup options. The system directory can be accessed by outside callers and subscribers by last name, first name, or extension. Additionally, the system provides the capability to choose the course of action to take if a unique match (by either name or number) is made, as well as whether or not extension numbers are spoken to callers. If the menu format is selected, the system presents a conversation similar to the following:

"To speak with Amanda, press 1; to speak with Emma, press 2; to speak with Beth, press 3; ..."

If extensions are configured to be announced, then each subscriber's extension number will be included in the conversation.

In a multiple Cisco Unity server network environment, those servers that are digitally networked can be configured to limit the search to a local Cisco Unity server or you can configure a dialing domain, which links several Cisco Unity servers together. It also makes it easier on the subscriber to address messages and for outside callers to find and be transferred to subscribers across Cisco Unity servers. The ability to do this depends on the ability of existing telephone systems to network together.

Beginning with Cisco Unity version 4.x, it is possible to create multiple directory handlers, which enables the Cisco Unity system to to present a subset of all subscribers based on settings such as Class of Service, Public Distribution Lists, Dialing Domain, and so on. They can be useful when you want to separate your directory, such as when you are using centralized call processing models, or a hub-and-spoke model.

Configuring the Operator Handler

The operator box is another important system configuration. An outside caller, in most cases, should have a way to connect to the operator during a system greeting, prompt, or message. Most users expect to be connected to an operator after pressing 0. This call handler is associated with the system ID of 0 by default. If a caller does nothing during the opening greeting, they also reach the operator. The Operator Call handler is found on the Call Handlers page. It must be searched out using the Search icon.

The operator may be an individual who uses a physical extension other than 0. To accommodate that, the transfer options of the operator call handler must reflect the extension of that individual. Also, keep in mind the need for an appropriate greeting on the operator box for when the operator is not available.

Chapter Summary

In this chapter, you learned about the Cisco Unity System Administrator and some of the configuration options available within the system. Specifically, you learned how to do the following:

- Plan and design the Cisco Unity installation using specific information that must be provided ahead of the actual installation.

- Use the Cisco Unity System Administrator to manipulate the Cisco Unity server.

- Use security to authenticate access to a network using Anonymous authentication or Integrated Windows authentication.

- Provide the necessary ports to support the needs of the network and subscribers, and the licensing to provide additional features and functions to those subscribers prior to installation.

- Handle calls when they arrive at a business and receive an automated greeting. This greeting can have a profound effect on the client relationship. If callers do not consider their first contact with your company to be a positive experience, then it is quite conceivable that it will be their only contact with your company.

- Give callers options, such as pressing 0 to get to a live operator, and at the same time, the ability to access a corporate directory to dial by name (first or last), as well as direct dialing of an extension to expedite the handling of the call through the system.

- Design an efficient menu structure that you have tested so that callers have a positive experience.

For additional information on the preceding topics, refer to these resources:

- Cisco Unity CD Pack
- Cisco Unity Installation Guide
- Cisco Unity Administration Guide
- Cisco Unity Design Guide
- Networking in Cisco Unity Guide

Chapter Review Questions

Use this section to test yourself on how well your learned the concepts discussed in this chapter. You can find the answers to the review questions for this chapter in Appendix A.

1　List the three basic sections of the Cisco Unity System Administrator page.

2　List the two basic methods of authentication that are available for Cisco Unity subscribers.

3　Which of the two authentication types is more easily configured? Why?

4　How many system administrator accounts can be logged in to the Cisco Unity System Administrator tool concurrently?

5　List at least three options available on the Configuration Settings page and their functions.

6　On a date for which the Cisco Unity server has been configured as a holiday, which greeting will callers hear upon calling in?

7　Instead of using a hardware key for Cisco Unity licensing, what is used in Cisco Unity 4.x?

8　Which tool can be used to retrieve near real-time port statistics?

9　List two methods that can be used to alter greetings.

10　List two predefined call handlers.

Upon completion of this chapter, you will be able to perform the following tasks:

- Describe and change Cisco Unity global subscriber accounts, templates, and settings
- Set up Cisco Unity subscriber accounts, templates, and settings

CHAPTER 4

Unified Communications Subscribers

Now that you have completed the general setup of the Cisco Unity system, it is time to begin adding subscribers. A number of options are available not only to the administrator but also to each subscriber who is added into the Cisco Unity system. This chapter discusses the features and options that are available to both the administrator and the subscriber.

The subscriber experience with Cisco Unity will be based largely on the manner in which the system is configured by the administrator at this point. Much of the work that has been accomplished in getting to this phase of the installation lays the groundwork to support subscribers. Software add-ons, call routing, system schedules, and all the other aspects of the system come down to this. The system should be subscriber- and caller-friendly. These two facets of the overall experience can have a profound effect on the usability of the system and, of course, on those who must use the system.

Understanding Cisco Unity Global Subscriber Accounts, Templates, and Settings

Global subscriber settings influence many aspects of Cisco Unity system behavior for individual subscribers. Changes made in these areas affect many, if not all, subscribers. There are a number of changes that can be made to an individual subscriber's account; however, these changes affect only that one account. There are areas of subscriber settings that affect a subset of subscribers or that may have a global effect on all Cisco Unity subscribers. These settings include:

- Account Policy
- Class of Service (COS)
- Public Distribution Lists
- Subscriber Templates

Good planning and preparation can make your administrative task of adding subscribers much easier. This section focuses on considerations you must keep in mind when planning and preparing to add subscribers.

To benefit fully from this section, it is recommended that you have the following prerequisite skills and knowledge. (If you need a quick review of either topic, see Chapter 3, "Setting Up Cisco Unified Communications," where you can find more information.)

- A working knowledge of the Cisco Unity System Administrator
- A basic understanding of Cisco Unity setup and configuration

Setting Account Policy

The settings made on the Account Policy page determine telephone password restrictions and how and when accounts become locked out. By default, the Number setting is set to six invalid attempts within 30 minutes. A locked-out account is reinstated after 60 minutes. There is also a setting to allow for "no account lockout." Each of these settings influences the security of the system and affects only telephone access to the subscriber's Cisco Unity account for the Cisco Unity system over the telephone. The settings have no effect on account policy for other Microsoft Windows or Exchange servers. When a setting is changed on the Account Policy page, it takes effect immediately.

Additionally, you can alter the minimum required length of a password. This setting takes effect for all accounts except those that are permitted a blank password. The last setting, which governs telephone password history, determines whether subscribers must generate a unique password each time they change it. You can also simply set the number of unique passwords that the subscribers need to generate.

It is highly recommended, as a security measure, to require subscribers to set passwords. These passwords should also expire on a regular basis, thereby forcing subscribers to change their passwords occasionally. The first setting, Maximum Password Age, is a setting that may not act in a global fashion. If a system administrator changes the number of days until the passwords expire, this will change for everyone on the system except those subscribers whose accounts are set with a password that never expires. The change takes effect immediately and all subscribers whose accounts do not match the setting are required to make the change at the next login over the telephone. Be aware that compulsory periodic password changes can cause some consternation among the subscriber population. Thus, you may need to temper the need for tight security in consideration of the subscribers' patience (or lack thereof).

Describing COS

COS is a subgrouping of users who share a collection of common system features and privileges. This concept of COS is familiar to most telephony installers. Figure 4-1 shows the COS page.

Figure 4-1 *Cisco Unity COS Page*

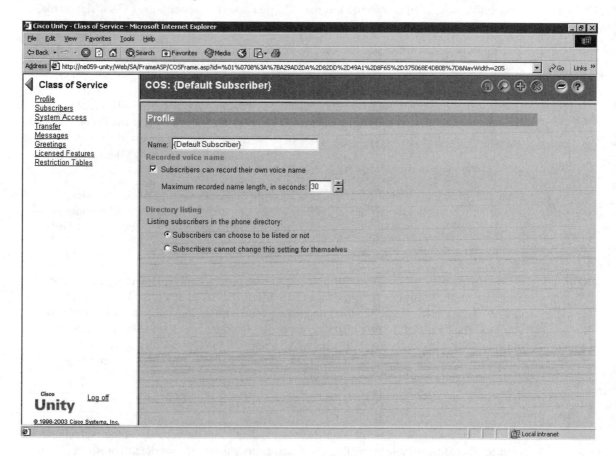

A COS defines limits and permissions for using Cisco Unity. Using a COS, the administrator can perform the following actions:

- Control access to the Cisco Unity Administrator, and add functionality such as text-to-speech e-mail or Live Reply.

- Control the manner in which subscribers interact with the Cisco Unity system. For instance, a COS can specify the maximum length of subscriber messages and greetings. It can also determine whether subscribers have the choice to be listed in directory assistance and can specify whether subscribers can send messages to a public distribution list.

- Specify the restriction table that is used to control the phone numbers that subscribers can use for fax delivery, message notification, call transfer, and other tasks.

A COS is specified in each subscriber template. When you create a subscriber account, you can use a template to assign common settings. This template can specify the COS assigned to the specific subscriber.

In telephony systems, COS can be used to provide, or deny, a group of subscribers a set of features and privileges rather than doing this on an individual basis. By grouping subscribers, the time needed to apply features and privileges is optimized.

COS gives an administrator an easy way to grant system access privileges and control licensing. If there are subscribers who will perform a subset of system administration tasks, it is possible to grant them access to only those portions of the console for which they will be responsible. If some groups within an organization need specific licensed features while others do not, it is easiest to control those licenses through a COS.

Changes made to a COS affect all users in a group. The COS settings affects profiles, subscribers, system access, transfer options, messages, greetings, licensing of features, and restriction tables. The changes are immediate and require no additional action to take effect.

NOTE COS settings may not be altered by individual subscriber accounts. However, a Cisco Unity System Administrator can reassign a user to a differing COS at any time. If, at any time, there ceases to exist at least one Windows domain account with membership in a COS that offers access to the Cisco Unity administrator, the ability to administer Cisco Unity may be lost entirely. In this instance, it will be necessary to reinstall the Cisco Unity system software. Always take steps to ensure that at least one account is associated with a subscriber account assigned to the Default Administrator COS.

The settings made for a Cisco Unity COS help to determine the security of the system and the features that are available to subscribers. Cisco Unity ships with two default classes of service: administrator and subscriber. It is possible to add as many classes of service as necessary. The classes can be based on workgroup membership, job function, or any other desired classification. A new COS can be based upon an existing definition or a new definition. It is often easier to base a new class on an already-existing or similar definition, to minimize necessary changes. In the subscriber template, the COS to be used must be specified. Subscriber COS membership can be reassigned at any time.

Every subscriber will not necessarily need every feature. Because many of the add-on features are licensed, it is useful to have the ability to modify the subscriber experience based on the needs of the individual. In this type of scenario, licensing can be controlled through COS. For example, an organization may grant access to the Cisco Unity Inbox, a visual messaging interface, for those members of a COS that have workstation access, while denying access to subscribers that use Cisco Unity only over the telephone, thus preserving licenses for subscribers who require the functionality.

Distribution Lists

It is possible to create lists, called distribution lists, that allow messages to be sent to multiple subscribers simultaneously. Cisco Unity creates a few distribution lists by default. These are known as public distribution lists.

The subscribers assigned to a public distribution list typically are subscribers who need the same information on a regular basis, such as employees in a department or members of a team.

Three public distribution lists are created by default:

- **All Subscribers**—All subscribers are automatically added to this list upon creation.

- **Unaddressed Messages**—Subscribers assigned to this list receive messages left in the Operator call handler mailbox. This is typically a repository for messages received when the operator is not available. Any message that is deemed undeliverable is also forwarded to this list (for example, when a subscriber mailbox is full).

- **System Event Messages**—Subscribers added to this list receive messages from the Event Notification utility. This could include error messages, problem notifications, or warnings about potential problems with the Cisco Unity server.

Initially, the Example Administrator account is the sole member of both the Unaddressed Messages and System Event Messages distribution lists.

NOTE   Do not delete the Example Administrator account until additional subscribers have been added to these two distribution lists.

You may alter the system-installed lists as you deem necessary. You can also create new lists if the existing lists do not meet the needs of your system or subscriber base, and you can import public distribution lists from Microsoft Exchange. You can include both subscribers and nonsubscribers as members of an imported distribution list. However, nonsubscribers will not be displayed in the Cisco Unity Administrator.

Any messages addressed to an imported list are forwarded to all members of the list. This includes nonsubscriber list members unless nonuniversal groups are imported from Microsoft Exchange 2000. With nonuniversal groups, not all of the public distribution list members may receive messages as expected.

Creating Subscriber Templates

A subscriber template allows you to predefine certain parameters regarding individual subscribers. This saves you time and tedious redundant input of information as you add new subscribers to the system. By default, there are two templates: the administrator and subscriber templates. Any changes made to the subscriber template affect only those subscribers added after the change. Therefore, individual subscriber changes must be made for each subscriber if they already existed under the template. To remedy this potentially painstaking process, Cisco has created the Bulk Edit Utility, a tool that performs mass alterations to subscriber accounts. The Bulk Edit Utility is covered in more detail in Chapter 11, "Unified Communications Backup and Utilities." Figure 4-2 shows the Subscriber Template page.

Figure 4-2 *Cisco Unity Subscriber Template Page*

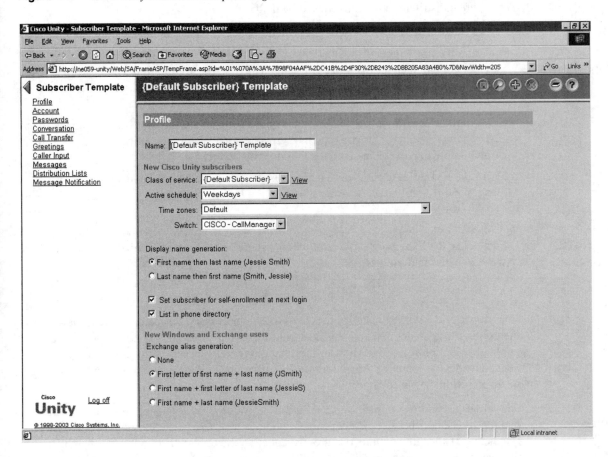

As shown on the left side of Figure 4-2, the information that can be input in either the Administrator or Subscriber Template page includes the following:

- Profile
- Account
- Passwords
- Conversation

- Call Transfer
- Greetings
- Caller Input
- Messages
- Distribution Lists
- Messages Notification

A subscriber template defines the rules for subscriber accounts and the settings for most users. Whereas account policy and COS settings take effect immediately and apply to subscribers retroactively, changes made to a subscriber template apply only to subscribers who are added after the changes are made. Multiple subscriber templates can be used, as many as 64 of them, to customize each one for a different group of subscribers. A recommended strategy for the use of subscriber templates is to define the settings as they will apply to most subscribers in a group, before you create the subscribers. This enables you to cover the needs of the masses more effectively. After you have completed the generic templates, you can address individual needs on an as-needed basis.

Many of the settings that are available for templates are also available for individual subscribers. To make subscriber template changes, navigate to **Subscribers > Subscriber Template**, indicate the desired template, and then specify the page to modify. To change a setting for an individual subscriber, navigate to **Subscribers > Subscribers**, find the individual subscriber, and then choose the appropriate page to modify.

The following is a list of the pages that the Subscriber Template link contains:

- Profile
- Account
- Passwords
- Conversation
- Call Transfer
- Greetings
- Caller Input
- Messages
- Distribution Lists
- Message Notification

Next, each of these pages is explained.

Understanding the Profile Page

The first page called Profile defines the settings on how Cisco Unity identifies a subscriber. Settings such as Name, COS, Active Schedule, Time Zones, Switch (for dual phone system integrations only), Display Name Generation, Set Subscriber for Self-Enrollment at Next Login, List in Phone Directory, and Exchange Alias Generation are stored here. Although some of these settings are defined in the subscriber template for subscribers that are created, most are defined in the Cisco Unity account for each individual subscriber that has been defined on the system.

Two particularly crucial settings are selected on the Profile page: the COS and Schedule that subscribers will use. It is possible to specify how display names are generated, and whether subscribers are selected for self-enrollment.

Also available is the specification of phone directory listing, as well as the option to Show Subscriber in E-mail Server Address Book. In addition, on the profile page is the pattern used to create aliases for new Exchange and Active Directory (AD) users. It is possible to customize the naming conventions; however, any account names created in Cisco Unity need to be edited to match the custom pattern. To "customize" the naming conventions, the users must be added to the Exchange/AD member list with the desired naming convention, then imported into Cisco Unity. This method makes for a rather cumbersome process to add users. A final option here would be to choose None and use no particular pattern. This is not recommended, but it is an option.

In any event, the naming convention should match the existing Windows accounts and Exchange mailboxes, if any. The Import utility searches for the Exchange mailbox that matches the alias when parsing a comma-separated value (.csv) file. The matching Exchange mailbox will be associated with the subscriber account.

When you are creating accounts for users who have neither a Windows account nor an Exchange mailbox, the ALIAS column is optional in the .csv file to be imported. If an alias is not specified in the .csv file, the Exchange alias is derived from this field in the subscriber template, using a combination of first and last name.

Alternatively, you can add users through the Exchange administration or AD console, and then import them as Cisco Unity subscribers. Adding users is not yet possible in Cisco Unity for Lotus Domino implementations, though, because all subscribers must be created in Lotus Domino and imported into Cisco Unity.

Setting Account Settings

The Account page is used to set an account as "locked" when it is initially created using a particular template. This page also includes options to associate billing ID information with the subscriber account.

Creating Passwords

The Passwords page enables you to specify a phone password policy and the default phone passwords for new subscribers. You also specify on this page the password change requirements to be used by subscribers. The change takes effect on the subscriber's next login. It is possible to create a default password to be changed at the first login. If a new AD account is created, the same default password can be used.

Setting Conversation Options

On the Conversation page, most of the settings are straightforward. The Conversation type choices, Full Menus or Brief Menus, may not be obvious at first. Full Menus is the setting to choose for users who do not have a great deal of experience with voice mail. Brief Menus is a more appropriate choice for "power" users who possess a clear understanding of the messaging system's capabilities and wish to operate in a more streamlined fashion.

Also included are settings for volume of played messages, language used for prompts, time forwarding, and a 12- to 24-hour clock or system default. Under the Conversation Style, you can specify the action to be taken when exiting a conversation. The template choices here can be configured to specify, once a subscriber has logged on, which conversations should be played and what information should be provided regarding messages (such as number of fax messages, voice messages, saved messages, new messages, and so on). Also specified here is the manner in which saved messages are sorted (by time sent or by source phone number).

Setting Call Transfer Options

The Call Transfer page presents call-handling settings, including whether calls are transferred to the subscriber's extension (most are) and which of the following two transfer types to use:

- **Release transfer**—Use this transfer type (also called blind transfer) in situations where the telephone switch (PBX) provides call forwarding. This allows Cisco Unity to process calls more quickly.

- **Supervise transfer**—Use this transfer type at times when Cisco Unity should act as a receptionist, keeping control of the call (and keeping a port used until the call is extended), and waiting the specified number of rings before answering the call. The number of rings is configurable and should be set to a realistic number, such as three rings, to provide adequate answer opportunity to the subscriber. Another recommendation is to set the number of rings to two less than the number the telephone switch will use to forward the call in a ring-no-answer (RNA) condition.

  You should use supervise transfer when you want to implement options such as call screening and call holding. Supervise transfer allows Cisco Unity to maintain control over the call so that it can implement these features.

In the event of a supervised transfer, the Gather Caller Information section of the page contains settings that can help individual subscribers manage incoming calls. Many of the options are self-evident, though a few, such as If the Call Is Busy, Always Hold and Announce, require some explanation.

The setting If the Call Is Busy allows the subscriber to specify options such as Always Hold. If enabled, the caller is placed on hold until the subscriber can pick up the call. You can also use the No Holding option. When selected, the caller is prompted to leave a message for the subscriber. Neither of these options is available when using release transfer, because the Cisco Unity system does not retain control of the call in that specific instance.

The Announce setting causes the voice mail to sound a tone, letting the subscriber know when an incoming call has been transferred to their telephone. If the box beside Ask Caller's Name is checked, the Cisco Unity system asks an outside caller "Who may I say is calling?" and records their answer for playback to the subscriber. This allows the subscriber to screen incoming calls by accepting or refusing the call. If the call is refused, the caller is asked to leave a message for the subscriber.

Setting Greetings

Cisco Unity offers the possibility of using five different greetings, depending on the date, time of day, various system settings, and the capabilities of the telephone switch. The greetings used most often include the standard (used during normal business hours), closed (used during all hours not defined as open for business), and alternate (used when out of the office for an extended period) greetings. Whether or not the internal or busy greetings are used depends on the capabilities of the telephone system. Administrators, as subscribers, have the option of using the system greeting supplied by Cisco or recording their own greeting.

Most subscribers on a system have the standard greeting enabled by default. If all users of the Cisco Unity system have the same greeting for a particular circumstance, such as while the business is closed, it would be appropriate to choose that greeting and record it on a Subscriber Template page. Otherwise, individual subscribers should record greetings as a part of self-enrollment (if enabled).

You must enable each greeting that is going to be used on the system and choose a source. If subscribers will be recording their own greetings, click the Recording radio button on the Greetings page. If you want to allow caller input during any greeting, check the appropriate box on the page.

Finally, set the After Greeting action. In most cases, the Take Message option is used, because that is the main function of a voice-messaging system. You also have the Send Caller To option, which provides additional options for managing the call.

Configuring Caller Input

There may be cases in which all users of the system have some keys enabled for caller input. In these situations, it is best to configure a subscriber template to define and allow the key presses.

For example, consider that an option is configured to allow all callers to skip the subscriber's greeting and proceed directly to recording their message by pressing the 1 key during the greeting. On the Caller Input page, simply select the 1 key, check the Lock This Key to the Action box, and select the Skip Greeting radio button. This, along with any other system-wide caller input options, is implemented here.

Setting Messages

On the Messages page, you can set the Maximum amount of time for voice message left by outside callers, as well as what options are available to them after leaving a message. In most cases, once an outside caller has left a message, they are ready to exit the system; choosing the Say Goodbye radio button is the appropriate choice in those circumstances. In addition, you can choose whether callers are offered the option of marking their messages as Urgent, what language your callers hear by default (or more than one language if properly licensed), and whether to use message waiting indicators (MWIs) for message notification. In almost every case, you will use MWIs, unless otherwise deemed necessary by the needs or demands of subscribers.

Creating Distribution Lists

If you need to add a group of subscribers to public distribution lists, it is easiest to do it in a subscriber template for that group. If you need to create distribution lists, you can do so on the **Subscribers > Public Distribution Lists** page before you attempt to add that list. All Cisco Unity Subscribers is a group that every subscriber on the system is a member of by default. It is not possible to remove a subscriber from this list, short of deleting the subscriber.

Setting Message Notification Options

If there is a need, you can use the Message Notification pages of a subscriber template to arrange for standardized notification and delivery of messages to any group of subscribers that shares the template. In most cases, message notification and delivery are different for every subscriber, so it is more likely that you will be making those changes on an individual basis.

Understanding COS Settings and Subscriber Interactions

It is important to understand the relationship that exists between account policy, COS, and subscriber templates. These three groups of settings all interact to provide a complete package of information that you use when adding subscribers. Though account policy applies to all subscribers on the system without regard to the COS or subscriber template used, it has an effect on all subscribers and must be taken into account. One of the first choices that you make in a subscriber template is the COS to which subscribers will belong. For this reason, all of your

COS settings should be in place before you define any subscriber templates. The account policy and COS settings combine to provide system security and subscribers' level of access to the system and its features. Subscriber templates control the way subscribers interact with the system on a daily basis. Once you have set up all your COS settings, you can define the settings that will apply to groups of subscribers in the subscriber templates. At this point, you can begin adding subscribers.

Understanding Cisco Unity Individual Subscriber Accounts, Templates, and Settings

Subscribers are the main reason voice-messaging systems exist. A large part of an administrator's job, once the initial system setup is complete, involves moves, adds, and changes to subscriber accounts. Knowing what kinds of accounts are available and how to set them up efficiently can make your life as an administrator much easier. Thus, augmenting individual subscriber accounts is discussed in the next section of this chapter.

To benefit fully from this section, it is recommended that you have the following prerequisite skills and knowledge. (If you need a quick review, see the designated chapter, where you can find more information on the topic.)

- A navigational understanding of the Cisco Unity System Administrator (see Chapter 3, "Setting Up Cisco Unified Communications")

- Cisco Unity standard features (see Chapter 1, "Cisco Unified Communications System Fundamentals")

Setting Subscriber Accounts Versus Subscriber Templates

A subscriber template is used as a "model" to specify the default settings of a new subscriber. You can think of it as a one-time filter that the subscriber's information passes through during the creation process. When adding or importing a new subscriber, you must choose a template to provide subscriber setting information. As you are adding the new subscriber, you supply information that is specific to that subscriber, the extension, and the first and last name. After the subscriber is added, you have other information that is available on an individual basis: private distribution lists, message notification, and alternate extensions. Once the subscriber is added to the Cisco Unity system, you can change any of the individual settings for that subscriber.

Once a subscriber has been added using a particular template, any changes you make to the account must be made on the individual subscriber's page. Changes made on the subscriber template apply only to subscribers added after the template is changed. This is the primary reason for verifying the proper template configuration during the initial system setup.

In addition to the settings included on the subscriber template (and on each individual subscriber's settings, once created), you can use the following settings:

- **Private Lists**—In Cisco Unity 4.0(2) or later, there is no defined limit on list membership. In previous versions of Cisco Unity, subscribers or administrators were limited to the creation of up to 20 private lists with 25 members each.

- **Alternate Extensions**—Each subscriber can have up to nine alternate extensions available.

- **Message Notification**—Up to 12 devices can be set up to receive notification of a message.

There are some settings that are available on individual subscriber pages that are not shown on any Subscriber Template page. Private lists and alternate extensions are features that are available to subscribers on an individual basis and make sense only in that context.

Using Private Lists

Private lists are available for each subscriber on a Cisco Unity system. The subscriber that owns these lists manages them either over the telephone or by using Cisco Unity Assistant. Cisco Unity Assistant (formerly known as Active Assistant) is a web page that allows subscribers to customize personal settings. This includes recorded greetings and message delivery options. The subscriber is the only person that may send messages to their private lists. When addressing a message to the list, the subscriber must use the group number, not the group name. Private lists significantly differ from Exchange personal distribution lists because information is stored in different locations. Exchange personal distribution lists are stored in the Microsoft Outlook client; Cisco Unity's private lists are stored on the Cisco Unity server with the subscriber's other settings. There is no reference to the private lists in Exchange. For this reason, a subscriber can address messages to their private lists only by using the telephone user interface (TUI).

NOTE   It is also possible to use the ViewMail for Outlook (VMO) or Domino Unified Communications Service (DUCS) clients to create a Unified Messaging (UM) message and use a list of names or distribution lists in the TO: field.

Using Alternate Extensions

Each subscriber can have up to nine different alternate extensions. This feature has two different purposes: It can provide easy message access for the subscriber. When you enter the subscriber's cell phone number in the Alternate Extension field, Cisco Unity recognizes the incoming digits of the subscriber's cell phone number and asks for the subscriber's password as if the person were using their desk extension. This happens as long as the PBX passes the Caller ID digits along to Cisco Unity.

The Alternate Extension field can also be used in an environment in which multiple Cisco Unity servers and multiple telephone switches are networked together. Cisco Unity servers are differentiated by the location data in the Cisco Unity System Administrator. If an alternate extension is added for subscribers that exactly mirrors the number other subscribers would dial when telephoning another subscriber directly through the networked telephone switches, then they are able to message each other through the telephone using that same number. A Cisco Unity system administrator can add alternate extensions for the subscriber.

Using Message Notifications

Cisco Unity has the capability to place a telephone call to any subscriber and notify that subscriber of new messages.

Subscribers can be notified of new messages via:

- Telephone
- Pager
- E-mail

Notifications can be set up by the following individuals:

- System administrator
- Individual subscriber by using the Cisco Unity Assistant
- Individual subscriber by using the TUI (four devices only, including home phone, work phone, spare phone, and pager)

Numerous different device names correlate to a type of call or a separate type of notification. A call to a "spare" phone would have a specific conversation indicating the presence of messages. A call to a "pager" would consist purely of sending touch-tones and pauses. A call to a "text pager" literally means sending an SMTP-type message. The Cisco Unity system administrator or the subscriber using Cisco Unity Assistant enters a string of text and an SMTP address in the appropriate field, and then Cisco Unity notifies subscribers of new messages by sending the text to the SMTP address.

Each device has settings for the time of day and day of week to notify you, as well as entries to specify for which type of messages to use the device. As an example, Cisco Unity could send a text message for regular voice messages that notifies the subscriber every 60 minutes. If an "urgent" message is left by a caller, Cisco Unity can send an Urgent text message notification every 5 minutes. As soon as the messages are collected, Cisco Unity stops notification, because Cisco Unity notifies only when new (unread) messages exist.

Via the TUI, and depending on the phone system's capabilities, a subscriber can set up only four devices: home phone, work phone, spare phone, and pager. The first three are labels only; the phone could be any one that Cisco Unity is capable of dialing while adhering to its Call Restriction tables.

Creating Default Cisco Unity Accounts

Cisco Unity automatically creates some default accounts:

- Installer account
- Example Administrator account
  - Default owner of new call handlers
  - Default message recipient of new call handlers
- Example Subscriber account (versions prior to Cisco Unity 4.0(3))

As part of the installation process, Cisco Unity for Exchange or Domino creates default subscriber accounts. Two of the accounts are the Example Administrator and the Example Subscriber. The main difference between the Example Administrator and the Example Subscriber accounts is the COS. The Example Subscriber account does nothing more than give an example of what a basic subscriber account looks like. The Example Subscriber account takes up a user license, but it can be deleted to recover the user license. The Example Administrator account is the "owner" and "message recipient" of all default call handlers. The Example Administrator account cannot be deleted via the Cisco Unity System Administrator tool. In a situation in which you need to recover a single user license or you encounter a security issue about the account, you can delete the Example Administrator account. However, you should first carefully consider and research the issue before you make a decision to delete the Example Administrator account. The deletion of the account can have a significant effect on the Cisco Unity system.

Another account that is created during the installation process is called the Unity "*server name*" messaging account. This is a hidden account and does not take a user license. This is the account that Cisco Unity uses to send messages from outside callers to a subscriber's inbox.

There is also a hidden Microsoft Structured Query Language (SQL) account that is secretly associated to the current logon account during installation. The SQL account is called the Installer account and has the administrator COS. This gives your Microsoft Windows 2000/ Exchange 2000 installer account the ability to log on to the Cisco Unity System Administrator and modify system and user settings. An analogous account is created for Cisco Unity for Domino.

Adding Cisco Unity Subscribers

The means by which the subscriber is defined will have an effect on their individual user experience. Each type of user is defined with variable traits and attributes.

Figure 4-3 provides a flowchart reference that is useful in deciding what type of subscriber to define for a particular situation.

Figure 4-3   *Choosing the Type of Subscriber Account*

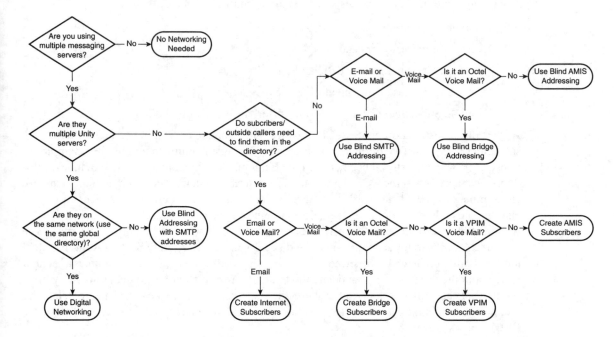

This flowchart can assist you in making the decision of what type(s) of subscribers to add to the system. In many cases, new user types will be defined and added as necessary. In every case, the target message server on which the subscriber holds an account dictates the type of subscriber to be created.

When you add new users to the Cisco Unity system, you have the choice of adding the following types of Cisco Unity subscribers:

- **New subscriber**—If you are adding a new subscriber, Cisco Unity creates a mail-enabled user account in Windows 2000 Active Directory.

- **Import Exchange user**—If you are importing an existing Exchange user, the system modifies the voice attributes of an existing user in AD.

- **Import Lotus Domino user**—Importing from the Lotus Domino system is the only method available for adding users from Lotus Domino. The system creates individual subscribers as with other imports. Any new Lotus Domino users have to be added to the Lotus Domino system, then imported to gain a Cisco Unity subscriber account.

The following list of subscriber types lists network subscribers. They have a spelled and recorded name and show up in the Exchange global address list (GAL) but cannot log on to Cisco Unity to retrieve messages, record greetings, or do several other normal functions that a full subscriber can do. Using these network subscribers is a method of making a remote person look like a subscriber. Messages to network subscribers are not actually stored on the local Exchange system, but instead are sent to the remote recipient's message store. The method that is used to send the message is based on the type of subscriber that is created and the licensing purchased.

- **Internet subscriber**—The messages that are sent to an Internet subscriber are e-mails with an attached .wav file sent to an SMTP address. Internet subscribers are a special type of Cisco Unity voice-mail user used specifically for networking and SMTP mail delivery. When you are adding a new subscriber in the Cisco Unity Administrator, a radio button option allows you to create an Internet subscriber and specify an SMTP address for that user. This is similar to Custom Recipient(s) (Contact(s) in Windows 2000/Exchange 2000); the Internet subscriber is actually a mailbox that has no local message store.

When you are creating an Internet subscriber, setup options relating to the local message store are not available. These options include phone password, private lists, conversation, and message notification. In other words, the mailbox acts as a pointer to the SMTP address that is specified when creating the Internet subscriber account. Both outside and internal callers benefit from the ability to address messages to the subscriber over the telephone in most cases, and internal users also have an option to address to them using the GAL. The Internet subscriber has a recorded voice name and greeting just like any other Cisco Unity subscriber. The main difference between a regular Cisco Unity subscriber and an Internet subscriber is that when mail is left for an Internet subscriber, the mail is delivered out the SMTP gateway (Internet Mail Service [IMS] for Exchange 5.5) to its Internet destination as specified within their account. The end location could be any other mail server or even another voice-mail system therefore, from the sender's perspective, offsite Internet subscribers with whom the sender is interacting appear as if they are actually *onsite*, such as field technicians or outside sales personnel.

Additionally, Internet subscribers can be used to link offices, without the need to set up messaging connectors and directory replication connectors between sites. However, the administrator must manually and individually set up Internet subscribers for each destination location. This requirement may be unacceptable if a large number of users exist in remote offices. For organizations with many users in various locations, using Blind Addressing is typically a better choice than using Internet subscribers.

- **AMIS subscriber**—The messages sent to an Audio Messaging Interchange Specification (AMIS) subscriber are delivered to another voice-mail system by using an analog telephone call. Cisco Unity Version 4.0 enables users to interface with third-party voice-mail systems by using the AMIS-analog protocol (AMIS-a). AMIS subscribers are much like Internet subscribers, with one important difference: whereas an Internet subscriber's off-box storage is generally another e-mail system, an AMIS subscriber's off-box storage is going to be a different voice-mail system. It would be set up as Custom Recipients in Exchange 5.5 or Contact(s) in AD.

  As with Internet subscribers, any options that relate to the local message store are unavailable. This means that AMIS subscribers cannot log on to Cisco Unity to check or send messages, log on to Cisco Unity via the telephone, or use Cisco Unity Assistant to change personal settings, own private lists, set up or receive message notification, or receive MWIs via Cisco Unity. Messages sent to AMIS subscribers are transferred to the target voice-mail system through telephone calls placed from one server to another server and messages played over the analog phone lines.

- **VPIM subscriber**—Cisco Unity Version 4.0 enables users to interface with third-party voice-mail systems using Voice Profile for Internet Messaging (VPIM). The messages sent to the VPIM subscriber are sent as an SMTP e-mail with an attached .wav file to a VPIM-compliant voice-mail system via the Internet. As with AMIS, a VPIM subscriber's off-box storage is going to be a different voice-mail system. They would be set up as Contact(s) in AD. A 5-minute message sent via SMTP takes no more than 1 minute to transmit, whereas the same message sent via AMIS takes more than 5 minutes to transmit. The main difference is that the messages are transmitted via SMTP rather than as an analog message over the Public Switched Telephone Network (PSTN).

  As with Internet subscribers, any options that relate to the local message store are unavailable. This means that VPIM subscribers cannot log on to Cisco Unity to check or send messages, log on to Cisco Unity via the telephone, use Cisco Unity Assistant to change personal settings, own private lists, set up or receive message notification, or receive MWIs via Cisco Unity.

- **Bridge subscriber**—The messages sent to a Bridge subscriber leave Cisco Unity as a VPIM message to the Bridge server. Cisco Unity Version 4.0 enables users to interface with Octel voice-mail systems using the Cisco Unity Bridge as a networking gateway to an analog Octel network. Bridge subscribers are much like Internet and AMIS subscribers with one important difference: whereas an Internet subscriber's off-box storage is generally another e-mail system and a VPIM or an AMIS subscriber's off-box storage is going to be a different voice-mail system, Bridge subscribers' messages reside on an Octel voice-mail system. They would be set up as Custom Recipients in Exchange 5.5 or Contact(s) in AD.

AMIS, VPIM, Internet, and Bridge subscribers share all other features with regular Cisco Unity subscribers. You can give them an off-campus telephone number, and calls will be transferred there. Outside callers may look up Internet, Bridge, VPIM, or AMIS subscribers in the directory (unless you have restricted this access) and leave them voice mail. They can be members of distribution lists. The main purpose of these recipients is to receive messages in a transparent manner.

Adding Subscribers

Once you have set the account policy, created your COS, set up your distribution lists, created your subscriber templates, and decided what types of subscribers to add, all you need to do is create a list of employees and their telephone extension numbers. To create this information, log on to the Cisco Unity System Administrator, click the Subscriber link, click the Add button, and enter the data. Figure 4-4 shows the Subscribers setup page.

Figure 4-4 *Cisco Unity Subscribers Setup Page*

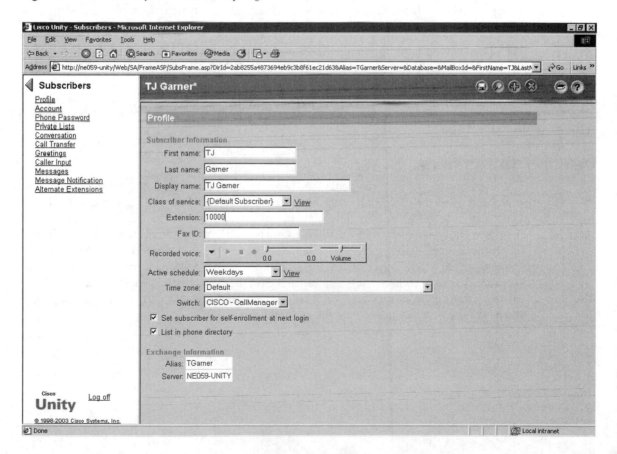

It is also possible to import subscribers in a bulk process from Exchange, Domino, or a properly formatted .csv file. There may be circumstances in which you need to upgrade from Cisco Unity for Exchange to Cisco Unity for Domino. Customers in a Domino environment may have purchased Cisco Unity in a Cisco Unity VoiceMail–only configuration while awaiting the Cisco Unity Domino release. Cisco Unity VoiceMail–only configuration is supported only in the Exchange environment. Note that the upgrade procedure to Cisco Unity 4.0 for Domino from Cisco Unity 3.xx Exchange is supported and documented on the Cisco TAC website. However, be aware that the upgrade essentially amounts to a reinstallation.

Currently, no way exists to carry over the database from Cisco Unity for Exchange to Cisco Unity for Domino or vice versa because they have two completely different messaging systems. To save the subscriber database, you must export it from Exchange, modify it to a form that is acceptable to Domino, import it into Domino, and then import the subscribers from the Domino server into Cisco Unity 4.0. The information that is exportable includes the subscribers' names and extensions, but not the spoken name recordings, greetings, and so on. Subscribers' messages are not carried over to the new system. Cisco does not offer a utility to accomplish this.

Other Cisco Unity database information such as call handlers, call routing tables, and restriction tables are also not carried over.

If you are creating subscribers individually and they do not have an existing Exchange account, Cisco Unity will create a mail-enabled Windows 2000 Active Directory account for them. It is not possible to add users directly in Cisco Unity for Domino due to restrictions on writing to the Domino database. You must first add them as users in Domino and then import them into Cisco Unity.

Deleting Subscribers

If you are deleting subscribers from Cisco Unity by using the System Administration tool, the tool will remove the Cisco Unity subscriber's information from the SQL database on the Cisco Unity server. It will not remove the mail accounts in Domino or Exchange; it will remove only the Cisco Unity–specific data from those accounts. The System Administration tool will not delete the account. To completely remove the account from the Domino Names.NSF file or the Windows 2000 Active Directory list, the appropriate administration tool must be used for that software. To delete a Cisco Unity subscriber, select the subscriber's account, click the red Delete button, and confirm the action. This does not delete the AD or Domino account; it only removes the Cisco Unity data from the account.

Chapter Summary

In this chapter, you learned how to do the following:

- Set Cisco Unity account policies.
- Describe a COS.
- Define a distribution list for Cisco Unity.
- Use subscriber templates.
- Define subscriber accounts versus subscriber templates.
- Add and delete Cisco Unity subscribers.

For additional information on the preceding topics, refer to these resources, found at Cisco.com by performing a search of the text:

- The Cisco Unity Administration Guide
- The Subscriber Template Settings—Cisco Unity
- The Cisco Unity Installation Guide

Chapter Review Questions

Use this section to test yourself on how well you learned the concepts discussed in this chapter. You can find the answers to the review questions for this chapter in Appendix A.

1 If Account Lockout is enabled, how many logon failures are required, by default, to lock a subscriber account?

2 When does a change made in the Account Policy page take effect?

3 A group of subscribers defined in the Cisco Unity system as sharing a common collection of system features and privileges is known as what?

4 Where do you specify a COS to place it into production to govern subscribers?

5 Cisco Unity provides three default distribution lists to provide the ability to send messages to multiple users simultaneously. List each of these three distribution lists and its purpose.

6 What information can be specified by a subscriber template?

7 Subscriber templates provide a powerful tool for setting user options. What should be configured prior to the creation of any subscriber templates?

8 A Cisco Unity subscriber can create private distribution lists. How many lists may be created by subscribers and administrators in Cisco Unity 4.0(2) or later? Where are they created?

9 Cisco Unity has the capability to place a call to any subscriber to notify them of new messages. What means of notification are available to subscribers when new messages arrive?

10 List the Cisco Unity accounts created by the Cisco Unity installation process.

Upon completion of this chapter, you will be able to perform the following tasks:

- Use Cisco Unity call handlers to manage sets of instructions for treating and forwarding calls from the Cisco Unity server, including predefined, special, and user-defined call handlers

- Set and plan call handler settings, and understand call routing rules

CHAPTER 5

Cisco Unified Communications System Customization

In this chapter, the topic of discussion centers on the use of call handlers in Cisco Unity, because they represent the basic building blocks of any Cisco Unity system.

Understanding Cisco Unity Call Handlers

Call handlers do exactly what their name implies, they handle calls. Calls that are not answered are forwarded to Cisco Unity, which in turn answers calls, greets callers with recorded prompts, provides callers with information and options, routes calls, and takes messages. Your plan for call handlers may fall anywhere within a wide range of options, from a simplistic plan that uses only the predefined Cisco Unity call handlers, to a complex plan that uses an unlimited number of new call handlers. Call handlers can be used in numerous ways, including as an Automated Attendant (autoattendant), as a message recipient, for prerecorded audio, or to transfer calls.

The call handler defines a set of call-processing instructions so that the system knows what to do when a call reaches a particular system ID. All the entities defined in a Cisco Unity system are call handlers, whether they are subscribers, the operator, the opening greeting, or some other user-defined box. Some of them may be considered special cases, or look different than a standard call handler, but they are call handlers.

There is no hard limit to the number of call handlers that a Cisco Unity system can define. The handlers allow administrators to provide a wide range of services beyond those included with standard voice mail, including (but certainly not limited to) audiotext applications of any size, emergency notification services, job lines, and call routing. Call handlers have a wide range of capabilities.

Virtually every entity in a Cisco Unity system has an ID. Whether discussing subscribers, extensions, mailboxes, or other objects within the Cisco Unity system, a unique ID exists that identifies each entity to the Cisco Unity system. A call handler does not require that a physical extension be associated with it. It can be distinguished simply by the given name. Additionally, the call handler can be selected by the system based on administrator-defined criteria, such as time of day or holiday schedules.

When Cisco Unity is set up with its default settings, it can use many of the standard features and it is highly customizable. You need to know what call handlers are and how to use them, and learn the procedures for creating call handler applications efficiently. This will enable you to customize a Cisco Unity system to the degree required to meet your business messaging needs.

To benefit fully from this section, it is recommended that you have the following prerequisite skills and knowledge (see Chapter 1, "Cisco Unified Communications System Fundamentals," for more information on either topic):

- Cisco Unity call flow
- Cisco Unity features

Defining Default Call Handlers

Cisco Unity defines three separate default call handlers, including Operator Greeting, Opening Greeting, and Goodbye Greeting. Figure 5-1 shows the Call Handler page for the Opening Greeting.

Figure 5-1   *Cisco Unity Call Handler, Opening Greeting Page*

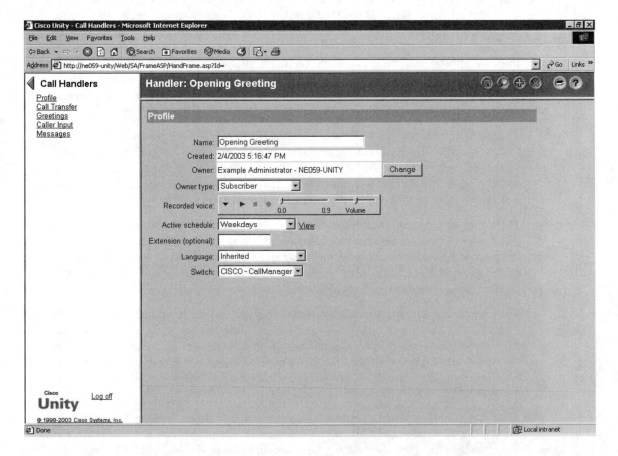

Table 5-1 defines and explains the default call handlers.

Table 5-1   *Default Call Handlers*

Call Handler	Function
Operator Greeting	The Operator box is a special call handler that is used exclusively for calls that go to the operator. The system ID of this box is usually 0. The extension that rings when 0 is pressed is dependent on the information you enter in the Call Transfer page. It can be any valid extension or phone number on your telephone system. It is also capable of simply taking a message rather than transferring the call. By default, the incoming call is sent directly to this handler's greeting.
	In terms of the greetings, the standard and closed greetings are enabled by default. The standard greeting cannot be disabled, but the closed greeting can. It is possible, however, to enable and customize an Alternate, Busy, and Internal greeting for this handler, as well as the others.
Opening Greeting	The Opening Greeting is a default call handler box that is used exclusively for automated attendant. The default greeting for this call handler is furnished by Cisco, so you probably should rerecord the opening greeting to customize your Cisco Unity system. Anyone, typically a nonsubscriber, could hear this greeting upon dialing into the Cisco Unity system directly. This could be an outside caller or an extension that has not been defined on the Cisco Unity system. That is, the Cisco Unity system does not recognize the number as that of a subscriber.
	The same Call Transfer options are available here as are available to the operator handler; however, it does not have an extension associated with it. By default, the only greetings enabled are the standard and closed greetings. The standard greeting cannot be disabled here, but the closed greeting can be.
	In terms of call input, when they are using this handler, the only keys (by default) that are configured include:
	4—Send Caller to Directory Handler
	*—Send Caller to Sign-In
	0—Send Caller to Attempt Transfer to Operator, which sends them to the Operator call handler
	#—Send Caller to Attempt Transfer to Operator
	All other keys are set to Ignore Key, meaning that if the caller presses 1, Cisco Unity will not take any action while the caller is in this handler.
	The following keys are also set to **Locked, *, 0,** and **#**. This means that Cisco Unity ignores additional input after callers press any of these keys. This option is configurable for any of the keys.
	By default, the active schedule for this greeting is set to Weekdays.

continues

Table 5-1   *Default Call Handlers (Continued)*

Call Handler	Function
Goodbye Greeting	This call handler is used at the end of a call cycle within the Cisco Unity system. The goodbye call handler can be configured with the same options as any other handler. A goodbye call handler is designed to be used with an audiotext application or to stop callers from being part of voice-mail jail. It also ends a call gracefully instead of just hanging up. By default, no extension is set. While the system plays the goodbye message, a caller can actually, by default, dial a subscriber's extension, or press *, 0, or # for the same functionality as the previous sections. By default, this greeting is set to All Hours—All Days.

Customizing Default Call Handlers

The Operator call handler is an important component. Callers have the expectation that they will be connected to an operator after they press 0. This call handler is associated with the system ID of 0 by default. If a caller does nothing during the opening greeting, they will also reach the operator. The operator may be an individual who uses a physical extension other than 0. That extension can simply be associated with the call handler. Keep in mind that a voice mailbox should be appropriated to the operator in case of missed calls.

The Opening Greeting call handler is installed with a default opening greeting. This default opening greeting should be altered and customized for individual needs. This will be the opening greeting that all callers hear, including outside callers and those who are not defined in the Cisco Unity system. It should direct them to the options that may be necessary to satisfy the purpose of their call, such as options to go to a directory of extensions (directory call handler), dial a desired extension, stay on the line, or press 0 for the operator. Other options, of course, are possible as deemed necessary in the configuration of one-key dialing.

The Goodbye Greeting call handler is used to play a short goodbye message and then hang up if it does not detect caller input. By default, the Goodbye call handler enables a caller to dial the applicable extension to reach the sign-in conversation, or the Operator call handler. If the After Greeting action is altered from the default of Hang Up to Take Message, the messages left in the Goodbye call handler will be sent to the Example Administrator account mailbox.

Using Special Call Handlers

Two special call handlers are typically used in Cisco Unity. These are the Directory call handler and the Interview call handler.

Using the Directory Call Handler

The default directory handler is used to search for subscribers in the Cisco Unity system. This call handler allows callers to search for subscribers by last name or extension. You can choose to let callers who know the name of the person they want to reach, but not their extension, search for the person's extension by pressing touch-tone keys whose letters correspond to as many of the letters of the subscriber's name as they wish to use. This allows callers to route themselves to extensions without burdening the operator or receptionist. It is possible to set this up to correspond to either first or last names.

The Cisco Unity directory status of each subscriber is determined systemwide but can be modified on an individual basis. When the directory handler is used (by a caller, for a subscriber search based on extension), the system searches the subscriber directory for matches as each digit is dialed. Once a unique or near match is found for a caller-dialed extension (and the directory handler is set to "request caller input first"), the system begins announcing the matched name(s). Be default, it uses a menu format, which announces the extension with each name. However, you can configure this to simply announce the extension alone, thus omitting the subscriber name. Caller input is slightly different here than for a standard call handler; you have four options to set here:

- **Timeout If No Input (in seconds: default is 5 seconds)**—The number of seconds that Cisco Unity waits for caller input when the caller does not press any key. If the caller does not press any key within this set time frame, Cisco Unity asks for confirmation that the caller is still there. If there is no response, Cisco Unity performs the action selected in the If Caller Exits, Send To field.

- **Timeout After Last Input (in seconds: default is 4 seconds)**—The number of seconds Cisco Unity waits after caller input before it performs the action indicated by the input.

- **Times to Repeat Name Entry Prompt (default is 1 try)**—The number of times Cisco Unity will reprompt the caller for input. When the caller does not press any key after being prompted, Cisco Unity asks for confirmation that the caller is still there. If there is no response, then Cisco Unity performs the action selected in the If Caller Exits, Send To field.

- **If Caller Exits, Send To (default is opening greeting handler)**—Can be selected from defined call handler on the system.

A new feature in Cisco Unity 4.0 is the capability to configure multiple directory handlers. This capability is most useful in systems with subscribers numbering in the hundreds or thousands. It is also quite useful in centralized call-processing environments that provide services to one or more remote sites.

You can use the default Directory handler as a template for the creation of new directory handlers. You can use location, class of service (COS), and public distribution list membership as filters for listing subscribers in a directory. Subscribers can be listed in more than one directory. In order for a subscriber to be listed in any directory, they must have a recorded voice name and have the List in Directory box checked on their Profile page.

There is also an option to use Search In. Options for Search In include Local Cisco Unity Server Only (default), Location, Class Of Service, Dialing domain and Public Distrubution List. The List in Directory is an option configured on the subscriber templates. By default, this option is checked on the default subscriber template. This means that when a subscriber is created and associated with this template, they become part of the directory. During first-time enrollment, the users are told, by default, that they are listed in the directory and that they may have the option to remove themselves from it.

Using the Interview Handler

Interview handlers are specialized call handlers that have up to 20 prerecorded questions for callers and can target the messages for different purposes, such as customer orders and preliminary job interviews.

An interview handler plays each question, in turn, followed by a beep. The interview handler then records the answer given by the caller. Once the caller stops speaking, or the maximum recording time has elapsed, the next question is presented. The process continues until the last question has been presented and a response has been provided.

When the message is delivered, the recipient hears only the answers, separated by beeps. For this reason, the recipients must know the order and content of the questions. If a caller does not answer a question, this shows up in the message as two beeps in a row without an intervening response.

Cisco Unity comes with a sample interview handler. The questions asked, their order, and how messages left are handled can be seen in the system. When using an interview handler, it is beneficial for the first question to contain any instructions or introductions that are necessary to complete the interview, such as the number of questions, response time, and so on.

Once you are done with the first recording, ask the questions in a logical order, making certain to leave callers an adequate response time. The system will truncate the recording based on its length if the entire response time has not been used.

Some of the specific onscreen settings for the interview handler include:

- **Optional Extension**—This is an extension that subscribers can dial to reach the interview handler. If the interview handler is reached only through the use of one-key dialing, do not enter an extension here.

- **To Whom the Response Should Be Delivered**—This can be a subscriber or public distribution list. (The default for the example interview is the Example Administrator.)

- **Response Urgency** — After you answer all the questions, you can configure Cisco Unity, to mark the message in a specific urgency response, or by using the Ask Caller setting, you can ask the caller if they want to mark the interview message as urgent. Your choices are: Mark as Urgent, Mark as Normal, or Ask Caller.
- **After Interview Action** — You can send the caller to any of the following, after the interview is complete: Send To: CVM Mailbox Reset, Call Handler, Directory Handler, Greetings Administrator, Hang Up, Hotel Checked Out, Interview Handler, Sign-In, or Subscriber. The default for a newly created interview is to Send to Goodbye Call Handler.

The example interview handler comes with five prerecorded prompts:

1 At the tone, please answer each of the following questions. At the end of each answer, you may press #. What person or department are you trying to reach?

2 What is your name?

3 What is your phone number?

4 What are the best times to reach you?

5 Is there any other information you would like to leave?

All are set to 30 seconds by default. If enabled, a warning tone sounds before the maximum message length is reached.

In addition, the recordings can be recorded/played back through either a phone or multimedia on a system using the Media Master Control.

The Question text field is limited to a maximum of 50 characters.

Before you record a message, it is a good idea to write the message out exactly as it is to be recorded.

Using User-Defined Call Handlers

Call handlers can be used to set up specialized call routing, create one-key dialing menus, or provide announcements of prerecorded information. As mentioned previously, call handlers can be as simple or as complex as you desire. An example of a simple application of a call handler is the delivery of prerecorded information, also known as *audiotext*.

The automated attendant is a call handler. The Opening Greeting, where callers first dial in, either can be very simple or can take advantage of some powerful features, such as *one-key dialing*. With one-key dialing, you can provide a menu of choices for incoming calls. Callers press one touch-tone key to route their call to the department or service they want. In the background, the one-key dialing menu routes the call to a system ID, whether it is to another menu, an extension, or any other system ID. One-key dialing is a shortcut available to callers that allows quick access to any listed system ID (entity).

One-key dialing and audiotext are in widespread use on a global basis. Everyone, at some time or another, has used such applications, whether calling someone at work or calling the local movie theater and choosing to hear the dates and show times for movies. For example, when you call to check what is showing at the movie theater, you may encounter a message such as the following:

Hello and thank you for calling Movie House Theaters. If you would like to check movie show times, press 1. To purchase tickets, press 2. For theater location and directions, please press 3. To speak to a customer service representative at any time, press 0.

Call handlers can be quite customized based on individual subscriber needs. Knowing how to customize them allows you to design and implement a structured audiotext application that meets specific corporate messaging needs.

To benefit fully from this section, it is recommended that you have the following prerequisite skills and knowledge. (If you need a quick review, see the designated chapter, where you can find more information on the topic.)

- Cisco Unity standard features (see Chapter 1)
- How Cisco Unity handles calls (see Chapter 2, "Using Your Cisco Unified Communications System")

Customizing Call Handler Settings

Call handlers have numerous customizable settings that you can employ to provide the highest level of service from the Cisco Unity system. These settings include a few basic pieces of information, such as the following:

- **Profile settings**—Specify ownership of the call handler, schedule to determine the times that standard and closed transfer rules and greetings are in effect, as well as the extension of the call handler.
- **Call transfer settings**—Specify how the call is transferred.
- **Greeting settings**—Specify which greeting plays based on predefined criteria, such as time of day, day of week, holiday, and so on.
- **Caller input settings**—Specify action(s) taken when a touch-tone key is pressed.
- **Message settings**—Specify who receives a message, the maximum message duration, and other settings.

Using Profile Settings

The Profile page defines the call handler. This page stores the name, time of creation, and system ownership information. Be sure to record the name of the box here, which will provide assistance in troubleshooting. The owner of the box is the subscriber or distribution list specified on the Profile page. This is the person (or group of persons) who may request that changes be made by the administrator. The owner can change the greeting in the box using the Cisco Unity Greeting Administrator (CUGA). The schedule can be set for this handler to follow what schedules the greetings and extension will be in effect when callers reach this call handler. Handlers in the middle of an application that are reached only from another handler do not need an extension number in your numbering plan. Figure 5-2 shows the call handler Profiles page. Table 5-2 lists and describes the fields on the Profile page.

Figure 5-2   *Cisco Unity Call Handler, Opening Greeting, Profile Page*

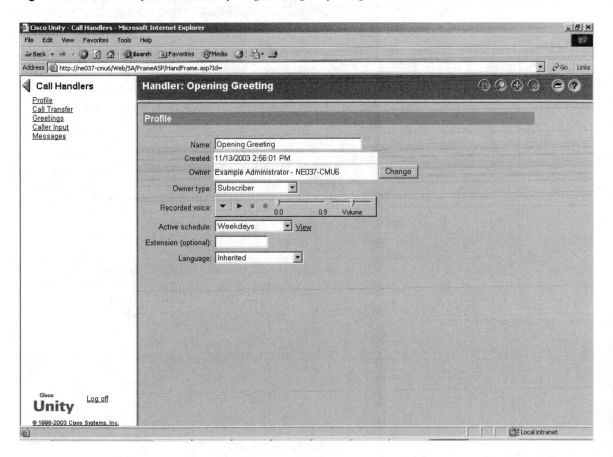

Table 5-2   *Profile Page Fields*

Field	Purpose
Name	Specifies the name of the call handler. To change the name, simply enter a new name and then click Save.
Created	*Display only.* Shows the date and time that the call handler was created.
Owner	The owner of the call handler can be specified as any valid subscriber or public distribution list. The owner (not necessarily the message recipient) of the call handler can record and change the call handler greeting over the phone. The owner can be changed here.
Owner Type	As mentioned, the owner can be a subscriber or distribution list. Select Subscriber or Distribution List in this field to assign ownership accordingly. Default: Subscriber
Recorded Voice	Specifies the recorded name of the call handler. The Media Master is used to record the name. If a prerecorded name is available, it is possible to select it by choosing **Options > Paste From File** on the Media Master control bar. The file should be in **.wav** format. Keep in mind that the Media Master will not function across a firewall.
Active Schedule	The schedule determines the times that standard and closed transfer rules and greetings are in effect for the call handler. These default settings are for new call handlers that are not based on existing handlers. If based on existing handlers, the new handler is created as a duplicate of the original. Default: Weekdays
Extension	The number that callers dial to reach the call handler. The extension should be supplied only if callers are allowed to dial it to reach the handler (not a one-key dialing situation). In addition, this is not an extension to which calls are transferred. This is used only to reach the handler itself. Default: Blank

Table 5-2   *Profile Page Fields (Continued)*

Field	Purpose
Language	The language in which system prompts are presented. Using the Inherited setting allows Cisco Unity to determine the language used for the call handler on a per-call basis, depending on the call handler or routing rule that processed the call. Using the Inherited setting also specifies that all system prompts will be presented in the same language for this handler. If the language is set to Inherited for every rule and handler that processes a call, then the system prompts are played in the default phone language. Default: Inherited
Switch	The phone system that the call handler uses. If set incorrectly, Cisco Unity will not be able to transfer calls to or from the call handler. This is used for dual phone system integrations only.

Using Call Transfer Settings

You use the settings on the Call Transfer page to specify whether unidentified callers are transferred to the call handler's greeting, to the recipient's extension, or to the subscriber at a particular number. Figure 5-3 shows the Call Transfer page.

Additionally, the Call Transfer page enables you to specify how Cisco Unity handles a transfer (release it to the phone system or supervise its transfer).

You can have three customizable transfer rules. One of these rules is for standard hours, one is for closed hours of the active schedule, and the third is an alternate transfer rule (in effect at all times) that can override the first two rules. By default, the standard and closed handlers are enabled and the alternate call handler is disabled, which is known as a supervised transfer.

Another type of transfer is a release transfer. Release transfer is a blind transfer of the call to its intended destination. In this case Cisco Unity releases the call.

When you are developing an audiotext application, typically you should ensure that callers hear the greeting in the box immediately. This can be accomplished by disabling the transfer. If the caller is transferred to an extension, a supervised or release transfer can be used.

Figure 5-3 *Cisco Unity Call Handler, Opening Greeting, Call Transfer Page*

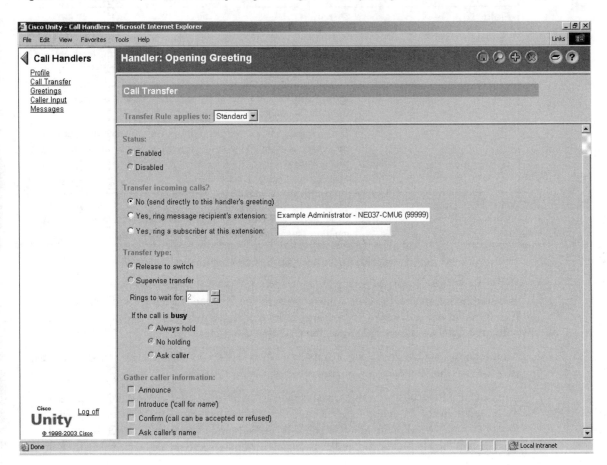

NOTE   If you create a large number of call handlers, all of which have been set to transfer directly to their greeting, and then you decide later that the calls should first transfer to an extension, you can use the Bulk Edit Utility in the Tools Depot to make the change. Call handlers can be edited in bulk to alter nearly any of the available options. More information on this is provided in the "Cisco Unity Administration Tools" section of Chapter 11. See the discussion on the Audio Text Manager (ATM). ATM provides an extremely useful tool in dealing with call handlers.

There are three basic options for handling calls:

- Send the caller directly to the handler's greeting (this is the default on a newly created handler that is not based on an existing handler).
- Ring the recipient's extension.
- Ring the subscriber at a particular number (this can be an internal or external phone, depending on the call restriction table settings).

When the administrator chooses either the second or third option, the this setting allows the setup of transfer to either release or supervised. If supervised is set, there is the option to set approximately how many times Cisco Unity will ring the destination before it brings back the call to the recipient's greeting. The default value is two rings, but it can be changed the same way on the **Subscribers page>Call Transfer page**, Subscriber template, or by using Bulk Edit.

When supervising transfers, Cisco Unity can provide additional control with call holding and call screening.

Call holding simply means that the system is set up to tell the user that the line is busy and the system places the caller on hold. The two options available for this on Figure 5-3 are called Always hold and Ask caller. With Always hold, the system will immediately place the caller on hold. The Ask caller option will ask the caller if they would like to wait.

When on hold the system can then play hold music (if Music On Hold is available) and tell the caller on hold how many callers are ahead of them and it also allows them to continue holding, leave a message, or try another extension. When these options are enabled, the caller is prompted every 30 seconds. There is no hard limit to the number of callers that can be on hold at a given point in time.

Call screening has the system ask for the caller's name prior to connecting the caller to a subscriber. Upon hearing the name of the caller, the subscriber can accept or refuse the call. These are found under the Gather caller information section of the Call Transfer page.

Using Greeting Settings

Settings on the Greetings page provide the capability to record appropriate greetings based on the set schedule from the Profile page. Greetings can be recorded for any number of possible scenarios and specified here. There is a default schedule set to include All Hours and All Days. Alternate greetings are typically used for holidays, emergencies, or any time the standard greetings need to be preempted. Using the CUGA, a call handler owner can toggle between the alternate and standard greetings or rerecord the standard greeting over the telephone. There are five greetings in all: Alternate, Busy, Closed, Internal, and Standard. When Alternate is enabled, it simply overrides the other greetings. Figure 5-4 shows the Call Handler, Greeting Settings page.

Figure 5-4 *Cisco Unity Call Handler, Opening Greeting, Greetings Page*

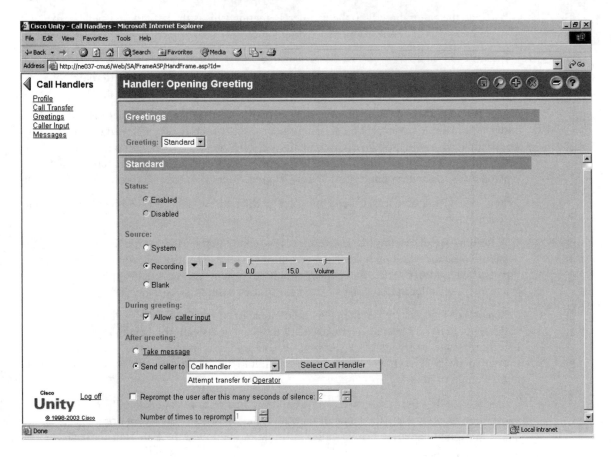

- **Alternate**—A substitute greeting that can be enabled or disabled as deemed necessary. It is typically used on special occasions, such as vacations or holiday. When enabled, the Alternate greeting overrides all other greetings.

- **Busy**—A greeting that plays when a subscriber extension is busy.

- **Closed**—A greeting that plays during the hours specified as closed in the active schedule (such as nonbusiness hours).

- **Internal**—A greeting that can be configured to play only to other subscribers, rather than the Standard or Alternate greeting.

- **Standard**—The greeting played during the standard hours specified in the active schedule unless overridden by another greeting.

If the Alternate greeting is disabled when a call is forwarded because the subscriber has set either the Call Forward All option or the Call Forward No Answer option, the Standard greeting is played. If the Internal greeting is enabled when a call is received from another Cisco Unity subscriber, the Internal greeting is played. If the subscriber has configured Call Forward Busy, the Busy greeting is played if the subscriber's line is in use.

For a Standard call handler, the only greetings that are turned on by default are Closed and Standard. All others need to be configured. For each greeting configured, several options need to be specified.

The configurable options in the CUA are as follows:

- **Status**—To enable a greeting, check the Greeting Enabled check box. The following are the possible settings:
  - **Enabled**—Turn on the selected greeting (check box checked).
  - **Disabled**—Turn off the selected greeting (check box unchecked).
- **Source**—The greeting source specifies how the greeting will be recorded. Three options are available for the greeting source setting:
  - **System Default Greeting**—The standard system default greeting.
  - **Recording**—Allows the recording of custom greetings with the Media Master control bar. It is possible to use either the subscriber telephone or a multimedia microphone to record the greeting. The appropriate source device should be selected. If the phone option is clicked, the Cisco Unity system places a call to the subscriber extension for which the greeting is being recorded. Once the phone is answered, the system plays a tone to indicate that recording has begun and that the subscriber should now speak the desired greeting into the handset. If the multimedia microphone option is chosen, the system plays a tone to indicate that recording has begun and that the subscriber should now speak the desired greeting into the microphone.

    Once the greeting has been recorded, by either method, it is necessary to click on the Stop button to end recording.
  - **Blank**—Allows the subscriber to choose a blank greeting.

    Once the recording and selection of a greeting have been completed, it is necessary to click the Save button.
- **During Greeting**—This setting dictates what the caller can do, if anything, during the playing of the greeting. This option has one setting:

Settings:

- **Allow Caller Input (default is checked)**—When checked, this setting uses the settings in the Caller Input page to allow the caller to use configured options. The caller selects presented options by pressing numbers on the telephone keypad. By default, this setting is enabled.

- **After Greeting**—After the greeting is played, this setting dictates what action should be taken by the Cisco Unity system. The following are the possible settings:

  - **Take Message**—The default on a newly created handler that is not based on an existing handler. It specifies that the Cisco Unity system should record the caller's message.

  - **Send Caller To**—Specifies that the caller should be transferred to the selected destination. Possible options here include: Send To: CVM Mailbox Reset, Call Handler, Directory Handler, Greetings Administrator, Hang Up, Hotel Checked Out, Interview Handler, Sign-In, or Subscriber.

  - **Reprompt the User After This Many Seconds of Silence**—Specifies the number of times to reprompt the caller if no input is received from the caller by voice or keypad number press. Two seconds is the default setting, if enabled.

  - **Number of Times to Reprompt**—Indicates the number of times the caller should be reprompted prior to performing the After Greeting action. The default is set to one reprompt.

Using Caller Input Settings

The Caller Input page is used to set up one-key dialing actions. A wide array of options is available for those times in which caller input is to be allowed. In such cases, callers must be presented with all possible options that they can use in reaching the appropriate subscriber or mailbox. The top of the screen provides a check box, Allow Callers to Dial an Extension During Greeting, for use along with the Lock This Key feature to allow access to some extensions while denying others during a greeting. Unchecking the Allow Callers to Dial an Extension During Greeting check box has the effect of locking all keys. Locking all keys used in the application allows the system to execute the instruction set more quickly. Locking the keys does not disable the ability to use one-key dialing. Figure 5-5 shows the Call Handler, Caller Input page.

With the keys unlocked, the system waits a set length of time (1 to 2 seconds) after every key to determine whether or not another key is to be pressed. This is a configurable option and is set in milliseconds. The default value for newly created handlers is 1500 milliseconds (1.5 seconds). The Allow Callers to Dial an Extension During Greeting check box is checked by default on newly created handlers. The action taken as a result of the key being pressed will, of course, depend on the call handler.

Figure 5-5   *Cisco Unity Call Handler, Opening Greeting, Caller Input Page*

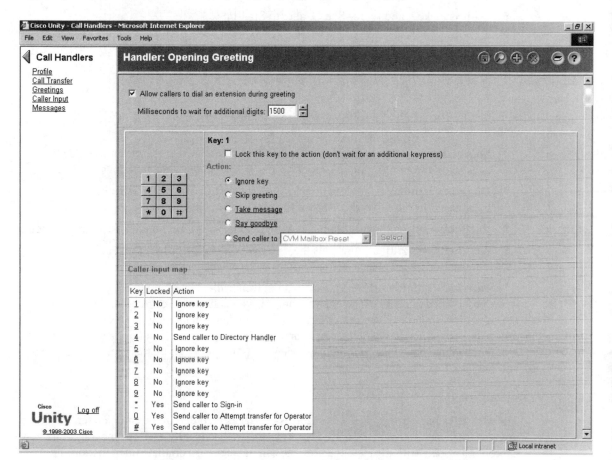

For every key press, 0 to 9, *, and #, the option of either locking the key to the action, such as specifying that 0 will go to the operator handler, is available. In this case, it will not wait for another digit. In addition, for each key, you can set it to include:

- **Ignore Key**—Cisco Unity does not take any action.

- **Skip Greeting**—Cisco Unity skips the greeting and performs the After Greeting action. By default, # is assigned to this action.

- **Take Message**—Takes a message for the caller.

- **Say Goodbye**—Takes the caller to the Goodbye call handler.

- **Send Caller To**—Sends the call to a conversation for changing call handler greetings over the phone.

On a newly created handler, not based on an existing handler, the only keys configured include:

- *—It is locked, and set for Send Caller to Sign-in.
- **0**—It is not locked, and set for Send Caller to Attempt Transfer to Operator (basically taking them to the Operator handler).
- **#**—It is locked, and set for Skip Greeting, taking the caller to whatever the After Greeting action is set to.

The call can be forwarded to one of several destinations, including the following, or you can hang up the phone. The destinations and their purposes are as follows:

- **Subscriber logon conversation**—Recorded instructions that are meant to guide the subscriber through the logon process to access system features, functions, and messages.
- **Directory handler**—Provides directory assistance, allowing callers to initiate searches of the subscriber base, and then forwards calls to the selected subscriber.
- **Particular subscriber**—Designates an individual subscriber in the Cisco Unity system.
- **Another call handler**—Presents the caller with recorded prompts and provides information and available options, routes calls, and takes messages.
- **Interview handler**—Collects information from callers by playing a sequence of prerecorded questions. The answers provided by callers are recorded in the system and then forwarded to a configured recipient. The default recipient is the Example Administrator. Do not delete the Example Administrator account unless other applicable subscribers have been assigned to review messages received by the interview handler.

Using Message Settings

The Messages page determines who receives messages recorded in the call handler. It also governs the length of said messages, actions taken by Cisco Unity after the message, and how Cisco Unity deals with the message after the call handler has completed its function. The message recipient can be either a subscriber or a public distribution list. Typical call handlers do not allow callers to leave messages; however, allowing them to do so provides a great deal of flexibility regarding delivery of the message. The owner of the call handler and the person(s) to whom the message is addressed do not have to be the same person.

Figure 5-6 *Cisco Unity Call Handler, Opening Greeting, Messages Page*

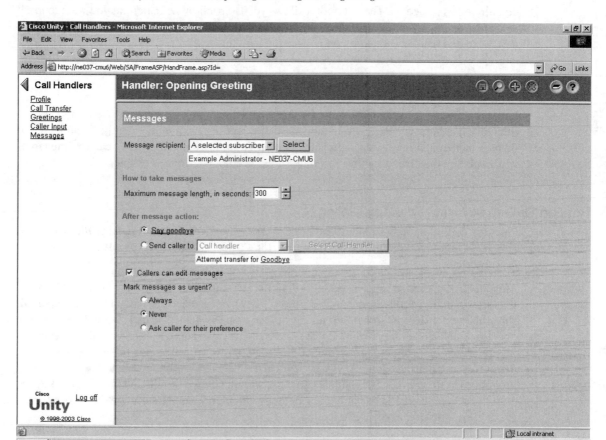

The default maximum message length is 300 seconds, and a warning tone sounds before the maximum message length is reached. The Max and Min for this option can be from 1 to 999 seconds. Messages less than 1 second in length are discarded. Discarded messages, in this case, generate an event that is recorded in the application event log. Figure 5-6 shows the Call Handler Messages page.

The After Message action settings, by default, on a newly created call handler is set to Say Goodbye; however, there is also the option to set it to one of the following options, which are similar to the Call Input one-key options: Send To: CVM Mailbox Reset, Call Handler, Directory Handler, Greetings Administrator, Hang Up, Hotel Checked Out, Interview Handler, Sign-In, or Subscriber.

The After Message actions also include the option to allow the caller to edit their messages; by default, this is turned on. The last option allows you to specify whether or not you want to mark the messages as urgent: Always, Never, or Ask Caller for Their Preference. The default on a newly created handler, not based on an existing handler, is Never.

Planning Call Handler Use

Careful planning for your system components, including call handlers, interview handlers, directory handlers, and call routing tables, is key to setting them up efficiently. Creating a call management map is a way to document your plan. Additional information on call routing tables is provided in the "Defining Call Routing Rules" section later in this chapter.

Routing Callers by Using One-Key Dialing

One-key dialing options include Send To: CVM Mailbox Reset, Call Handler, Directory Handler, Greetings Administrator, Hang Up, Hotel Checked Out, Interview Handler, Sign-In, or Subscriber.

This menu of choices designates a single digit to represent a subscriber extension, call handler, interview handler, or directory handler. The one-key system can be bypassed by entering a full subscriber extension or by pressing no keys in the menu system. The call should be sent to the operator call handler automatically. The system can be set to pause a certain number of seconds for additional key presses before routing the call to allow for full extension dialing. As mentioned previously, certain keys can be locked to take the caller directly to the action programmed for that key. The handler greeting should be used to tell callers what one-key options are available. In this handler, as in many others, it is important to give callers every available option in the recorded greeting.

Creating a Call Management Map

As with network designing, the design of the Cisco Unity menu structure should be planned out and documented. A good way of doing both concurrently is to create a call management map. In this map, include a menu of one-key dialing options, all possible navigation choices, and, if desired, the predefined call handlers.

Figure 5-7 illustrates a sample call management map. As is evident in the figure, the call management map is a simple, logically flowing tiered structure that allows the caller to actively choose how the call is treated.

Figure 5-7   *Call Management Map*

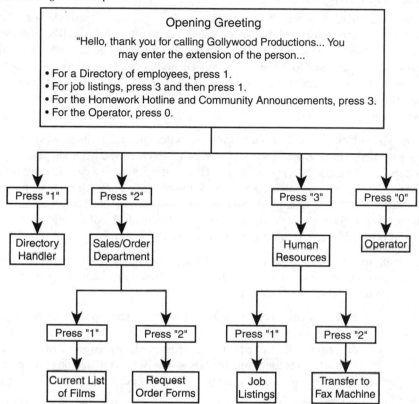

After you create the map, you need to create detailed scripts for use by each call handler during the recording session. It is recommended, for simplicity's sake, that you implement the map from the bottom tier working up to the top tier, as follows:

Step 1   Create the system subscribers and distribution lists.

Step 2   Create each call handler, beginning with those that route calls to subscribers and/or distribution lists, as shown in the bottom tier of the call management map in Figure 5-7.

Step 3   Create each tier of the call map in the Cisco Unity system. Continue working from bottom to top in the hierarchy of the call map until the top tier is complete. Again, refer to Figure 5-7 for a brief example.

Defining Call Routing Rules

When calls arrive, they must be acted upon according to the defined rule sets. The rules specify that calls need to be forwarded to specific destinations, therefore a call routing table is used. All calls are forwarded in some form or fashion, even if the call is forwarded to Hang Up. Call routing tables are used to direct incoming calls to the operator, specific subscribers, call handlers, directory handlers, or interview handlers. Call routing tables also route subscribers to the subscriber logon conversation. Default routing rules come with the system, each with its own settings.

When Cisco Unity receives a phone call, the system must determine whether the call is direct or forwarded. This is done based on the information received from the phone system. The routing is done on a "first match" basis. That is, the first time a call matches all of the criteria of a particular rule, the call is forwarded. If the call fails to match even a single portion of the rule criteria, that rule is skipped and the next rule is processed. The process continues until a match is made. The last rule in the table is the Default Call Handler. Any call that has not already been processed by a rule in the table is processed by this rule.

Although the order of the rules can be altered, the predefined call routes cannot be modified. A call can be forwarded to a number of potential destinations. Each has a particular function in the call routing table. These include:

- **Live Record**—Enables the recording of a conversation while talking to another caller. The recorded conversation is stored in the recording subscriber's inbox as a message. As any other message, it can be reviewed, redirected, or forwarded to another subscriber or distribution list. This functionality may not exist in some phone systems and may be subject to legal implications if all parties are not informed of the recording in progress.

- **Attempt Forward**—Forwards the call if the forwarding station belongs to a subscriber. If the subscriber extension can be found, the call is sent to the subscriber greeting. If no extension is found, the call is compared to the next rule in the routing table.

- **Attempt Sign-In**—If the calling number matches that of the subscriber, the call is sent to the subscriber logon conversation. If not, the next rule in the table is applied to the call.

- **Call Handler**—Sends the call to a selected call handler.

- **Directory Handler**—Sends the call to a selected directory handler.

- **Greetings Administrator**—Sends the call to a conversation that allows a subscriber to alter their configured greetings over the phone rather than from the web interface.

- **Interview Handler**—Sends the call to a selected interview handler.

- **Sign-In**—Sends the call to the subscriber logon conversation. This differs from Attempt Sign-In in that the system prompts for the subscriber extension rather than checking the calling number. This allows a sign-in from any phone or extension.

- **Subscriber**—Sends the call to a specified subscriber.

Cisco Unity has two call routing tables:

- **Direct Calls**—Handles calls from subscribers and unidentified callers that are directly dialed to the Cisco Unity system; for example, a subscriber who is calling to check their voice mail and retrieve messages. Table 5-3 illustrates the rules for direct calls.

Table 5-3   *Direct Call Routing Rules*

Rule	Status	Call Type	Port	Trunk	Dialed Number	Calling Number	Schedule	Send Call To	Language
Live Record	On	Both	Any	Any	Any	Any	Always	Start Live Record	Inherited
Attempt Sign-In	On	Both	Any	Any	Any	Any	Always	Attempt Sign-In	Inherited
Default Call Handler	On	Both	Any	Any	Any	Any	Always	Attempt Transfer for Opening Greeting	Inherited

- **Forwarded Calls**—Handles calls that are forwarded to Cisco Unity from a subscriber extension or an extension that is not associated with a subscriber account; for example, an external call that is forwarded to the Cisco Unity system because the subscriber has set the Call Forward No Answer option. The subscriber extension does not ring. Instead, the call is automatically redirected to the subscriber's configured greeting. Table 5-4 illustrates the routing rules for forwarded calls.

Table 5-4   *Forwarded Call Routing Rules*

Rule	Status	Call Type	Forwarding Station	Dialed Number	Calling Number	Schedule	Send Call To	Language
Attempt Forward to Greeting	On	Both	Any	Any	Any	Always	Attempt Forward to Greeting	Inherited
Default Call Handler	On	Both	Any	Any	Any	Always	Attempt Transfer for Opening Greeting	Inherited

Obviously, call routing rules make decisions regarding the destination of a call. These call routing tables contain the routing rules. You can add additional rules as you deem necessary. You should modify routing tables only after you have created the call handlers, directory handlers, and other necessary components.

Using Direct Calls

Direct calls are those that are sent directly to Cisco Unity. The default rules for direct calls are Attempt Sign-In and Default Call Handler. Neither of these rules can be altered.

This section provides additional information on the numerous fields in Table 5-3. They are as follows:

- **Rule**—The name of the rule (for example, Live Record). This field accepts words or numbers. The name should probably reflect the purpose.
- **Status**—The choices are Enabled and Disabled. The default on a new rule is Enabled.
- **Call Type**—The choices are Internal Calls, External Calls, and Both. The default is set to Both.
- **Port**—A fill-in parameter that specifies to which port it applies this rule to as the call arrives. If left blank (which is the default), it considers all ports on a direct call when trying to match the rule. You can also specify a range of ports
- **Trunk**—These are present only on the Direct Calls rules.
- **Dialed Number (known as Distribute Network Information Services [DNIS])**—The called-party number. Wildcards can be used in this field, for instance, 800*, or it can be left blank for all numbers dialed.
- **Calling Number (known as Automatic Number Identification [ANI])**—The calling-party number. It uses the same parameters as DNIS.
  - **Schedule**—Specifies whether to Always use this rule, use All Hours–All Days schedule, or Weekdays schedule. The default is Always. Any schedule that is defined in the Cisco Unity system may be used. These two schedules are provided by default when the system is installed.
  - **Send Call To**—Specifies what action to take. Here, there are additional options, including Attempt Forward, Attempt Sign-In, CVM Mailbox Reset, Call Handler, Directory Handler, Greetings Administrator, Hotel Checked Out, Interview Handler, Sign-In, Start Live Record, and Subscriber. The default when a rule is first created is Directory Handler.
  - **Language**—Specifies which languages to use; the default is Inherited.

The call type, port, trunk, DNIS, ANI, and schedule settings all allow the limiting of the call or to direct specific calls to particular destinations.

For example, consider the CUGA. A Cisco Unity administrator can arrange to have a specific DID number ring directly to Cisco Unity. When calls come in with that particular DNIS information, the Send Call To destination can be CUGA. In that way, only people who know the CUGA phone number can use it.

The set of call routing rules is one of the most powerful and least understood features of Unity.

Using Forwarded Calls

Forwarded calls are those that are sent to the Cisco Unity system from either a subscriber extension or an extension that is not associated with any subscriber account. The predefined rules for forwarded calls are Attempt Forward to Greeting and Default Call Handler. You cannot modify these two rules, although you can add additional rules.

This section provide additional information about the numerous fields in Table 5-4. They are as follows:

- **Rule**—The name of the rule (for example, Attempt Forward Greeting). This field accepts words or numbers. The name should probably reflect the purpose.

- **Status**—The state of the rule, Enabled or Disabled. The default on a new rule is enabled.

- **Call Type**—The source of the call. Options are Internal Calls (such as calls from subscribers), External Calls (such as calls from unidentified callers), or Both. The default Call Type for a new rule is Both.

- **Forwarding Station**—(Forwarded Calls page only.) The extension (station) that the call was forwarded from. Wildcards can be used in this field, for instance, 3*, or it can be left blank for all numbers dialed.

- **Dialed Number (DNIS)**—The called-party number. Wildcards can be used in this field, for instance, 800*, or it can be left blank for all numbers dialed.

- **Calling Number (ANI)**—The calling-party number. It uses the same parameters as DNIS.

- **Schedule**—Specifies whether to Always use this rule, use All Hours–All Days schedule, or Weekdays schedule. The default is Always.

- **Send Call To**—Specifies what action to take. The options here include Attempt Forward, Attempt Sign-In, CVM Mailbox Reset, Call Handler, Directory Handler, Greetings Administrator, Hotel Checked Out, Interview Handler, Sign-In, Start Live Record, and Subscriber. The default when a rule is first created is Directory Handler.

- **Language**—Specifies what languages to use. The default is Inherited.

In cases where there is an integration of Cisco Unity and telephone switches, call routing tables and rules are even more important. There are some issues that may arise in any integration. Some of these lie in the realm of call routing. Call routing rules are not meant to repair broken integrations. Call routing may work better because of the types and amounts of information capable of passing between the Cisco Unity system and the phone switch, but the rules do not provide a fix for a flawed integration. However, you should understand that improper call routing can break or impair a properly executed and implemented integration.

Call routing tables are processed from top to bottom, and from left to right. First, the Live Record rule is processed. Live Record allows the recording of a call conversation and is very dependent on the capabilities of a telephone system. When Live Record is requested, the call is handed back to Cisco Unity and recorded as the conversation progresses.

The phone system must be able to transmit a barge code and an extension as the call is arriving at the Cisco Unity port. A *barge code* is a short sequence that tells Cisco Unity to open a silent conference with the call already in progress at the specified extension. The setting Start live record begins recording a message that contains whatever is being spoken at the extension.

If no barge code and extension are passed, the rule fails and Cisco Unity moves on to the next, Attempt Sign-In. If the PBX passes a sequence of * and a subscriber's extension, then it begins the sign-in process. This is how Easy Message Access (one of the three main features of an integration) is accomplished. If Cisco Unity does not receive a sequence of * plus a valid extension, then it uses the last rule and sends the caller to the Opening Greeting. You may have as many call routing rules on a system as you wish. There is no practical limit to the number that will execute in a very short period of time.

Chapter Summary

In this chapter, you have learned how to do the following:

- Describe how call handlers can be used for audiotext applications
- Set up one-key dialing
- Describe interview handlers
- Define call routing rules

For additional information on the preceding topics, refer to these resources, found at Cisco.com by performing a search of the text:

- *Cisco Unity Installation Guide*
- *Cisco Unity Administration Guide, "Call Management"*
- *Cisco Unity Administration Guide, "Call Management Tools"*

Chapter Review Questions

Use this section to test yourself on how well you learned the concepts discussed in this chapter. You can find the answers to the review questions for this chapter in Appendix A.

1 List the three predefined call handlers.

2 Which default call handler is used to allow callers to search for subscribers in a Cisco Unity system?

3 Which call handler page provides detailed information about ownership, ownership type, and name of a call handler?

4 If a voice message is less than 1 second in length, how does the Cisco Unity system handle it?

5 If a call is compared to all rules in the call routing table, and it matches none of the defined rules, how will the call be routed?

6 In call routing rules, a call can be forwarded to a number of potential destinations. Among these are destinations known as Attempt Sign-In and Sign-In. What is the difference between these two call destinations?

7 What page can be used to set up one-key dialing on a call handler?

8 The Cisco Unity system provides two default routing tables. List them along with a brief description of each.

9 List the five greetings you can use on a call handler.

10 Which call handler is typically used at the end of a call cycle within the Cisco Unity system?

Upon completing this chapter, you will be able to perform the following tasks:

- Use Cisco Unity Status Monitor
- Use diagnostic traces, reports, and logs to monitor the health of the Cisco unified communications systems
- Choose which report to run to collect specific Cisco Unity information

CHAPTER 6

Cisco Unified Communications System Maintenance

After setting up your Cisco Unity system with your subscribers added and your system configured, the next step is to put it into production and start using it.

Proper maintenance and monitoring are very important to the continued health of Cisco unified communications systems. This chapter provides information about implementing maintenance practices, and introduces the different monitoring tools available in Cisco Unity and Personal Assistant (PA).

Understanding Cisco Unity System Monitoring and Maintenance

You can use Cisco Unity monitoring tools to capture current real-time activity and information.

Once you have that information, it is important to maintain and monitor a Cisco Unity system after placing it in a production environment, to ensure that it continues to perform at the level it is able to, while maintaining optimal performance.

To fully benefit from this section, it is recommended that you have the following prerequisite skills and knowledge. (If you need a quick review, please see the designated chapter, where you can find more information on the topic.)

- Knowledge of the different Cisco Utility tools and utilities (see Chapter 11, "Unified Communications Backup and Utilities")
- Ability to navigate Microsoft Windows 2000 (refer to Chapter 3, "Cisco Unified Communications General Setup")
- Ability to use monitoring tools (see Chapter 11)

Defining Cisco Real-Time Monitoring Tools

Complex systems such as Cisco Unity and Cisco PA need consistent monitoring to maximize their effectiveness over time. Information that is monitored falls into two categories: real-time and historical.

Real-time monitoring means exactly that, monitoring the system functions as they happen. Issues to monitor in real time on a frequent basis include such things as how much space is left on the hard drive and what ports are dialing out to notify users of messages and lighting the lamps on their phones.

Historical monitoring is the gathering of information for a system over a specified time period. It could also be a snapshot of a system's data at a given time.

Here is a quick list of some of the real-time monitoring tools that can be used with Cisco Unity that is discussed in this chapter:

- Status Monitor (HTML)
- Status Monitor.exe
- Port Status Monitor program

Here is a list of some of the tools used to capture historical data:

- Cisco Unity Performance Information and Diagnostic (CUPID)
- Cisco Unity Reporting Tools

Knowing When to Use Cisco Real-Time Monitoring Tools

When developing information, the type of data you are trying to gather determines the type of tool you will use to collect that information. You would use real-time monitoring to collect information when trying to duplicate a specific failure, such as a user who collects all messages but whose lamp does not turn off.

Using Status Monitor (HTML)

Status Monitor, shown in Figure 6-1, is a Cisco Unity application with an HTML interface that runs separately from the Cisco Unity System Administrator. It is possible to run both the System Administrator and Status Monitor at the same time. The class of service (COS) in Cisco Unity controls access to Status Monitor. On the **Class of Service > System Access** page for those administrators who will use Status Monitor, ensure the Access Status Monitor check box is selected. Status Monitor requires the use of Internet Explorer 6.0 or later.

Figure 6-1   *Status Monitor (HTML)*

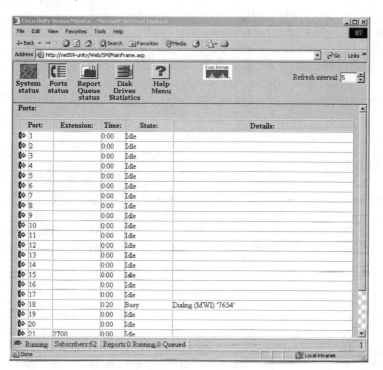

When you first start Status Monitor, the first page you will see is the system status page. Across the top of the page is a set of five icons at the upper-left corner and a Refresh interval box in the upper-right corner. Because HTML is not capable of showing dynamic data in a constant real-time stream, you must tell Status Monitor how often to update information on the screen. You can set it to refresh from 2 to 99 seconds, with 5 seconds as the default. Setting this too low will result in excess network traffic with no appreciable reporting benefit. This also affects the performance of the CPU. Setting it too high may provide information that is not granular enough; if the reporting interval were higher than the system's average call length, it is possible that you would miss some calls altogether. The following is the Status Monitor web address:

http://unity-server-name-or-ip/status/default.asp

Understanding the System Status Page

The main body of the System Status page shows whether or not Cisco Unity is running and enables you to shut it down in one of two ways. You can either wait until all current calls are finished or send a voice message to interrupt the calls and shut the system down. One way to find out how many calls are active in the system before shutting down is to look at the Ports page.

The Ports Page

A port attached to a Cisco Unity system is capable of carrying one call at a time. The Ports page gives you a quick look at the current state (within the latest refresh interval) of the ports on the system. You can see at a glance which ports are active and how long they have been so. You also get information about the state of the call and details about which part of the system conversation the call is currently in. If the port appears locked in an off-hook state (and therefore unavailable to the rest of the system), you can select the port, and then click the Reset button in the lower-right corner of the page body to attempt to make the port available again.

The Reports Page

The Reports page shows the status of reports submitted. It provides information about which state the report is in, who ran it, and whether or not the report has been started or is complete. The information on this page can be quite useful because some reports on the system have the potential to take a long time to complete. You can choose to cancel a report that is already in queue by selecting the report and clicking the Cancel Report button.

The Disk Drives Page

The Disk Drives page gives you a quick look at how much disk space the Cisco Unity system has and how much of it is currently free. You can see all the disk drives on the system, including physical or logical drives. It does not include floppy and CD-ROM drives. If you wish to get more details about the physical drives on the system, including their partitioning and formatting information, you can use a tool such as the Microsoft Windows Computer Management tool.

The last page on the Status Monitor tool is the online Help. It is a pop-up web page that gives you more information about Status Monitor, the Cisco Message Store Manager utility, and the Cisco Event Monitoring Service (EMS).

Using the Status Monitor Program

The Status Monitor program is another real-time tool that you can use to watch what is happening on each of the ports, as shown in Figure 6-2. This includes when a Cisco Unity subscriber calls in to listen to new messages, when Cisco Unity dials out to light the message waiting indicator (MWI) or calls a cell phone to deliver a message, and when an outside caller calls in and navigates through a one-key audio-text application. This tool is found in the \commserver\techtools folder and is called StatusMonitor.

Figure 6-2   *Port Status Monitor Program*

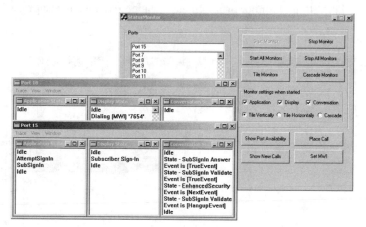

When you start a monitor, the monitor settings control the state information that is shown. You can monitor port status based on Application, Display, or Conversation:

- **Application**—Displays the state of the Cisco Unity application during the monitoring session. States include Idle, Attempt Sign-in, Transfer, and Greeting. This is the same information you would see if you were using the HTML Status Monitor. As an example, when a user is attempting to log in to their mailbox, using a port that is being monitored, the Application display will show Attempt Sign-in. This is useful information when troubleshooting a call to know at what stage of the application the call is in.

- **Display**—Displays a high-level overview of activity during the monitoring session, including Dialing, MWI (with extension), Notification (with extension), and so on. This comes in handy when you are troubleshooting MWI issues. You can see when an MWI message was sent out and for what extension.

- **Conversation**—Displays detailed events that occur during the monitoring session. Events include Call Handlers in use, Action by Subscribers, Greetings, Dual-tone Multifrequency (DTMF), and so on. It is useful when troubleshooting items like when a user enters an extension, but it cannot be transferred to it from Cisco Unity's general greeting. By using the Conversation display, you can see what is coming in from the telephone system (for example, whether Cisco Unity actually is seeing all of the digits when a user dials 1000).

Status Monitor also allows you to log status information to a text file. You can also busy-out a port, or disable it. It also has "Show New Calls" and "Show Port Availability" buttons, which will display that information in real time.

Cisco Unity also comes with another tool called the Port Status Monitor program. It provides the same information as the Status Monitor application. In addition, it allows you to clear all traces from the Status Monitor window and turn on/off the auto-scroll feature, and it has a real-time display option, which gives you more description information about what is occurring on a port. It also gives you the option to specify the maximum traces in the trace window and maximum traces in a log file. This tool is found in the Cisco Unity Tools Depot. Figure 6-3 shows the Port Status Monitor program and a caller leaving a message on Cisco Unity port 5.

Figure 6-3   *Status Monitor Program*

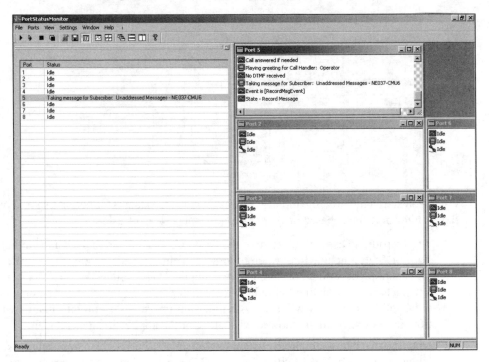

Maintaining a Cisco Unity Server

This section provides information about the proper maintenance of a Cisco Unity system. Here is a quick list of the tasks to consider when maintaining a Cisco Unity server:

- Forward unaddressed messages to the appropriate recipients.

- Scan for viruses.

- Keep virus-scanning definitions up to date.

- Check for mailboxes that exceed their storage limit.

- Run Exchange Optimizer on Exchange 5.5 when more than 100 subscribers are added.

- Keep up to date with Cisco Unity qualified service packs and hot fixes. Service packs that are installed on a Cisco Unity system go through a Cisco qualification process before they are supported on this system.

- Twice a year run the Exchange Eseutil utility from Microsoft, available at http://support.microsoft.com. This is a Microsoft maintenance utility for Exchange Server databases.

- Verify that the backup medium used has enough available space to back up the Cisco Unity server.
- Back up Cisco Unity and message stores regularly.
- Include Cisco Unity servers in the schedule if you are restarting other network servers.
- Run the DbWalker utility.
- Check that messages left in the Unity Messaging Repository (UMR) are delivered to subscriber mailboxes.
- Check whether Cisco Unity System Administrator sessions are not being released and whether any are not being used.
- If using Exchange, check for mailboxes that are over their size limits.
- If using Exchange, schedule mailbox maintenance tasks using the Message Store Manager.
- Update the system clock.
- Monitor forums that are available for Cisco Unity.

All the software and hardware associated with the Cisco Unity server require ongoing maintenance to ensure high performance. The pieces affected by this can also affect server performance in general. Performing regular maintenance on the Cisco Unity server may ensure continuous reliability and performance.

Messages that are not delivered in Cisco Unity return to the Unaddressed Messages distribution list. The following are possible reasons why messages may go to this distribution list: the network is not available, the server assigned to the intended subscriber is not available, the intended subscriber exceeded its message storage limit, or someone left a message using the Operator call handler because the operator was unavailable.

Once these messages arrive in the Unaddressed Messages distribution list, a designated person should manually forward the messages to the proper recipients. This should be done on a continual basis. By default, the only member of the Unaddressed Messages distribution list is the example administrator. Someone responsible for monitoring the system for undelivered messages should also be a member of this distribution list. This person should have no message storage limit on their mailbox, to avoid unaddressed messages not being sent to them. You can add a subscriber by performing the following steps:

Step 1   Open the Cisco Unity System Administrator web page.

Step 2   On the left side, click the Public Distribution Lists link.

Step 3   On the Find and View Distribution list, click Find.

Step 4   On the resulting list, click Unaddressed Messages.

Step 5   On the left side, click Members.

Step 6   Select Add and Find the subscriber you would like to add to this distribution list.

Step 7 Select the subscriber and click the "Add to List" button. This automatically saves this information. So, there is no need to click the standard Save button on the SA.

For more information about forwarding unaddressed messages to the correct recipients, perform a search on Cisco.com for "Forwarding unaddressed messages to the correct recipients."

When running virus scanning and backups on a daily basis, it is good practice to run them during off hours, when the Cisco Unity server is less busy. Some things to consider, however, when running backups are the delivery of messages for Audio Messaging Interchange Specification (AMIS) and Bridge networking, which may occur off hours as well. The virus-scanning software should be set up to notify you every week or two to check with the manufacturer for updates to its virus-scanning definitions. If there is a policy in place to do so for other systems on the network already, you can include the Cisco Unity server with them. If there is no policy in place, Cisco recommends that you update the definitions on the Cisco Unity server whenever the virus-scanning software alerts you of new definitions. "Cisco Unity Requirements, and Supported Hardware and Software," available at Cisco.com, contains a list of virus-scanning software that is qualified for use with Cisco Unity.

For Microsoft Exchange 5.5, when 100 or more Exchange mailboxes or Cisco Unity subscribers are added, you should run Exchange Optimizer. More information on this can be found on Microsoft's website. Refer to Article ID 266051, "Understanding the Microsoft Exchange Server Performance Optimizer" (white paper), at http://www.microsoft.com.

Microsoft regularly provides updates for Microsoft Windows 2000, Microsoft Exchange, Microsoft SQL Server 2000/MSDE 2000, Microsoft Internet Explorer, and Microsoft Internet Information Server (IIS). These updates (which Microsoft also refers to as security updates, patches, or hot fixes) are limited to changes that fix specific problems. They do not include general defect fixes or new functionality. Cisco recommends that these updates be applied to the Cisco Unity server as they are released.

Microsoft also occasionally releases service packs that contain fixes generated since the last general product release. Because the service pack scope is broad, each service pack must go through thorough testing to ensure that changes do not adversely affect Cisco Unity. Cisco Technical Assistance Center (TAC) does not support new service packs until they have been qualified for use with Cisco Unity. You must uninstall unqualified service packs before Cisco TAC provides assistance in resolving issues.

For information on which service packs have been qualified for use with Cisco Unity, refer to "Cisco Unity Requirements, and Supported Hardware and Software," available at Cisco.com.

Microsoft Exchange Eseutil is a defragmentation utility for use with Microsoft Exchange Server 5.5 and Exchange 2000. This utility helps to keep Exchange running efficiently. You should run a backup before running this utility. The time to complete may, however, be lengthy. Run it on a regular basis, at least once every six months. For more information, refer to Article

ID 192185, "XADM: How to Defragment with the Eseutil Utility (Eseutil.exe)," available at http://www.microsoft.com.

On a monthly basis, you should check that the backup medium that is used to back up your Cisco Unity system has enough space.

Proper backup of your Cisco Unity system is important in case a system recovery is required. The backup software used for Cisco Unity should provide the ability to also back up the software products that Cisco Unity uses as well as their data. These include Microsoft Windows 2000 Server, Microsoft SQL Server 2000, Microsoft SQL Server 2000 Desktop Engine (MSDE 2000), and, for some setups, Microsoft Exchange Server 2000. Cisco Unity also includes the Cisco Unity Disaster Recovery Backup tool, which can be used to back up and restore Cisco Unity data. It can be found in the Cisco Unity Tool Depot on the Cisco Unity server.

For more information on backing up and restoring a Cisco Unity server go to Cisco.com and perform a search on "Backing Up and Restoring a Cisco Unity System (Version 4.0)."

If you restart your servers on a regular basis on your network, you should include the Cisco Unity servers also. Cisco Unity comes with a Cisco Unity Schedule Restart Tool, which allows you to schedule a restart for the Cisco Unity server. Cisco recommends that you use this tool to schedule automatic restarts for the Cisco Unity server. The Cisco Unity Schedule Restart Tool is found in the Cisco Unity Tools Depot.

Running the DbWalker utility will ensure the integrity of the Cisco Unity database. It checks for unassociated (orphaned) call handlers and invalid links caused by not removing all references to already deleted call handlers in the database. It also checks each subscriber, subscriber template, interview handler, location object, and directory object for values not present, broken links, and other issues. These can cause instability in the Cisco Unity server and system lockups if left unattended. They will affect any attempt to restore a database made from a backup that contains a corrupted database. You should also run a backup before you run this utility.

Another maintenance item to consider on your Cisco Unity server is to verify that messages left in the UMR are being processed on a daily basis. One way to check this is by looking at the \Commserver\UnityMTA folder to see if messages have not been processed.

There may be times where Cisco Unity Administrator sessions are not being released. You can check this by running a report using the CUPID tool. CUPID can collect the following data for this:

- \Active Server Pages\Sessions Current
- \Active Server Pages\Session Duration
- \Active Server Pages\Sessions Total

If you are using Exchange as your message store and you have set limits to the maximum size of the subscriber mailboxes, on a monthly basis you should also monitor which mailboxes are full or have met their maximum size. This will help you determine whether mailboxes have the appropriate maximum size. You can monitor this by scheduling a Subscriber Message Store Status report using the Message Store Manager utility. This tool can be found in the Cisco Unity Tools Depot or at http://www.ciscounitytools.com.

Use the Message Store Manager to also schedule mailbox maintenance tasks for Exchange. You can schedule items such as deleting old messages and archiving messages.

The system clock should also be updated on the Cisco Unity system if it is connected to the network. An authoritative time server can be set up on the network to make sure all the computers on the network use the same time. You can find more information on how to set up a time server on Microsoft's website, Article ID 216734, "How to Configure an Authoritative Time Server in Windows 2000." When the time on the Cisco Unity server is significantly behind the actual time, message delivery may seem to be slow for subscribers, when it is actually not.

If the Cisco Unity system is not on the network, on a monthly basis you should check the system clock for accuracy. It should be within one minute of the actual time. You can change it by going to the Windows Start menu and clicking **Settings > Control Panel > Date/Time**.

NOTE   If you change the time on the system clock while using the Cisco Unity Administrator, this may produce inconsistencies in the data. There may be values that you have changed that still appear as if they have not been changed. It is recommended not to change the system time while using the Cisco Unity Administrator.

There are many forums available for Cisco products. Forums are great sources to find answers to specific questions. The following is the link to the Cisco Networking Professionals Connection:

http://forums.cisco.com/eforum/servlet/NetProf?page=Voice_and_Video_discussion

Cisco Unity Additional Maintenance Resources

Additional maintenance resources can be found in the following white papers at Cisco.com

- "Maintaining a Cisco Unity System"
- "Security Best Practices for Cisco Unity"

The white papers listed, as well as others listed go into much greater depth about these topics. You can also perform a search on the same website for "Cisco Unity White Papers" to find the latest available white papers for the Cisco Unity product. Please check it regularly for the most current and new information.

Understanding Cisco Unified Communications System Reporting

Cisco Unity Administrator reporting tools show historical system activity and information.

Cisco Unity administrators must understand how to use these tools, analyze the performance of their Cisco Unity system, and put the information in context. An administrator can come to understand what is normal for their system when using reporting tools. Once you establish a normal baseline, it is easier to establish a context for interpreting real-time information captured from the system.

To fully benefit from this section, it is recommended that you have the following prerequisite skills and knowledge. (If you need a quick review, please see the designated chapter, where you can find more information on the topic.)

- Knowledge of how to navigate through the Cisco Unity Administrator web pages (refer to Chapter 3)
- Knowledge of the difference between real-time and historical reporting (see Chapter 11)

Defining Cisco Unity Reporting Tools

Cisco Unity reporting tools provide historical information about functions on the system. Cisco Unity provides the historical information in two broad categories: activity that has taken place over a specified period of time and information that is a "snapshot" in time.

Port activity is a good example of information you can capture over a specified period.

A Subscribers report is an example of information you can collect to look at a snapshot of the state of the system's subscribers at a given period.

Knowing When to Use Cisco Reporting Tools

The type of data that you want to gather determines the type of tool that you should use to collect that information. If you want to see, for example, how many times a specific user received calls that the automated attendant transferred, you use a reporting tool to gather historical information. In addition, if a report indicates that there were particular times during the day when system bottlenecks occurred, it would be useful to observe the system as it is running during those times.

Historical information is data that was previously collected, which you can use to create reports. The report-generating tools go back through the logs and look at events from the Cisco Unity or Cisco PA point of view. You can use reports to develop information about two broad categories: information that is related to subscribers and information that concerns system activity.

Specifying Settings on Cisco Unity Administrator Reports

You can specify different settings on Cisco Unity Administrator reports, depending on the type of report. You can choose what subscribers, administrators, and distribution to include, the date and time range to use, and what data field to sort on. In addition, you also specify the file format that Cisco Unity will use when it generates the report.

What file format you should use depends on what you want to do with the report after you generate it. You can have the report delivered in either web page (HTML) or comma-separated values (CSV) format. If you will be doing some post processing on the report for further analysis or charting, then setting it up as a comma-delimited file is best. If you want the information in the report with no further need of processing, then select the web page format. At present, web browsers are limited to opening files of no more than 220 MB. If you suspect that your report will be larger than that, use the comma-delimited format.

Each individual component in Cisco Unity runs its own log file. The event log reads all the components and combines them into a readable form. You can configure how long to keep the log files saved in the system by using the Cisco Unity System Administrator. The **System > Configuration > Settings** page has three separate settings for log file cleanup. Each of the settings defaults to 7 days, but you can make them longer or shorter as you require. There is a setting for data, diagnostic, and report files. If you wish to run reports that encompass more than the last 7 days, then you must make the Cleanup interval for the logger data files longer. If you do not keep reports after they are generated, then you can shorten the Cleanup interval for report files from the initial 7 days. In Figure 6-4, Status Monitor is showing two reports.

Any report that is run in Cisco Unity draws its data from two different sources: the continuous data represented by the log files and on-demand data. On-demand data is information present in the Exchange database that the reports can extract as needed. Examples of this are subscriber names, aliases, public distribution list membership, and disk space used by each subscriber. Once the report has been started, you can monitor its progress from Status Monitor, or you can wait to be e-mailed when it is ready.

When the report is finished, Cisco Unity sends an e-mail to the account of the person who started the report. Depending on the size of the message store being queried and how busy both message store and Cisco Unity are, the amount of time that is needed to generate the report can be highly variable. Some reports, because of their complexity, may take as long as 18 hours to run. The best time to generate reports is when the system is not busy taking calls or when no other system-intensive process (such as a backup) is in progress. In the present release of Cisco Unity, you cannot schedule reports in advance. In addition, if Cisco Unity is stopped while processing a report, all reports in the queue will be deleted.

Figure 6-4   *Status Monitor, Reports Page*

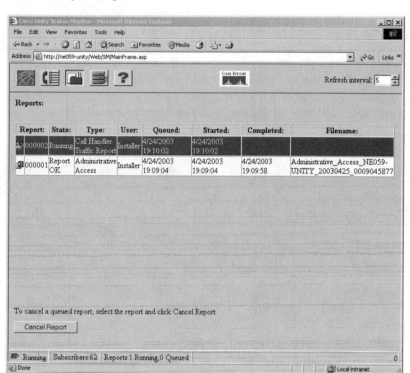

Using Cisco Unity Subscriber Reports

The following is a list of the different Subscriber Reports available for Cisco Unity:

- Subscribers
- Subscriber Message Activity
- Distribution Lists
- Failed Login
- Storage Usage
- Transfer Call Billing
- OutCall Billing

Subscribers Reports

You can run Subscribers reports for all subscribers, for a selected subscriber, or for a public distribution list. The report contains profile and account information on the subscriber(s) selected. This information includes their name, mail alias, COS, extension, and inbox size. This report can be useful in determining which subscribers are using Cisco Unity and the degree to which they are using it. Running the report a week or so after introducing the system will give you an idea of which subscribers may need some extra training or encouragement. Figure 6-5 shows the Cisco Unity Administrator, Subscriber Reports page.

Figure 6-5 *Cisco Unity Administrator, Subscriber Reports Page*

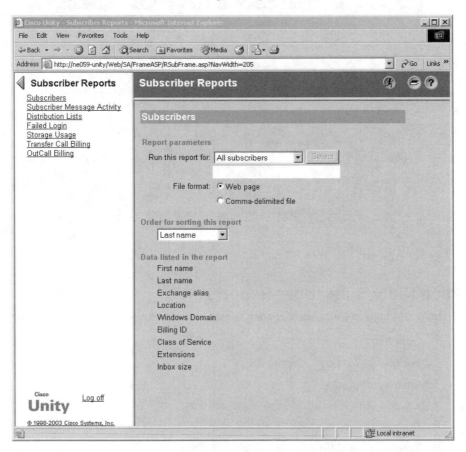

Subscriber Message Activity Reports

A subscriber may report that they are not getting their messages or that their MWI is not turning on or off in a timely fashion. If that is the case, this is the report to run. When gathering information from a subscriber about delayed messages, you should get information about when the problem occurred, whom the message was from, and what they did in response to the message. You can then set up the report to bracket the time. You can run the report only for a specified subscriber at a time. Once run, the report will tell you everything it knows about the message activity of that subscriber, including when they responded to it, what telephone DTMF digits they pressed (if they accessed it over the telephone), what application generated the message, and when the message arrived in their inbox. Armed with this information, you should be able to address most reports of delayed messages. Our experience indicates very few verified cases of delayed messages. In most cases, the perception of a delayed message can be traced to either a misunderstanding on the part of the subscriber or an error they made in using their account.

Distribution Lists Reports

You can generate a report for any single distribution list or all distribution lists on your Cisco Unity system. When you do, you'll know its creation date, the name of the list's owner, the total number of members, and, optionally, the members of the list. If the distribution list has other public lists as a member, the report lists them as well. This report only tells you about public distribution lists; private lists of subscribers are not included in this report.

Failed Login Reports

One responsibility of system administrators is to monitor the system against intrusion by unauthorized callers. The Failed Login report provides the information you need to accomplish this task. The report can track both failed telephone logins and failed system administrator logins. To get the failed system administrator logins, you must enable auditing in Windows security policies.

The report can list all subscribers or a selected subscriber. If a subscriber calls with a locked account, it would be important to find out how the account came to be locked. You can use this report to list all login failures for the selected subscriber, which might be helpful in establishing a pattern or determining a need for further end-user training.

Here are items listed in the Failed Login report:

- For each telephone login failure:
  - Subscriber name
  - Alias
  - Caller ID (phone number called from)
  - Subscriber DTMF
  - Date and time of failure
  - Maximum failures exceeded
  - Failure number

- For each System Admin login failure:
    - Username
    - Computer
    - User domain
    - Event ID
    - Date and time of failure
    - Failure number

Storage Usage Reports

Another administration responsibility is to track the amount of disk space that is used by each subscriber. You can run the Storage Usage report for all subscribers or a selected one. It will tell you how much space is currently in use and how much is still available for use. The amount of space allotted to each subscriber is set through Active Directory, and you can change it if necessary.

Transfer Call Billing Reports

You can use the Transfer Call Billing report to obtain information about calls that are transferred from a subscriber's account or from a call handler. You could use this report for billing purposes or to keep track of transfers to long distance phone numbers. You can generate the report for all subscribers, billing IDs, or call handlers or for a specific subscriber, public distribution list, billing ID, or call handler. The report tells you when the call was made, what number was called, and the result of the call (whether it was connected, busy, unanswered, or some unknown condition occurred).

OutCall Billing Reports

Another report, similar in function to the Transfer Call Billing report, is OutCall Billing. You use it to obtain information about outbound calls made by Cisco Unity for message notifications. This report also provides information about outbound calls when subscribers use the Media Master control over the phone. You can use this report for billing purposes, or to keep track of message notifications sent to long distance phone numbers.

You can generate the report for all Cisco Unity subscribers or billing IDs, or for a specific subscriber, billing ID, or public distribution list. You can generate a summary version of the report or a detailed version, which includes additional information about each call. The summary version contains the time and length of each call. The detailed version contains information on the time the call was made, the notification device used, the dialed number, the result of the call (busy, connected, failure, port disabled, port unavailable, no answer, release, which typically happens for notifications sent to pagers), or unknown, and how much time the call took.

NOTE   The devices for message notification are specified on the subscriber's message notification page and can be a home phone, work phone, spare phone, or pager. The Telephony Record and Playback (TRaP) is listed as the delivery device for Media Master recording by phone.

Using Cisco Unity System Reports

The following is a list of the different System Reports available on Cisco Unity:

- Administrative Access Activity
- Event Log
- Port Usage
- System Configuration
- Unresolved References
- Call Handler Traffic
- AMIS Outbound Traffic
- AMIS Inbound Traffic

Administrative Access Activity Reports

When you need to track which system administrator changed values in Cisco Unity and what values they changed, use this report. You can run the report for all administrators or a selected one and you can set the report for a particular date and time range. The report tells you whether data was created, updated, or deleted, and, if so, who did it and when. In addition, it gives you details about the name of every setting changed and what its new value is. With the hectic pace of business today, a tool like this that helps track the changes made in the system can be very useful.

Event Log Reports

You can use this report to list events from the Windows event log. You can look at all events in the log, or you can filter it so that only Cisco Unity events show up. All the events shown are application events, because Cisco Unity does not write system or security events. Of course, you can view the same information using the Microsoft Windows Event Viewer; Cisco Unity is giving you a way to do it so that you can either maintain a record (by keeping the file) or do it without leaving the Cisco Unity Administrator interface.

Port Usage Reports

To have a clear picture of whether or not your Cisco Unity system is running close to its full capacity, you should run this report on a regular basis. It would be best to run it each week for a few weeks after installing a new system, to gauge whether the ports have been set up correctly for your system traffic. You can run this report for all ports or a selected range of them. The report tells you how many calls arrived on the port, their length and average length, the percentage that the port is being used, and how many calls per day and calls per hour are coming in. If you find that a majority of your ports are running at or above 80 percent capacity during the busiest times of your working day, this may indicate a need for either more port capacity or a rearrangement of port status. Rearrange port status only in consultation with the installer of the system, because, as with simple changes, it could have a profound effect on the way Cisco Unity works.

System Configuration Reports

The System Configuration report gathers information from several places in the Cisco Unity Administrator and makes it accessible all in one place. You can view all of this information (and much more) in the **System > Configuration** section of the Cisco Unity Administrator on several of its pages. This would be a good report to print out before a call to the Cisco TAC.

Here are some of the items listed in the System Configuration report:

- Cisco Unity serial number
- OEM code
- Number of languages
- Version numbers for Cisco Unity and Windows Server
- Number of voice ports
- Available licenses and total licenses
- Leading silence for recordings
- Trailing silence for short and long recordings
- Minimum length for a recording
- Computer name and Windows domain
- Hard drive space used and total
- Additional settings such as:
  - Switch integration type
  - Cisco Unity Assistant licensing
  - Text-to-speech engine

Unresolved References Reports

When you delete subscribers by using the Microsoft Windows 2000 Active Directory Users and Computers console without first deleting the subscriber by using the Cisco Unity Administrator, call handlers can be left in an invalid state. Use the Unresolved References report to locate primary call handlers (call handlers associated with a subscriber's account) and other call handlers, and to interview handlers that are left in this way.

The Unresolved References report examines the Cisco Unity information stored in the SQL database and reports any problems that it finds. The report identifies the errant handler, describes the problem, and suggests a solution.

If the report finds an invalid primary call handler, you need to run Cisco Unity's SysCheck utility to remove it. To access the SysCheck utility, on the Cisco Unity server, select **Start > Programs > Unity > Cisco Unity Tools Depot** and double-click **SysCheck**.

The DbWalker tool can also be used to find call handler references with invalid states.

The Unresolved References report contains information about the handler's name, what kind of call handler it is, the handler's access ID (if any), who "owns" the handler, and who receives messages (if any) left for this handler.

Call Handler Traffic Reports

Once you have built an audio-text application using call handlers, you can use the Call Handler Traffic report to track the number of calls handled by it. The report shows the number of calls going through a particular call handler, and how callers are choosing to exit that handler.

A caller can exit a call handler in four ways: hang up, choose a one-key dialing option, dial an extension that transfers the call to another call handler (or subscriber), or be routed automatically by the after-greeting action (for example, be routed to the Good-bye call handler). The Call Handler Traffic report contains columns for each exit method and a tally of how many times each method is used for the handler (or handlers). You can run this report for a particular handler or for all of them on the system, as well as for a particular timeframe.

AMIS Outbound Traffic Reports

The AMIS Outbound Traffic report provides a variety of data for the system administrator. This report provides the following information:

- When the subscriber submitted the message for transmission
- Whether the message is marked urgent
- The sender's primary extension
- The delivery phone number Cisco Unity dialed to deliver the message
- When the message transmission started
- The number of seconds it needed to transmit the message

- Whether the delivery was a success or a failure
- Total number of messages Cisco Unity delivered successfully
- Total number of messages Cisco Unity delivered unsuccessfully

AMIS Inbound Traffic Reports

The AMIS Inbound Traffic report provides information about the progress of inbound AMIS messages. The following information is included:

- Date and time when Cisco Unity receives transmission of incoming messages
- Cisco Unity location ID of the node sending the messages
- Target user of the AMIS message
- Number of seconds required for the transmission of messages
- Whether the delivery is a success or failure
- Cisco Unity port number receiving the transmission
- Total number of messages received successfully
- Total number of messages that failed

Monitoring Performance Counters

There are several tools that can be used to monitor the performance of a Cisco Unity system. Among them are Microsoft Performance Monitor and Cisco Unity Performance Information and Diagnostics (CUPID), shown in Figure 6-6.

Microsoft Performance Monitor can be used to track items such as processor usage information, memory, Cisco Unity authentication, Cisco Unity integration, and so on. Cisco Unity integration contains counters to track voice mail port usage, total port usage percentage, ports locked, and current ports used.

You can also use CUPID to track the Cisco Unity performance items such as system memory, outgoing calls/sec, and many other things. It is a service that logs its data into a CSV output file and can be used to do performance analysis. Once you start CUPID, it creates a CSV file in the \Commserver\logs folder. If you open it, you see all the items it keeps track of. It requires less system resources than Microsoft Performance Monitor. Once installed, it starts automatically on a system restart. You can change this default behavior by using the Services applet and changing the status of the CUPID service. It can be found in the Cisco Unity Tool Depot of the Cisco Unity System, and it is also available at http://www.ciscounitytools.com.

Figure 6-6   *Cisco Unity Performance Information and Diagnostics (CUPID)*

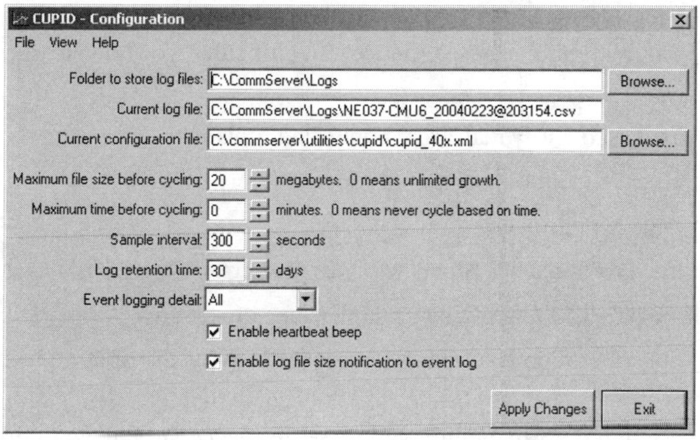

Monitoring PA

This section provides information about monitoring the performance of Personal Assistant.

The Cisco PA performance statistics are collected and displayed by using Microsoft Windows Performance Monitor. You can use more than 25 counters to monitor PA, including items such as the following:

- Total number of calls made to Cisco PA
- Number of errors in the speech system while callers were trying to dial a party by name
- Total number of times callers were asked to access voice mail

All the counters are renewed when the Cisco PA server is restarted.

You can use Call History Information logs to help identify toll fraud on your system. You can use the CiscoWorks2000 Syslog facility to write the collected information to syslog. If not, Cisco PA writes the call history records to a series of 2-MB files called PACallHistoryxx.log. Their numbers range from 00 to 99. Cisco PA will begin reusing the logs once they reach the 2-MB limit.

Chapter Summary

In this chapter, you have learned about real-time and historical monitoring tools, Subscriber and System reports, and maintenance practices. In particular, you have learned how to do the following:

- Describe Cisco Unity real-time monitoring tools
- Use the real-time monitoring tools appropriately
- Use Status Monitor
- Describe how to use the Status Monitor program
- Describe effective Cisco Unity maintenance procedures
- Use Subscriber reports to manage message activity, distribution lists, storage usage, and message traffic
- Use System reports to monitor system performance through administrative access, events on the system, port usage, and system configuration
- View Cisco PA logs and counters

For additional information on the preceding topics, refer to these resources:

- Cisco Unity System Administration Guide
- White papers available at:

    http://www.cisco.com/univercd/cc/td/doc/product/voice/c_unity/whitpapr/index.htm

- Chapter 7 of this book, "Cisco Unified Communications System Hardware"
- Cisco Personal Assistant Administration Guide

Chapter Review Questions

Use this section to test yourself on how well you learned the concepts discussed in this chapter. You can find the answers to the review questions for this chapter in Appendix A.

1 What are Cisco Unity real-time monitoring tools?

2 What information does the HTML-based Status Monitor application provide?

3 List the items to consider when maintaining a Cisco Unity server.

4 When generating a Cisco Unity report, which two file formats can you choose from to have Cisco Unity generate the report?

5 When running a Cisco Unity report, if you suspect that it will be larger than 220 MB, which file format should you use?

6 If there are some Cisco Unity reports in queue and an administrator stops Cisco Unity, what happens to the reports?

7 A user is stating that their MWI does not turn on immediately after they receive a message on their Cisco Unity voice mailbox. Which Cisco Unity Subscriber report can you run to help troubleshoot this issue?

8 When you want to track which system administrator changed values in Cisco Unity and what values they changed, which System report will help you track these changes?

9 Which Cisco Unity report will help you determine how many times callers simply hung up from the opening greeting?

10 What are some of the PA statistics you can monitor by using Performance Monitor counters?

PART II

Cisco Unity Engineering

Upon completing this chapter, you will be able to perform the following tasks:

- Select the server platform specifications for Cisco Unity deployment and understand how the choice of server platform affects the efficiency of the Cisco Unity Voice Mail (VM) only and Unified Messaging (UM) capabilities

- Use voice cards in Cisco Unity integrations with either a PBX alone or in combination with a Cisco CallManager

- Install additional hardware functionality that may or may not be supported by the Cisco Technical Assistance Center (TAC)

Understanding Cisco Unified Communications System Hardware

A Cisco Unity server will be a heavily used network host in your network. The hardware platform that you select should be constructed with this in mind. It is imperative that you meet the minimum system specifications supported for use with Cisco Unity. To facilitate ease of construction and to support issue resolution, Cisco has specified hardware platform overlays. *Platform overlays* are varying options of hardware and machine horsepower that are necessary for a variety of installation scenarios or missions. Essentially, the platform overlays specify configuration of processors, hard disk space, and memory for a specific server size or Cisco Unity user population.

Cisco Unity support is not your sole concern overall in selecting a hardware platform. Other functionality offered, but not necessarily deployed in every instance, can also factor into the necessary horsepower of a server platform. An example of this is the Cisco Personal Communications Assistant (CPCA) server functionality, discussed later in this chapter.

Understanding Cisco Unity Server Hardware—Platform Overlays

As mentioned, Cisco has opted for a platform overlay model to specify platforms for Cisco Unity servers. The platform overlays that are available provide a wide range of functionality and cost. The intent here is to make basic, acceptable Cisco Unity performance available to all customers, from single server users to corporate enterprise services.

Knowing the proper hardware to choose for specific deployments is important, to ensure that it performs properly and meets your customer needs.

Cisco has created a five-level template. Beginning at level 1 and moving up to level 5, the robustness and performance of the server increases. The basic configuration and specifications for each level are set for "acceptable" performance.

To further facilitate ease of support, Cisco has certified specific hardware vendors. Each of these vendors offers a server solution according to each platform overlay. These vendors are Hewlett-Packard/Compaq (one company now that they have merged, referred to as HP for the remainder of the chapter) and IBM. Specific solutions will be discussed along with each platform overlay. Dell solutions were previously sold, however they are no longer available for purchase through Cisco for the Cisco Unity 4.0 product.

To benefit fully from this section, it is recommended that you have the following prerequisite skills and knowledge. (If you need a quick review of either topic, see Chapter 3, "Setting Up Cisco Unified Communications," where you can find more information.)

- A solid understanding of the numbers and system needs of subscribers.

- In-depth knowledge and understanding of the tasks necessary to install and configure the Cisco Unity system.

Table 7-1 shows the five levels of Cisco's platform overlay model. In the table, the amount of message storage time is presented in hours. Two compression algorithms (coder/decoder [codecs]) are in use on Cisco Unity servers, G.711 and G.729a. These two specifications are defined by the International Telecommunication Union (ITU) for voice encoding/compression and transmission in digital form.

G.711 is a pulse code modulation (PCM), which uses a 64-kbps encoding scheme. G.729a is Conjugate Structure Algebraic–Code Excited Linear Predicting (CSA-CELP), which uses an 8-kbps encoding scheme. G.711 is known as "toll-quality" in the telephony world. This is typically the quality of the voice that is heard in day-to-day phone calls on the legacy PSTN. G.729a provides near-toll-quality voice at 8-kbps per-call encoding, compared to G.711's 64-kbps per-call encoding. The encoding bit rate is not necessarily proportionate to bandwidth utilization when discussing voice over data networks. The encoded portion is carried as payload in data packets and therefore requires additional overhead. The additional overhead varies based on several factors, including, but not limited to, TCP header compression and Layer 2 of the Open System Interconnection (OSI) model framing type (not all frames are created equally).

In Mean Opinion Scoring (MOS), a voice quality comparison study, most participants find it difficult to distinguish between calls made using G.711 and calls made using G.729a. The difference between them is important due to bandwidth restraints experienced across WAN links with Voice over IP (VoIP) calls (again referring to bandwidth utilization per call). G.711 offers the best quality, but at a high bandwidth cost, whereas G.729 provides nearly the same quality utilizing a fraction of the bandwidth, but with an increased latency of 10 to 20 ms due to compression/decompression processing.

These codecs work in conjunction with IP telephony integration: Cisco CallManager and Session Initiation Protocol (SIP). These codecs are important because when an integrated system is present, bandwidth utilization is a consideration. Cisco CallManager 4.0 can be configured for G.729, G.711, G.723, G.728, G.722, wideband, and global system for mobile communication (GSM). Cisco Unity only accepts G.729 and G.711 calls from a Cisco CallManager, though. If Cisco CallManager is configured with any other codec to use with Cisco Unity, voice-quality issues will likely arise. Bandwidth considerations are especially important if the Cisco Unity system and Cisco CallManager exist at different sites.

NOTE	For a single call, Cisco CallManager allocates 80 kbps for a G.711 call and 24 kbps for a G.729 call. These should be considered when planning a deployment.

Most significant to the needs of a Cisco Unity system is the dramatic effect of the codec selection on the size of the message store, in minutes. Table 7-1 illustrates this point.

Table 7-1   *Cisco Unity Platform Overlay Levels*

Platform Overlay	Platform Overlay Level 1	Platform Overlay Level 2	Platform Overlay Level 3	Platform Overlay Level 4	Platform Overlay Level 5
Platform	MCS-7815I-ECS1 MCS-7825H-ECS1 IBM x205	MCS-7835H-ECS1 MCS-7835I-ECS1 HP DL380-G3 single processor HP ML370-G3 single processor IBM x235 single processor IBM x345 single processor	MCS-7845H-ECS1 MCS-7845H-ECS2 MCS-7845I-ECS1 MCS-7845I-ECS2 HP DL380-G3 dual processor HP DL370-G3 dual processor IBM x235 dual processor IBM x345 dual processor	MCS-7855I-ECS1 MCS-7855I-ECS2 HP DL580-G2 dual processor HP DL570-G2 dual processor IBM x255 dual processor	MCS-7865I-ECS1 MCS-7865I-ECS2 HP DL580-G2 quad processor HP DL570-G2 quad processor IBM x255 quad processor
Description	Single processor 512 MB RAM	Single processor 512 MB RAM	Dual processors 1 GB RAM	Quad capable Dual processors 2 GB RAM	Quad capable Quad processors 4 GB RAM
VM users	499	1100	2200	3000	3000

continues

Table 7-1   *Cisco Unity Platform Overlay Levels (Continued)*

Platform Overlay	Platform Overlay Level 1	Platform Overlay Level 2	Platform Overlay Level 3	Platform Overlay Level 4	Platform Overlay Level 5
UM users VM with off-box message store users	499	1599	2500	7500	7500
Ports	16	32	48	72	72
Message store users	499	1100	2200	3000	3000
CPCA sessions	50	100	150	200	300
TTS sessions	8	16	24	36	36
Approx. message storage (minutes) G.711	25,604 or 28,580 (platform dependent)	25,604	67,270	134,731	134,731
Approx. message storage (minutes) G.729	204,832 or 228,640 (platform dependent)	204,832	538,160	1,077,848	1,077,848

Selecting Cisco Unity Voice Messaging and UM Configurations

As shown in Table 7-1, some models of Cisco Media Convergence Server (MCS) platforms are offered in two enterprise communications configuration options for Cisco Unity. These are known as ECS1 and ECS2 configurations. The ECS1 configurations are optimized for VM-only deployments, because each has extra hard drive capacity and a redundant array of independent disks (RAID) configuration to support storage of messages on the same server. In contrast, ECS2 configurations are optimized for UM deployments or for VM deployments in which messages are stored on a separate server. These ECS2 configurations typically possess fewer RAID-configured hard drives, which makes them more cost effective when the additional on-box message store capacity is not needed.

Understanding Cisco Unity Server Physical Storage Configurations

The new Cisco 7800 Series of MCSs showcase the updates in Cisco's recommended configuration for physical hard disk and mass-storage devices for the Cisco Unity application. The ECS2 platforms are configured with 2 X RAID 1 hard drives for off-box message storage, whereas ECS1 versions typically have either 3 X RAID 1 or 2 X RAID 1 plus RAID 10 arrays. These mass-storage configurations are designed to optimize platform input/output performance by separating binaries, transaction logs, and databases onto their own RAID arrays.

All multiprocessor Cisco-supported servers carry multiple RAID volumes. A configuration with three RAID-1 volumes is a server that has three RAID volumes and is optimized for installing Cisco Unity in a VM configuration with Exchange 2000 on the same system. This setup allows binaries, transaction logs, and databases to reside on separate hard drives.

A configuration with two RAID-1 volumes is a multiprocessor server (in Platform Overlays 4 and 5) that is configured for a Cisco Unity system, which does not have the message store on the same system (off-box message store). The binaries and transaction logs can be separated, but a third RAID volume is not necessary for the Exchange databases.

The reference to two RAID-1 volumes in Platform Overlay 3 refers to a multiprocessor server, which can have Exchange 2000 either on the same Cisco Unity system or on a separate system.

NOTE   A RAID 10 array is formed using a dual-layer hierarchy of RAID types. At the lowest level of the hierarchy is a set of RAID 1 subarrays (for example, mirrored sets). These RAID 1 subarrays, in turn, are then striped to form a RAID 0 array at the upper level of the hierarchy. The collective result is a RAID 10 array, as mentioned above.

When you are ordering the hardware for each platform, the part numbers will be formatted with ECS1 or ECS2 as a suffix, such as:

```
MCS-7845H-ECS1
MCS-7845H-ECS2
```

Each of these is a 7845 MCS. However, the suffix of each platform immediately brings its capabilities into focus.

As is evident in Table 7-1, the selection of a hardware platform for just about any Cisco Unity subscriber-based need is realistic. From single- to quad-processor solutions, varying degrees of RAID, and varying quantities of RAM, the configuration of the server hardware is fairly straightforward. That, when coupled with the part-numbering scheme, makes specification of customer requirements easier.

When you are using the failover options that are available to some platform overlay models, it is necessary for the primary and secondary systems to have identical hardware specifications and the same number of voice-mail ports. This allows the secondary system to take over voice-mail functionality if the primary Cisco Unity system becomes unavailable on the network. These systems function at the traditional 10/100-Mbps Ethernet speeds, and are soon to incorporate 1-Gbps Ethernet capabilities.

When you are configuring Cisco Unity failover, you must always install the message store off-box, on a separate system, to make sure that messages are available even if one of the Cisco Unity systems becomes unavailable. Also note that the TAC does not support any Cisco Unity server installation that is not running on a supported platform.

The following sections discuss each platform overlay separately. The discussion does not include all server models currently available from each vendor. Table 7-1 lists the currently supported platforms for each platform overlay.

Using Platform Overlay 1

Obviously, Platform Overlay 1 is designed to provide the most basic needs of the deployment. These servers are specifically designed, built, and tested for each individual deployment. These are lower-end servers, capable of running Cisco Unity for a smaller implementation.

Platform Overlay 1 supports up to 16 ports, 499 VM/UM users (message stores), 8 TTS sessions, and 50 Cisco PCA sessions. Typically this system assumes that you are using an 8-GB system partition for recovery and you are using Exchange (voice-mail run-time) Standard edition. In UM deployments, the amount of storage time available for messages is, of course, dependent on the Microsoft Exchange or Lotus Domino physical disk space capacity. Refer to Table 7-1 for storage time specifications.

The MCS 7815 and MCS 7825 fall into Platform Overlay 1. These systems have a single processor and 512 MB RAM. They ship with DVD-ROM and hard drives. The 7815 contains a single 40-GB hard drive, whereas the 7825 ships with two 36-GB hard drives. IBM and HP have equivalent systems as well.

These systems fit the minimum requirements for Platform Overlay 1 in Cisco's model and are appropriate for small office implementations.

Using Platform Overlay 2

Platform Overlay 2 is similar, in many ways, to Platform Overlay 1. The primary difference is in the hard drive configuration. Whereas Platform Overlay 1 implements a single hard drive, Platform Overlay 2 implements a dual drive system using RAID 1. This system represents an implementation suitable for moderately sized office deployment.

Platform Overlay 2 supports 32 voice-mail ports, 1100 VM or 1599 UM users, 16 TTS sessions, and 100 Cisco PCA sessions. This system assumes that you are using a 8-GB system partition for recovery and are using Exchange (voice-mail run-time) Standard edition. In UM deployments, the amount of storage time available for messages is, of course, dependent on the Exchange or Domino physical disk space capacity. Refer to Table 7-1 for storage time specifications.

The MCS 7835 falls into Platform Overlay 2. This system ships with 512 MB RAM, a DVD-ROM drive, and dual 36-GB hard drives that use RAID 1 drive mirroring. Also available is the IBM x345 server with 512 MB RAM, a DVD-ROM drive, and a hard drive configuration that is identical to that of the MCS 7835.

Platform Overlay 2 offers some fault tolerance; however, it is somewhat limited on storage space.

Using Platform Overlay 3

For midsize to large deployments, Platform Overlay 3 is appropriate. This is a higher-end system that offers higher redundancy and performance than Platform Overlays 1 and 2. This overlay specifies 1 GB RAM and five hard drives.

Platform Overlay 3 supports 48 ports, 2200 VM or 2500 UM users, 24 TTS sessions, and 150 Cisco PCA sessions. This system assumes that you are using a 8-GB system partition for recovery and are using Exchange (voice-mail run-time) Standard edition. In UM deployments, the amount of storage time available for messages is, of course, dependent on the Exchange or Domino physical disk space capacity. Refer to Table 7-1 for storage time specifications.

Cisco ships the MCS 7845 with dual processors, 1 GB RAM, and a DVD-ROM drive. The ECS1 version is built to handle voice mail only with an on-box message store. It contains four 36-GB plus two 72-GB hard drives in a 3 X RAID 1 mirrored configuration. The ECS2 version is built for unified messaging and an off-box message store. It contains four 36-GB hard drives in a 2 X RAID 1 configuration.

IBM and HP offer comparable options as well. All have sufficient system specifications to match the requirements of Platform Overlay 3.

Platform Overlay 3 systems can offer higher redundancy and symmetric multiprocessing capabilities along with adequate storage space for user data.

Using Platform Overlay 4

For large deployments, those consisting of up to 7500 unified messaging users, 3000 voice-mail users, or 3000 message store users, Platform Overlay 4 is appropriate. Platform Overlay 4 offers the option of quad processors, but requires only dual processors. This overlay specifies a 2-GB RAM minimum requirement.

Platform Overlay 4 supports 72 ports, 3000 VM or 7500 UM users, 36 TTS sessions, and 200 Cisco PCA sessions. Refer to Table 7-1 for storage time specifications.

Cisco ships the MCS 7855 with dual processors, 2 GB RAM, and a DVD-ROM drive. The ECS1 version of this model is optimized for VM-only deployments and on-box message store. The hard drive configuration contains four 36-GB hard drives configured for 2 X RAID 1 arrays along with four 72-GB hard drives configured for RAID 10.

Platform Overlay 4 is suitable for larger deployments where redundancy and dependability are vital for the voice-messaging system. The additional mirror set allows the separation of the Exchange transaction logs from the application logs to minimize Exchange log stalling.

Using Platform Overlay 5

Platform Overlay 5 is the pinnacle of performance and redundancy in the Unity server arena. This system is suitable for large to very large deployments of VM and UM.

Platform Overlay 5 supports 72 ports, 3000 VM or 7500 UM users, 36 TTS sessions, and 300 CPCA sessions. Refer to Table 7-1 for storage time specifications.

The flagship of the Cisco server line is the MCS 7865, which ships with quad processors, 4 GB RAM, and a DVD-ROM drive. The ECS1 version of this model is optimized for VM-only deployments and on-box message store. The hard drive configuration contains four 36-GB hard drives configured for 2 X RAID 1 arrays along with four 72-GB hard drives configured for RAID 10.

As with all platform overlays, IBM and HP offer equivalent server platforms.

Cisco Unity Supported Platforms List

Cisco keeps an updated list of certified platforms at Cisco.com. This site includes information on legacy server platforms, current server platforms, and working customer platforms. For questions concerning issues of whether or not Cisco Unity will run on a particular platform, go to

http://www.cisco.com/en/US/products/sw/voicesw/ps2237/
products_data_sheet09186a008009267e.html

The web page can also be reached by navigating to Cisco.com and clicking **Products & Services > Voice and Telephony > Cisco Unity > Product Literature > Data Sheets > Cisco Unity Supported Platforms List**.

This page is updated regularly with the most current information regarding hardware platform support for Cisco Unity servers. This page provides some of the best information available regarding Cisco Unity systems.

When ordering Unity 4.0, you can choose to order it as software-only or with all the items, such as the servers and voice cards, as needed to build your complete system. The software-only version does not include Windows 2000 Server.

Cisco Systems provide an online tool called the Dynamic Configuration Tool that can assist you in choosing the proper options for your Cisco Unity requirements. It also includes a configuration guidance option. When enabled, it can determine system incompatibilities as you choose your options. You can access this tool by going to http://www.cisco.com/order/apollo/configureHome.html. You must log in.

For more information on ordering guidelines for Cisco Unity 4.0, go to

http://www.cisco.com/en/US/products/sw/voicesw/ps2237/
products_quick_reference_guide09186a008011c984.html

Additional Hardware Considerations

There are several additional items you should consider when choosing a Cisco Unity server.

You can have multiple NICs for adapter fault tolerance (AFT) on a Cisco Unity system (this is also referred to as network fault tolerance (NFT) by some server manufacturers). This technology provides a second backup connection between your server and the hub or switch it is connected to. This is done by assigning one of your NICs as the primary and the other as the backup (or secondary) NIC. In a typical setup, if your primary NIC fails, the connection to the secondary NIC automatically becomes the active link. To use AFT/NFT you need two NICs installed in the Cisco Unity system and they must be connected on the same network segment. One IP address is assigned to both NICs and the operating system identifies only one NIC on the system.

There are some Cisco Unity servers and switch blades that come with Gigabit Ethernet. You can use this technology with a Cisco Unity server. However, it is not required.

Understanding Cisco PA Hardware Requirements

The Cisco PA package has been mentioned previously in passing. The PA functions were discussed in Chapter 2, "Using Your Cisco Unified Communications System." For now, however, it is important to understand the hardware requirements that are necessary to properly deploy Cisco PA.

The MCS 7825H and MCS 7835H are well suited to run PA. Any of the overlay qualified systems will perform adequately with PA. Figure 7-1 shows the MCS 7825H.

Figure 7-1 *Cisco MCS 7825*

Figure 7-2 *Cisco Unity Voice Card*

The Cisco PA server software package includes ten user licenses and two speech-recognition sessions. Customers can add more users by purchasing additional user licenses and increase automatic speech recognition (ASR) capabilities by purchasing speech-recognition expansion sessions. Most customers require one speech-recognition session for approximately 50 users; however, Cisco recommends a lower user-to-session ratio for enterprise customers with high speech-recognition usage. Tables 7-2 and 7-3 summarize system capacity per server for the Cisco PA server and the speech-recognition server.

IP Phone Productivity Services should be deployed on a corporate web server or a separate server from the Cisco PA server and speech-recognition servers.

To properly understand the information represented in Tables 7-2 and 7-3, some terminology must be defined first:

- **Busy hour call attempts (BHCA)**—The BHCA is the number of calls placed (or attempted) in a continuous 1-hour period, lying wholly in the time interval concerned, for which the traffic or the number of call attempts is greatest. BHCA capacity is one of the primary metrics in determining the capacity and capabilities of a telephone switch.

- **Acoustic model**—Used with ASR in the Cisco PA, the acoustic model is essentially the language database or dictionary to be used (or recognized as the case may be). Currently, Cisco Unity contains acoustic models for American English, U.K. English, French, French Canadian, and German.

Table 7-2   *MCS 7825 and 7835 Capacity*

Server Installation	MCS-7825			MCS-7835		
	Cisco PA Users	**Speech-Recognition Sessions**	**TTS Sessions**	**Cisco PA Users**	**Speech-Recognition Sessions**	**TTS Sessions**
Cisco PA server, speech-recognition server, and enhanced TTS server installed on different systems of the same type	Up to 2500 users	Supports 60 sessions	Supports 12 sessions	Up to 2500 users	Supports 88 sessions	Supports 12 sessions
Cisco PA server, speech-recognition server, and enhanced TTS server installed on the same system	Up to 2500 users	Supports 48 sessions	Supports 12 sessions	Up to 2500 users	Supports 52 sessions	Supports 12 sessions

Table 7-3 *Server System Capacity Using Acoustic Model English.America*[*]

Server Installation	20,000 Names in Corporate Directory		45,000 Names in Corporate Directory	
	Cisco PA Users*	Speech-Recognition Sessions	Cisco PA Users*	Speech-Recognition Sessions
Cisco PA server and speech-recognition server installed on different MCS-7835H or MCS-7835I systems	Up to 2500 users	Supports 60 sessions	Up to 2500 users	Supports 72 sessions
Cisco PA server and speech-recognition server installed on the same MCS-7835H or MCS-7835I systems	Up to 2500 users	Supports 48 sessions	Up to 2500 users	Supports 40 sessions

* Cisco PA supports 15,000 BHCA. Divided by an estimated six calls per person per hour, approximately 2500 users can be supported. See the *Cisco Personal Assistant Design Guide* for detailed deployment scenarios.

For acoustic models other than English.America, a Cisco Unity administrator can expect performance capacity ranges as follows:

- Approximately the same performance capacity for other locales with a similar acoustic model (plus or minus 5 percent).

- Approximately 5 to 10 percent reduced performance capacity for each additional locale running on the same PA speech server (for example, multiple acoustic models in simultaneous operation on one server).

In a typical enterprise, Cisco PA servers can be scaled into N+1 configurations to provide redundancy. They can also be deployed in distributed environments. Multiple Cisco PA servers can be configured into a single environment and then associated with a single Cisco CallManager cluster or multiple clusters, if desired.

For further information on provisioning, refer to the *Cisco Personal Assistant Design Guide* available at Cisco.com. As with all products associated with Cisco CallManager, the Cisco PA system administrator must understand the impact of configuration decisions on the Cisco CallManager environment.

The ASR server can support a maximum of 45,000 entries for accurate recognition in the standard configuration with the English.America.3 acoustic model. Cisco PA can be configured to allow users to clarify duplicate name matches (when searching for subscribers in the directory) by department or location. Refer to the *Cisco Personal Assistant Design Guide* for instructions on procedures that handle larger deployments.

Using Unified Communication Voice Cards

Voice cards are used in Cisco Unity integrations with a circuit-switched PBX either alone or in combination with a Cisco CallManager. Using voice cards is also necessary in the implementation of a Cisco Unity Bridge server to communicate with an Octel voice-mail node. The type of PBX used in the integration dictates the type of voice card(s) necessary for the integration. The total number of voice-mail ports that will be connecting the PBX is the determining factor in calculating the number of cards necessary to provide adequate port capacity for the integration. When integrating solely with a Cisco CallManager or SIP, voice cards are not required.

Knowing the proper voice cards to choose for specific deployments is important, to ensure that they meet your customer needs.

To benefit fully from this section, it is recommended that you have the following prerequisite skills and knowledge. (If you need a quick review, see the designated chapter, where you can find more information on the topic.)

- Basic knowledge of Cisco Unity system integrations (see Chapter 1, "Cisco Unified Communications System Fundamentals")
- Understanding of available Cisco Unity integration methodologies (see Chapter 9, "Cisco Unified Communications Integrations")

A voice card can be seen essentially as a collection of 4, 12, or 24 single-line extensions on a single card. These voice cards are used in Cisco Unity integrations with a circuit-switched PBX either alone or in combination with a Cisco CallManager. All communications between the PBX and the Cisco Unity server occur across the voice card connections. This is not the case with CallManager integrations because all communications take place over the IP network infrastructure.

It is also possible to use voice cards in the implementation of a Cisco Unity Bridge server to communicate with an Octel voice-mail node. Cisco Unity Bridge communicates with Octel voice-mail systems over the PSTN using Octel's analog messaging protocol. The Cisco Unity Bridge uses a four-port Brooktrout voice card.

The installed voice cards in a Cisco Unity system run as a software service in Microsoft Windows 2000 Server. Each voice card is dependent on its individual service for functionality. As the boot process of the Cisco Unity server completes, the voice cards initialize and start their services. If the services do not properly initialize, the Cisco Unity services will be unable to start.

Through the combined efforts of the hardware and software, voice cards perform the same functions as a typical telephone user. The voice card can initiate a call, send dual-tone multifrequency (DTMF) tones, and interpret tones on the phone line as dial-tone, ringback, or busy signals. The voice card can interpret DTMF tones it receives to perform digit analysis. Each function allows it to coexist with, and send/receive information to/from, the Cisco Unity server.

A second function that voice cards perform is modulation and demodulation. This is the process of converting digital signals to analog (and back) as necessary when performing playback of digital files that the voice card receives from Cisco Unity (either system prompts or a subscriber's recorded greeting). This is necessary because the greetings and system prompts must be played over the analog PSTN to the subscriber or outside caller. The same is true when analog-to-digital conversion takes place. That is when a message, greeting, or voice name is spoken over the telephone network and is then converted into a digital file residing on a server's hard drive.

Installing Voice Card Hardware

As mentioned, the voice cards are available in 4-, 12-, or 24-port versions. The cards can be installed in any Cisco Unity server that meets the minimum hardware requirements mentioned in any of the five overlay templates. Each voice card is manufactured by Intel/Dialogic. Industry Standard Architecture (ISA) voice cards are not supported for new Cisco Unity 4.0 installations or upgrades. Use the documentation provided with each voice card, and make sure to follow the warnings and precautions so that you do not damage the hardware during installation and configuration.

If the Cisco Unity system installation is performed outside the United States and is connecting directly to a central office using an analog loop, it may be necessary to install inline telco filters on the Intel/Dialogic voice cards to filter tax impulse signals. You can find more information about this in the Intel/Dialogic documentation that ships with the voice cards.

The Intel/Dialogic D/41EPCI, D/41JCT-LS, and D/41JCT-Euro voice cards are meant for use with all circuit-based switches using DTMF or Simplified Message Desk Interface (SMDI) integration. Each card provides

- Four-port analog digital signal processor (DSP) card.
- Four RJ-11 connectors.
- All cards in one system share the same interrupt request (IRQ) and base memory address.

- Set SW2 switches to off as shown in the *Cisco Unity Installation Guide.*
- Set jumpers JP2 through JP7 as shown in the *Cisco Unity Installation Guide.*
- A 16-position rotary switch (SW1) manually identifies each card in a system; the first card is set to ID 1, the second is set to ID 2, and so on.
- Each card is configured using Dialogic Configuration Manager (DCM), Dialogic's configuration utility. This utility writes information into the Registry.

The Intel/Dialogic D/120JCT-LS (uPCI, Rev 2) and D/120 JCT-Euro (uPCI) voice cards are quite similar to the four-port version. They provide the following:

- 12-port analog DSP card.
- Uses six RJ-14 connectors; ports 1 and 2 use the top connector and ports 11 and 12 use the bottom connector.
- All cards in one system share the same IRQ and base memory address.
- A 16-position rotary switch (SW100) manually identifies each card in a system; the first card is set to ID 1, the second is set to ID 2, and so on.
- Set SW1 to On-hook for each card; otherwise, they will not answer calls.
- Each card is configured using -DCM. This utility writes information into the Registry.

Cisco recommends using the newer Universal (3.3Vdc or 5Vdc dual voltage) Peripheral Component Interconnect (PCI) versions of the D/120JCT-LS and the D/120JCT-Euro cards, rather than the older, single-bus voltage (5Vdc) versions of the cards. Note that older (Revision 1) LS cards are still supported for use with Cisco Unity version 4.0(x).

The Intel/Dialogic D/240PCI-T1 voice card provides 24-port service. This connection is accomplished via a single RJ-48 (8-pin modular) connector. This connection uses T1 TDM technology. It provides the following:

- 24-port T1 DSP card.
- Uses one RJ-48C connector.
- All cards in one system share the same IRQ and base memory address.
- A 16-position rotary switch (SW100) manually identifies each card in a system; the first card is set to ID 1, the second is set to ID 2, and so on.
- Each card is configured using the Dialogic Configuration Manager (DCM). This utility writes information into the Registry.

The Intel/Dialogic voice cards are useful in many configurations. These represent the core of the Cisco Unity voice card options.

The Brooktrout Technology TR114+P4L voice card, while similar to the Intel/Dialogic, offers additional flexibility. It is a four-port card that uses a single RJ-45 connector and is used only with a Cisco Unity Bridge. It cannot be used in any other capacity with a Cisco Unity system.

Each card is supplied with a cable that has an RJ-45 plug at one end and four RJ-14 connectors at the other end. All cards in one system share the same IRQ (10) and base memory address.

Because Brooktrout PCI analog voice-and-fax cards are designed for the PCI expansion bus, the interrupts and memory (I/O) addresses used by the cards are assigned by the platform BIOS, not by configuring jumpers or switches.

Refer to the Cisco Unity Bridge server hardware documentation to determine how to configure the platform to assign IRQ 10 to expansion slots used by PCI voice-and-fax cards. Figure 7-2 shows a typical voice card.

Installing Optional Hardware

Occasionally, you may need additional hardware functionality for your Cisco Unity system. In such situations, you need to make sure to choose hardware that is supported by Cisco Unity. It can range from the simple external modem to virtually any functional configuration that can be contrived. This section focuses on the optional hardware that is supported and unsupported with Cisco Unity.

Knowing the proper optional hardware to choose for specific deployments is important, to ensure that it performs properly and meets your customer needs.

Optional Supported Hardware

The following optional hardware is supported for use with Cisco Unity 4.0(x):

- **External modem**—This is used with the Symantec pcAnywhere, which has been selected as the Cisco TAC remote-access method. Note that modems and Symantec pcAnywhere software must be provided by the customer. The option may also exist to use Remote Desktop capabilities. Cisco recommends an external V.34 modem rather than an internal modem because the external modem does not use a slot in the system or the PCI subsystem resources, which an internal modem may require. This is more of a concern when integrating Cisco Unity with circuit-switched telephone systems that require voice cards. An external modem uses system resources, but it uses only one IRQ and I/O port map.

- **Allocation**—Some configurations may require three serial ports (Cisco Unity servers normally have two serial ports). You may have a situation where you need a serial port for an external modem, a UPS, and a serial data connection for your telephone system. In this case, an internal modem may be used instead.

- **Tape drives for system backup**—A tape autoloader may also be attached to a Cisco Unity server, although network backup to a dedicated backup server is recommended for high-capacity backup and recovery scenarios.

- **Uninterrupted power supply**—A UPS can be connected to a Cisco Unity server by a serial cable.
- **Additional storage**—Directly connected chaining of additional mass storage onto a RAID channel or channels hosted via a Small Computer System Interface (SCSI) controller or a Fibre Channel host bus adapter inside the server.

Note   Cisco TAC is unable to assist with this hardware setup or with problems related to this storage configuration. Consult with the server vendor for any issues related to this configuration.

- **Dual NICs**—You can use two or more network interface cards (NICs) to form a fault-tolerant team, sharing the same IP address (active-passive configuration).
- **Out-of-band management cards**—The following cards are supported for use with Cisco Unity 4.0(x):
  - HP Remote Insight Lights-Out Edition, all versions
  - IBM Remote Supervisor Adapter, all versions

Optional Unsupported Hardware Configurations

Hardware that has not been qualified for use with Cisco Unity is not supported for use on or connected to a Cisco Unity server. Cisco TAC will ask that it be removed, disconnected, or disabled during troubleshooting.

The following are hardware configurations that are not supported:

- **Multiple NICs for load balancing**—When a Cisco Unity server has dual NICs and each is set up for different network segments, messages may not be delivered when using Exchange 2000. In addition, when someone calls into Cisco Unity, they may hear the standard prompts, but Cisco Unity may not hear the caller speaking.
- **Storage area networking**—Remote data storage connectivity through frame or packet switch fabrics or networks, such as Fibre Channel, InfiniBand, or IP packetization, is not supported. Installation or relocation of Cisco Unity software, required Microsoft components, or the associated log files onto disks other than the physical disks that are a part of a Cisco Unity server are not supported.
- **Multiple IP addresses**—Multiple IP addresses for two or more load-balanced NICs (active-active configuration) is not supported. Note that active-passive NIC configuration is supported.

Chapter Summary

In this chapter, you have learned about the following:

- The hardware specifications necessary to support Cisco Unity and PA
- The voice cards used for Cisco Unity and Cisco Unity Bridge server
- Optional hardware for Cisco Unity
- Optional unsupported hardware for Cisco Unity

For additional information on the preceding topics, refer to these resources:

- Cisco Unity Supported Platforms List, at http://www.cisco.com/en/US/products/sw/ voicesw/ps2237/products_data_sheet09186a008009267e.html
- Cisco Personal Assistant Data Sheet, at http://www.cisco.com/en/US/products/sw/ voicesw/ps2026/products_data_sheet09186a00800a1763.html
- Cisco Unity, Selecting Hardware, at http://www.cisco.com/en/US/products/sw/voicesw/ ps2237/products_implementation_design_guide_chapter09186a00801187ca.html
- *Cisco Unity System Requirements, and Supported Hardware and Software,* available at Cisco.com.

Chapter Review Questions

Use this section to test yourself on how well you learned the concepts discussed in this chapter. You can find the answers to the review questions for this chapter in Appendix A.

1 List two hardware manufacturers that are certified to provide Cisco Unity server and PA server functionality.

2 Which overlay template supports quad-processor capabilities, but does not require it?

3 Which voice card provides the highest density of ports available for a Cisco Unity server?

4 Which voice card(s) provides four-port connectivity?

5 List three types of optional hardware that are supported by the Cisco TAC.

6 List two types of unsupported hardware configurations that are not supported by the Cisco TAC.

7 What codecs can you use when integrating Cisco CallManager with Cisco Unity?

8 What type of modem is typically recommended for use with the Cisco Unity system?

9 How many voice ports does the Intel/Dialogic D/240PCI-T1 card provide?

Upon completing this chapter, you will be able to perform the following tasks:

- Describe Cisco Unity for Microsoft Exchange and Lotus Domino architectures
- Describe the Cisco Personal Assistant (PA) architecture
- Describe the software needed to perform a successful installation of Cisco Unity for Exchange and Domino configurations
- Describe the Cisco Unity system installation
- Describe the use of Cisco Unity Server Preparation Assistant (CUSPA) and Cisco Unity Installation and Configuration Assistant (CUICA)
- Describe the upgrade process for Cisco Unity and Cisco PA

CHAPTER 8

Cisco Unified Communications System Software

This chapter starts by describing different types of unified communications architectures offered by Cisco, including Cisco Unity for Exchange, Cisco Unity for Domino, and Cisco PA. It then describes the software requirements that are necessary to successfully install these products, and explores the installation process for a Cisco Unity installation, including the steps for using CUSPA and CUICA. Finally, it examines the upgrade process for the Cisco Unity Unified Messaging (UM) systems.

Cisco Unity and Cisco PA are built upon an involved architecture. Knowing the structures will help you perform a smooth and healthy installation and maintain the system. Understanding how the different software components interact with the Cisco unified communications products will help you to troubleshoot the products.

To benefit fully from this section, it is recommended that you have the following prerequisite skills and knowledge. (If you need a quick review, see the designated chapter, where you can find more information on the topic.)

- Knowledge of the different unified communications hardware (see Chapter 7, "Understanding Cisco Unified Communications System Hardware")
- Knowledge of the way Cisco Unity and Cisco PA handle calls (see Chapter 2, "Using Your Cisco Unified Communications System")
- General knowledge of Cisco Unity and Cisco PA features (see Chapter 1, "Cisco Unified Communications System Fundamentals")
- General knowledge of Cisco CallManager and Telephone systems (see Chapter 1)

Understanding the Cisco Unity for Exchange Architecture

The foundation of the Cisco Unity architecture is the hardware. You can purchase Cisco Unity on several different platforms. (For more information or to review this topic, take a look at Chapter 7, "Cisco Unified Communications Server Hardware.") Cisco Unity uses Microsoft Windows 2000 Server (or Windows 2000 Advanced Server) as its operating system. Cisco Unity stores a small amount of user data on Windows 2000 Server or

Microsoft Windows Server 2003 Active Directory (AD); however, it uses an SQL database to store all of its information.

Figure 8-1 illustrates the Cisco Unity 4.0 unified architecture with Exchange message store.

Figure 8-1 *Cisco Unity 4.0 Unified Architecture with Exchange Message Store*

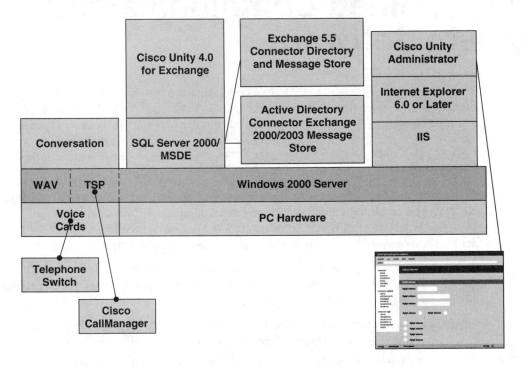

The Cisco Unity system console screens are HTML-based windows. It uses Microsoft Internet Explorer 6.0 with Service Pack 1 (SP1) to provide the HTML screens. Netscape is currently not supported.

When you use the Cisco Unity Administration Active Server Pages (ASP) to add, delete, or modify a Cisco Unity subscriber, you are modifying the SQL database. Cisco Unity stores information about Cisco Unity subscribers, as well as selected Cisco Unity configuration data, in a Microsoft SQL Server 2000 server. Cisco Unity uses either Microsoft Data Engine (MSDE 2000) or Microsoft SQL Server 2000 software depending on your Cisco Unity configuration and customer requirements. This is really based on the number of subscribers and number of ports the configuration requires. If the system will be set up with 32 ports or less, then MSDE can be used. For systems that require more than 32 ports, MS SQL Server 2000 is required.

When there are two or more Cisco Unity servers on an AD forest or Microsoft Exchange 5.5 directory, a small amount of information is stored on each SQL database of the other subscribers. The Cisco Unity Directory Monitor synchronizes the information in the MS SQL

Server 2000 database with information in AD or in the Exchange 5.5 directory. If Cisco Unity information is changed by using another type of application, such as when you modify subscriber data by using AD Users and Computers, then the Cisco Unity Directory Monitor automatically discovers the change and propagates the change to the MS SQL Server 2000 database accordingly. If it is changed in SQL first, the information is then passed to Microsoft Windows AD through either the Microsoft Active Directory Connector (ADC) for Exchange 5.5 or the AD Connector for Microsoft Exchange 2000 or Microsoft Exchange 2003. This choice is made during the Cisco Unity installation process.

Cisco Unity has the ability to store voice-mail messages in an Exchange 2000, 2003, or 5.5 Message Store, or in a Lotus Domino message store. On some Cisco Unity configurations, Exchange is installed on the same system as the Cisco Unity server. In this type of configuration, the message store that Cisco Unity uses is local to the server. In other Cisco Unity setups, Exchange can be installed on one or more other servers, where the message store may or may not be local to the Cisco Unity system.

In these solutions, some or all of the subscribers may have their Exchange mailboxes on other Exchange servers. Cisco Unity can have subscribers on multiple Exchange servers. When you create a subscriber from Cisco Unity, you specify which message store it will use or you can import a user from any message store that is visible to Cisco Unity.

If Cisco Unity is using an off-box Exchange server as its message store and the Cisco Unity Message Repository (UMR) discovers that it is unavailable, new subscriber messages will be stored on the Cisco Unity server until the Exchange server becomes available again.

Cisco Unity can also have subscribers on either active/active or active/passive clusters. When using active/passive clustering, Cisco Unity can have subscribers only on two-node clusters. Cisco Unity cannot be installed on an Exchange server cluster. Cisco Unity does not support Exchange 5.5 clustering.

Cisco Unity 4.0 can reside within a Windows Server 2003 AD network. You can upgrade your existing Microsoft Windows 2000 Domain Controller (DC), Global Catalog (GC) servers, and member servers to Windows 2003 servers . Before you do so, review the notes in the following online document, which provides more details on the types of upgrade and current options and limitations: http://www.cisco.com/warp/public/788/AVVID/MS_2003.pdf

Telephone Systems and Cisco Unity with Exchange

Whether you integrate Cisco Unity with a Cisco CallManager or a circuit-based telephone system, you need a physical connection between the two. The physical connection for the Cisco CallManager integration is a connection to the site's LAN or WAN. This is also true when you are connecting to a SIP proxy server.

The connections for a circuit-based telephone system are physical; voice cards are installed on the Cisco Unity server and, in some integrations, a serial link is installed that carries call information and message waiting indicator (MWI) information. A discussion of various voice cards appears in Chapter 6.

You also need software drivers and a TAPI service provider (TSP) to run the hardware, and a software interface to configure and modify the TSP settings. The Cisco Unity Telephony Integration Manager (UTIM) installs the TSP provided by the manufacturer of the device that communicates with the telephone system. It can also be used to manage the different types of integrations configured on the Cisco Unity system, such as for Cisco CallManager or Session Initiation Protocol (SIP). A maximum of two integrations is currently supported. This means that you can have a telephone switch and one or more Cisco CallManagers installed on the system. Or you can have a SIP proxy server and also Cisco CallManager integration.

Once Cisco Unity is configured, you can reach UTIM in either of two ways. You can go to the Control Panel and click **Phone and Modem Options**, click the **Advanced** tab, choose **Cisco Unity-CM TSP**, and click **Configure**. The second way is to go through the Tools Depot: choose **Start > Programs > Unity > Cisco Unity Tools Depot**.

Here are some of the actions that you can perform with UTIM for Cisco CallManager configurations:

- Assign the IP address of the primary CallManager and secondary servers.
- Assign the Cisco CallManager device name prefix of the voice-mail ports.
- Assign the IP port number used to connect to CallManager.
- Verify the connection between CallManager and Cisco Unity. Basically, UTIM pings the CallManager and verifies that each voice-mail port is configured correctly on the primary server. If there is a secondary server, UTIM will verify that configuration as well.
- Assign the MWI numbers.
- Add/remove ports to a particular integration. You can have more than one Cisco CallManager cluster configured on a Cisco Unity system.
- Choose to schedule MWI synchronization or manually force it.
- Set up automatic gain control. Cisco Unity automatically adjusts the volume of phone messages or subscriber greetings to match a specific target volume. You can choose to disable this feature.

Figure 8-2 illustrates UTIM with a CallManager integration and a telephone system integration setup.

Figure 8-2   *Cisco UTIM Tool*

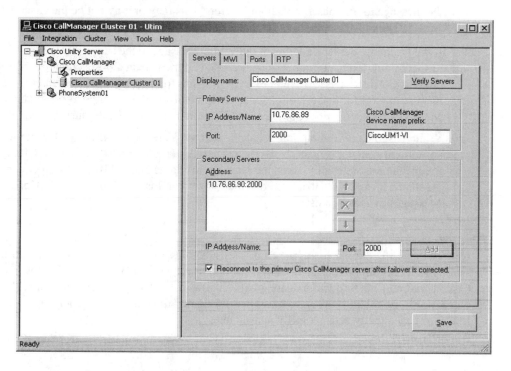

When Cisco Unity receives a voice-mail message, it passes the subscriber messages to the appropriate Exchange message store. The message is then placed into the Cisco Unity subscriber's Exchange Inbox, which is part of the Exchange Information Store (IS).

The following example indicates what happens when an outside caller (also known as an unidentified caller) leaves a message for a subscriber:

1 The caller dials a subscriber's extension. If the extension is busy or set to forwarded-all, or the subscriber is away from their desk (also known as no answer in Cisco CallManager), the call is forwarded to Cisco Unity with the information of who called, the intended subscriber, and the reason why the call was extended to Cisco Unity.

2 When Cisco Unity receives the call, it answers it, looks up the subscriber's information that is stored in the MS SQL server, finds the subscriber's greeting, and plays it for the outside caller. Then, it prompts the caller to leave a message. The Cisco Unity server keeps the subscriber greeting locally in a file instead of in AD.

3 After the caller hangs up, the message is temporarily stored locally on the Cisco Unity server's hard disk.

4 Cisco Unity attempts to send the message to the Exchange server, which in turn delivers the message to the subscriber's home server. (This may or may not be the Cisco Unity server.) Then the Exchange server stores the message in the subscriber's mailbox.

If the Exchange server's attempt to deliver the message to the subscriber's home server is unsuccessful, Exchange queues the message and tries again at a specified interval. By default, this interval is set to retry every 10 minutes for a period of 24 hours. If the message is unsuccessful for that period, Exchange then delivers the message to the Unaddressed Messages public distribution list, which is created by Cisco Unity during installation.

While Cisco Unity is temporarily storing that message locally, if network issues exist or Cisco Unity cannot contact the Exchange server that it communicates with, Cisco Unity retains the message until Exchange becomes available again. If the subscriber's mailbox is full, the message is not delivered to that subscriber. Instead, it is sent to the Unaddressed Messages distribution list.

NOTE   Cisco Unity will continue to answer calls, play greetings, and record messages for subscribers as long as it is running. This gives callers the opportunity to perform these things even though Cisco Unity may not be communicating with an off-box Exchange server at the time. However, when a subscriber calls to retrieve messages during this time, they receive a greeting that indicates Cisco Unity is temporarily unavailable.

---

5 Cisco Unity continually monitors all subscriber mailboxes. When it notices a change in state for a mailbox, it uses the Messaging Application Programming Interface (MAPI) to find out what happened. If it identifies the change as a new voice-mail message, it generates an MWI request (on or off, depending on the state change). By default, Cisco Unity will notify subscribers only of new voice-mail messages. Subscribers can, however, configure their mailbox to receive notification on new e-mails by using **Cisco Unity Assistant > Message Notification** and choosing the e-mail option.

Cisco Unity can be set to use several different methods to notify subscribers:

- When a subscriber has a phone that is connected to a phone system or Cisco CallManager, Cisco Unity turns on the subscriber MWI on the subscriber's phone.

- When Cisco Unity is set up for UM, the messages appear in the subscriber's e-mail inbox.

- Cisco Unity also has other Message Notification options that are configurable through the Cisco Unity Assistant. A subscriber can configure their personal options to have Cisco Unity call one or more phones or pagers, or send an e-mail to a text pager to notify the subscriber that they have received a new voice-mail message.

When a subscriber leaves a message over the phone, Cisco Unity responds very similarly to how it responds when an outside caller leaves a message, as just described. The conversation played for the subscriber is slightly different because the subscriber has extra options that the outside caller does not have, such as the ability to change personal settings. The message left is also identified by the subscriber's information instead of from arriving from the Cisco Unity Messaging System mailbox. For example, Cisco Unity can play the following before the message is heard: "From extension one, zero, zero, one."

The main differences in how Cisco Unity responds come into play when either the network is having issues or one or more of the Exchange servers on the network are not up and working properly. In these situations, the following can occur:

- When the intended subscriber's home Exchange server is down, or the caller's home Exchange server and Cisco Unity cannot contact the recipient's home Exchange server because of network issues, the message resides on the caller's home Exchange server until both Exchange servers start communicating again.

- When subscribers are configured on multiple Exchange servers, and a voice-mail message is left for a subscriber, Cisco Unity sends out the message to one of the Exchange servers. If the intended Exchange server is down or there are network issues preventing connection to that server, then all subscriber-to-subscriber messages are stored locally on the Cisco Unity server until that Exchange server becomes available on the network again.

The following example indicates what happens when a subscriber listens to a message over the phone:

1 A subscriber calls into Cisco Unity over a phone by entering their extension followed by their password. If the calling party's call is identified by Cisco Unity as a direct call from a subscriber, then Cisco Unity prompts for their password only.

2 When the subscriber enters their password, Cisco Unity checks its SQL database to verify whether the password entered is correct.

   When the password is correctly entered, Cisco Unity logs in to the subscriber's mailbox using MAPI. If the subscriber's home Exchange server is down or there are network issues preventing connection to that Exchange server, Cisco Unity tells the subscriber that the mailbox is currently unavailable. If messages were left for that subscriber during the down time, Cisco Unity asks the subscriber if they would like to listen to those messages. These messages are being held by Cisco Unity locally until it can communicate with the targeted Exchange server again.

   In a normal situation, however, the subscriber simply follows the Cisco Unity conversation to listen to their messages. When a voice-mail message is played, it streams from the subscriber's home Exchange server to Cisco Unity (which can actually be the same server, depending on the configuration) and then to its targeted phone system to play on the subscriber's phone.

NOTE   When a subscriber listens to messages over the phone, either by calling Cisco Unity directly or by using ViewMail (or the Domino Unified Communication Services [DUCS] client) to call a phone and then listens to a message, a voice-mail port is used on the Cisco Unity server. However, if the subscriber uses ViewMail and their computer speakers to listen to the messages, a port is not used. This decreases the load on the Cisco Unity server and keeps more ports available on the Cisco Unity system for other purposes.

   3 After hearing the complete message, the subscriber has the option to follow the Cisco Unity prompts to save, delete, or listen to the message again. While the message is playing, the subscriber also has the option to delete it without hearing the entire message.

A guide to the software components that make up the Cisco Unity system is provided later in this chapter in the "Understanding Unified Communications Software" section.

Understanding the Cisco Unity for Domino Architecture

The Cisco Unity for Domino architecture is very similar to the Cisco Unity for Exchange architecture; however, this configuration uses Domino as the message store. MS SQL Server 2000 or MSDE components communicate with Domino through a Domino connector, which is specified during the Cisco Unity installation process. Lotus developed the Domino Unified Communications Service (DUCS) for Domino, which can be used to integrate Domino with Cisco Unity. The collaboration between Cisco Systems and IBM/Lotus resulted in the Cisco Unity UM for Domino. This enables Cisco Unity to provide UM capabilities in Domino.

DUCS must be installed on a Domino directory server in every domain and on each Domino messaging server where a Cisco Unity subscriber mailbox resides. Currently, DUCS requires Domino Version 5.0.10 or 5.0.11 for Cisco Unity 4.0(1). In addition, Cisco Unity 4.0(2) supports Domino 5.0.12, and Cisco Unity 4.0(3) and later supports Domino 6.0.0, 6.0.1, and 6.02.

Lotus Notes software, which is the e-mail client for Domino, must also be installed on the Cisco Unity platform. This supplies the message notification function for Cisco Unity for Domino.

The Cisco Unity for Domino configuration is supported only in a UM environment in which Domino services are installed off the Cisco Unity platform. Failover is currently not supported for Cisco Unity UM for Domino.

Figure 8-3 illustrates the Cisco Unity 4.0 unified architecture with a Domino message store.

Figure 8-3   *Cisco Unity 4.0 Unified Architecture with a Domino Message Store*

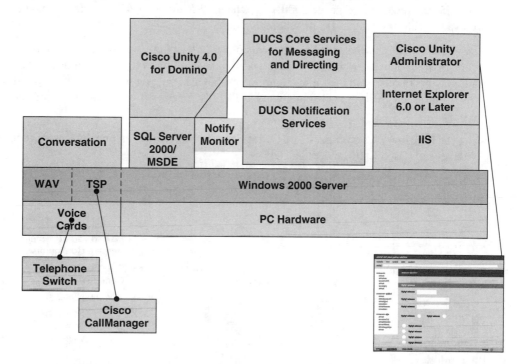

Understanding Cisco PA Architecture

Windows 2000 Server is also used for Cisco PA 1.4. It is installed on a separate server with Cisco-supported hardware. The supported platforms are discussed in Chapter 7.

Cisco PA software consists of three major components: Cisco PA Server, PA Web Administration, and PA Speech Recognition Server. For performance purposes, you may choose to install the optional Speech Recognition software on a separate server. In addition, Cisco IP Phone Productivity Services can be installed on a separate server. This enables some of the PA features to be accessed from the display of Cisco 7940, 7960, and 7970 phones. The integration options to either view your Microsoft Outlook calendar on the display phone or to use routing rules based on your calendar require Exchange 5.5 or later. These features are currently not supported with Domino.

Cisco PA 1.4 integrates with Cisco CallManager 3.2 or later. For name lookups in the corporate directory, a directory server such as Cisco CallManager's DC directory server is required. (You can use a third-party directory service, such as Microsoft Active Directory or Netscape Directory Services).

Voice-mail functionality is added through the integration of Cisco Unity Version 3.1 or later with Exchange 2003, Exchange 2000, or Exchange 5.5 and PA 1.4(3) or later. Or you can use Ayaya Octel Messaging as the messaging system.

PA works together with several components on an IP telephony configuration. Some components, such as Cisco CallManager, need to be configured to work with PA. Other components do not have the same requirements, but also interact with PA. Before you deploy this solution, it is recommended that you have a fully functional Voice over IP (VoIP) network in place.

You can have one PA server per Cisco CallManager cluster. However, one PA server can interact with several Cisco CallManager clusters.

Figure 8-4 illustrates the Cisco PA architecture.

Figure 8-4   *Cisco PA Architecture*

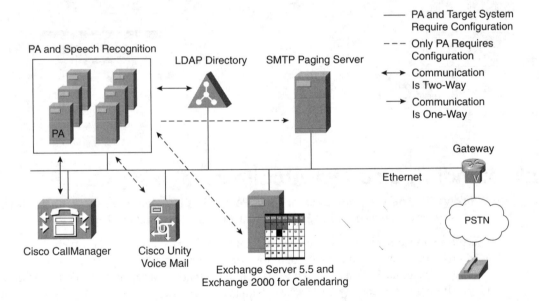

Understanding Unified Communications Software

Being familiar with the structures that Cisco Unity and PA are built upon will help you to perform a smooth and healthy installation and maintain the system. Understanding how the different software components interact with the Cisco unified communications products will help you when you are troubleshooting the products.

To benefit fully from this section, it is recommended that you have the following prerequisite skills and knowledge. (If you need a quick review, see the designated chapter, where you can find more information on the topic.)

- Understanding of the models presented in the "Understanding the Cisco Unity for Exchange Architecture" and "Understanding the Cisco Unity for Domino Architecture" sections of this chapter and how they work together to provide solutions
- Familiarity with the different hardware overlays (see Chapter 7)

Using System Software for Cisco Unity for Exchange

As previously mentioned, Cisco Unity systems have Windows 2000 Server installed. When installing it, you choose different options depending on what platform you install it on.

If you use Cisco Unity Platform Overlay 1, 2, and 3 servers (in English, German, or French), Windows 2000 Server is required.

For Cisco Unity Platform Overlay 4 and 5 servers, Windows 2000 Advanced Server (in English, German, French, or Japanese) is required when performing a new installation, replacing an existing system, or purchasing an additional Cisco Unity Platform 4 or 5 server.

If the system is not purchased from Cisco, you must purchase Windows 2000 Advanced Server for these platforms. Windows 2000 Advanced Server is also supported, but not required, on Platform Overlays 1, 2, and 3. Microsoft Windows 2000 Professional, Microsoft Windows 2000 Datacenter Server, and any edition of Microsoft Windows Server 2003 are currently not qualified to be installed on a Cisco Unity server itself. However, Cisco Unity can reside on a Windows 2003 Active Directory network. Upgrading existing Platform Overlays 4 and 5 to Windows 2000 Advanced Server is not required, but is recommended.

Cisco Unity Software Requirements with Exchange

For Cisco Unity to function properly, the following Windows 2000 Server components must also be installed: Internet Information Server (IIS), Microsoft Windows 2000 Service Pack 3 (SP3), Message Queuing Services, and Network News Transfer Protocol (NNTP). Microsoft Windows Terminal Services should also be installed for troubleshooting purposes. Service Pack 4 (SP4) can also be installed after Cisco Unity has been successfully installed. Microsoft AD needs to be installed on the Cisco Unity server if Cisco Unity will be in VoiceMail–only configuration and, therefore, in its own domain. If, however, Cisco Unity will be joining an existing domain as a member server, the AD option is not installed on the Cisco Unity server. The Cisco Unity server should not act as a Domain Name System (DNS) or Dynamic Host Configuration Protocol (DHCP) server for the network.

Which Windows 2000 Server CD-ROM you should use for installation of the operating system depends on from whom you purchased the Cisco Unity server. If the server you intend to use for Cisco Unity was purchased from Cisco, you would install Windows 2000 Server from the Platform Configuration CD-ROM that came with the Cisco Unity server bundle. However, if only the hardware was purchased from Cisco, or the server was not purchased from Cisco, you would use the original equipment manufacturer (OEM) CD-ROM that came with the system. This CD-ROM contains OEM drivers for Compaq, Dell, or IBM computers that allow you to use a retail version of Windows 2000 Server.

The following are some of the required components for a Cisco Unity system:

- **Internet Explorer 6.0:** This Web browser must be installed on Windows 2000 Server when using IIS. Cisco Unity does not support Netscape Navigator. Microsoft Internet Explorer supports Windows authentication, which is one of the items used by Cisco Unity.

- **eXtensible Markup Language (XML):** Microsoft's MSXML3 and MSXML SP1 parsers are installed and can be found on Cisco Unity CD 1.

- **Microsoft .NET Framework:** .NET supports the Tabular Data Stream (TDS) protocol. This allows client applications to securely access the Cisco Unity database in SQL, without having to set up mixed authentication on the MS SQL server.

The following is a list of other, optional software components that can be installed on Cisco Unity 4.0 for Exchange:

- Cisco Unity 4.0 for Exchange software.
- Windows 2000 SP3.
- Items installed during Window 2000 Server installation: Microsoft Message Queuing service, NNTP, and IIS 5.0.
- Internet Explorer 6.0 SP1.
- Exchange 2000 SP3 or Exchange 5.5 SP4 (message store software shipped only with voice-mail systems).
- Microsoft MSXML 3.0 and MSXML 3.0 SP1.
- Symantec pcAnywhere Version 10.0 or later (should be used with external modem) and Microsoft .NET Framework, Version 1.1.
- The Windows hot fix described in Microsoft Security Bulletin MS03-007 and Microsoft Knowledge Base article 815021.
- The Windows hot fix described in Microsoft Security Bulletin MS03-026 and Microsoft Knowledge Base article 823980.
- On a system that has more than 32 voice ports or that is using Cisco Unity Failover, MS SQL Server 2000 Standard Edition (other editions of SQL Server are not supported).
- On a system that has 32 or fewer voice ports or that is not using Cisco Unity Failover, MSDE 2000 (other editions of MSDE are not supported).

- For Cisco Unity 4.0(2) and later, MS SQL Server 2000 SP3 or MSDE 2000 SP3, depending on which software package you are using.

- For Cisco Unity 4.0(1), MS SQL Server 2000 SP2 and MS SQL Server 2000 Security Rollup Package (SRP) 1 August 2002. (SP2 and SRP1 are required both for a system running MS SQL Server 2000 and for a system running MSDE 2000.)

- If you are integrating with Cisco CallManager, a compatible Cisco Unity-CM TSP version is required. For more information on which TSP to use, go to the following link:

  http://www.cisco.com/univercd/cc/td/doc/product/voice/c_unity/tsp/index.htm

- Windows Terminal Services (optional). This is the default remote access software included with Windows 2000 Server.

- Cisco Security Agent for Cisco Unity 1.1 (optional).

NOTE   The Cisco Unity-CM TSP used for Cisco CallManager/Cisco Unity integration is not the same TSP included with Cisco CallManager. It is the one included with Cisco Unity.

NOTE   When running Cisco Unity Failover, the system requires MS SQL Server 2000 Standard Edition even though it may have less than 32 ports.

These software requirements also do change. For the latest requirements, go to Cisco.com and search for "Cisco Unity Software Requirements."

NOTE   A Cisco Unity Failover configuration requires that the Exchange message be installed off-box on a separate server from the Cisco Unity primary and secondary servers.

Supported Microsoft Exchange Software with Cisco Unity

Microsoft's e-mail servers include Exchange 2003, Exchange 2000, and Exchange 5.5. Cisco Unity uses the Exchange 2003, 2000, or 5.5 message store to store subscriber messages, and uses the AD in Windows 2000 Server or Windows Server 2003. Cisco Unity can also be installed to integrate with Microsoft Exchange 5.5 SP4, Exchange 2000, or Exchange 2003. Beginning with the release of Cisco Unity 4.0, Cisco Unity, installed in the UM mode, supports Exchange 2000 only in an "off-box" configuration, and the message store software is not shipped with the other Cisco Unity software. The term *off box* means the message store that Cisco Unity will use is installed on a system other than the Cisco Unity server.

With the introduction of Cisco Unity 4.0(3), Cisco Unity supports Exchange 2003 as the message store for UM configurations. However, Exchange 2003 is not supported for VoiceMail-only configurations. Also, Exchange 2003 is not supported when installed on the Cisco Unity system itself, because Cisco UM requires the message store to be off box. The Cisco Unity Voice Connector for Exchange 2000, which is used for the networking options such as Audio Messaging Interchange Specification (AMIS), Bridge, Simple Mail Transfer Protocol (SMTP), and Voice Profile for Internet Messaging (VPIM), can be used with Exchange 2003. Currently, there is not a separate version of the Cisco Unity Voice Connector for Exchange 2003.

Windows Terminal Service is the default remote access software for the Cisco Unity servers and comes in Windows 2000 Server. pcAnywhere Version 10.0 or greater, which is optional software on the Cisco Unity system, allows the Cisco Technical Assistance Center (TAC) to access the Cisco Unity server for maintenance and repair. Cisco recommends that an external modem be used with pcAnywhere.

Cisco UM with Exchange requires that the Exchange server be installed on a server other than the server on which Cisco Unity 4.0(x) resides. You must either move the Exchange users to another off-box Exchange server or install Exchange on another server to move those users to the new system. If your Cisco Unity system is configured for Voice Messaging, Exchange 5.5 is supported only if you are upgrading from a previous version of Cisco Unity. However, Exchange 2000 is supported for upgrades and new installations.

Cisco Unity Service Pack CD-ROM

Cisco.com offers a Cisco Unity Service Pack CD-ROM, the contents of which can also be downloaded as an image, and posts updates periodically. The image is available in multiple languages, which are noted by the three-letter language acronym in the filename. For example, ENU in the filename CiscoUnity4.0-ServicePacks-ENU-CD1 stands for U.S. English.

The following list shows what the CiscoUnity4.0-ServicePacks-ENU-CD1 image contains:

- Cisco Unity System Preparation Assistant
- Internet Explorer 6.0 SP1
- Microsoft .NET Framework
- MSDE SP3
- MSXML3 SP1
- MS SQL Server 2000 SP3
- Windows 2000 Server SP3
- The Windows hot fix described in Microsoft Security Bulletin MS03-007 and Microsoft Knowledge Base article 815021
- The Windows patch described in Microsoft Security Bulletin MS03-026 and Knowledge Base article 823980 (in the Patches directory)

- Exchange 5.5 SP4
- Exchange 2000 SP3
- March 2003 Exchange 2000 Server Post-SP3 Rollup, described in Microsoft Knowledge Base article 813840 (in the Patches directory)

Exchange 2000 SP2 is currently the required service pack for Exchange 2000. It is recommended that you install SP3 and the March 2003 Exchange 2000 Server Post-SP3 Rollup, in that order, because they resolve an intermittent issue with message notification.

NOTE   If you install SP3 and the Post-SP3 Rollup on the Cisco Unity server, it is recommended that you install them on all the Exchange 2000 servers to which the Cisco Unity subscribers are homed. The reason for this is that if they are not installed, Exchange will send additional User Datagram Protocol (UDP) packets to ports on the Cisco Unity server that are not expecting packets. This scenario is observed by intrusion-detection systems (IDSs) as attacks or port scans.

The Cisco Security Agent for Cisco Unity v1.1 is a standalone agent that provides intrusion prevention, malicious code protection, operating system integrity assurance, and audit log consolidation. This agent should be considered an additional line of defense that can improve security when operating with other defenses, such as firewall and virus-scanning software. Cisco Systems currently provides it free of charge for Cisco Unity servers that meet system requirements. Make sure that you read the release notes before you install and use it.

For more information, go to Cisco.com and perform a search for "Cisco Security Agent for Cisco Unity."

Using System Software for Cisco Unity for Domino

Cisco Unity for Domino uses most of the same software components that are used on a Cisco Unity Exchange installation. The main difference is the message store that is used in each.

Domino is the IBM Lotus database and messaging product. Cisco Unity for Domino resulted from the collaboration between Cisco Systems and IBM Lotus. IBM Lotus created DUCS for Cisco Unity as part of this collaboration. This component enables Cisco Unity to deliver UM in a Domino environment.

Software components installed with Cisco Unity 4.0 for Domino (some are optional) include the following:

- Cisco Unity for Domino software components.
- Windows 2000 Server SP3.

- Items installed during Window 2000 Server installation: Message Queuing Services, NNTP, and IIS 5.0.

- Internet Explorer 6.0 SP1.

- Microsoft MSXML3 and MSXML3 SP1.

- Lotus Notes Client 5.0.10 or later.

- DUCS on every Domino server with Cisco Unity subscribers.

- pcAnywhere 10.0 (host only) (optional).

- Microsoft .NET Framework, Version 1.1.

- The Windows hot fix described in Microsoft Security Bulletin MS03-007 and Microsoft Knowledge Base article 815021.

- The Windows hot fix described in Microsoft Security Bulletin MS03-026 and Microsoft Knowledge Base article 823980.

- On a system with more than 32 voice ports, Microsoft SQL Server 2000 Standard Edition (other editions of SQL Server are not supported).

- On a system with 32 or fewer voice ports, MSDE 2000 (other editions of MSDE are not supported).

- For Cisco Unity 4.0(2) and later, MS SQL Server 2000 SP3 or MSDE 2000 SP3, depending on the Cisco Unity configuration setup you have or will be setting up.

- For Cisco Unity 4.0(1), MS SQL Server 2000 SP2 and MS SQL Server 2000 SRP 1 August 2002. (The service pack and SRP are required both for a system running MS SQL Server 2000 and for a system running MSDE 2000.)

- If you are integrating with Cisco CallManager, a compatible Cisco Unity-CM TSP version is required.

- Microsoft Windows Terminal Services (optional). This is the default remote access software included with Windows 2000 Server.

- Cisco Security Agent for Cisco Unity 1.1 (optional).

DUCS can be purchased through IBM Lotus; it is not supplied by Cisco Systems. DUCS is currently qualified by IBM Lotus to work on Windows 2000 Server. However, this can change. Any Domino server hosting a message store for Cisco Unity subscribers needs Windows 2000 Server as its operating system. Cisco Unity for Domino currently is supported only in a UM configuration with Domino installed off-box. DUCS requires Domino Version 5.0.10 or later.

The Domino directory server requires DUCS in each Domino domain. You must install DUCS on every Domino message store server where Cisco Unity subscribers' mailboxes reside. The Windows OS is currently the only operating system supported.

The key features of DUCS include the following:

- Single, unified Domino message store

- Native Notes Address Book support

- Message notification and MWIs
- Native Lotus Mail Template for voice-mail message playback/record
- iNotes web access to messages
- Message categorization
- Integrated voice player/recorder and voice inbox

Which versions of Domino, DUCS, and Lotus Notes that are supported on the Cisco Unity server varies slightly for each of the Cisco Unity 4.0(x) versions prior to Cisco Unity 4.0(3). The following is a list of the supported versions with Cisco Unity 4.0(3) and later:

- Domino versions: 6.02, 6.0.1, 6.0.0, 5.0.12, 5.0.11, and 5.0.10
- DUCS versions: 1.2.1 (the download on the IBM Lotus website is called Version 1.2)
- Lotus Notes versions: 6.0.1, 6.0.0, 5.0.12, 5.0.11, and 5.0.10

Using System Software for Cisco PA

Cisco PA 1.4 consists of the following software:

- Cisco PA Server
- Cisco PA Speech Recognition Server
- Cisco PA Web Administration

Cisco PA Server software is installed on its own server, separate from any other Cisco Architecture for Voice, Video, and Integrated Data (AVVID) product. The PA Server software provides Lightweight Directory Access Protocol (LDAP) directory lookups, rule-based call transfers, and voice-mail access. It allows users to synchronize personal address books with their Exchange contact lists. This can be achieved through either the PA Web Administration software or the optional IP Phone Productivity Services software.

The Cisco PA Server software is compatible with Cisco CallManager 3.2, 3.3, and 4.0 starting with PA 1.4(3); Cisco Unity 3.x and 4.0 for voice-mail features; and Exchange 5.5, Exchange 2000, and Exchange 2003 for calendar, e-mail, and contact synchronization features.

The Cisco PA Speech Recognition Server software enables users to verbally perform directory lookups, verbally ask for your voice-mail box, and configure routing-rule instructions verbally. Speech Recognition Server software can be installed on the PA server or its own server. As previously mentioned, installing the Speech Recognition Server software on its own server enhances system performance. Speech Recognition engines are available in U.S. English, British English, French, French Canadian, and German. Currently, the limit is 45,000 directory entries for accurate recognition of names.

The Cisco PA Web Administration software is installed on the same server as PA and allows for web-based administration from either the PA server or a client workstation. This allows clients to administer their own PA features. The client requires either Internet Explorer 6.0 (or later) or Netscape Navigator 7.0. The web-based GUI is available in English, French, and German.

Software components installed on a Cisco PA system include the following:

- Windows 2000 Server
- Cisco PA Server
- Cisco PA Speech Recognition Server
- Cisco PA Web Administration
- Cisco IP Productivity Services

Software requirements for PA include the following:

- Cisco CallManager on a separate server: Version 4.0, 3.3, or 3.2.
- An LDAP-enabled directory service for storing business and personal directory information, such as names, phone numbers, and e-mail addresses. This can be a service such as the Cisco CallManager integrated with DC directory, Microsoft AD, or Netscape Directory Services.
- An Internet browser, either Internet Explorer 6.0 (or 5.x), or Netscape Navigator.
- Cisco Unity with Exchange 5.5 or Exchange 2000, Version 3.x or later. (Only one version is required when you are integrating Cisco PA with a messaging system.)
- When e-mail paging is a requirement for a setup, an SMTP-compliant paging server is necessary.
- If you would like to collect error messages to SysLog for analysis purposes, CiscoWorks 2000 Resource Manager Essentials (RME) 3.3 is supported.
- If you are using Cisco Unity as the message store, Cisco Unity messages and recorded names must be encoded in G.711 Mu-Law format.

NOTE   When voice-mail browsing is a requirement for a setup, Cisco Unity with Exchange is also required. Users will not be able to browse if another messaging system is used.

Optional software includes:

- Cisco Security Agent for Cisco PA 1.1(1) and 1.1(0).
- McAfee NetShield Version 7.0.

Cisco IP Phone Productivity Services software enhances the capabilities of the Cisco 7940, 7960, and 7970 IP phones through the use of scrolling keys for checking e-mail, voice mail, personal contacts, and calendar information from the Exchange server. Through the

CalendarView feature of the IP Phone Productivity Services software, the user can view appointments either by day or week on the IP phone display.

The MailView features allow access to e-mail and Cisco Unity voice messages. Users can scroll through and read e-mail messages on the IP phone display. They can also listen to and delete voice-mail messages by using the IP phone soft keys.

IP Phone Productivity Services software allows users to activate or deactivate their routing Rule Sets directly from the IP phone and synchronize their personal address book with their Exchange contacts list. IP Phone Productivity Services software is installed on its own server and requires IIS 4.0 or later.

For more information about the most current software requirements for Cisco PA Server, go to the following link:

http://www.cisco.com/univercd/cc/td/doc/product/voice/assist/assist14/relnote/pa141rn.pdf

Using Client Software for Cisco Unity for Exchange

Cisco Unity ViewMail for Outlook (VMO) is a special form in Outlook that has a set of control buttons. With these controls and the toolbar of buttons on the form, you can listen to, send, reply to, and forward voice-mail messages. VMO can be used with Microsoft Outlook 98, Microsoft Outlook 2000, and Microsoft Outlook XP. VMO cannot be used with Microsoft Outlook Express or Microsoft Outlook Web Access because these clients do not support Microsoft Outlook forms.

VMO software can be found on the Cisco Unity Installation CD 1 in the ViewMail folder, and is installed on the client workstations, not the Cisco Unity server. Although VMO is not required, it makes listening to voice-mail messages much easier. If VMO is not installed, voice-mail messages appear as .wav attachments in your in box. UM can be deployed without losing any functionality at the client workstations.

Clients may also want to access their mailbox settings through the Cisco Personal Communications Assistant (CPCA). The two Cisco PCA components are the Cisco Unity Assistant and Cisco Unity Inbox, which allows the user to change their mailbox settings through a user-friendly web-based GUI, rather than over the phone. Any mailbox settings that are available through the telephone are available through Cisco PCA. Class of service (COS) in Cisco Unity controls access to CPCA. Additionally, the client workstation must be running Internet Explorer 5.5 or later. With the introduction of Cisco Unity 4.0(3), upgrades from Cisco Unity 3(x) to 4(x) no longer require subscribers to have special CoS privileges to use VMO. Subscribers that have ViewMail installed can take advantage of these features.

Site administrators of Cisco Unity can also access the Cisco Unity Administration windows through their desktops. Clients must have Internet Explorer 6.0 or later on their workstations.

Figure 8-5 illustrates the client view of a Cisco unified architecture—with a Microsoft Exchange message store.

Figure 8-5 *Cisco Unified Architecture—Client View with Exchange Message Store*

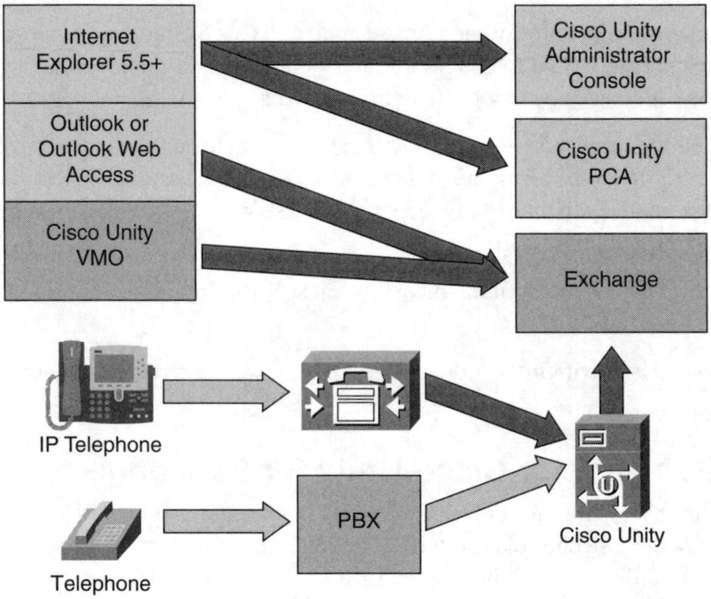

Using Client Software for Cisco Unity for Domino

The software required on the client side for Cisco Unity for Domino configurations is very similar to the software that is required for Exchange configurations. The Lotus Notes client is used instead of Outlook. Figure 8-6 illustrates the client view of a Cisco Unified architecture with a Lotus Notes message store.

The current qualified software versions for use on Cisco Unity subscriber workstations include IBM DUCS for Cisco Unity Version 1.2. This version is supported with Cisco Unity 4.0(3) and later in the following languages:

- English
- French
- German
- Japanese (with Cisco Unity with Domino)

The current qualified software versions of IBM Lotus iNotes are 6.0.2, 6.0.1, 6.0.0, and 5.0.12, and Lotus Notes Versions 6.0.2, 6.0.1, 6.0.0, 5.0.12, 5.0.11, and 5.0.10 (with Cisco Unity with Domino).

Figure 8-6   *Cisco Unified Architecture—Client View with Lotus Notes Message Store*

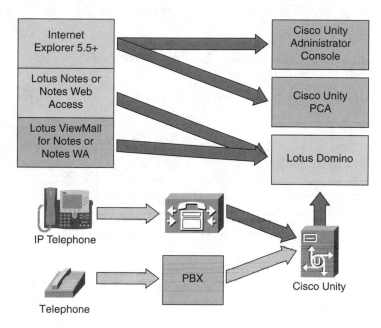

For the most current version combinations of software that are qualified for Cisco Unity 4.0, go to the following link:

http://www.cisco.com/univercd/cc/td/doc/product/voice/c_unity/cmptblty/clientmx.htm

As with VMO, DUCS client software gives the end user an easy GUI from which to check their voice mail and e-mail, and to send, reply to, or forward either type of messages. DUCS client software is a Notes Mail template built and supported by IBM Lotus.

CoS controls access to Cisco PCA features and the Cisco Unity Administration windows and requires Internet Explorer 6.0 or later to function.

Using Client Software for Cisco PA

Once Cisco PA is set up on your network, it works like a virtual assistant. Cisco PA can forward and screen your incoming calls based on the rules you set using the Cisco PA web GUI. These rules tell Cisco PA which calls you would like forwarded, which calls you would like screened, if any, and where you would like to receive calls, enabling you to receive a call on a phone number other than your extension. These rules can be activated by using either the Cisco PA web GUI or spoken commands over your phone handset or headset. With spoken commands, Cisco PA can also assist you in placing and receiving calls and browsing your voice mail.

The following is an example of what a phone dialog would sound like when user "John" performs a directory dialing and call screening takes place:

John already is on the Cisco PA menu.

Cisco PA: John, welcome to Personal Assistant. What would you like to do? Say the full name of the person you are trying to call.

(When Cisco PA plays John's name, it plays the recorded name of the person.)

John: Mr. Davis.

Cisco PA: I'm sorry, I didn't understand. Say the first and last name of the person you want to call or say "Voice mail."

John: "Michael Davis."

Cisco PA: "Michael Davis." Is this correct?

(When Cisco PA plays the name, it plays the recorded name of the person.)

John: Yes.

Cisco PA: *(Cisco PA starts to locate Mr. Davis.)* Please wait while locating.

Mr. Davis: Hi John.

John: Hi. Did you set up Cisco PA to screen your calls? Because Cisco PA said to "Please wait while locating" before you answered.

Mr. Davis: Yes, it's a very easy feature to set too. All you need to do is go to your Rule page on the Cisco PA user website and select call screening.

John: When I set it up, what will it sound like?

Mr. Davis: When I picked up, Cisco PA said, "You have a call from John." It included your recorded name. Then Cisco PA said, "Press 1 to connect, or press 2 to transfer the call to a different number." There's also an option to send the call to voice mail.

John: That will be useful.

Mr. Davis: You can set your call screening to all the calls you receive or to individual callers, based on the rules you set up.

John: I will set that up.

Mr. Davis: OK.

You can find more information on this topic at Cisco.com by searching the *Cisco Personal Assistant User Guide* text.

Installing Cisco Unified Communications Software

Understanding the installation process of the software will help you to perform a smooth installation of the Cisco Unity system and PA. In addition, the installation process for Cisco Unity is different from previous versions.

To benefit fully from this section, you should be familiar with the concepts and software components presented in the "Understanding the Cisco Unity for Exchange Architecture" and "Understanding the Cisco Unity for Domino Architecture" sections of this chapter.

Setting Up a Cisco Unity System

As part of installation process you must gather general system information. The setup process needs this information to install the correct languages on the system, including the correct text-to-speech language, and to install Cisco Unity in the correct folder and partition on the hard drive. It loads the default database, which consists of the Cisco Unity Installer account, the Example Administrator account, the default call handlers, and all the other default objects.

The Cisco Unity system setup steps are as follows:

- Gathers basic system information
- Chooses a language
- Creates the default database
- Loads TTS and system prompts

Using Cisco Unity Server Preparation Assistant

CUSPA is a preparation tool that helps you to prepare your Cisco Unity system for a Cisco Unity installation. This tool, located on the Service Pack CD-ROM, checks the Cisco Unity server for the required software and service packs. CUSPA asks for your Cisco Unity server characteristics, such as UM or VM, Failover, and the number of Cisco Unity ports.

CUSPA checks for the proper versions of SQL, MSXML, Windows, NNTP, Internet Explorer, and .NET Framework, and checks for the proper service packs. If a software component or service pack is not installed on the system, you can choose to install it through CUSPA. CUSPA does not check to make sure that the AD Schema has been extended for an Exchange 2000 installation. Extending the AD Schema is required before you begin the Cisco Unity installation in an AD/Exchange 2000 environment. In addition, CUSPA does not check the Exchange or Domino version.

When you first open CUSPA, it prompts you with a welcome window that indicates it will do the following:

- Determine whether your server is ready to have Cisco Unity installed and configured
- Install any needed software

CUSPA checks for the following items on Cisco Unity 4.0(3) and later:

- XML3 SP1
- IIS
- Windows Terminal Services
- NNTP Service
- SMTP Service
- Message Queuing Services
- Windows 2000 Server SP3
- Internet Explorer 6.0 SP1
- Cisco Unity Data Store (SQL/MSDE)
- Cisco Unity Data Store SP3
- .NET Framework v1.1
- Some Windows 2000 IIS security patches

In the following example, CUSPA checks the system and reports what is and is not installed on the system. It also gives you the option to click the service/software component that is not installed and configure it. CUSPA provides a link to the component so that you can install it from there.

Figure 8-7 illustrates CUSPA showing which components are not installed.

Figure 8-7   *The CUSPA Utility*

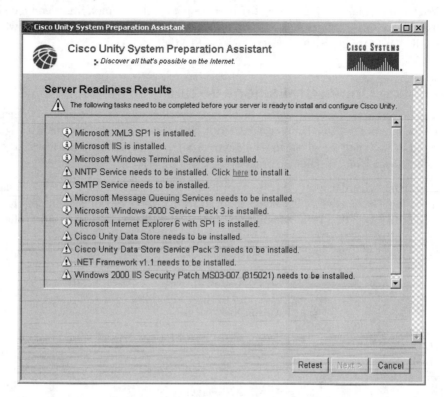

Using Cisco Unity Installation and Configuration Assistant

CUICA replaces the two-part Cisco Unity installation introduced in Cisco Unity 3.0. You run CUICA after CUSPA and it guides you through the entire setup process, from setting the correct permissions to installing Cisco Unity to integrating Cisco Unity with a telephone system.

CUICA is actually five individual wizard utilities, listed next, combined with the Cisco Unity Setup program:

- Permissions Wizard
- License File Wizard
- Service Configuration Wizard
- System Setup/Message Store Configuration Wizard
- Cisco UTIM

After you have installed Cisco Unity, you can run all but the Message Store Configuration Wizard individually by accessing the Tools Depot of Cisco Unity. It is recommended that you use the Service Configuration Wizard to install Cisco Unity 4.0. The final step when using CUICA is to set up Secure Sockets Layer (SSL) for Cisco Unity.

Using the Cisco Unity Permissions Wizard

The Permissions Wizard enables you to set the permissions that are needed to install Cisco Unity and for the Cisco Unity services to log on and run properly. It is the first wizard executed by CUICA. Using the wizard to set the correct permissions will help you to avoid complications as the Cisco Unity installation proceeds.

Before the wizard can set the correct permissions, you need to tell it which message store you are using: Exchange 5.5, Exchange 2000, Exchange 2003, or Lotus Domino. This is the first step of the wizard, shown in Figure 8-8. After you select your message store, click Next.

Figure 8-8 *Selecting the Message Store*

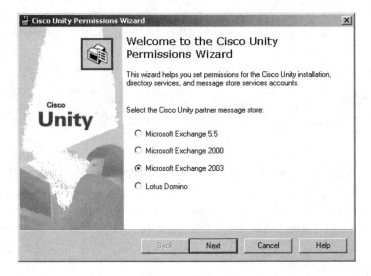

Depending on your configuration, the wizard asks different questions, such as which account should be given permissions to install and configure Cisco Unity, which account Cisco Unity directory services will log on with, and which account to log on with to the message store.

NOTE   The Permissions Wizard can be run individually without the use of CUICA. The version that comes with Cisco Unity 4.0(3) and later cannot be used with earlier versions of Cisco Unity for new installations, because the new Permissions Wizard limits the permissions granted to certain accounts. It can, however, be used on Cisco Unity Versions 3.1(1) through 4.0(2) for systems that have Cisco Unity installed already.

The next step is choosing a Windows Account that will be responsible for the Cisco Unity message store services.

Figure 8-9 illustrates selecting a Microsoft Windows account that will own Cisco Unity message store services.

Figure 8-9   *Selecting a Windows Account that Will Own Cisco Unity Message Store Services*

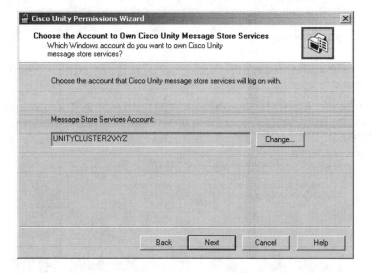

The next step is choosing an account that will be used to install Cisco Unity.

Figure 8-10 illustrates selecting a Windows account to install Cisco Unity.

Figure 8-10 *Selecting a Windows Account to Install Cisco Unity*

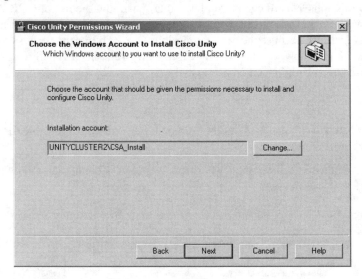

The next step is choosing a Windows Account that will be responsible for the Cisco Unity directory services.

Figure 8-11 illustrates selecting an account that will own the Cisco Unity directory services.

Figure 8-11 *Selecting an Account that Will Own the Cisco Unity Directory Services*

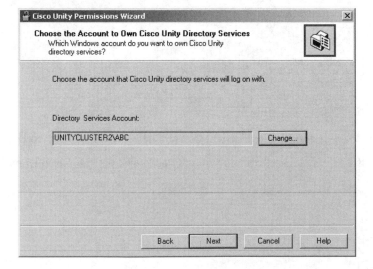

Installing the License File Wizard

At least 24 hours before you install Cisco Unity, you need to contact Cisco to register and obtain your Cisco Unity license file. You need to have the Media Access Control (MAC) address (physical address) for the network interface card (NIC) in the Cisco Unity computer and the product authorization key (PAK), which is listed in the *Cisco Unity Software Keys* booklet that is shipped with the software CD-ROMs or on the bottom from corner. With that information, you can access the license file generator website at http://www.cisco.com/pcgi-bin/Software/FormManager/formgenerator.pl.

You must first log in to the Cisco website to have access.

It is not enough to simply copy license files onto the file system of the Cisco Unity server. You need to run and complete the License File Wizard in order for Cisco Unity to use the information in the files. You specify the names of each of your license files in the wizard. You should specify all the files you want Cisco Unity to use from that point forward, even if some of the files were installed previously. The wizard extracts the information from the files and checks the data for errors. If no errors are found, you may complete the wizard. Please check that what you have purchased is included in the license file.

Once you complete the wizard, Cisco Unity begins using the license information from the files. If the wizard detects errors in the files, it tells you what the problems are and does not permit you to proceed to the completion page. If you encounter problems, you should contact Cisco TAC.

Configuring the Service Configuration Wizard

The Service Configuration Wizard helps you to configure three groups of Cisco Unity services that are installed by your system. The wizard uses the selections you made during the Permissions Wizard as default accounts for the services. Because these are the accounts that have the correct permissions associated with them, it is best to accept the defaults. If you are not changing the accounts, you must enter the password for the accounts when asked. If, however, you change which accounts to use, make sure they have the proper permissions.

The first wizard window prompts you to choose whether you are configured for Exchange 5.5, Exchange 2000, Exchange 2003, or Lotus Domino. This leads to different wizard setup versions, depending on which configuration you chose. The Directory Services sets the Cisco Unity account it will use to access the AD or the Domino database. The message store services need to run under an account that is allowed access to Exchange 2000 and 2003 mailboxes. The Cisco Unity local services, in an Exchange or Domino configuration, run under an account that allows them access to registry files, the file system, and the MS SQL Server 2000.

The Service Configuration Wizard configures the following three services:

- Directory services
- Message store services
- Local services

Setting Up the Message Store Configuration Wizard

The Message Store Configuration Wizard section of CUICA is where you choose Exchange 5.5, Exchange 2000, Exchange 2003, or Lotus Domino R5/R6. You need to decide where to home new mailboxes in your message store when they are added through the Cisco Unity System Administration windows. The Directory Service account would be the same account you chose in the Cisco Service Configuration Wizard as the account that will run the Cisco Unity Directory Service, which passes information back and forth between Cisco Unity and the message store.

The Message Store Configuration Wizard asks you to choose the following:

- A message store
- The location for new mailboxes
- Your directory services account

Integrating Cisco Unity with Telephone Systems

Cisco UTIM steps you through the process of integrating Cisco Unity with your telephone system. Cisco Unity supports integrations for IP telephony (Cisco CallManager), circuit-switched PBXs, and SIP. You can find a list of supported circuit-switched PBXs and integration methods in Chapter 1.

If you choose TSP for Cisco CallManager integration, before you can run UTIM, you must have your Cisco CallManager configured to integrate with Cisco Unity. UTIM asks for the Cisco CallManager IP address, the display name for the voice-mail ports created, and the Message Waiting On and Off directory numbers. At the end of the process, you can run a test to ensure that the integration process was successful. You can find instructions on setting up Cisco CallManager to integrate with Cisco Unity in the *Cisco CallManager Integration Guide* by performing a search for "Cisco CallManager" at Cisco.com.

UTIM pings the CallManager server and checks that each port is configured correctly. If there is an issue, you normally receive an error message that indicates there is a problem.

TIP   One of the most common issues when configuring the TSP on Cisco Unity for Cisco CallManager is the prefix spelling of the voice-mail port names. Make sure that the spelling used on both Cisco CallManager and Cisco Unity is identical.

SIP is an important emerging Internet protocol that is designed to easily build up and tear down IP sessions. Numerous vendors are embracing SIP as the next big Internet protocol for VoIP. Currently, Cisco Unity's SIP integration supports interactions with Cisco SIP Proxy Server, as well as Cisco SIP-enabled 7960 phones, Pingtel Expressa phones, and MSN Messenger.

Using Resources to Guide the Cisco Unity Installation

A copy of the *Cisco Unity Installation Guide* is shipped with each Cisco Unity system. The installation manual contains information on installing the Cisco Unity system as a baseline (server purchased from Cisco) and as a component system (server supplied by the customer). It also includes instructions for upgrading earlier versions of Cisco Unity to Version 4.0.

If you are integrating Cisco Unity with Cisco CallManager, the Cisco CallManager integration guides are extremely helpful. There are different versions of the guides depending on your version of Cisco CallManager. Included are instructions for setting up your CallManager to integrate with Cisco Unity, and instructions for setting up dual-switch integration.

There are also various integration guides for supported circuit-switched telephone systems. These guides cover the programming that is necessary to integrate the various circuit-based telephone systems with Cisco Unity. You can view these guides at http://www.cisco.com/univercd/cc/td/doc/product/voice/c_unity/integuid/index.htm. CUICA contains Read Me files to help guide you through the installation.

Additional installation resources include the following:

- *Cisco Unity 4.0 Installation Guide*
- Cisco Unity 4.0 Release Notes
- *Cisco CallManager Integration Guide*
- Cisco Unity integration guides
- Cisco Unity Installation and Configuration Assistant (CUICA)

You can find these resources by going to Cisco.com and searching for the corresponding text.

Installing the Cisco PA Software

Cisco PA has three components that you can install separately or together:

- PA Web Administration interfaces for end users and administrators
- Cisco PA Server
- Cisco PA Speech Recognition Server

Most of the configuration process for PA takes place after installation. Be sure to use the *Personal Assistant Installation Guide* when performing an install. Before you perform a new installation of PA, follow these steps:

Step 1   Determine how many users the system will need to support and which of the three PA configurations is the most appropriate. You need this information during the installation. For more information on planning for PA, go to the following link:

http://www.cisco.com/univercd/cc/td/doc/product/voice/assist/assist14/ag/ag141/paplan.pdf

Step 2   Find the hardware and software requirements for PA 1.4 and your users. You can find out more information about this in the latest release notes at Cisco.com by searching for "Cisco Personal Assistant Release Notes."

Step 3   Find out whether there are any system limitations and restrictions on how PA may be configured on your network and, if so, whether they affect the setup you will be installing. You can find more information about this in the release notes at Cisco.com by searching for "Cisco Personal Assistant Release Notes." If your system is using AD for the business directory, you must prepare the directory system to work with PA. This information can be found in the "Setting Up Active Directory as the Corporate Directory for Personal Assistant" section of the "Installing and Upgrading Personal Assistant" document located at Cisco.com.

Step 4   Disable the McAfee NetShield services and the Cisco Security Agent on the PA server if they are installed. Doing so ensures that they will not interfere with the PA installation program.

After you have performed the previous steps, install Cisco PA Server, PA Speech Recognition server, and user and administrative interfaces. Instructions on how to install these are found in the *Cisco Personal Assistant Installation Guide*, which is located at Cisco.com.

Step 1   When you install these components, the next step is to install the enhanced Text to Speech server. This may or may not be one of your configuration requirements.

Step 2   Configure the Cisco CallManager to work with PA.

Step 3 Configure your PA system.

Step 4 Refresh your PA system. To do so, log on to the PA administration interface and select **System > Speech Services > Refresh Now**.

NOTE When refreshing a PA server, it can take up to an hour to refresh the service configuration and reload the directory and speech-recognition grammars. This depends on the size of the corporate directory.

Step 5 Re-enable the McAfee NetShield services and Cisco Security Agent if they are installed on the PA server.

Upgrading Cisco Unified Communications Software

Understanding the supported upgrades and the upgrade process will help you to successfully upgrade Cisco Unity and PA. Some upgrades require more steps than others, and not all upgrades from previous versions of Cisco Unity to Cisco Unity 4.0 are supported. This is also true when upgrading to PA 1.4. Being familiar with this will help you to avoid possible configuration issues and problems that may occur during the upgrade process.

To benefit fully from this section, it is recommended that you should already be familiar with the following information. (If you need a quick review, see the designated chapter or section, where you can find more information on the topic.)

- The new features that come with Cisco Unity 4.0 (see Chapter 1)
- The features that come with Cisco PA (see Chapter 1)
- The Cisco Unity and Cisco PA software components covered in the "Understanding Unified Communications Software" section of this chapter

Upgrading from Cisco Unity 2.4x or 3.x to Cisco Unity 4.0

The upgrade to Cisco Unity 4.0 from previous versions of Cisco Unity is supported. However, versions of Cisco Unity prior to 3.0 require a reinstallation of Cisco Unity, which includes re-entering the database. Versions prior to Cisco Unity 3.0 stored database attributes in Exchange's custom attributes 12 to 15, because the Exchange Directory Service was not extensible. With the release of Cisco Unity 3.0, Microsoft SQL Server 2000 or MSDE became the main database store. It is not possible to move the attributes from Exchange to SQL without reinstalling the database.

The procedures for performing the supported upgrades are discussed later in this section.

When upgrading, as an option you can choose to prepare for a possible downgrade if there are problems with the upgrade. There are instructions for this in the *Cisco Unity Installation Guide*, which you can find at Cisco.com. (You can also choose to make a backup.)

Supported upgrades to Cisco Unity 4.0 for Exchange are as follows:

- Cisco Unity 3.0(1–3)
- Cisco Unity 3.1(X)
- Cisco Unity 2.4(5–6)—requires a Cisco Unity reinstallation

Upgrades from Cisco Unity Versions 2.3(4.104) and earlier are not supported. The utilities used to export and import the database, subscriber, and other information from a Cisco Unity 2.x system and import into a 4.0(x) system do not work on systems that have Version 2.3(4.104) or earlier. Cisco Unity must be installed as a new system and must be reconfigured. The previous data will be lost.

NOTE   When upgrading from Cisco Unity 2.4(x), you must first upgrade to Cisco Unity 4.0(2), then upgrade to the latest version of Cisco Unity.

Determining the Cisco Unity Software Version Number

To determine the software versions for Cisco Unity and the Cisco Unity-CM TSP, you must find the Cisco Unity version number and the Cisco Unity-CM TSP version.

Locating Cisco Unity Version Number

There are two ways you can find the Cisco Unity version used on your system. The first way is to use the Cisco Unity Administrator. Go to the **Cisco Unity Administrator > System > Configuration > Software Versions** page.

The second way is to look at the properties of the AvCsMgr.exe file. This list is for Cisco Unity 3.0(4) and later:

Step 1   Find the CommServer directory.

Step 2   Find the AvCsMgr.exe file, right-click it, and then choose **Properties**.

Step 3   Within the Properties window, click the **Version** tab.

Step 4   In the Item Name list, click **Product Version**.

The Cisco Unity version is shown in the Value field.

Locating the Cisco Unity-CM TSP Version Number

To check the Cisco Unity-CM TSP version, you can either use UTIM or check the properties of the AvSkinny.tsp file.

To check the version by using UTIM, follow these steps:

Step 1 Double-click the Cisco Unity Tools Depot icon on the desktop.

Step 2 Find UTIM under Switch Integration Tools and double-click it.

Step 3 Go to the Cisco **CallManager > Properties** page.

The Cisco Unity-CM TSP version is shown in the TSP Version field.

To determine the Cisco Unity-CM TSP version by checking the AvSkinny.tsp file, do the following:

Step 1 Go to the WinNT\System32 folder.

Step 2 Right-click **AvSkinny.tsp**, and then click **Properties**.

Step 3 In the Properties window, click the **Version** tab.

Step 4 In the Item Name list, click **Product Version**.

The Cisco Unity-CM TSP version is shown in the Value window.

Upgrading from Cisco Unity 3.0 to Cisco Unity 4.0

To upgrade from Cisco Unity 3.0 to Cisco Unity 4.0, you need to obtain a new license file from Cisco, because the upgrade procedure itself does not upgrade the license file (as it has done in the past).

You should also ensure that Exchange 2000 SP3 has been installed on the message store that you will use for your subscribers. CUSPA does not check for the Exchange version; however, CUICA does, and the Cisco Unity installation will not continue if it does not find the correct version. However, it does inform you of what could be the problem.

The AD Schema Extension utility, which is run on the domain controller to extend the AD Schema for Cisco Unity, has a new option to extend the AD Schema for the VPIM option. You need to run the utility for the VPIM option to function properly.

You need to run CUICA to load the new Cisco Unity 4.0 files. During this process, there will be no database loss. During the upgrade process, the Cisco Unity system will be out of service, so you need to plan accordingly. If you have Cisco Failover set up, do not use your secondary server to provide voice-messaging services while the primary is being upgraded, and vice versa.

The following is a list of the general items to keep in mind when you are upgrading to Cisco Unity 4.0 for Exchange:

- Obtain a new license file if you are upgrading Cisco Unity from an earlier version of 4.0.
- Verify that Exchange 2000 SP3 has been installed on the message store.
- Run AD Schema Extension on the domain controller.
- Use CUSPA.
- Use CUICA.
- There is no database loss during this process.

Upgrading from Cisco Unity 3.0 Voice Mail (Exchange) to Cisco Unity 4.0 UM (Domino)

There may be circumstances in which you need to upgrade from Cisco Unity for Exchange to Cisco Unity for Domino. Customers in a Domino environment may have purchased Cisco Unity in a VoiceMail-only configuration while awaiting the Cisco Unity Domino release. Cisco Unity VoiceMail-only configuration is supported only in an Exchange environment.

When attempting to perform an upgrade from Cisco Unity 3.x for Exchange to Cisco Unity 4.0 for Domino, keep in mind that this is basically a reinstallation. There is no way to carry over the database from one to the other because you have two completely different messaging systems. If you would like to save the subscriber database, you must export the subscriber database from Exchange, modify the subscriber database to a form acceptable to Domino, import it into Domino, and then import the subscribers from the Domino server into Cisco Unity 4.0. The information that will be exportable includes the subscribers' names and extensions, but not information such as spoken names and greetings. Subscribers' messages will not be carried over. Cisco does not offer a utility to accomplish this.

Other Cisco Unity database information such as call handlers, call routing tables, and restriction tables are also not carried over.

The following is a list of the items to keep in mind when preparing for a Domino upgrade from Cisco Unity 3.x:

- Perform a new Cisco Unity 4.0 installation.
- No database is carried over.
- Export the subscriber database from Exchange.
- Modify the subscriber database into a form acceptable to Domino.
- Import the subscriber database into Domino.
- Import the subscriber database into Cisco Unity 4.0.
- Subscribers' messages are not carried over.

Upgrading from Cisco PA 1.3 to Cisco PA 1.4

The Cisco PA upgrade procedure is very straightforward. The upgrade process automatically shuts down the PA services and restarts them after the upgrade is complete. There should be no need to reprogram the database.

If you are upgrading from PA Version 1.2, you must first upgrade to Version 1.3, then apply the patch for Version 1.3(3).

WARNING   Upgrading from Cisco PA 1.2(x) to 1.4 is not recommended. A Cisco PA 1.2 to 1.3 upgrade is required first before upgrading to 1.4. Also, upgrading from Version 1.1(x) is not supported.

Detailed instructions for upgrading Cisco PA can be found in the *Cisco Personal Assistant Installation Guide,* which you can find on Cisco.com.

The following is a list of items to keep in mind when you are performing a PA upgrade:

- Upgrade to 1.3(x) first if it is an earlier version of PA.
- Apply the appropriate PA patches.
- Install PA 1.4.
- Installation can be done from CD.
- There is no reprogramming of Cisco PA required.

When you are performing a PA upgrade, keep the following tips in mind:

- Disable the McAfee NetShield services and the Cisco Security Agent on the PA server, if they are installed, so that they will not interfere with the PA installation program.
- Upgrade Cisco CallManager to the appropriate software version if required.

More information on this can be found in the Cisco *Personal Assistant Installation Guide*.

Step 1   Remove PA from the network by stopping all PA services.

Step 2   After all PA services are stopped, install the new PA server, speech recognition server, and user and administrative interfaces.

If you are performing the upgrade to the enhanced Text to Speech server, install the enhanced server.

Step 3   Refresh your PA system. To do so, log on to the PA administration interface and select **System > Speech Services > Refresh Now**.

Step 4   If you have McAfee NetShield or the Cisco Security Agent installed, enable these services.

Chapter Summary

In this chapter, you learned about the different Cisco unified communications architectures, the software that is needed to perform a successful installation of the unified communications products, the Cisco Unity system installation process, the use of CUSPA and CUICA, and the upgrade process for the Cisco unified communications products. Specifically, you learned how to do the following:

- Describe the architecture of Cisco Unity for Exchange
- Describe the architecture of Cisco Unity for Domino
- Describe the architecture of Cisco PA
- Identify where to find additional help and information
- Describe the software required to install Cisco Unity for Exchange
- Describe the software required to install Cisco Unity for Domino
- Describe the software required to install Cisco PA
- Describe the client software for both Cisco Unity for Exchange and Domino
- Describe the resources available to assist with the Cisco Unity installation
- Describe the use of CUSPA
- Describe the use of CUICA and its components
- Describe the process of installing PA
- Use supported upgrades for Cisco Unity
- Use supported upgrades for Cisco PA
- Use upgrade procedure for Cisco Unity
- Use upgrade procedure for Cisco PA

For additional information on the preceding topics, refer to these resources:

- *Cisco Unity Installation Guide (with Domino), Release 4.0*
- *Cisco Unity Installation Guide (with Exchange), Release 4.0*
- *Cisco Unity System Administration Guide (with Domino), Release 4.0*
- *Cisco Unity System Administration Guide (with Exchange), Release 4.0*
- *Cisco CallManager Integration Guide*
- *Cisco Personal Assistant Administration Guide*
- *Cisco Unity Design Guide*

You the can find these guides at Cisco.com by searching for the preceding titles.

Chapter Review Questions

Use this section to test yourself on how well you learned the concepts discussed in this chapter. You can find the answers to the review questions for this chapter in Appendix A.

1 Name the different message stores that you can choose when installing Cisco Unity 4.0.

2 When is the Microsoft SQL Server 2000 software required for a Cisco Unity installation, as opposed to the MSDE?

3 Which component developed by IBM Lotus can be used to integrate Cisco Unity 4.0 with Domino R5/R6?

4 Name the three major components of Cisco PA.

5 When is Windows 2000 Advanced Server required for Cisco Unity 4.0?

6 What configuration setup is supported with Cisco Unity for Domino?

7 When installing Cisco PA 1.4, where can the Cisco PA Speech Recognition Server software be installed?

8 When preparing to install VMO on a client machine, where is this software found?

9 What does the CUSPA tool do?

10 Which version of PA must your system be on to upgrade to PA 1.4?

Upon completing this chapter, you will be able to perform the following tasks:

- Describe the attributes and types of Cisco unified communications integrations with telephone systems
- Describe uses of messaging ports in a Cisco messaging system
- Configure messaging ports in a Cisco messaging system

CHAPTER 9

Cisco Unified Communications Integrations

This chapter discusses the different types of communication used between a Cisco unified communications server and a telephone system.

This chapter starts by discussing the elements of Cisco unified communications integrations. This includes the integration between Cisco Unity, Cisco CallManager (CCM), circuit-switched PBXs, and Session Initiation Protocol (SIP) integration. It also discusses the integration between CCM and Cisco Personal Assistant (PA). It then moves on to discuss the attributes of communications integrations between Cisco Unity and a telephone system, as well as between Cisco PA and CCM.

The chapter continues by discussing the telephone integrations supported for Cisco Unity 4.0. It also includes examples of IP, dual-tone multifrequency (DTMF), Simplified Message Desk Interface (SMDI), PBXLink, and SIP integrations.

Defining a Communications Systems Integration

A telephone system and a voice-processing system communicate with one another via integration. Integration between Cisco Unity and a PBX takes place when the following three essential features are present, as shown in Figure 9-1:

- Call forward to a personal greeting
- Easy message access
- Message waiting indication

These features are present when the PBX and the voice messaging system are exchanging information with each other in an agreed upon manner. The delivery of this information between the two systems varies from integration to integration.

Figure 9-1   *Attributes of an Integration*

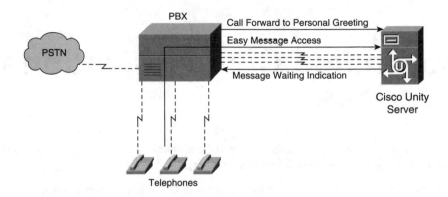

The basic integration types are IP-based, in-band DTMF, SMDI, PBXLink, and SIP. Cisco messaging systems currently integrate with the majority of telephone systems in the business telephone market. Once an integration is made, the PBX and the voice-mail system work together, sharing information regarding call routing and message notification.

- **Call Forward to Personal Greeting**—This feature is essential to voice-mail functionality. Call forward to personal greeting is the way that the telephone system tells Cisco Unity what greeting to play. To route a call to the correct greeting, the PBX must send information along with a call to instruct Cisco Unity about what to do with that call. The Cisco Unity integration packages enable information regarding station identification to be sent to Cisco Unity, which then plays the appropriate greeting. If this information were not present, the caller would hear the Opening Greeting. In this case, by default, the caller would then need to enter the mailbox ID of the person they are trying to reach. Usually this is the phone extension.

The different integrations function in various ways:

  — An IP integration sends call information to Cisco CallManager via Skinny packets across the LAN.

  — In-band integration requires DTMF station identification (audio tones) for caller ID. The phone extension is sent as DTMF tones to identify the calling party.

  — An SMDI integration passes information along in a small packet of data sent via a serial cable or over a combination of modems and phone lines. This is used along with analog lines that connect the PBX and Cisco Unity for its voice path.

—   PBXLink integrations must have special digital lines installed that will transmit this information.

—   A SIP integration uses requests and responses to set up, maintain, and end sessions (calls). This information is sent in ASCII-based packets through the network cable connecting Cisco Unity with another endpoint for each session.

- **Easy message access**—Cisco Unity typically recognizes a subscriber when they enter a one- or two-button code on their extension, without them having to enter their Personal ID. This is possible with the Cisco Unity integrations because the telephone system has been programmed to download the digits of a subscriber's Personal ID in response to that particular key sequence. In Cisco CallManager, for example, the Messages button can be programmed to dial the pilot number of the Cisco Unity system. Generally, if you press one or two keys at your extension, for example 72 or possibly the Messages button, the telephone system transfers the call to the hunt group for the voice-mail system, and then sends along the digits for a Personal ID, such as *1408. The next thing you hear in the conversation is either a request for your password or the beginning of the subscriber conversation. With this feature present, it is a very good idea for subscribers to password-protect their voice mailbox. By default, Cisco Unity assigns a standard password to all subscribers.

- **Message waiting indicators**—To inform users of new voice mail messages, Cisco Unity sends code to the PBX to activate and deactivate message waiting indicators (MWIs). That indication will take different forms depending on the telephone system and the telephone sets attached to it. The indication can be a steadily lit or flashing light, a word on a liquid crystal display (LCD) panel, or a special tone heard when you pick up the handset.

When a call is sent from a PBX to Cisco Unity, the following call information is typically also sent:

- The number of the called party.

- The telephone number of the calling party, which may be an extension or phone number of an external call (if the phone system supports caller ID).

- The reason code why the call was sent to Cisco Unity. This can either be because the extension was busy on the other line and it was forwarded to Cisco Unity, did not answer because they were away from their desk, or the extension is set to forward all calls to voice-mail because they are on vacation. Another reason could be when an extension calls Cisco Unity directly to check their messages.

Understanding the Attributes of Cisco Unified Communications Integrations

Understanding the attributes of a communications integration will help you during installation and while analyzing integration issues that may arise. This understanding will enable you to save valuable time when troubleshooting these issues.

To fully benefit from this section, it is recommended that you have the following prerequisite skills and knowledge (see Chapter 1, "Cisco Unified Communications System Fundamentals," for a quick review of any of these topics):

- Understand basic telephone system terminologies
- Understand Cisco Unity standard features
- Understand Cisco Unity basic call flow

Integrating Cisco Unity and CCM

Computer-based telephone systems are becoming more and more popular. Most of them communicate via an Ethernet connection. This new method requires new ways of integrating voice mail with them. Cisco Unity uses the Skinny Client Control Protocol (SCCP) to communicate directly with Cisco CallManager. Because Cisco Unity and CCM are on separate servers, each requires some information from the other to communicate. CCM, for example, must know information such as the names of the voice-mail ports and the extensions that should be assigned to the voice-mail ports. The Cisco Unity side requires information such as what the IP addresses are of the CCMs that Cisco Unity will be servicing and what Message Waiting on and off numbers are assigned in CCM. With each voice-mail port given a specific name by using a number suffix incremented for each, Cisco Unity must also know what common prefix has been assigned to the group of ports being configured.

You can configure Cisco Unity and CCM in many ways, depending on the customer's requirements and the site's existing network topology.

The issues involved are normally focused on WAN deployments. Most LAN deployments are very flexible because they have fewer bandwidth constraints. It is important to understand how all the components interact to determine what works best for the customer. Figure 9-2 illustrates a Cisco Unity and CCM integration.

Figure 9-2   *Cisco Unity and CCM Integration*

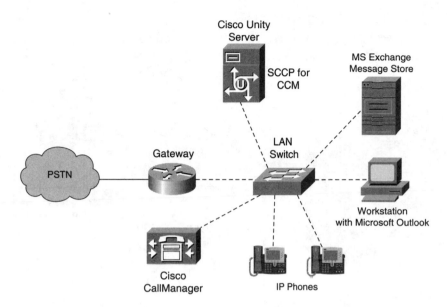

Integrating PA and CCM

The information that passes between the Cisco PA and CCM is basically call information carried as IP packets over a company's LAN. The PA uses interceptor ports to identify the telephone extensions that PA will intercept from CCM. You must configure these ports as computer telephony integration (CTI) route points and translation patterns in CCM to identify them in the PA server configuration. The CTI route point's configuration allows PA to intercept the call; the translation patterns allow calls to go through to the extension if the PA server is unavailable.

Figure 9-3 illustrates the following steps to complete a Cisco PA and CCM integration:

1 A call arrives for an extension from the Public Switched Telephone Network (PSTN).

2 Because this extension has a PA interceptor port (CTI route point) configured for it, CCM routes the call to PA.

3 PA retrieves the user information from the Lightweight Directory Access Protocol (LDAP) directory and checks whether the user has any rules set.

4 In this example, the user has a rule set to have calls sent to a branch office where the user is working. The call extends to a phone on the branch office.

Figure 9-3 *Cisco PA and CCM Integration*

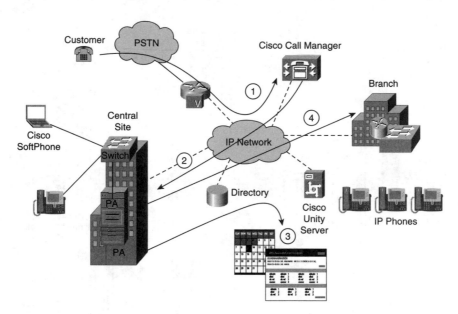

Understanding the Types of Cisco Unified Communications Integrations

A Cisco Unity system uses the services of a telephone system, either circuit-switched or packet-switched, to perform its essential functions. Functions such as automated attendant, voicemail, and audiotext work because of an established relationship with a telephone system.

Understanding the relationship between a telephone system and a Cisco Unity voice-processing system and its integrations contributes to the proper installation and troubleshooting of Cisco Unity.

To fully benefit from this section, it is recommended that you have the following prerequisite skills and knowledge (see Chapter 1 for more information on any of these topics):

- Knowledge of the basic telephone features used with voice mail

- The ability to list the telephone switch integrations supported by Cisco Unity 4.0

- Knowledge of the standard features of Cisco Unity

- Knowledge of the standard features of Cisco PA

Integrating with IP

Cisco Unity messaging systems integrate with CCM by using the Cisco Unity-CM TAPI service provider (TSP) in a pure IP environment. Because Cisco Unity and CCM communicate without the use of traditional voice boards, all call information, including session, signaling, and audio, travels as packets across the network. Figure 9-4 illustrates a Cisco Unity and CCM integration.

Figure 9-4   *Cisco Unity and CCM Integration*

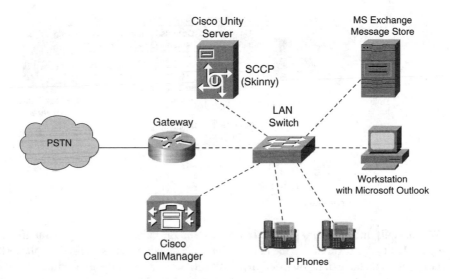

Most Cisco IP telephone models connect to virtual station ports on CCM using the Skinny Client Control Protocol (SCCP). Cisco developed a TSP that connects to the SCCP layer of CCM. The SCCP layer is similar to the CTI layer and provides a communication channel to CCM. All integration functionality remains the same when using this protocol and all TAPI session and call control is served through the Cisco Unity-CM TSP and SCCP.

NOTE   The Cisco TSP referred to is one that comes with the Cisco Unity product. This is different from the Cisco-TSP that comes with Cisco CallManager.

Cisco Unity 4.0 uses SCCP to provide the call session and signaling information between CCM and itself. This bidirectional communication between Cisco Unity and CCM takes place via the Cisco Unity-CM TSP, a piece of software that opens and maintains that communication channel. The TSP is installed on the Cisco Unity system. You can configure it by using the Cisco Unity Telephony Integration Manager (UTIM) application.

Integrating with DTMF

A telephone system (PBX, using a DTMF integration) sends a series of DTMF tones to the voice-processing system that communicates information needed for call forwarding to personal greeting and easy message access. The voice-processing system in turn sends DTMF packets over the analog lines to the telephone system to tell it to turn the MWI on or off. It does not use an RS-232 serial cable connection. Figure 9-5 illustrates a DTMF integration.

Figure 9-5 *DTMF Integration*

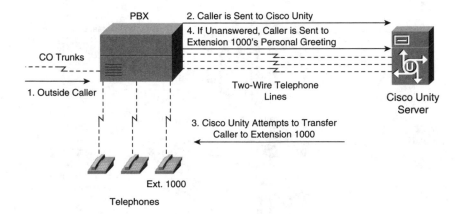

When a call initially comes in to Cisco Unity and the caller hears the general greeting from the Cisco Unity AutoAttendant, the caller enters an extension. The system then places the caller on hold and dials the extension listed in the subscriber's page for the extension ID (extension 1000 in Figure 9-5). Once the caller is on hold, Cisco Unity pulses out the extension and then either waits on the line and listens for ringing (supervised transfer, as referred to in the System Administrator [SA] web page) or releases the call (release to switch, sometimes also referred to as blind transfer). If the call goes unanswered for the specified number of rings (either in Cisco Unity's or the PBX's programming, dependent on the transfer type used), the call comes back to Cisco Unity. In the case of a supervised transfer, Cisco Unity still has control of the call, so it sends the call directly to the personal greeting. In the case of a release to switch, Cisco Unity answers as if it is a new incoming call and the PBX pulses out in DTMF packets the call forwarding digits needed by Cisco Unity to play the correct subscriber's personal greeting.

Integrating with SMDI

An SMDI integration usually uses an RS-232 cable to connect the voice-mail system and the telephone system. The serial cable plugs into the voice-processing system, which in this case can be a Cisco Unity system on one end and the telephone system on the other. This is also known as out-of-band signaling because the information about the call is carried on a different path than the voice traffic. In contrast, an in-band (DTMF, for example) solution carries the information about the call on the same path that carries the voice traffic.

SMDI integrations (using a serial cable) have a 100-foot connection limit that is determined by the technical specifications of the RS-232 standard. If you are using Centrex lines, where the central office serves, in effect, as an off-site PBX, having a dedicated line connected by modems at each end allows you to bypass the 100-foot limit. You can also use modems on site to bypass the RS-232 limit. The serial packets sent are sometimes referred to as SMDI packets. This is the standard protocol used by Centrex, but it is also used by the NEC 2000 and the NEC 2400 telephone systems, among others.

A serial integration is more difficult to configure because of the variables involved: telephone system programming, cable configurations, and COM port configurations. Once it has been set up, it is both extremely reliable and quicker than a DTMF integration, particularly in the area of servicing MWI requests. Figure 9-6 illustrates an SMDI integration.

Figure 9-6   *SMDI Integration*

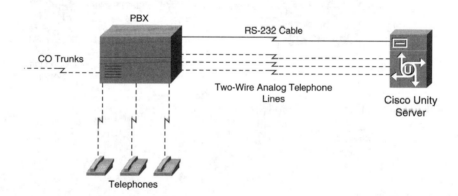

Integrating with PBXLink

The PBXLink box provides an integration solution for several telephone systems, among which are the Avaya Definity Gx and the Nortel Meridian 1. The PBXLink box works in conjunction with the voice boards inside Cisco Unity. The voice boards used in the integration are the standard boards available for Cisco Unity systems. Which boards are used depends on a configuration that makes most efficient use of slots in the server.

The voice boards used with the PBXLink use PCI slots. The PBXLink connects to the telephone system by using digital lines. Analog lines connect the PBX to the voice boards, which together provide a channel for all the voice and DTMF traffic. The integration information travels to Cisco Unity via an RS-232 cable between it and the PBXLink box.

You attach the PBXLink to the PBX via digital lines and program them on the PBX side. The PBXLink uses the busy indicators to determine which analog lines between the PBX and the voice-mail system are busy. Also, when calls arrive at the voice-mail system, the PBXLink gathers the call information from the display of the digital set.

The PBXLink reads the digital information about the call (the called party's extension, the reason for the forward, and the calling party's extension on internal calls), translates that into SMDI packets, and sends the information through the RS-232 cable to voice mail. The PBXLink box sends the information about the call (for example, which personal greeting to play when a call forwards to voice mail on a ring with no answer) across the RS-232 cable. The PBX sends the call to the voice-messaging system through the analog lines that connect the voice boards and the telephone system. Figure 9-7 illustrates a PBXLink integration.

Figure 9-7   *PBXLink Integration*

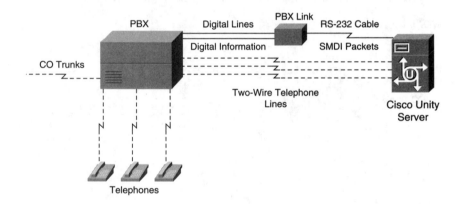

Integrating with SIP

SIP is a peer-to-peer Internet Engineering Task Force (IETF) standard that is designed for multimedia calls over IP.

A SIP proxy server is a system that receives SIP requests from a client, such as a SIP-enabled IP phone, and then forwards the requests on behalf of the client. These proxy servers receive SIP messages, and then can forward them to other SIP servers. SIP proxy servers can provide capabilities such as authentication, authorization, network access control, routing, reliable request retransmission, and security. Figure 9-8 illustrates a SIP integration.

Figure 9-8   *SIP Integration*

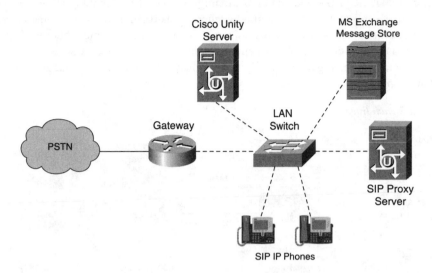

A Cisco Unity SIP integration uses a SIP proxy server to set up communication between the voice messaging ports on the Cisco Unity server and the appropriate endpoint, such as an IP-enabled phone. The communications occur through an IP network (LAN, WAN, or Internet) to all SIP-enabled devices connected to it, a SIP-enabled gateway to the PSTN, and all phones connected to it.

The proxy server sends the following information in the SIP message along with the forwarded call:

- In the Diversion header, the extension of the called party
- In the Diversion header, the reason for the forwarded call
- In the Form header, the extension of the calling party (for internal calls) or the SIP URL of the calling party (if it is an external call and the system uses caller ID)

You can use the UTIM to configure this integration.

Integrating with Dual Phone Systems

Compatibility among voice and unified messaging systems, the existing PBX equipment, and IP telephony solutions is a primary concern for most enterprises. Users must experience uninterrupted service and be offered a familiar interface to ensure a smooth migration from a traditional PBX system to an IP telephony environment.

Dual-switch integration provides an integration for customers who currently have a traditional circuit-switched PBX and would like to migrate to CCM. This integration preserves a customer's investment in its circuit-switched infrastructure while simultaneously allowing for migration to packet-switched technology at any pace the customer chooses. This allows enterprises to operate in a hybrid environment while maintaining consistent voice-messaging service across the organization. Figure 9-9 illustrates a dual-switch integration using Cisco Unity and CCM.

Figure 9-9   *Dual-Switch Integration*

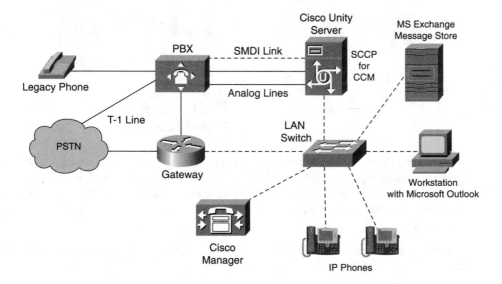

Cisco Unity solutions are designed to provide connectivity with CCM and existing PBX equipment at the same time. In addition to connectivity, Cisco Unity solutions also support complete voice-mail integration between both systems simultaneously.

Dual-switch integration can be used to connect CCM and a Cisco SIP proxy server. It is also available for a Cisco SIP proxy server and a supported traditional circuit-switched PBX when connecting with Cisco Unity.

The best source for information about the Cisco Unity and CCM integration in a dual-switch environment is the *Cisco CallManager Integration Guide* series. These guides are available in Adobe Acrobat PDF format from several sources. They are available at Cisco.com by performing a search on "Cisco CallManager Integration Guide."

Integrating with Telephone Systems

The following are the currently supported telephone systems for Cisco Unity 4.0:

- Alcatel 4400 (DTMF)
- Avaya Definity G3 (DTMF)
- Avaya Definity Gx (PBXLink)
- Avaya Definity ProLogix (DTMF)
- CCM (IP)
- Cisco SIP Proxy Server (SIP)
- Centrex (SMDI)
- ECI Coral III (Serial)
- Ericsson MD-110 (Serial)
- Fujitsu 9600 (Serial)
- Intecom E14 Millenium (Serial)
- Matra 6500 (DTMF)
- Mitel SX-200, SX-2000 (DTMF) ONS
- NEC NEAX 2000, 2400 (Serial) MCI
- Nortel Meridian 1 (PBXLink)
- Siemens 9751 9006i (DTMF)
- Siemens Hicom 300 (DTMF)
- Syntegra ITS (SMDI)
- Syntegra ITS (SMDI)

You can find this list by visting the following website:

http://www.cisco.com/en/US/products/sw/voicesw/ps2237/
prod_configuration_guides_list.html

Cisco conducts extensive testing before qualifying a telephone system for use with Cisco Unity. Telephone systems are tested under many different call scenarios, and troubleshooting information is created. Therefore, Cisco TAC will not support systems that are not first qualified. If you do decide to install Cisco Unity with a nonsupported telephone system, you will be responsible for all integration issues on that system.

Using Messaging Ports in a Cisco Messaging System

The Cisco Unity voice-mail ports are a crucial part of general setup. Ports are also referred to in many of the Cisco Unity documents as sessions. The term *port* is from the telephony world, referring to when a physical connection is made between the voice-mail system and the telephone system. *Session* is the term used in the IP telephony world.

In essence, a messaging port is an open communications channel between the telephone system and Cisco Unity. When Cisco Unity answers a PSTN call or a user calling to check messages, Cisco Unity uses a port. In other words, Cisco Unity requires one port for every simultaneous telephone call you expect it to handle. Determining how many ports you require depends on your client's corporate messaging needs. Such features as AutoAttendant, Audiotext, and Message Notification, and whether it is a DTMF integration, all can affect the number of ports required.

In CCM, you configure each Cisco Unity messaging port as a voice-mail port. In circuit-based PBX integrations, the Cisco Unity messaging ports are analog extensions with one extension used per port.

Defining Messaging Ports Configuration Options

There are various settings for the Cisco Unity messaging ports.

Figure 9-10 shows the Ports Configuration page from the System Administrator (SA) tool. When you open the SA, on the left-hand side you will see a list of links. Scroll to the bottom and you will see the Ports link. Click it to go to the Ports page.

Figure 9-10 *Ports Configuration*

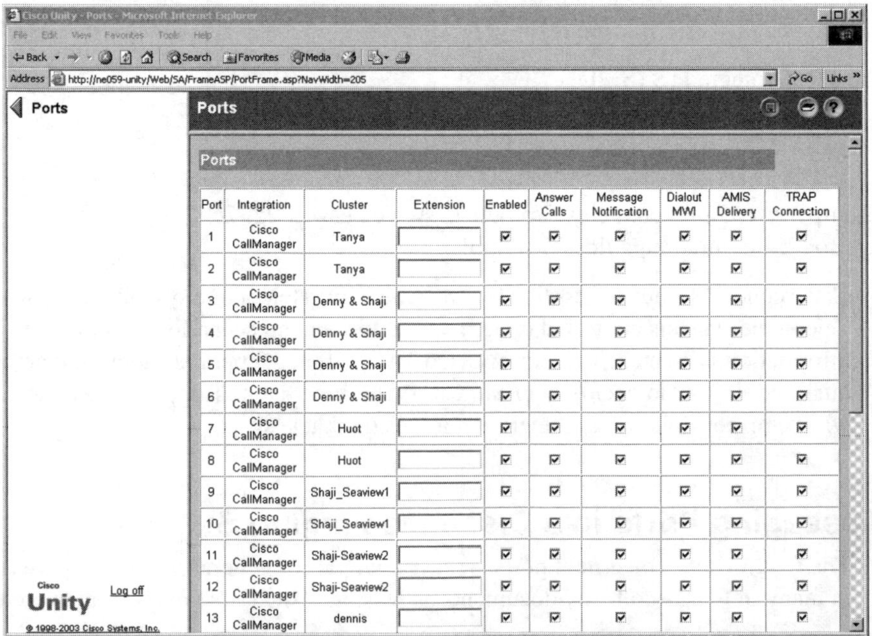

The following is a list of the settings configured for each messaging port:

- **Enabled**—This setting means that the port is in service. If this setting is unchecked, the port is out of service. In that scenario, the caller who reaches that port receives ringing tones but Cisco Unity does not answer. You might uncheck this setting if you are having issues with that particular port or extension from the telephone system and you do not want callers to access that port. You should remove that port from the hunt group you created, to prevent such a scenario from happening.

- **Answer Calls**—This setting means Cisco Unity will answer a call received on this port. This can be either a call coming in from the PSTN or an internal call coming from a subscriber's office extension number. Unchecking this setting means Cisco Unity will not accept an incoming call on this port.

- **Message Notification**—This setting allows the Cisco Unity port to dial out calls for message notification, such as to a pager, mobile phone, or text pager. Dialouts are subject to Restriction Table settings. Simply saving this information will enable this function.

- **Dialout MWI**—This setting allows the Cisco Unity port to dial out the message lamp on and off codes that are associated with telephone systems. Typically, the last few ports are reserved for dialout and outbound MWI traffic only because this type of traffic will not interfere with calls Cisco Unity is receiving. By default, however, all ports are enabled for this functionality. The number of recommended ports varies for this depending on the size of the deployment and how Cisco Unity will be used.

- **TRAP (Telephony Record and Playback) Connection**—This setting is used during telephone recording and playback of greetings through the Media Master in Cisco Unity. The Media Master is used when recording or playing greetings using the Cisco Unity Assistant or through System Administration screens. Unchecking this setting for all ports would require each user to use the microphone of their PC's multimedia device for record and playback.

- **AMIS (Audio Messaging Interchange Specification) Delivery**—AMIS is a protocol that uses analog lines to exchange voice messages between voice-mail systems that support AMIS. Cisco Unity supports the Audio Messaging Interchange Specification analog (AMIS-a) protocol. The AMIS Delivery setting is available on systems that are licensed for AMIS. When using AMIS Networking, this setting affects outbound AMIS calls only. This is used for delivering voice-mail messages to target voice-messaging systems. More information is available in Chapter 10, "Unified Communications Networking."

Each Cisco Unity messaging port can be configured to one or more of these five settings: Enabled, Answer Calls, Message Notification, Dialout MWI, and TRaP Connection. AMIS Delivery is an optional setting that is available if your Cisco Unity system contains an AMIS license. How the individual ports on your Cisco Unity are configured will depend on your corporate messaging needs. Some considerations are discussed in the next section.

Configuring Messaging Ports

The determining factor on how to configure the Cisco Unity ports is your client's corporate messaging needs. As you have seen, Cisco Unity is feature rich and your use of these features directly impacts how the ports will be configured.

The AutoAttendant feature can affect the port configuration by requiring the Answer Calls setting to be used on all ports. To ensure that callers do not receive a busy signal when calling, you would want as many ports as possible set to answer those calls.

The Message Notification feature of Cisco Unity can greatly increase the dialout usage of the ports. As you know, subscribers have the option of having up to 13 different message notification devices configured to notify them when they have messages in their mailbox. If a port is not available, the message notification will be queued and a user's notifications may be delayed. How long the delay is will depend on how many message notifications are queued.

If the Dialout MWI setting is not selected on a sufficient number of Cisco Unity ports, there will be a delay of the lighting and extinguishing of MWIs on the user's telephone. This may result in user complaints of delayed messages (messages in their mailboxes but the lamps not being lit) or that lamps are not going out after they retrieve their messages. These scenarios can occur on those installations that use DTMF or (to a much lesser extent) IP integrations. (Serial- and PBXLink-type integrations do not use Cisco Unity messaging ports to light message waiting lamps. However, at least one messaging port must be configured for MWIs).

As a guide, 25 percent of Cisco Unity messaging ports should be set for Dialout MWI for DTMF integrations. This can be adjusted if issues arise or if corporate needs have specific requirements.

As a guide for IP integrations, one Dialout MWI port should be configured for every 16 ports of the Cisco Unity system. Although the Cisco Unity port is not sending out Touch-Tones to light lamps on an IP integration, the channel still needs to be open.

Using TRaP for hearing voice messages can also have an impact on port usage. If not enough ports are configured for TRaP, some users will receive an error such as, "Unknown problems are preventing the completion of this call." Those users then need to use their PC's multimedia microphone to record greetings during that session, or they can call back when a port becomes available.

Chapter Summary

In this chapter, you learned the attributes that make up Cisco unified communications integrations, the types of Cisco unified communications integrations, and the different uses and types of configurations for messaging ports in a Cisco messaging system. Specifically, you learned the following:

- The attributes of a communications integration
- The integration between Cisco Unity and CCM
- The integration between Cisco PA and CCM
- A dual telephone system integration
- The supported Cisco Unity telephone systems
- Define a Cisco Unity messaging port
- Describe Cisco Unity messaging port configurations
- Define guidelines for Cisco Unity messaging port settings

For additional information on the topics presented in this chapter, refer to the following resources:

- *Cisco CallManager Integration Guide*
- *Cisco Personal Assistant Administration Guide*
- Various Cisco Unity Integration guides
- *Cisco Unity System Administration Guide*

These references can be found by going to Cisco.com and performing a search.

Chapter Review Questions

Use this section to test yourself on how well you learned the concepts discussed in this chapter. You can find the answers to the review questions for this chapter in Appendix A.

1 Name the three main integration features present when integration between Cisco Unity and a PBX takes place.

2 What communications protocol does Cisco Unity use to communicate with Cisco CallManager?

3 When using PA, what type of ports must you configure in CCM?

4 List at least three types of integration that Cisco Unity 4.0 uses to integrate with telephone systems.

5 When using DTMF integration, what mechanism does Cisco Unity use to turn on a lamp on a phone?

6 What type of cable does the SMDI integration usually use to send information about a call?

7 When using PBXLink integration, you attach the PBXLink box to the PBX using what type of lines?

8 In Cisco Unity, what is another name for a messaging port?

9 What is the TRaP Connection setting used for on the Cisco Unity messaging ports?

10 List at least three telephone systems that Cisco Unity 4.0 currently supports.

Upon completing this chapter, you will be able to perform the following tasks:

- Describe how messages are delivered and directories are replicated
- Describe how Simple Mail Transfer Protocol (SMTP), Audio Messaging Interchange Specification (AMIS), Voice Profile for Internet Messaging (VPIM), and the Cisco Unity Bridge are used to deliver messages
- Describe addressing options in Cisco Unity
- Select which scenarios would appropriately use blind addressing in Cisco Unity from a list of possible scenarios
- Describe the advantages of the Cisco Unity networking capabilities
- Create and use Internet, AMIS, VPIM, and Bridge subscribers

CHAPTER 10

Unified Communications Networking

This chapter covers the networking components that are used with Cisco Unity to establish communication with other messaging systems for voice mail, e-mail, and fax.

Messaging within an organization is vital for everyday business, with each organization having specific requirements and needs to exchange information internally and externally. This chapter explores the different ways in which Cisco Unity can be set up to provide connectivity to other Cisco Unity systems and to non–Cisco Unity recipients, and describes the components involved. It contains basic and advanced areas of Cisco Unity networking with Microsoft Exchange and Lotus Notes.

Cisco Unity Networking Fundamentals

This section explores the areas that are important to networking with Cisco Unity. It explains directory replication, location objects, dialing domains, and the different types of networking offered by Cisco Unity.

Before you implement networking between Cisco Unity and other messaging systems (which may include another Cisco Unity server), you must first understand the basic concepts and terminology on which it is built. This section defines all the fundamental concepts for each of the later sections that concentrate on specific implementations of networking.

To benefit fully from this section, it is recommended that you have these prerequisite skills and knowledge. (If you need a quick review of either topic, see Chapter 1, "Cisco Unified Communications System Fundamentals," where you can find more information.)

- An understanding of the standard features of Cisco Unity
- An understanding of the Cisco Unity call flow

Defining Cisco Unity Networking

In Cisco Unity, "networking" is the general term for defining messaging between Cisco Unity servers and Cisco Unity and other messaging systems. In these cases, messaging systems may include voice mail, e-mail, and fax messaging.

In Cisco Unity Version 3.x and earlier, networking had a limited meaning. It referred only to the capability of one subscriber to call into voice mail and address a message to another subscriber residing on a remote Cisco Unity server. This server may have been in a remote Exchange site. Cisco Unity 4.0 expands the definition of networking by adding more capabilities, which are described next. Whether or not you can use each of the new capabilities depends on the type of telephone switch network you are using and the configuration of your mail store.

In a Cisco Unity networked environment, any subscriber can leave a message for any other subscriber in the organization by name or extension. Callers can dial into any Cisco Unity server and the Cisco Unity Automated Attendant will transfer that call to the correct subscriber in the organization, regardless of which Cisco Unity server the called subscriber is associated with. Outside callers can also dial into any Cisco Unity server and find any subscriber by name in the directory and be transferred to them, regardless of which Cisco Unity server the subscriber is homed to. Finally, any number of Cisco Unity servers can be bound together in a dialing domain so that subscribers can address messages and perform auto-attendant transfers simply by dialing the same number they use to reach that person through the telephone system.

Figure 10-1 illustrates the different types of networking that Cisco Unity is capable of handling.

Figure 10-1 *The Different Types of Cisco Unity Networking*

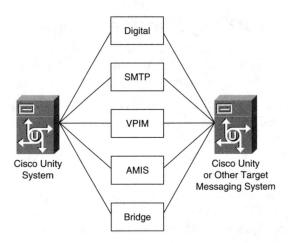

The main goal of networking in Cisco Unity is to deliver messages from a Cisco Unity server to a target, and from the target to a Cisco Unity server. The experience that a user has is very simple: the caller leaves a message for someone who is a subscriber on the system. The caller does not need to know what type of server the subscriber resides on, nor where they are physically located. The target server may not even be a Cisco Unity server, in which case communication protocols and software setup are used to make that message transfer to the remote messaging system once the user leaves the message. This makes it transparent to the user who is leaving a message.

Understanding Cisco Unity Networking Communication Methods

Cisco Unity has five different types of networking communication methods available, each of which enables Cisco Unity to be connected to a variety of other messaging systems for delivery of messages. The type of networking used with Cisco Unity depends on the target server the subscriber's message needs to be delivered to. The following list presents a brief look at each type of target server and the method used to reach it:

- **Digital networking**—Can be used if an organization has several Cisco Unity servers and requires that subscribers communicate with each other. It is implemented when all the servers are part of the same global directory on a network.

- **SMTP**—Can be used if the target server is a Cisco Unity system and it uses a separate global directory. If the target server is a different type of messaging server that is capable of receiving SMTP mail, it is also a candidate for SMTP networking. The major difference in sending messages to another Cisco Unity server and sending messages to any other server is the appearance of the message when it arrives at the target server. If a voice message is sent to a Cisco Unity server, it retains all of its voice-mail attributes (that is, a subscriber can listen to it over the telephone). If the other target server is a different e-mail server, then the voice message arrives as an e-mail message with a WAV file attachment.

- **AMIS-analog (AMIS-a)**—Can be used to connect Cisco Unity and other AMIS-a-compliant voice-mail systems. It is a widely available type of networking. This protocol uses an analog method to exchange messages between each messaging system. Phone calls are placed between the voice-mail systems to deliver voice messages.

- **VPIM**—If the target voice-mail system supports the VPIM protocol, then this is the preferred method of transferring messages between voice-mail servers. This is a digital standard based on SMTP and the Multipurpose Internet Mail Extension (MIME) protocol. Voice, text, and fax messages may be transferred between target servers.

- **Bridge networking**—The ideal method for transferring messages between Cisco Unity and Octel voice-mail servers if the target voice-mail system is a supported Octel server. Bridge networking uses VPIM and the MIME protocol with some proprietary extensions to exchange messages with Cisco Unity. It uses the Octel analog messaging standard to communicate with Octel servers. Voice messages can be transferred between messaging systems.

Cisco Unity Digital Networking with IBM Lotus Domino

Digital networking can be used in a Cisco Unity 4.0 and Domino environment. It is enabled on every Cisco Unity server, and it can be easily configured. Besides the digital networking requirements, the other required configuration is of the primary location object on each server. The primary location object is a system object, created by default when Cisco Unity is installed, and it cannot be deleted. It contains the information each Cisco Unity server requires to send messages to other servers. You can find the primary location object in the Cisco Unity Administrator, located under Network.

Figure 10-2 illustrates the Primary Location page of a Cisco Unity system.

Figure 10-2 *Primary Location Page*

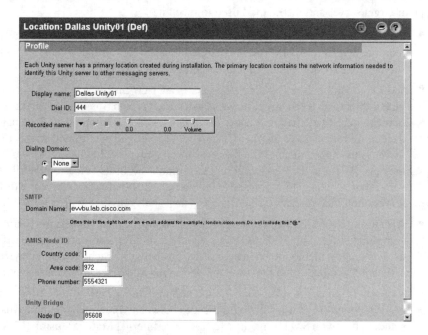

A dialing domain is a collection of Cisco Unity servers that are either served by the same telephone system or are attached to a networked telephone system. Dialing domains allow an organization to deal with overlapping dial plans.

Further information about the requirements for, and configuration of, digital networking is given in the section "Implementing Digital Networking in Cisco Unity" later in the chapter.

Understanding Cisco Unity for Exchange Networking

With the addition of Internet Voice Connector (IVC), Cisco Unity 4.0 for Exchange is capable of the full range of networking solutions. Users may send messages to subscribers residing on other Cisco Unity servers, on SMTP servers, on VPIM-compliant messaging servers, on AMIS-a-compliant voice-mail servers, or on Octel voice-mail systems that are using the Octel analog protocol. The following sections explore the capabilities and configuration of each of these networking solutions. They also discuss when and how the IVC software is used with Cisco Unity and the other messaging systems.

Using IVC for Exchange

IVC allows two Cisco Unity systems to send and receive voice messages as SMTP mail, while preserving the Cisco Unity attributes within the message. It also allows Cisco Unity to communicate with SMTP servers, Octel voice-mail systems, VPIM-compliant voice-mail servers, and AMIS-a-compliant voice-mail systems. The data objects within the location object define the type of communication used. Whenever you specify another Cisco Unity as the destination type, the SMTP message is packaged with binary data that identifies the mail as a Cisco Unity voice-mail message to the receiving machine (another Cisco Unity server). The end result is that the message may be played over the telephone, as well as played and managed by ViewMail for Outlook (VMO). The messages do not appear as an attached WAV file to subscribers.

IVC is a separate installation from Cisco Unity and is located on the Cisco Unity Installation CD-ROM. After you install IVC, it appears as an Exchange connector object similar to Internet Mail Service (IMS in Microsoft Exchange 5.5) or SMTP Connector (Microsoft Exchange 2000, and is a Windows NT service as well). Thus, an entry is created in the Exchange Gateway Address Routing Table for a message type of VOICE. Because IVC uses SMTP, it requires the IMS connector to function properly in Exchange 5.5.

If you are upgrading to Cisco Unity 4.0, then you should use the latest connector. It is also important that you have only one connector installed. Instructions for removing earlier versions of the connector differ from the instructions for removing the most current connector. You can find these instructions at Cisco.com in the *Networking in Cisco Unity Guide* (with *Microsoft Exchange*).

If you install IVC after you have established subscribers on your Cisco Unity system, and that system will be a remote location (or AMIS location) to other Cisco Unity systems, you need to run the Extension Address Utility to generate the proper addresses for your subscribers. To locate this utility, choose **Start > Programs > Unity**. It creates user addresses of the type VOICE and SMTP, both necessary for blind addressing. Once you install IVC, any new subscribers who are added to Cisco Unity automatically have those addresses generated for them as a part of the normal subscriber creation process. If you change your location ID or domain name after creating extension addresses, you need to rerun the utility to create correct addresses. Instructions for running the utility are located in the *Cisco Unity System Administration Guide*.

Understanding Message Transfer and Directory Replication

This section explains in general the message transfer and directory replication process in a messaging environment. In addition, this section describes Cisco Unity's interactions with Active Directory (AD) in Microsoft Windows 2000.

Figure 10-3 illustrates the message transfer and directory replication process.

Figure 10-3 *Message Transfer and Directory Replication Process*

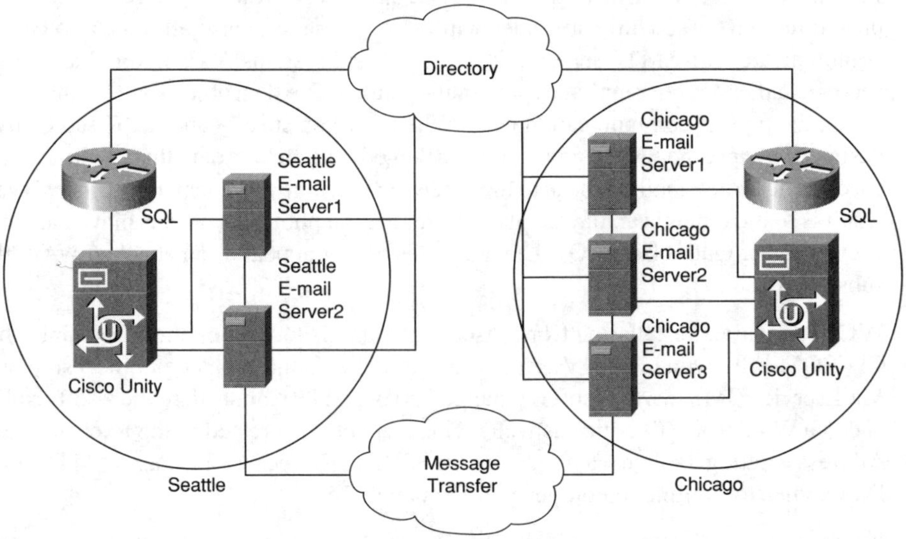

Figure 10-3 is a high-level, conceptual diagram of the connection between two Cisco Unity servers installed on a corporate network. It contains a Cisco Unity server on each site, Chicago and Seattle. In addition, there are several back-end e-mail servers at each site. These servers all share a global directory that contains information about the mail users. This is also the subscribers' mail store where users can gain access to their messages, monitor their mailboxes, and leave messages. The key to this model is that all the employees in this organization share a single directory, which is the global directory; thus, other sites can be added while maintaining the same model.

Cisco Unity servers synchronize information in this directory with their local SQL database. Information such as all mail users, Unity objects, and public distribution lists are examples of the data that is kept in the SQL database. As a result, directory lookups across the organization can take place very quickly because a copy is stored locally on each Cisco Unity server.

Earlier versions of Cisco Unity copied a large amount of information from SQL to the directory. In Cisco Unity 4.0, that information has been reduced to a smaller set. Only information that is needed to address messages to subscribers, find subscribers, and transfer calls to subscribers' phones is now stored in the directory. The rest of the information is on the SQL database. The type of information copied to the directory includes the following:

- First name.
- Last name.
- Display name.
- Recorded voice name.

- E-mail alias.

- Fax ID. This ID is used when using third-party fax integrations. It allows faxes that are intended for a particular subscriber to be sent directly to their mailbox.

- Primary ID. This ID is used when subscribers log on to their voice-mail boxes. It is usually their extension number.

- Up to nine alternate IDs.

- Location object assignment.

- System ID. This identifies the Cisco Unity server the subscriber is associated with.

- Transfer string. This field identifies the exact digits that are necessary to ring the subscriber's phone during a transfer. This can include dual-tone multifrequency (DTMF) digits, trunk access codes, and pauses. Each subscriber can have only one string.

If a subscriber is added in Seattle, the previous information, along with all the other subscriber information, is written to the local SQL database. Replication is set between the database and directory so that the items listed above are transferred to the directory periodically.

Now that the Seattle local SQL database and directory are in sync, the next step is to have the SQL database in Chicago pick up the updated information from the directory. (If there were another site, the same method would be used.) After all the SQL databases have received the new information, a subscriber in Chicago can look up the new Seattle subscriber while in voice mail. The subscriber can perform this either by name or by extension. When addressing a message, the Chicago subscriber can also choose to hear the voice name of the intended subscriber as confirmation.

In Figure 10-3, the direct message connections are limited to the servers in the local site. Any subscriber can send messages to users outside the site by using the message transfer "cloud" (that is, the Message Transfer Agent [MTA] in Exchange 5.5). However, you can log in and access messages only on a server at your site. The same sort of limitations apply to Exchange 2000/2003 and Domino. Only the names of the defined boundaries will change.

The following sections examine how messages are transferred within and between Exchange sites (for Exchange 5.5) and routing groups (for Exchange 2000/2003). Then, you learn how Cisco Unity interacts with AD in Windows 2000 in terms of the directory replication process.

Intrasite Messaging in Exchange 5.5

If a particular site has only one Exchange server, all messages and directory information reside on that server. However, if that site has more than one server, messages need to be delivered to the appropriate home server, and each of the directories must be replicated across the servers. To achieve this, Exchange relies on the Directory Service (Exchange 2000/2003 uses AD instead) to provide information about where the recipient is homed.

The home server for a recipient is specified when they are created. However, an administrator may modify which server is the recipient's home server at any time. This server is where the recipient's mail is physically kept on disk for retrieval. Once a server is added to a site, directory replication occurs automatically so that each server on the site knows the list of recipients on every other server at that site. Directory replication occurs approximately every 5 minutes and typically does not need to be modified. Figure 10-4 illustrates the process of delivering a message within an intrasite messaging Exchange 5.5 environment.

Figure 10-4   *Intrasite Messaging Exchange 5.5*

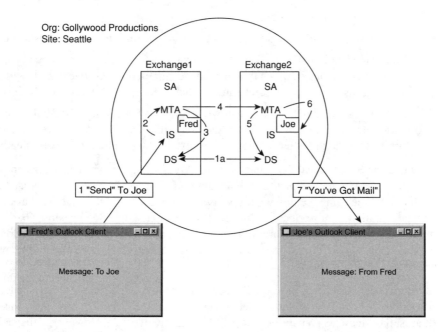

The numbers of the steps in the following list correspond to those in Figure 10-4:

1 Fred, in Exchange1, composes a message, addresses it to Joe, and sends it. (Step 1a is a recognition that Exchange 5.5 servers within a site replicate information automatically.)

2 The Exchange1 IS (Information Store) sends a message to the MTA for delivery to a remote Exchange server.

3 Exchange1's MTA performs a directory lookup in the DS and finds the distinguished name of the remote server's MTA.

4 The Exchange1 MTA opens an association (connection) with the Exchange2 MTA and delivers the message.

5 The Exchange2 MTA performs a directory lookup in the DS and finds that Joe's mailbox is homed locally.

6 The Exchange2 MTA delivers the message to the IS.

7 Joe sees a new message from Fred show up in his mailbox.

All directory services within a site communicate with each other directly to maintain the Exchange directory synchronization. This occurs about 5 minutes after a change.

Intersite Message Passing and Directory Replication

There are many similarities between connecting multiple servers in a site and connecting multiple servers at multiple sites, but a few differences do exist. In a multiple-site environment, an Exchange administrator between the sites must set up messaging connectors and directory replication connectors. Some of the messaging connectors for Exchange 5.5 are site connectors, X.400 connectors, IMS connectors, and Dynamic Remote Access Service (DRAS) connectors. Determining the best messaging connector is important because each provides different sets of features and functionalities. For example, some connectors for Exchange 5.5 have user and message size restrictions.

After you set up the site connectors, your next step is to configure the proper directory replication connectors. This configuration varies based on the organization's topology. The directory replication connector uses the messaging connector to send its directory replication messages. Therefore, the messaging connector must be in place before the directory replication connector is set. Directory replication between sites is scheduled to occur every 3 hours by default, but may be accelerated. Upon initial installation of the directory replication connector, directory replication occurs within a few minutes and typically does not need to be accelerated. After the initial replication, only changes are sent on subsequent updates to the directory. Once directory replication is completed, subscribers can address messages to anyone in the organization by accessing either the Cisco Unity telephone directory conversation or the Exchange-based global address list (GAL).

Figure 10-5 illustrates how messages are passed within an Exchange 5.5 organization with multiple sites and servers.

The numbers of the steps in the following list correspond to those in Figure 10-5:

1 Fred composes a message, addresses it to Joe, and sends it.

2 The Exchange1 IS sends a message to the MTA for delivery to a remote Exchange server.

3 Exchange1's MTA performs a directory lookup in the DS and finds the distinguished name of the remote server's MTA.

4 The Exchange1 MTA notices that Joe's home server is at the remote site Los Angeles and selects the site connector. The Exchange1 MTA sees that it must send all mail using the site connector to the site connector bridgehead, Exchange2.

5 The Exchange2 MTA performs a directory lookup in the DS, realizes that it must pass this message to the remote site Los Angeles, and uses the site connector.

Figure 10-5 *Intrasite Message Passing and Directory*

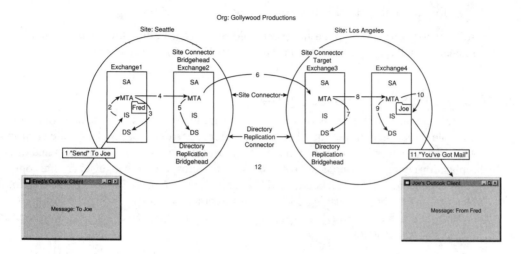

6   Because Exchange2 is the site connector bridgehead, MTA makes a connection to the Los Angeles site connector target server, Exchange3, and delivers the message.

7   Exchange3's MTA performs a directory lookup and sees that Joe's home server is Exchange4.

8   Exchange3's MTA passes the message to the Exchange4 MTA.

9   Exchange4's MTA performs a lookup and sees that Joe is homed on Exchange4.

10   Exchange4 MTA passes the message to the IS.

11   Joe sees a new message appear in his inbox.

12   Directory replication occurs.

In order for directory replication to occur between sites, you must install the directory replication connector after you install a site connector. As part of the installation process, you must define a bridgehead server at each site. Replication between these bridgehead servers then occurs once every 3 hours by default. This number may be changed in the connector's properties pages. All directory service changes are sent between bridgeheads as mail messages. The local MTAs are responsible for delivery.

Intrarouting Group Message Passing and Directory Replication

Routing groups are used in Exchange 2000 to carry out functions that are similar to what is referred to as sites in Exchange 5.5. If a server in a routing group is the only server, all messages and directory information reside on that server. However, if two or more servers exist in a routing group, messages must be delivered to the correct home server and the directories must be accessed.

To accomplish delivery of messages, Exchange 2000 relies on AD to provide information about where the recipient is homed. The home server for a recipient is specified when the recipient is created, but may be modified by an administrator at any time. This is the server where the recipient's mail is physically kept on disk for retrieval. Once a server is added to a site, directory information is shared automatically so that each server at the site knows the list of recipients on every other server. Directory information is available automatically to all servers that are members of the same forest. The manner in which messages are passed within an Exchange 2000 routing group with multiple servers is illustrated in Figure 10-6 and described next.

Figure 10-6 *Routing Group Messaging: Exchange 2000*

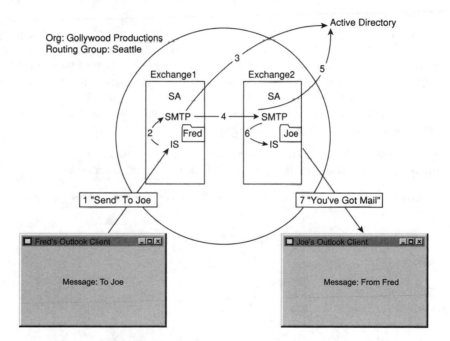

The numbers of the steps in the following list correspond to those in Figure 10-6:

1 Fred composes a message, addresses it to Joe, and sends it.

2 The Exchange1 IS sends a message to the SMTP server for delivery to a remote Exchange server.

3 Exchange1's SMTP server performs a directory lookup in AD and finds the distinguished name of the remote server's SMTP server.

4 The Exchange1 SMTP server opens an SMTP connection with the Exchange2 SMTP server and delivers the message.

5 The Exchange2 SMTP server performs a directory lookup in AD and finds that Joe's mailbox is homed locally.

6 The Exchange2 SMTP server delivers the message to the IS.

7 Joe sees a new message from Fred show up in his mailbox.

AD handles all directory services within a Windows 2000 forest, which maintains a one-to-one correspondence with the Exchange organization. The time it takes to replicate information varies depending on the links between servers and groups in Windows 2000. Inside a routing group, all servers should be on fast, permanent LAN links, so that replication of updated attributes for the directory objects takes place every 5 minutes.

Routing Group Message Passing

There are many similarities between connecting multiple servers in a routing group and connecting multiple servers in multiple routing groups, but there are a few differences. In a multiple routing group environment, routing group connectors must be set up between the groups. The Exchange administrator configures this. Bridgehead servers must be set up in both routing groups, and a cost needs to be configured for each route. Multiple routing group connectors can also be set. This enables you to continue to deliver messages if the primary link between the routing groups is not available.

The manner in which messages are passed within an Exchange 2000 organization with multiple routing groups and servers is illustrated in Figure 10-7 and described next.

Figure 10-7 *Routing Group Message Passing and Directory Replication: Exchange 2000*

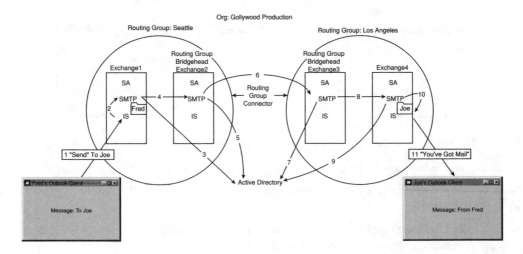

The numbers of the following steps correspond to those in Figure 10-7:

1 Fred composes a message, addresses it to Joe, and sends it.

2 The Exchange1 IS sends a message to the SMTP server for delivery to a remote Exchange server.

3 Exchange1's SMTP server performs a directory lookup in AD and finds the distinguished name of the remote server's SMTP server.

4 The Exchange1 MTA notices that Joe's home server is in a different routing group, Los Angeles, and, after consulting its internal link-state table, selects the least-cost routing group connector. The Exchange1 SMTP server sees that it must send all mail using the routing group connector to the group bridgehead, Exchange2.

5 The Exchange2 SMTP server performs a directory lookup in AD, realizes that it must pass this message to the routing group Los Angeles, and uses the connector.

6 Because Exchange2 is the connector bridgehead, its SMTP server makes a connection to the Los Angeles connector target server, Exchange3, and delivers the message.

7 Exchange3's SMTP server performs a directory lookup and sees that Joe's home server is Exchange4.

8 Exchange3's SMTP server passes the message to the Exchange4 SMTP server.

9 Exchange4's SMTP server performs a lookup and sees that Joe is homed on Exchange4.

10 Exchange4's SMTP server passes the message to the IS.

11 Joe sees a new message appear in his inbox.

Replicating AD

AD is a directory service that is supported and used by Windows 2000. It stores a large and customizable set of objects, such as user objects. These objects can then be tracked and located on the network. Objects contain attributes, such as first name and last name. This service is fully integrated with Exchange 2000 and takes advantage of it by storing its directory information within AD. The ability to be customized is what Cisco Unity takes advantage of. This is why the AD schema is extended during installation. All domain controllers in a forest contain a copy of the same AD database. Once the initial directory is built, AD replicates changed or updated attributes of an object to all other domain controllers in its forest. Once directory replication is complete, subscribers can address messages to anyone in the organization by accessing either the Cisco Unity telephone directory conversation or the Exchange-based GAL.

This section gives a detailed look at the way Cisco Unity interacts with AD.

Figure 10-8 illustrates two Cisco Unity systems in one AD forest.

Figure 10-8 *Two Cisco Unity Systems in a Forest*

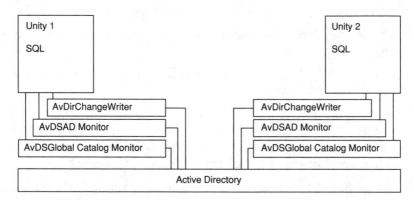

A typical administrative action might be to add a new subscriber using the Cisco Unity Administrator. Figure 10-9 illustrates adding a new user on the server called Unity 1.

Figure 10-9 *New User Added in Unity 1*

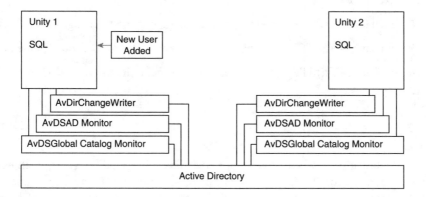

Once the administrator saves the data, it is written to Unity 1's local SQL database. Figure 10-10 illustrates the process of user data being added to the SQL database.

Figure 10-10   *Data Added to SQL Database*

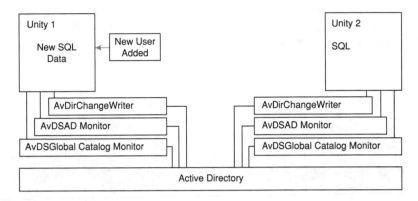

The Unity 1 Directory Change Writer (the Cisco Unity AvDirChangeWriter service) sees the data and sends the relevant pieces of it (detailed earlier, in the section "Understanding Message Transfer and Directory Replication") to AD, as shown in Figure 10-11.

Figure 10-11   *AvDirChangeWriter Sends Data to AD*

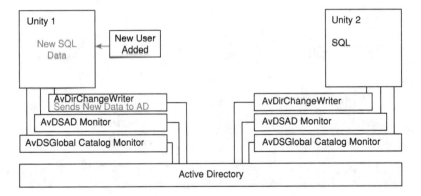

Now that the data is located in AD, it is replicated through the forest on its already established schedule. Figure 10-12 illustrates how the information is distributed across AD.

Figure 10-12 *Information Distributed Across AD*

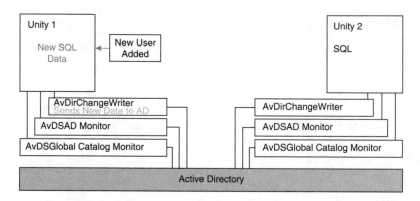

The Unity 2 server's Global Catalog Monitor (the Cisco Unity AvDSGlobalCatalogMonitor service) is a service that continuously monitors AD and notes any changes. Figure 10-13 illustrates how the Global Catalog Monitor service gathers new data from AD.

Figure 10-13 *Global Catalog Monitor Picks Up the Change*

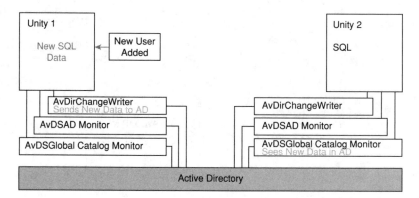

The Global Catalog Monitor passes a message to the Directory Change Writer to send the changes to the local SQL database in Unity 2. Figure 10-14 illustrates how new data is passed on to the SQL database.

Figure 10-14 *AvDirChangeWriter Sends the Data to SQL Database*

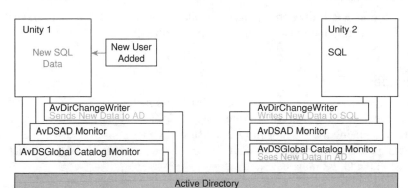

Any subscriber or outside caller who reaches Unity 2 can now address and send messages to the new subscriber on Unity 1. Figure 10-15 illustrates how Cisco Unity becomes aware of a new user on Unity 1.

Figure 10-15 *Unity 2 Knows About the New Unity 1 User*

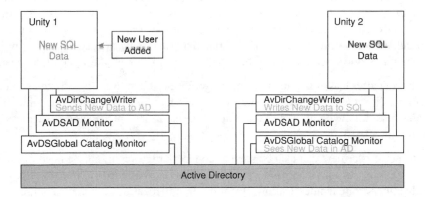

Digital networking in Cisco Unity 4.0 uses the process previously explained. Each Cisco Unity server has a primary location object configured. All subscribers homed on that server are known to all subscribers in the forest, and messages addressed from any Cisco Unity server in the forest will be delivered. This makes digital networking easy to set up and efficient in terms of handling delivery of messages.

Network Subscribers

This section details the options that are available for adding subscribers and presents a decision tree for selecting the most appropriate type of subscribers.

Internet Subscribers

Internet subscribers are used for users who do not have a mailbox in the local message store. They are used for digital networking and SMTP delivery. These subscribers can be manually created by using the Cisco Unity Administrator, under Subscribers. The key parameters when creating these subscribers are that the Subscriber Type must be set to Internet Subscriber and the SMTP address must be set.

Exchange custom recipients, which are called contacts in Windows 2000 and Exchange 2000, are the underlying mechanisms to implement Internet subscribers.

Internet subscribers do not have a local message store. That is because this subscriber's message store is actually located in a remote server. As a result, items such as phone passwords, private lists, conversations, and message notification information are not kept in Cisco Unity.

Internet subscribers do have the option of having a recorded name and greeting, though. The mailboxes created for these users in Cisco Unity are basically pointers to the remote server. The SMTP address is the key information that allows messages to be addressed to the other server. Basically, when a message is left for an Internet subscriber, that message is packaged and sent to the user via e-mail using the Exchange 2000 SMTP gateway, called IMS in Exchange 5.5. The end location could be any other mail server or even another voice-mail system.

When a caller leaves a voice-mail message for an offsite user, the offsite user appears to the caller as if they are actually on site, whereas in fact they may be field technicians or outside sales personnel who are not in the office. Internal users can also address a message to them by using the GAL.

Internet subscribers can also be used to connect offices, without the need of directory replications and message connectors. The administrator needs to individually define Internet subscribers for each destination's location. In organizations that have a large number of users, blind addressing typically is the ideal choice because of the possible administrative overhead involved.

AMIS Subscribers

AMIS-a is a voice-mail standard that is used between AMIS-a-compliant voice-mail systems for communication. Cisco Unity 4.0 has the capability to interface with voice-mail systems that support this protocol. AMIS subscribers, which are similar to Internet subscribers, are used in Cisco Unity to represent a user on a remote messaging server. The main difference is that the AMIS subscriber message store is homed on a different voice-mail system whereas the Internet subscriber message store is set up on another e-mail system. AMIS subscribers are set up as contacts in AD or custom recipients in Exchange 5.5.

AMIS subscribers contain items that have similar limitations as Internet subscribers. All options that relate to the local message store are unavailable. AMIS subscribers cannot log on to Cisco Unity via the telephone or use the Cisco Unity Assistant to change personal settings. They also cannot own local private lists, receive message notification, or receive message waiting indicators (MWIs) through Cisco Unity. When messages are sent to an AMIS subscriber, the message is sent to the other voice-mail system through calls via analog lines. Once the message is sent to the other voice-mail system, it is up to the receiving server to provide a message store and its features (that is, MWI and so on).

When you create an AMIS subscriber, you must set three key parameters: you must set the Subscriber Type to AMIS subscriber, populate the remote mailbox number extension, and select the location of the remote voice-mail system. (Normally, this would be the subscriber's extension number on the remote voice-messaging server.)

VPIM Subscribers

VPIM is another specification that is used by messaging systems to communicate with each other. Cisco Unity 4.0 has the capability to interface with voice-mail systems that support this standard. VPIM subscribers are similar to AMIS subscribers, as each does not have a local mail store on the local Exchange server. The VPIM subscriber's message store is located in a different voice-mail system. The main difference between AMIS and VPIM subscribers is that VPIM uses SMTP to deliver messages to the other voice-mail systems whereas AMIS uses analog lines. VPIM subscribers would be set up as contacts in AD.

VPIM subscribers contain items that have similar limitations as AMIS subscribers. All options that relate to the local message store are unavailable. VPIM subscribers cannot log on to Cisco Unity via the telephone or use Cisco Unity Assistant to change personal settings. They also cannot own local private lists, receive message notifications, or receive MWIs through Cisco Unity.

When you create a VPIM subscriber, you must set three key parameters: set the Subscriber Type to VPIM subscriber, populate the remote mailbox number extension, and select the location of the remote voice-mail system. (Normally, this would be the subscriber's extension number on the remote voice-messaging server.)

Bridge Subscribers

Bridge subscribers in Cisco Unity 4.0 are used when interfacing with an Octel analog voice-mail system. The Cisco Unity Bridge server is used as a networking gateway to connect to an analog Octel network. Bridge subscribers are very similar to AMIS and Internet subscribers. The main difference is that the Bridge subscriber's message store resides on the Octel voice-mail system.

Bridge, VPIM, and AMIS subscribers all share the other features that regular Cisco Unity subscribers do. An off-campus telephone number can be assigned to them and calls will be transferred to that number. Callers can perform a directory lookup and leave a message for these subscribers, although this can be restricted. They can also be part of distribution lists. The availability of these different types of subscribers enables you to connect Cisco Unity to other voice-mail systems while maintaining a transparent look and feel to outside callers.

Selecting Subscriber Addressing

This section provides information on the choices that are available when determining the best implementation for particular scenarios.

The flowchart shown in Figure 10-16 represents a decision tree for choosing what type(s) of subscribers to create on a Cisco Unity server. The choices are not mutually exclusive.

Figure 10-16 *Choosing Subscriber Addressing*

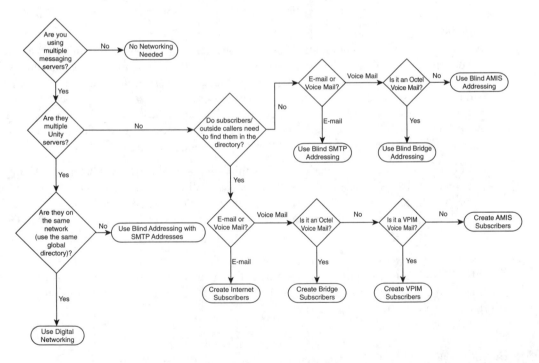

If you connect messaging servers that are not Cisco Unity servers and you want callers to be able to find those messaging servers' subscribers in the directory, then you would implement them as AMIS, VPIM, Internet, or Bridge subscribers. The one you should choose depends on the target server. If the target servers are not Cisco Unity servers and you do not wish to have the subscribers listed in the directory, then blind addressing is your best option.

Blind addressing can be defined by; when a subscriber addresses a message to a location, once the subscriber receives a confirmation that it has reached the proper location (the other messaging server), the subscriber can blindly address a message to a remote subscriber.

If there are multiple different messaging targets in an organization, it may require several of the subscriber addressing options.

After asking the administrator a series of three or four questions, you can determine which type of target server and what kind of addressing to use. First, find out whether all the target servers are Cisco Unity servers and, if they are, whether they all use the same global directory. If they do, then implementing digital networking is the best choice. If not, blind SMTP addressing will work best for you.

Implementing Digital Networking in Cisco Unity

Digital networking is a feature that allows subscribers to exchange voice messages among one another in organizations that have multiple Cisco Unity servers in one global directory. This section presents how to implement digital networking and the different components involved based on organizational requirements.

Digital networking by default is enabled on every Cisco Unity server. It is important to understand the basic concepts of digital networking and the details of how to implement it in order to provide customers with the best solution for their specific needs.

To benefit fully from this section, it is recommended that you have these prerequisite skills and knowledge:

- Knowledge of the Cisco Unity standard and optional features (see Chapter 1)
- Knowledge of Cisco Unity messaging call flow (see Chapter 1)
- Understanding of concepts presented in the "Cisco Unity Networking Fundamentals" section of this chapter

Understanding Location Objects and Digital Networking

Location objects play an important role when you are using digital networking. When Cisco Unity is first installed, the installation creates a default location called the primary location object. It cannot be deleted, because it represents the local subscribers. As subscribers are added to Cisco Unity, they become members of this location. The Cisco Unity Administrator allows you to create additional location objects, called delivery locations, that represent other remote messaging servers, including Cisco Unity systems. If a location is created on a Cisco Unity server, the other Cisco Unity servers on the same AD forest will be able to see the new location. Locations can be found in the Cisco Unity Administrator under Network.

When a new location is created, this information is passed along to the global directory. Each Cisco Unity server has a Directory Monitor service that checks the global directory for any changes every 15 minutes. As a result, other Cisco Unity servers may not immediately see that information.

NOTE   The primary location object contains information that Cisco Unity needs to route messages between Cisco Unity servers. Its name should reflect a geographical location.

Location objects can be grouped together using a property called a Dialing Domain ID. The grouping together of location objects allows you to create a virtual group that spans multiple Cisco Unity servers by assigning them all the same Dialing Domain ID. Location objects are used to easily span sites or other networking boundaries and to provide "transparent" dialing capabilities to customers that have networked telephone switches.

NOTE   A Dialing Domain ID provides a way to group locations for purposes of performing searches. This makes searches efficient because they do not have to be performed for the entire global directory.

In Cisco Unity, subscribers and any other system objects can be associated only with the primary location object that is created during initial installation. All other location objects are used solely for addressing purposes.

When outside callers use the Cisco Unity directory, they are presented with a list of names that includes members of the primary location object. Directory search options, which are also called addressing options, can be configured so that all other administrator-created locations are available to callers. Users who are associated with any location object other than the default object may be added to public and private distribution lists or added to message address lists by subscribers only.

When you define the primary location object, you give it a unique Dial ID. Creating a dial plan for your organization that will result in callers reaching subscribers correctly and efficiently is very important, so be sure that the Dial IDs do not conflict with previously assigned IDs.

NOTE   A Dial ID for a location is a unique numeric location identifier. By default, the minimum length is three digits, but that can be changed. Its maximum is ten digits. If Dial IDs are set with one or two digits, they may conflict with private distribution list IDs when searches are performed.

In the Cisco Unity Administrator, all location objects are visible within one global directory. However, only the administrator can edit and delete the delivery location objects that were created on their Cisco Unity system. Location objects that replicate from other sites are read-only.

The original location object that is installed with the system (the primary location object) can be edited but not deleted from the system. When primary location objects are replicated to the other Cisco Unity servers, they appear as delivery location objects there. Primary location objects should contain a meaningful name so that when they appear as delivery locations on the other servers, they can easily be identified.

Implementing Digital Networking

Before you set up digital networking, you must meet some prerequisites, which this section explains for both Domino and Exchange environments.

Subscribers who require digital networking must be able to access and address each other. Practically, this means that in a Domino environment, all the partner servers must be in the same Notes domain. Each Cisco Unity server monitors the primary Domino directory for the domain names.nsf file. In an Exchange environment, all servers must be members of the same AD forest, be members of the same Exchange 5.5 site, or be members of sites in an Exchange 5.5 organization that are connected through directory replication.

When these conditions are met, all subscribers will be able to see all locations and subscribers at the other locations.

Setting Up Digital Networking

Here is a quick list of the general steps involved when setting up digital networking:

Step 1   Make dial plan decisions based on the specific organizational requirements.

Step 2   Customize primary location objects on all Cisco Unity servers, which controls which subscribers local users will be able to find.

Step 3   Set search options.

Step 4   Add alternate extensions (optional).

Step 5   Set up Cisco Unity Automated Attendant transfers (optional).

An optional step would be to assign alternate extensions. One reason you may want to implement the optional fourth step is to match an extension address with the number that other subscribers use to call that extension directly. For example, if someone's extension is 5445222 but subscribers dial 85445222 to reach them directly, you would enter 85445222 as an alternate extension. Another reason you may want to add alternate extensions is to provide easy message access (automatic sign-in to a subscriber account) from telephones other than the subscriber's primary extension.

If the Cisco Unity servers are attached to a networked telephone system, then you should follow the optional fifth step to set up Cisco Unity Automated Attendant transfers. If each Cisco Unity server is integrated with a separate phone system, this step is not necessary.

Using Search Options

Search options (also called addressing options) are configured on each of the primary locations. These options are used to define how extensive a search may be in several cases, such as when a local subscriber is addressing a message, when local subscribers are being added to public or private distribution lists, when callers reach the local opening greeting for your company, or when an outside caller is looking for a subscriber in the directory. The primary location on each of the other servers performs the same function for that server's local subscribers. These locations work in conjunction with the dialing domain and global directory.

The administrator can limit the searches to the local server, the dialing domain (when the server is part of one), or to the entire global directory, as shown in Figure 10-17. The searches are normally configured based on the customer's requirements. In addition, locations can also be included when subscribers are searching for a subscriber. Basically, this allows them to dial the Dial ID that is assigned to the remote location, before they enter the subscriber extension. These options are located on the primary location addressing options. If the locations check box is unchecked, the Dial ID of the remote location will not be found during a search.

Figure 10-17 *Search Options*

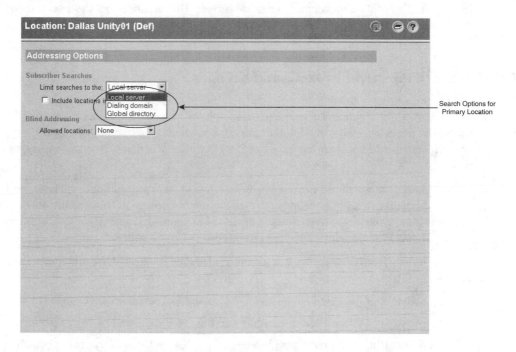

Understanding Dialing Domains

In a networked phone system, subscribers can dial one another without having to use a trunk access code or prefix. On a networked phone system, all extensions must be unique. If a company has several Cisco Unity servers, with some attached to a networked phone system and others attached to separate phone systems, then the networked phone systems and the separate systems may have an overlapping dial plan. Cisco Unity addresses this issue by introducing dialing domains in Cisco Unity 4.0. A dialing domain is a collection of Cisco Unity servers that are integrated with the same phone system or phone system network. A dialing domain is a group scheme that allows Cisco Unity to handle overlapping dial plans by having multiple dialing domains.

Subscribers can address messages directly to subscribers who reside on other Cisco Unity systems (and if alternate extensions are implemented, this number may be the same number they use to reach the subscriber directly by telephone). Subscribers who are on any Cisco Unity server within the dialing domain can be added to public or private distribution lists. Outside callers who dial in to any Cisco Unity server in the dialing domain can look up any subscriber in the directory and be transferred to that subscriber. This assumes that the search scope has been expanded to include the dialing domain.

Understanding SMTP Networking

SMTP networking is yet another powerful instrument that Cisco Unity uses to allow local subscribers to send voice-mail messages to recipients who reside on remote servers. E-mail users who are connected to the Internet can be sent voice mail. Even other Cisco Unity subscribers who do not share the same directory as the local server can be sent messages in this way.

Your organization may have specific needs for some of its voice-mail users. These needs may require that you extend to someone outside the directory on which Cisco Unity resides the ability to send a message. To meet these needs, SMTP networking enables you to extend this capability to any messaging system on the Internet that uses SMTP.

To benefit fully from this section, it is recommended that you have these prerequisite skills and knowledge:

- Knowledge of the Cisco Unity standard and optional features (see Chapter 1)
- Knowledge of Cisco Unity messaging call flow (see Chapter 1)
- Understanding of the concepts presented in the "Cisco Unity Networking Fundamentals" section of this chapter

Using SMTP Networking

SMTP, which is defined by Internet Engineering Task Force (IETF) RFC 821, is a messaging service that enables mail servers to deliver messages among one another. This service works in conjunction with Post Office Protocol version 3 (POP3) and Internet Message Access Protocol 4 (IMAP4) to provide end users the availability of e-mail to their desktops. POP3 provides end users the ability to retrieve their messages even if they are not connected to the messaging server on the Internet. Normally, users have some type of dial-up connection to the Internet, using an Internet service provider (a point-of-presence provider). Once they have established that connection, they can connect to the mail server and download their messages. IMAP works basically the same way; however, instead of first downloading all the messages, it first downloads the header of each message for purposes of reducing the amount of data that is sent to the client. IMAP and POP3 are not required if there is a permanent connection to the messaging servers.

Exchange 5.5 uses the IMS connector to provide Internet messaging capabilities. IMS uses the SMTP, POP3, and IMAP4 protocols to provide this service. By default, IMS is not configured on a new Exchange 5.5 server; you use the Exchange Administrator tool to configure it. Before you configure it, though, IMS requires a Domain Name System (DNS) server for the purpose of resolving the fully qualified domain name (FQDN) and delivering the messages.

When users are created in Exchange, an SMTP address is automatically generated for them also. By default, Exchange uses the user's alias followed by @ExchangeSiteName.ExchangeOrganizationName.com. The format of this address can by modified to accommodate organizational needs. For example, if the organization is a university, the address requires an .edu extension. It is common for administrators to remove ExchangeSiteName from the default naming address for purposes of simplifying the sending of SMTP mail.

IMS is used to deliver messages to Exchange and non-Exchange servers. DNS is used to help locate the domain for the intended recipient. Once the domain is located, Exchange connects to the remote e-mail server on that domain and sends the message across.

In Exchange 2000, SMTP is used in a variety of ways. SMTP is one of the services installed when setting up Internet Information Server (IIS). Exchange 2000 uses SMTP as its message transport method, even before the administrator installs the SMTP connector. Exchange 2000 uses SMTP for the delivery of messages. When the SMTP connector in Exchange is installed, it enhances the functionality and manageability of the existing SMTP service for Exchange. Some examples of these enhancements are the capability to relay messages to particular domains, add inbound/outbound security, and define routes for traffic.

To ensure that AD and Exchange 2000 work well in an organization, DNS must be designed and configured correctly.

Cisco Unity uses the SMTP connector provided in Exchange 2000 (known as IMS in Exchange 5.5) to deliver messages to other Cisco Unity servers that do not share the same local directory. The SMTP connector also delivers messages to messaging servers that are not Cisco Unity servers but that also use SMTP. The SMTP connector is used to send and receive messages from messaging servers that also support SMTP. This can be either an Exchange server or a non-Exchange server on the Internet. This functionality is extended to Cisco Unity when the connector is properly installed.

Using SMTP to deliver messages to remote mail servers has many advantages over using other protocols. However, one of its disadvantages is the fact that when Cisco Unity sends a voice-mail message to a subscriber on a remote server using the SMTP connector, the Cisco Unity voice attributes are not preserved. This means that when the message arrives at the remote server, the message appears as a regular e-mail with a WAV attachment. In addition, if the Cisco Unity subscriber does not belong to the same local Exchange organization directory, then they need to be configured in Exchange in a specific way to preserve the Cisco Unity attributes. They must either be added manually to the Exchange directory as custom recipients or be added on each local e-mail client such as Microsoft Outlook. They can be added as address book entries in the personal address book on the client.

Cisco Unity addresses these concerns by using IVC along with SMTP networking to retain the Cisco Unity voice attributes when messages are sent across the Internet. When installed, IVC registers with the local Exchange server so that it may handle all the messages with type VOICE. When Exchange receives a VOICE message, it redirects it to IVC. IVC repackages the message in MIME format and hands it off to the SMTP service, which then sends it across to the intended recipient. Once the message is received by the target server (assuming that the server also is Cisco Unity with IVC implemented), it is sent to IVC, which in turn reconverts the message while maintaining the VOICE attributes. The message then is delivered to the subscriber as a voice-mail message. This means that the subscriber gets an MWI lamp and can pick up the message over the phone or the desktop. If the target server does not have IVC installed, then these messages are sent as e-mail with a WAV file attachment.

Setting Up SMTP Networking

Here is a quick list of the general steps that are involved when you set up SMTP networking:

Step 1   Make dial plan decisions.

Step 2   Install IMS (Exchange 5.5).

Step 3   Verify SMTP connectivity.

Step 4   Install IVC (if remote subscribers are on Cisco Unity).

Step 5   Customize the primary location object.

Step 6   Set addressing and search options.

Step 7   Create delivery locations (if remote subscribers are on Cisco Unity).

Step 8   Create Internet subscriber accounts.

The steps required to set up SMTP networking between a Cisco Unity server and another messaging system are similar to the steps required to set up digital networking. The only difference is that with SMTP, IVC must be installed.

Dial planning is also an important factor when you are implementing SMTP networking. Dial planning means making sure that there are no conflicting IDs that could potentially confuse someone who is searching for a subscriber. If Exchange 5.5 is the server used, IMS must be installed on the server that IVC will be installed on. However, this is not required in Exchange 2000 because SMTP is the default messaging transport method used.

After you install IMS and confirm successful connectivity, the next step is to install IVC, which should be installed if one or more of the remote servers are Cisco Unity systems. There should be only one installation of IVC for an Exchange 5.5 or AD forest. Make sure the latest version of IVC is installed. If a previous version is already installed, you must remove it before you install the latest version.

Figure 10-18 shows the first menu that you see when you start the IVC setup for Exchange 2000.

Figure 10-18 *IVC Setup for Exchange 2000*

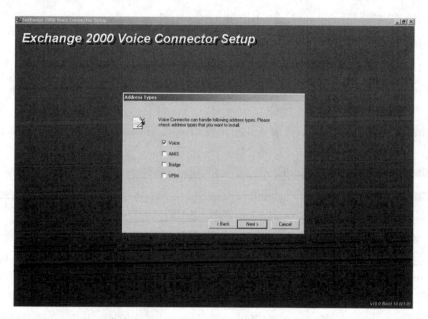

The next step after you install IVC is to customize the primary location object on the Cisco Unity server. This includes populating the name field and Dial ID and recording a voice name. If suitable, you can also make the location object a member of the dialing domain. The dialing domain needs to be entered only once from a Cisco Unity server if you are creating a new one. The rest of the servers in that domain will be able to select it after replication takes place.

The next step is to enter the SMTP domain name. If the domain has more than one Cisco Unity server using SMTP networking, then you must configure the primary location of all the servers, especially the SMTP domain name. If this is not configured, then SMTP networking will not work for subscribers on the other Cisco Unity servers.

SMTP networking carries the same set of considerations as digital networking when you are setting up addressing and search options. You should create delivery locations for each remote Cisco Unity server also.

The following is the general information included in a delivery location object: the location name, a Dialing Domain ID, a recorded name, the destination type, and the SMTP domain name. Each specific delivery location, however, such as SMTP, AMIS, and VPIM delivery locations, has its own specific settings. The settings for each type of delivery location are covered later in the chapter in each of their own delivery location section.

The following are the steps for creating a delivery location object for SMTP:

Step 1 Open the Cisco Unity Administration tool.

Step 2 Under Network, select Delivery Options.

Step 3 Click the plus command icon to create a new delivery location.

Step 4 Fill in the Name, which will represent the remote messaging server (for example, UNITY04).

Step 5 Assign a Dial ID that will be used to reach this remote location (for example, 555).

Step 6 For the purpose of this exercise, select SMTP as the location type.

Step 7 Fill in the SMTP with the domain of the remote messaging system, without adding the @ sign, such as unity40Domain.cisco.com.

Step 8 Click Add to insert the delivery location into the database.

Adding the location object is one of several steps involved in setting up networking for Cisco Unity. As a reminder, you create delivery locations for remote messaging systems that are not part of the same global directory.

Just as in dialing domains, you should create the delivery locations on one server in the network. If there are multiple Cisco Unity servers in the same directory, they will be able to access the newly created location because the location data is stored in the global directory and will be replicated to the entire Cisco Unity server there.

Adding Internet Subscribers

Internet subscribers are another type of voice-mail recipient used in Cisco Unity. They are used with SMTP networking for users who do not have a local message store in Exchange. In other words, they are used for sending mail to users homed on remote messaging servers. When you add a new subscriber through the Cisco Unity Administrator, if you change the Subscriber Type to Internet, a new field called SMTP Address appears at the bottom of the page, as shown in Figure 10-19. This basically is the e-mail address of the remote user, such as JohnDoe@evvbu.lab3.cisco.com. When Internet subscribers are created in Cisco Unity, they are created in Exchange 2000/Windows 2000 as mail-enabled contacts and in Exchange 5.5 as Exchange custom recipients. These users do not have a local Exchange message store.

Figure 10-19   *Adding a New Internet Subscriber with Internet Subscriber Key Components*

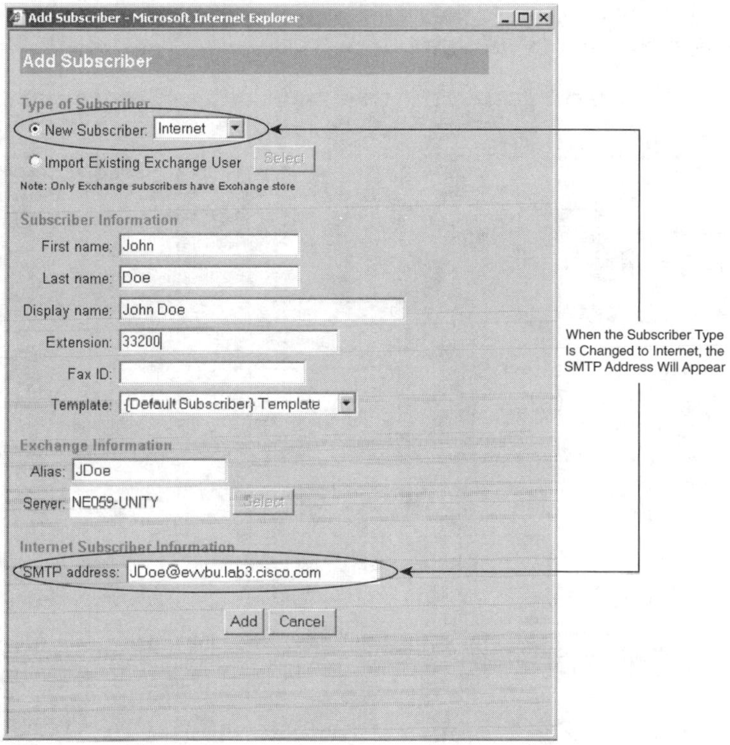

Making good dial plan decisions before you implement SMTP networking is very important. When you create Internet subscribers for another remote Cisco Unity server, you assign to them the Dial ID of the remote server (delivery location) within their SMTP address. If the administrator of the remote server changes its Dial ID, you need to manually change the Dial ID assignment of each of the existing Internet subscribers. The Extension Addresses Utility, which is normally used to modify subscribers, cannot be used to modify this action.

Internet subscribers in Cisco Unity enable users to send a voice-mail message to a user even though the Internet Subscriber's message store is not local. Because the message store is not local, the setup options that normally are available with the message store are not available, as identified in Figure 10-20. That means the following personalized options are not configurable for these subscribers using the Cisco Unity Administrator: view and set account status, set a billing ID, set a logon password, create and edit personalized groups of message recipients, set options for what callers hear when interacting with Cisco Unity, and set device and schedule options.

Figure 10-20 *Options for an Internet Subscriber*

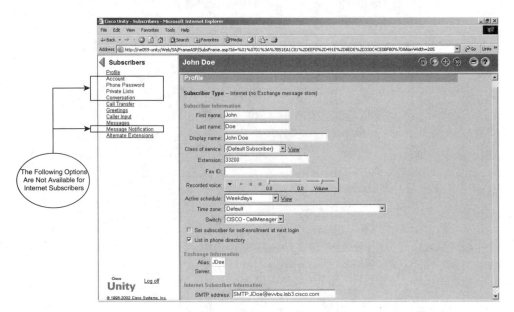

An Internet subscriber is a pointer to a remote mail server. The SMTP address for these subscribers is the key element. Internal and outside users can send voice-mail messages to these subscribers. Internal users benefit even further because they can address Internet subscribers by using the GAL. Internet subscribers also have the option of having a recorded name and the different types of greetings that are available to regular subscribers. Because Internet subscribers do not have access to Cisco Unity via the Telephone User Interface (TUI) or Cisco Personal Communications Assistant (CPCA), the administrator must record these for them. When a message is left for the Internet subscriber, the message is actually delivered out of the SMTP gateway (IMS), to the Internet, and then to IMS. The messaging server can also be a mail server of another voice-mail system. For the person who is leaving the voice-mail message, an Internet subscriber is presented just like any other regular subscriber on the Cisco Unity system.

With Internet subscribers, you also have the option to link offices without setting up messaging connectors and directory replication connectors between sites. The administrator must set up Internet subscribers for each destination location. If the organization has a large number of users, blind addressing would be more practical to use.

When Internet subscribers are used, the remote messaging server can be a Cisco Unity system also. If it is not, the voice-mail messages that are sent will arrive at the other messaging server as WAV attachments in e-mails.

Internet subscribers have certain limitations in terms of using Cisco Unity. They cannot log on to Cisco Unity either over the phone or using Cisco Unity Assistant. As a result, they cannot adjust personal settings identified earlier in Figure 10-20. In addition they cannot use VMO or Cisco Unity Inbox. The underlying reason for these limitations is that Internet subscribers do not have a local mailbox in Exchange.

Understanding VPIM Networking

VPIM is a standard used by different messaging systems to exchange voice, fax, and text messages among different systems over the Internet or a TCP/IP network. VPIM networking enables Cisco Unity to exchange this type of information with other systems that are also using VPIM. This section presents the basic concepts and procedures involved with VPIM networking and Cisco Unity.

If your organization needs to exchange messages between Cisco Unity and a VPIM-compliant messaging server, then you need to understand how VPIM works and the procedures for setting it up in Cisco Unity. Once it is set up, callers will have a transparent experience when messaging across the systems.

To benefit fully from this section, it is recommended that you have these prerequisite skills and knowledge:

- Knowledge of the standard and optional Cisco Unity features (see Chapter 1)
- Knowledge of how Cisco Unity messaging handles calls (see Chapter 2, "Using Your Cisco Unified Communications System")
- Understanding of the concepts presented in the "Cisco Unity Networking Fundamentals" section of this chapter

VPIM Networking and VPIM Messages

VPIM is a standard that was introduced in the industry for the intended purpose of having a common format for exchanging different types of messages digitally among messaging systems. It is based on the SMTP and MIME protocols. Voice, fax, and text can be exchanged over the Internet or on a TCP/IP network. As a result, organizations can potentially save on long-distance toll charges for messages sent among messaging systems.

VPIM defines the format of the messages, the protocols used, and the message addresses exchanged between two VPIM-compliant messaging systems. It is up to the messaging servers to specify how these messages are handled and presented to the end users. The type of client application used is an example of an item that varies depending on the actual messaging system used. Some servers may provide access to these messages through a telephone, an e-mail client application, or both. More information about the VPIM standard is available at http://www.ema.org/vpim.

VPIM networking is a licensed feature in Cisco Unity and is used with Microsoft Exchange 5.5/2000 integrations. If multiple Cisco Unity servers are networked together, then only one Cisco Unity server requires the VPIM license and configuration for VPIM networking. Licensing information can be viewed by using the Cisco Unity License Manager.

Figure 10-21 shows where you can check whether you are licensed for VPIM.

Figure 10-21 *VPIM Licensing*

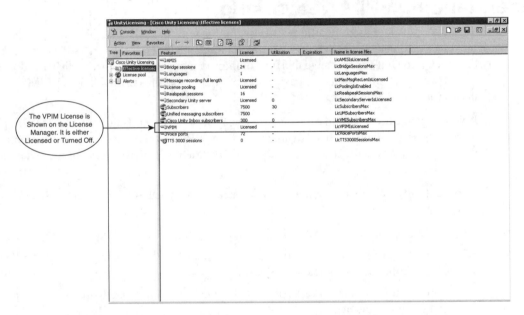

VPIM messages can contain several different types of MIME-encoded pieces, such as a voice message, a fax message, a text message, the sender's spoken name, or even a vCard, which is an electronic business card.

TIP

Cisco Unity can be configured to include the spoken name and vCard for outgoing messages. This is set using the Cisco Unity Administrator tool on the VPIM Delivery Location page.

For incoming messages, Cisco Unity allows the spoken name to be included in the message if it is attached as a WAV file. This means, for example, that when a subscriber receives a voice message, the subscriber can hear the spoken name of the sender first, then the actual voice message. In addition, a vCard sent to Cisco Unity can be viewed from a subscriber's Outlook client using VMO. Voice messages that are sent across VPIM are encoded using the International Telecommunication Union (ITU) G.726 Adaptive Differential Pulse Code

Modulation (ADPCM) standard, and fax messages are encoded using the Tagged Image File Format, class F (TIFF-F) standard.

When Cisco Unity records a message, it records it in the format defined in Cisco Unity. When a message is addressed to a subscriber on a remote VPIM-compliant messaging system, the VPIM connector converts the message into the G.726 standard. The same is true when a subscriber receives a message from a messaging system. Cisco Unity receives the message in the G.726 format, and then IVC converts it to what Cisco Unity is defined to, so that its local subscribers will be able to hear the message correctly.

NOTE   Cisco Unity is able to accept from a VPIM-compliant messaging system messages that are encoded using the G.711, G.726, and GSM standards. The default is G.726.

When you are setting up VPIM, you must insert a VPIM delivery location object. When VPIM messages are addressed, VPIM uses the information set up in the VPIM delivery location object to format the To: field of the message. It also uses the information from the primary location object to format the From: field of the message being sent.

Setting Up VPIM Networking

Here is a quick list of the general steps that are involved when you set up VPIM networking:

Step 1   Make dial plan decisions and gather network information.

Step 2   Verify SMTP connectivity.

Step 3   Extend the AD schema.

Step 4   Install IVC and SMTP Transport Event Sink.

Step 5   Customize the primary location object.

Step 6   Set addressing and search options.

Step 7   Create delivery locations for the remote system for VPIM.

Step 8   Create VPIM subscriber accounts (optional).

Step 9   Set up the remote system for VPIM.

The steps required to set up VPIM networking are similar to the steps required to set up SMTP and digital networking. Dial planning is an important factor when implementing VPIM. Dial planning means making sure that there are no conflicting Dial IDs that could potentially confuse someone who is searching for a subscriber. One of the first things you need to test is the SMTP connectivity between the messaging servers. VPIM is dependent on this because it uses MIME and SMTP.

NOTE Be sure that the SMTP service is running on the Exchange server that the VPIM connector will be installed on and also that the SMTP service or gateway is properly installed on the remote messaging server. More information on this can be found at Cisco.com in the *Networking in Cisco Unity Guide (with Microsoft Exchange).*

The next step is to further extend the AD schema specifically for VPIM networking. You accomplish this by using the AD Schema Setup utility found on the Cisco Unity CD 1. Instructions for this are located in the *Networking in Cisco Unity Guide (with Microsoft Exchange)*, which is available at Cisco.com.

Extending the schema for VPIM means adding information to the Cisco Unity location object class. Keep in mind that this may not be the same extension performed while first installing Cisco Unity. More information about the schema changes made are located in a file called vpimgateway.ldf, which is located on Cisco Unity CD 1 in the Schema\LdifScripts directory.

TIP Creating a VPIM delivery location will be unsuccessful if you do not extend the schema for VPIM first. If you attempt to create this delivery location and it does not appear locally on your server, the schema may be the issue.

After you extend the schema and test connectivity, the next step is to install IVC on an Exchange 2000 server. Although the installation is only supported on Exchange 2000, it is also supported on a mixed-mode environment that includes Exchange 2000. There should be only one installation of IVC for an AD forest. Also make sure the latest version of IVC is installed. If a previous version is already present, you must remove it before you install the latest version. During the installation, you are prompted to choose whether to install the SMTP Transport Event Sink, using the check box option shown in Figure 10-22. By default, this option is unchecked. Install this component on all the messaging servers that will be accepting incoming VPIM messages. This means that if only one server will be receiving these types of messages in the organization, that system is the only one that requires the SMTP Transport Event Sink.

Figure 10-22   *VPIM IVC Setup Option to Install the SMTP Transport Event Sink*

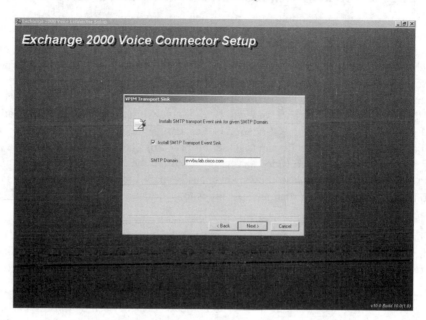

The next step after you install IVC is to customize the primary location object on the Cisco Unity server. This includes populating the name field and Dial ID and recording a voice name. If suitable, you can also make the location object a member of the dialing domain. The dialing domain needs to be entered only once from a Cisco Unity server if you are creating a new one. The rest of the Cisco Unity servers in that domain will be able to select it after replication takes place.

Entering the SMTP domain name is the next step. If the domain has more than one Cisco Unity server using digital networking, then you must configure the primary location of all the servers, especially the SMTP domain name. If this is not configured, then VPIM networking will not work for subscribers on the other Cisco Unity servers.

VPIM networking carries the same set of considerations as digital networking when you are setting up addressing and search options. You should create VPIM delivery locations for each remote voice-messaging server. Just as in dialing domains, you should create the delivery locations on one server in the network. If multiple Cisco Unity servers are networked together, they will be able to access the newly created location because the location data is stored in the directory.

Creating the VPIM subscribers is the next step. These are created only for users who would like to appear in the corporate directory. The final step is to configure the remote system for VPIM networking.

Understanding Location Objects and VPIM Networking

Location objects play an important role when you are using VPIM networking. When you install Cisco Unity, the installation creates a single default location referred to as the primary location object (named Default Location Object when Cisco Unity is first installed). As subscribers are added to Cisco Unity, they become members of this location. The Cisco Unity Administrator allows you to create additional location objects that represent other messaging servers, including Cisco Unity. If you are on the same AD forest, you do not need to create additional locations, because they will be available within minutes of their creation as default objects on the other systems. Location objects can be linked together using a property called a Dialing Domain ID. The linking together of these objects allows you to create a meta-location that spans multiple Cisco Unity servers by assigning them all the same Dialing Domain ID. Using Dialing Domains also allows you to easily span sites or other networking boundaries and to provide "transparent" dialing capabilities to customers who have networked telephone switches.

On a Cisco Unity system, subscribers and any other system objects can be associated only with the primary location object that is created by the setup program. All delivery location objects are used solely for remote addressing purposes.

When outside callers use the Cisco Unity directory, they are presented with a list of names that includes members of the primary location object. Directory search options can be configured so that all other administrator-created delivery locations are also available to callers. Users who are associated with any location object other than the default object may be added to public and private distribution lists or added to message address lists by subscribers only.

When you define the primary location object, you assign a Dial ID. Creating a dial plan for your organization that will result in callers reaching subscribers correctly and efficiently is very important, so be sure that the Dial IDs that you create do not conflict with previously assigned IDs. Another key setting on the primary location when using VPIM is the SMTP domain name. The domain is likely to be the same that is used when setting up the Event Sink domain.

Within the primary location, you also define the addressing options. Addressing options are relevant when Cisco Unity subscribers are addressing messages using the telephone. The default search limit is to the local server. This means that local subscribers can address only local subscribers from the Cisco Unity server. This option can be changed to search on the global directory or dialing domain if you have other Cisco Unity servers networked together.

Another option that can be configured on the Primary location page is the Blind Addressing ability of local subscribers to send messages to other locations.

NOTE   When you record a name for the delivery location, and someone is blind addressing, the confirmation they will receive of that location is that location's recorded name.

When you are creating location objects in Cisco Unity, they are all visible in the Cisco Unity Administrator from the Cisco Unity servers within the same global directory. However, only the administrator can modify or delete the locations created on their Cisco Unity server. Locations that are created on other servers are replicated, but they appear as read-only on the rest of the other servers. In addition, the primary location object can be modified but not deleted from any of the Cisco Unity systems.

Figure 10-23 illustrates a VPIM delivery location object.

Figure 10-23 *Delivery Location Object*

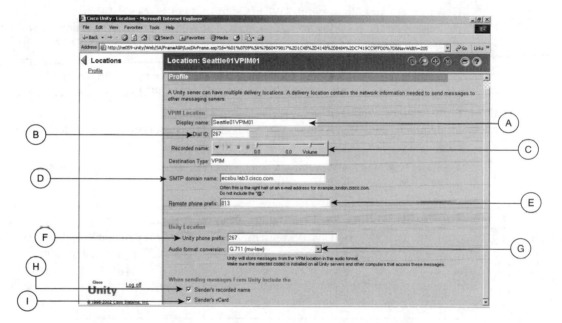

Figure 10-23 is an example of a VPIM delivery location setup on a local Cisco Unity server. The following fields are shown:

- **A. Display Name**—The name given to the delivery location object and the name by which other Cisco Unity servers identify this location.

- **B. Dial ID**—A unique ID given to the delivery location for the purpose of blind addressing to this location.

- **C. Recorded Name**—The recording that is played if a caller dials the Dial ID of this location to find a subscriber. The recorded name is played to the caller so that they can determine whether they have reached the proper location before they search for a subscriber there.

- **D. SMTP Domain Name**—The domain of the remote messaging system.

- **E. Remote Phone Prefix**—Used to prefix the address of the intended recipient for delivery. It is added to the outgoing messages intended to this remote location. The number 813 appears in Figure 10-23. Normally, this number represents the remote location Dial ID number. It is used in conjunction with the SMTP domain name, along with the sender's extension number. An example of the address of a message being delivered to remote subscriber 5000 would be 8135000@ecsbu.lab3.cisco.com.

- **F. Unity Phone Prefix**—This is the number that is used to construct addresses for Cisco Unity subscribers that send messages to the VPIM voice-mail system associated with this location.

- **G. Audio Format Conversion**—When Cisco Unity receives a message from a remote messaging server, it arrives in G.726 format. The Audio Format Conversion parameter allows you to change that to G.711 (mu-law), the default, G.729a, or GSM 6.11, or you can choose not to convert it at all. The purpose of this is to change the format to one defined for your local subscribers. Also, if you choose not to convert the incoming messages, be aware of the format in which the remote VPIM systems are sending the messages.

- **H. Sender's Recorded Name**—When this check box is checked, the sender's recorded name is sent along with the voice message that is sent.

- **I. Sender's vCard**—When this check box is checked, the sender's vCard is sent along with the voice message that is sent.

NOTE Regarding the Audio Format Conversion setting, if you choose not to convert your incoming VPIM voice messages, you may receive all your messages in G.726 format, depending on your remote messaging server. If this is the case, then the messages are delivered to the subscribers in that format, meaning that every workstation and Cisco Unity server must have that coder/decoder (codec) installed to play the message.

VPIM Networking and IVC

Exchange 2000 is a VPIM-compliant messaging system. When IVC is installed and registered to the Exchange server, VPIM messages are passed to IVC when Exchange is handling these messages. The first thing IVC does is convert the messages from Exchange's native format, MAPI, to MIME. It then formats the To: field by adding the SMTP domain name and prefix of the remote phone prefix specified, based on the correct VPIM Delivery Location page. It also formats the From: field of the message by adding the prefix of the correct Delivery Location page and the Primary Location page's domain name. The outgoing voice message is also converted to G.726 format. If a vCard and a recorded voice name are specified, then they are also attached to the message. Once the message is packaged, it is then placed in the SMTP pickup folder for it to be delivered.

When Cisco Unity receives a message, the SMTP Transport Event Sink first detects it and then redirects the message to IVC. The Event Sink is a component that is used with Cisco Unity to readdress messages and send them to IVC. When IVC receives a message, it checks whether the message was sent by a defined delivery location and whether the intended extension is in fact defined. If any of these do not match, the message is rejected and sent back to the sending original messaging system with a nondelivery report (NDR). If the message is validated and the delivery location is found, IVC starts to prepare the message for local delivery. IVC removes the prefixes placed on the To: and From: fields. IVC then checks that the recipients of the message exist. The message is then converted back from MIME to MAPI. Voice attachments are also converted into the format specified in the VPIM Delivery Location page. The last step is to send the message to Exchange so that it can handle the delivery of it to the subscriber's mailbox.

Adding VPIM Subscribers

VPIM and Internet subscribers are very similar in terms of the information stored in Exchange. They are Cisco Unity subscribers with no mailbox storage on the Exchange mail store. Before you create VPIM subscribers, make sure the delivery locations are created on the server where they will reside.

When you are creating these subscribers, you must specify the VPIM delivery location and the remote mailbox number of the subscribers. Although a Cisco Unity local extension is required, it does not need to be the same as the remote extension.

AD stores VPIM subscribers as contacts. These subscribers can be deleted either individually or by deleting the VPIM delivery location associated with them. This also deletes any VPIM subscriber associated with that delivery location. In any of these cases, the contact information is preserved in AD. Cisco Unity Administrator does not remove this information.

Figure 10-24 shows the window that you use to add a new VPIM subscriber with the VPIM key components.

TIP   The Bulk Import tool can be used to add multiple VPIM subscribers at one time.

The message store options are not available to VPIM subscribers, because they do not have a local message store. Like Internet subscribers, VPIM subscribers cannot log on to Cisco Unity via the telephone or use the Cisco Unity Assistant to receive message notifications, receive MWIs, or own private lists.

Figure 10-24   *Adding a New VPIM Subscriber*

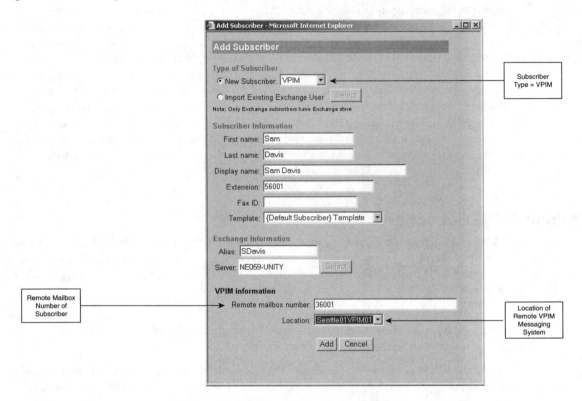

Understanding AMIS Networking

AMIS-a is a Cisco Unity–supported protocol that is used to transfer voice-mail messages among AMIS-compliant messaging systems. This section covers AMIS networking concepts and the overall actions that you take to implement AMIS networking with Cisco Unity.

If you plan to implement Cisco Unity in an environment that requires interaction with an AMIS-compliant voice-messaging system, you need to understand its model and its implementation process.

To benefit fully from this section, it is recommended that you have these prerequisite skills and knowledge:

- General knowledge of the Cisco Unity standard and optional networking features (see Chapter 1)

- Knowledge of Cisco Unity messaging call flow (see Chapter 1)

- Understanding of the concepts presented in the "Cisco Unity Networking Fundamentals" section of this chapter

Using AMIS Networking

The AMIS-a protocol is an industry-standard protocol that allows the exchange of voice messages among voice-messaging systems by using the Public Switched Telephone Network (PSTN) to place calls to transfer the messages. The voice-messaging system uses standard analog telephone lines to accomplish this. AMIS uses nodes to identify each of the voice-mail servers it connects to. Cisco Unity, for example, can be one of the nodes in an AMIS network. The node is a unique identifier that is assigned to each server on this network.

When an AMIS-compliant voice-mail server is ready to transfer a message to a target server, it places a call to the destination node. When the destination answers, the originating node sends its Node ID by sending a sequence of DTMF tones (also called touch-tones). If the destination node identifies the originating node and accepts the call, the originating node sends another series of DTMF tones that identify which subscriber the message is for. The destination node then opens a new message. The originating node proceeds to play the message. Finally, a series of DTMF tones that confirm the call are exchanged.

More information on the DTMF tones that are transmitted during a call can be found in the following white paper at Cisco.com: "AMIS Analog Networking Definitions (for Cisco Unity with Microsoft Exchange)."

AMIS networking is a licensed feature in Cisco Unity. Only one server requires the AMIS license in an organization with multiple Cisco Unity servers. The server with AMIS enabled is treated as the AMIS server. For load-balancing purposes, more AMIS servers can also be added to a network.

Figure 10-25 illustrates Cisco Unity in an AMIS-a mixed environment.

Figure 10-25 *Cisco Unity: AMIS-a*

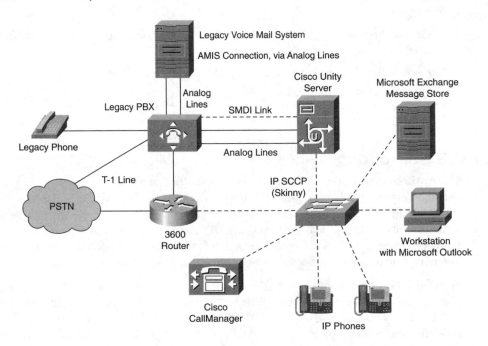

Figure 10-25 shows the versatility that Cisco Unity has as a messaging server. It is capable of assisting an organization that is transitioning its circuit-switched (legacy) PBX to an IP-based PBX network. The drawing contains two switches that are connected to Cisco Unity. One is a circuit-switched telephone system that is connected to Cisco Unity via analog interfaces. The other is a Cisco CallManager, an IP-based PBX that connects to Cisco Unity by using the Cisco IP-based network protocol called Skinny Client Control Protocol (SCCP). Cisco Unity can manage subscribers from both IP telephones and standard single-line extensions attached to the circuit-switched PBX. Cisco Unity can also send and receive voice-mail messages using the AMIS-a protocol through the analog lines connected to the circuit-switched PBX and voice mail.

Setting Up AMIS Networking

Here is a quick list of the general steps involved when setting up AMIS networking:

Step 1 Verify that the destination server is AMIS compliant.

Step 2 Install IVC.

Step 3 For each Cisco Unity server that is handling AMIS calls:

        (a) Create a UAmis mailbox on the AMIS server.

        (b) Designate ports for outbound AMIS calls.

        (c) Customize the primary location object.

        (d) Set addressing and search options.

        (e) Set AMIS delivery options.

        (f) Customize the AMIS restriction table.

        (g) Create delivery locations for each remote AMIS system.

        (h) Create AMIS subscriber accounts.

        (i) Set up a remote system for AMIS.

SMTP, digital, VPIM, and AMIS networking share similarities in terms of their setup, including the IVC installation. However, one distinction AMIS has is that it uses analog telephone lines to exchange voice-mail messages with other systems. As a result, AMIS networking has different setup instructions.

Before you begin, it is important to verify that the destination server is AMIS compliant. A list of supported AMIS servers is available in the *Cisco Unity Pre-Installation Guide* found at Cisco.com.

Installing IVC on an Exchange server is one of the first things to do. As mentioned earlier in the section "Setting Up SMTP Networking," only one installation of IVC should exist on an AD forest, Exchange site, or multisite organization. If an earlier version is already installed, you must remove it before you install the newest version.

NOTE

If you are preparing to install IVC on an Exchange 5.5 server, make sure that your Cisco Unity server is on the same site. Also, verify that IMS is installed.

TIP

Is IVC already installed on your Exchange 5.5/2000 system?

On Exchange 2000, open the Exchange System Manager and locate the Tools instance, within which is a folder called Monitoring and Status. Highlight the subfolder called Status. If IVC is installed, you will see an "AVExchangeIVC_" entry.

On an Exchange 5.5 server, open the Exchange Administrator. Go to **Site > Configuration > Connections**. There you will see an instance of IVC if it is installed.

After you install IVC, you must complete several other steps on each of the AMIS servers on which you will be installing AMIS (if your setup requires multiple AMIS servers).

Step 1   Create the UAmis mailbox on the AMIS server and designate which ports will be used for outbound AMIS calls. In terms of receiving AMIS calls, any port can be used to accept incoming calls.

Step 2   Customize the primary location object on the Cisco Unity server. This includes populating the Name and Dial ID fields and recording a voice name. If suitable, you can also make the location object a member of the dialing domain. The dialing domain needs to be entered only once from a Cisco Unity server if you are creating a new one.

The primary location also contains settings that are specific to AMIS. These are called the AMIS Node ID settings (see Figure 10-26) and they are present only if you are licensed for AMIS. The AMIS Node ID contains the country code, area code, and phone number. When combined, they make up the Node ID, which is sent through DTMF tones along with any voice messages that are intended for a remote AMIS node. This is how the remote AMIS node identifies the calling node. The only required field of these three is the phone number, because some voice-messaging systems only require this number. When configuring the country code and area code, they must match what is expected on the target system (which may not be called area code). This is important for international numbers.

Figure 10-26   *Primary Location with AMIS Options*

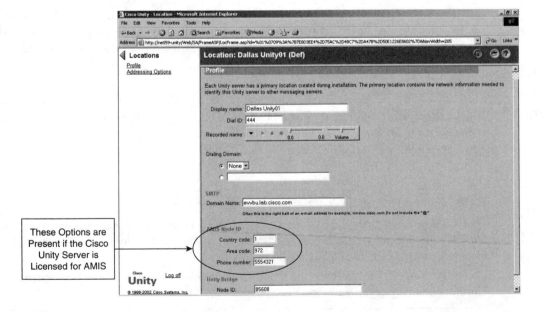

AMIS networking carries the same set of considerations as digital, SMTP, and VPIM networking when you are setting up addressing and search options. Whenever there is an incoming AMIS message to a Cisco Unity server, it will use the search and addressing settings on the primary location to locate the subscriber.

In addition, you must create a delivery location for the remote AMIS messaging system. If multiple Cisco Unity servers are networked together, they will be able to access the newly created locations, because the location data is stored in the directory.

The next step is to decide whether to create the AMIS subscribers or use blind addressing. You create AMIS subscribers only for users who would like to appear in the corporate directory. The final step is to configure the remote system for AMIS networking.

Assigning Port Usage and Schedules

A Cisco Unity system that will be used for outgoing AMIS calls must be assigned ports to use for this purpose. All ports that are set for outgoing calls can be used for inbound AMIS calls as well. By their nature, AMIS calls can be lengthy; a 5-minute message sent to a target AMIS server takes 5 minutes to transmit the message, plus the time needed for the two servers to set up the transfer. Some of this overhead takes place with every call. A 2-minute message, for example, that is sent to a distribution list of 200 AMIS recipients is sent individually to each recipient. That message will take at least 6 hours and 40 minutes to successfully transmit $((2\times200)/60)$.

TIP	When logged in as a Cisco Unity administrator, you can use these tools to configure AMIS delivery ports: Cisco Unity Administrator–Ports page, and UTIM. Each offers the same configuration functionality for this.

When multiple ports are set up to handle outbound AMIS calls, the load is spread out among them. When multiple messages are queued for a single destination, messages are grouped in batches of nine and each batch is sent to a different port for load balancing. When multiple destinations are involved, separate ports are used for each destination.

You can set up AMIS schedules so that transmission of voice-mail messages takes place at times of lower system activity. After-business hours are generally times of less activity. You can base this consideration on how many AMIS calls and how much activity are taking place, because AMIS transmissions can be lengthy. One possible advantage of using a schedule is to have transmissions take place during times of lower long-distance rates. You can also configure AMIS schedules so that all urgent messages are sent immediately. Users should be informed when AMIS schedules are set for after-hours so that they may choose to send an e-mail instead if the matter requires a faster response. AMIS schedules are set within the AMIS Options menu using the Cisco Unity Administrator.

Figure 10-27 illustrates the AMIS Options Delivery Options page.

Figure 10-27 *AMIS Options*

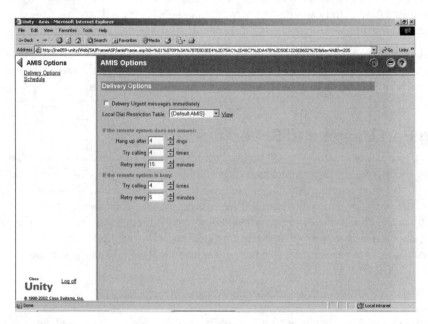

The AMIS restriction table specifies which delivery locations you will deliver messages to immediately, and which will use the standard AMIS schedule.

AMIS Options are settings that are used to place restrictions and create schedules for sending outbound messages to remote AMIS nodes. These settings determine when and where AMIS calls will be delivered.

Within the AMIS Options area, there are two sections: AMIS Delivery Options and Schedule Settings. This can sometimes be misleading because AMIS Delivery Options seem similar to the options found within the AMIS Delivery Location page. However, they are separated into a different section within the Cisco Unity Administrator because of their functionality. The AMIS Delivery Options enable you to configure whether urgent messages are going to be allowed for immediate delivery, set restriction tables based on administrator-defined dial strings, configure what actions to take when the remote system rings but does not answer, and configure what actions to take when the remote system is busy.

The Schedule Settings section allows you to configure when delivery of messages will occur if you have set up a schedule. The AMIS Schedule Settings schedule works in a similar way to the System Schedule in Cisco Unity. If you check a half-hour interval on the Schedule Settings page, it means delivery of messages will occur within that time period. If it is unchecked, then any messages left within that time frame are queued until the available time period. By default, all AMIS nodes are allowed to deliver messages at all times. The restriction table on the AMIS Delivery Options page and the Schedule Settings page determines this.

NOTE   AMIS restriction tables are used to control when messages will be transferred to the remote AMIS node(s). Because AMIS places calls to transfer messages, organizations may choose to limit when these calls can be placed due to the possible long duration of the calls. Although AMIS restriction tables are used to restrict when transfer takes place, they do not restrict the actual placing of the calls.

Figure 10-28 illustrates the AMIS Schedule Settings page.

Figure 10-28   *AMIS Schedule Settings*

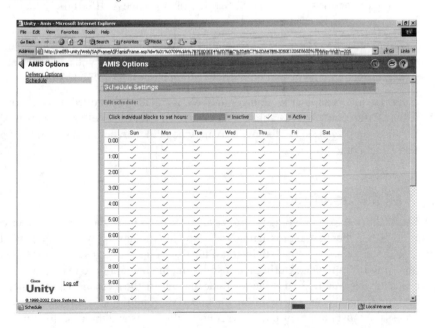

Understanding the UAmis Mailbox

When messages are sent from the Cisco Unity server to a remote AMIS system, they are first placed in the UAmis mailbox. The mailbox is created on the Exchange server that contains the Cisco Unity AMIS license.

NOTE   The UAmis mailbox is created using the ConfigMgr tool located in the Cisco Unity server \Commserver folder. It is not created using the Cisco Unity Administrator, because it is a special type of mailbox. In addition, this mailbox should be created on the AMIS bridgehead server or on AMIS servers that will be handling inbound and outbound AMIS messages.

Outgoing AMIS messages are placed in the UAmis mailbox for delivery. This mailbox is created on the Exchange server that is associated with the Cisco Unity server that is licensed for AMIS. Storage limits for this mailbox are important because AMIS transmissions can be lengthy. By default, mailboxes that are created in Exchange use the storage defaults put in place by the system administrator. This can be changed for individual mailboxes and it should be considered for the UAmis mailbox. Items that you should consider include any dialing and scheduling restrictions placed on AMIS, times of day when AMIS traffic spikes occur, and drive space limits on the Exchange server.

It is recommended to also monitor outbound AMIS traffic by using the AMIS Out traffic report, available on the Cisco Unity Administrator. The report can give you a baseline as to peak times of AMIS usage, which you can then use to set up the limits on the UAmis mailbox.

Because UAmis is another Exchange mailbox, it can also be moved. If you move it, you need to restart Cisco Unity to reestablish the connection with the mailbox in its new location. Otherwise, messages sent to the mailbox may be held there and not transmitted during the regularly scheduled time.

Delivering AMIS Messages

In Cisco Unity, AMIS outgoing messages are queued by node and sent in batches of a maximum of nine. When there are more than nine, Cisco Unity hangs up, waits a short while, and then places another call to continue delivery of the rest of the messages. Each of these messages has a time limit of 8 minutes. During a transmission, the length of the message is sent first. If it exceeds the maximum, the destination node may refuse the message. Cisco Unity, however, will accept messages that exceed that limit under certain conditions. The subscriber who is receiving the message must have their mailbox set up to allow this and their mailbox must have enough free space to accept the message.

Also, incoming AMIS messages can be delivered only to subscribers and not to public distribution lists.

Understanding Location Objects and AMIS Networking

As is true for digital networking and VPIM networking, location objects are key elements when using AMIS networking. Each Cisco Unity server has a default primary location, to which local subscribers are added when they are created. You can create more locations to represent other messaging systems that you want to communicate with. You can use a Dialing Domain ID to link several locations, to provide a more transparent dialing mechanism for businesses that have telephone switches that are networked.

In Cisco Unity, subscribers and any other system objects can be associated only with the primary location object that is created by the Setup program. All delivery location objects are used specifically for addressing remote messaging systems.

When outside callers use the Cisco Unity directory, they are presented with a list of names that includes members of the primary location object. When you define the primary location object, you assign it a Dial ID. Creating a dial plan for your organization that will result in callers reaching subscribers correctly and efficiently is very important, so be sure that the Dial IDs that you create do not conflict with previously assigned IDs.

All location objects that are created are visible in the Cisco Unity Administrator. However, only the administrator can modify or delete locations that are created on the Cisco Unity server they manage. Locations that are created on other sites are replicated and appear as read-only to the rest of the other sites. The primary location object can be modified but not deleted from Cisco Unity.

A delivery location must be configured for every remote AMIS node to exchange messages. The AMIS delivery location contains two key items to ensure delivery of AMIS messages: the Delivery Phone Number and Node ID. The Delivery Phone Number is the digits that Cisco Unity dials out when attempting to deliver a message to this remote voice-mail system. This number may include a trunk access number, depending on your setup. The Node ID setting is used when receiving messages from the remote voice-mail system. When Cisco Unity receives an AMIS call, the remote voice-mail system identifies itself by sending its Node ID. Cisco Unity tries to match that ID with the delivery location AMIS Node ID. If it does not match, the message is not accepted.

TIP

If you need to change the Dial ID of an existing AMIS delivery location, it can be changed. However, you also need to update with the new Dial ID all the AMIS subscribers who are using that location. In this case, the Extension Address Utility comes in handy. You can update the AMIS subscribers with the new information.

The delivery location needs to be created on only one Cisco Unity server. It is then replicated in the directory, where all the other servers in that directory will be able to access it.

Using IVC and AMIS Networking

Cisco Unity uses IVC to send and receive AMIS messages. When a subscriber addresses a message to an AMIS recipient, the message is passed to the IVC that is registered with Exchange. IVC formats the To: and From: field addresses and places the message in the UAmis mailbox for delivery.

When you are using Cisco Unity in an all–Exchange 5.5 environment, IVC for Exchange 5.5 is required. However, if it is an all–Exchange 2000 environment (or is mixed with Exchange 5.5), then use IVC for Exchange 2000 instead. When in a mixed environment, do not use the Exchange 5.5 Administrator program to manage IVC for Exchange 2000. Instead, use the appropriate Microsoft Management Console (MMC) snap-in.

Adding AMIS Subscribers

AMIS subscribers are similar to VPIM subscribers in terms of the information stored in Exchange. They are Cisco Unity subscribers with no mailbox storage on the Exchange mail store. Before you create these subscribers, you must create the AMIS delivery location object for them, because when you add a new AMIS subscriber, you must select a defined AMIS delivery location and remote extension number of the subscriber. Although a Cisco Unity local extension is required, it does not need to be the same as the remote extension.

AD stores AMIS subscribers as contacts. These subscribers can be deleted either individually or by deleting the AMIS delivery location associated with them. This also deletes any other AMIS subscriber associated with that delivery location. In any of these cases, the contact information is preserved in AD. Cisco Unity Administrator does not remove this information.

Figure 10-29 shows the window that you use to add a new AMIS subscriber with AMIS key components.

TIP   The Bulk Import tool can be used to create multiple AMIS subscribers at a time.

The message store options are not available to AMIS subscribers, because they do not have a local message store. Like VPIM and Internet subscribers, AMIS subscribers cannot log on to Cisco Unity via the telephone or use the Cisco Unity Assistant to receive message notifications, receive MWIs, and own private lists.

Figure 10-29   *Adding a New AMIS Subscriber*

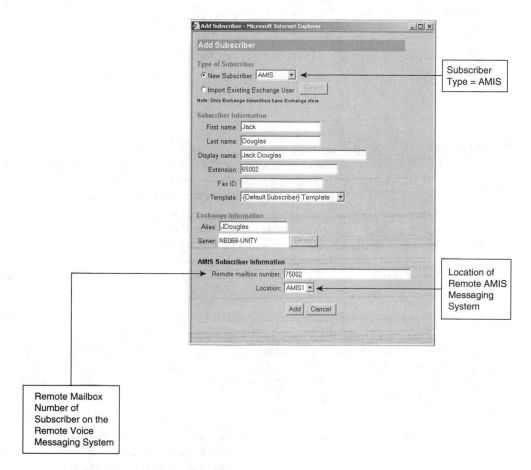

Understanding Bridge Networking

Bridge networking with Cisco Unity allows messages to be transferred between Cisco Unity and Octel voice-mail servers within an Octel analog environment.

If you plan to implement Cisco Unity in an environment with Octel voice-mail servers, you need to understand Bridge networking concepts and how it is implemented. This section provides the information that you need to effectively and efficiently provide customers with Bridge networking.

To benefit fully from this section, it is recommended that you have these prerequisite skills and knowledge:

- Knowledge of Cisco Unity messaging call flow (see Chapter 1)
- Knowledge of how Cisco Unity handles calls (see Chapter 2)
- Understanding of the concepts presented in the "Cisco Unity Networking Fundamentals" section of this chapter

Defining Bridge Networking

Cisco Unity Bridge is a gateway that runs on a server that allows Cisco Unity to communicate with Octel nodes within an Octel analog network. On the Octel network, the Bridge appears as another node on the network. This is similar to how Cisco Unity appears as a node on an AMIS network. The Cisco Unity Bridge's main function is to translate messages between two different protocols. When the Bridge communicates with an Octel node, it actually places a call to the Octel system, and then it uses the Octel analog protocol. When it communicates with the Cisco Unity system Octel uses VPIM with proprietary extensions for added functionality. Because VPIM uses TCP/IP to communicate, messaging between Cisco Unity and the Bridge can be done over the Internet or a TCP/IP network using SMTP.

Bridge networking is a licensed feature of Cisco Unity and requires a separate Bridge server. If you have multiple Cisco Unity servers in your organization, only one server needs to be licensed for and designated as the Bridge server. For purposes of load balancing, you can add more bridge servers. Bridge servers exist in a one-to-one relationship with Cisco Unity servers, which means that if there are two Bridge servers, two Cisco Unity servers are required to be configured for Bridge networking.

TIP   To check whether your Cisco Unity server contains a license for Bridge networking, open the license Manager by going to **Start > Run > Programs > Unity > Licensing**.

There, you will see all the features that are licensed, including the Bridge sessions. If the value of Bridge sessions is greater than 1, then you are licensed for at least one session on the Cisco Unity server.

You can find a list of supported Octel systems in the *Cisco Unity Pre-Installation Guide* found at Cisco.com.

Figures 10-30 and 10-31 illustrate how the Cisco Unity Bridge can be implemented in an enterprise's messaging infrastructure.

Figure 10-30 illustrates using Cisco Unity Bridge with dual integration.

Figure 10-30   *Cisco Unity with Dual Integration*

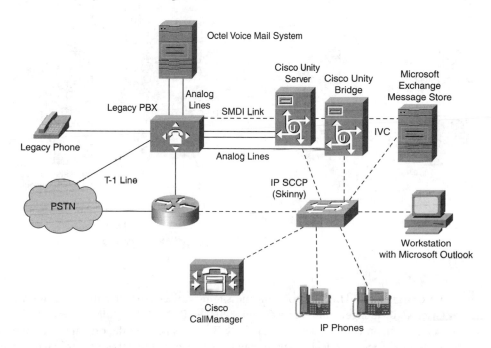

When Cisco Unity is combined with Cisco Unity Bridge, it is a solution that is capable of helping an organization manage the transition from legacy telephone equipment to a converged IP network. In the diagram, Cisco Unity is integrated with two switches: a circuit-switched (legacy) PBX and a Cisco CallManager. It can manage voice-mail accounts for subscribers with either IP telephones or standard single-line extensions attached to a circuit-switched PBX. In addition, Cisco Unity Bridge can send and receive voice-mail messages using Octel's analog messaging protocol through the analog lines that connect the legacy PBX and voice-mail system. In this manner, an enterprise may maximize its return on investment on older telephone equipment, while transitioning subscribers to an IP telephone network at a planned pace.

Figure 10-31 illustrates using Cisco Unity Bridge with Cisco CallManager.

Figure 10-31 *Cisco Bridge with Cisco CallManager*

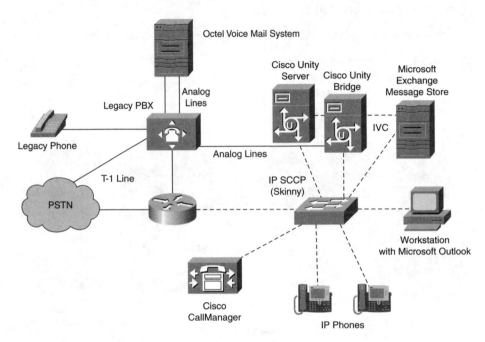

In this design, Cisco Unity is providing messaging services to subscribers who are being served by Cisco CallManager. However, a circuit-switched PBX is providing voice-mail services to the subscribers on an Octel system. Cisco Unity Bridge is helping the organization to manage the transition from legacy telephone equipment to a converged IP network. Cisco Unity can use the Cisco Unity Bridge to send and receive voice-mail messages using Octel's analog messaging protocol. These are provided through the analog lines that connect the legacy PBX and voice-mail system.

Setting Up Bridge Networking

Here is a quick list of the general steps involved when setting up Bridge networking:

Step 1 Make dial plan decisions and gather information.

Step 2 Provide network connectivity between the Exchange server with IVC installed and Cisco Unity Bridge.

Step 3 Extend the AD schema for Bridge delivery locations.

Step 4   Configure SMTP options.

Step 5   Install IVC on an Exchange 2000 server.

Step 6   Create the UOmni mailbox on the Cisco Unity bridgehead server.

Step 7   Customize the primary location object.

Step 8   Set addressing and search options.

Step 9   Set Bridge subscriber creation and synchronization options.

Step 10 Create delivery locations for each remote Octel system.

Step 11 Create Bridge subscriber accounts (optional).

Step 12 Set up remote system(s) with Bridge's Octel node information.

SMTP, digital, VPIM, AMIS, and Bridge networking share similarities in terms of their setup, including the IVC installation. Bridge networking uses analog communication to interact with other Octel systems. Therefore, Bridge networking has its own unique set of important setup instructions.

Before you move to other steps, be sure the server meets the requirements in the *Cisco Unity Bridge System Requirements, and Supported Hardware and Software* document available at Cisco.com. Designing a dial plan before you implement Bridge networking will result in a system that does not have any conflicting IDs that can confuse those searching for subscribers' addresses.

The next step is to provide network connectivity between the designated Exchange 2000 server for the IVC connector and the Cisco Unity Bridge.

The next step is to extend the AD schema for Bridge networking by using the AD Schema Setup utility. The schema changes that you make are additions to the Bridge delivery location object class. If this is not done, then Bridge delivery locations will not be able to be inserted using the Cisco Unity Administrator. A full description of the schema changes is provided in the file vpimgateway.ldf located in the Schema\LdifScripts directory on Cisco Unity CD 1.

On step 2 you may need to grant the Bridge server permissions to relay e-mail through the Exchange SMTP virtual server and you may need to configure an SMTP connector to route messages to the Bridge. Once this is done, you can install IVC on the Exchange 2000 server. There should be only one installation of IVC in an AD forest. If a previous version was installed, you must remove it before continuing.

There are a number of things that you must do after installing IVC. The following should be performed on every Bridge networking server installed.

1 Create the UOmni mailbox on the Cisco Unity bridgehead. This mailbox is used to deposit incoming and outgoing Bridge messages.

NOTE The UOmni mailbox is created using the ConfigMgr tool located in the Cisco Unity server \Commserver folder. It is not created using the Cisco Unity Administrator because it is a special mailbox. When you run the ConfigMgr tool, it also adds the Bridge subscriber template, which is used when auto-creating Bridge subscribers.

2 Configure the primary location object on the Cisco Unity server. This includes giving the location a name, Dial ID, and recorded voice name and, if appropriate, making it part of the dialing domain. The name for the domain needs to be inserted on only one server. There are two other key components defined on this page that are specific to Bridge networking, the Node ID and the server address of the Bridge server.

3 The Node ID is the serial number, which is also configured on the Cisco Unity Nodes page in the Bridge Administrator. This number is also used to configure the Bridge server. The Bridge server and the Cisco Unity server both share this ID on the Octel network. They are basically acting as one node on the Octel environment.

4 The server address of the Bridge server is populated with the FQDN, or full computer name, of the Bridge server. Here is an example: ne059-unity.unity40.ipcbu.cisco.com.

5 Configuring search and addressing options carries the same set of considerations as in AMIS, VPIM, SMTP, and digital networking.

6 Configure the Bridge options using the Cisco Unity Administrator. They are located under Network, Bridge Options. The first option is called Subscriber Creation. The Bridge server uses these options when it automatically creates Bridge subscribers. Here, you can select the subscriber template that the Bridge server will use to create a subscriber. There is also a check box that can be checked to allow newly created subscribers to be shown in the e-mail server address book.

NOTE These settings apply only to Bridge subscribers that will automatically be created due to directory propagation of the Bridge server and Octel systems. These settings do not affect the existing Bridge subscribers in Cisco Unity or subscribers who are manually created using the normal subscriber menu.

7 The Synchronization options allow you to choose the scope of synchronization you would like to perform between the subscriber directory on the Bridge server and the subscriber directory on Cisco Unity. The Bridge server will receive notification of changes made on all the servers within the scope specified. There are three options to select from:

— **Local Server**—Subscriber information for subscribers on the local Cisco Unity server is propagated to the Bridge server. Use this option when each Cisco Unity server is connected to a separate Bridge server.

— **Dialing Domain**—Subscriber information is propagated to the Bridge server for those Cisco Unity servers that are part of the dialing domain. Use this option when this server acts as a bridgehead server for the other Cisco Unity servers in the dialing domain.

— **Global Directory**—Subscriber information from the entire global directory is propagated to the Bridge server. Use this option when this server acts as the bridgehead server for other networked Cisco Unity servers.

NOTE   If you click the Synchronize button on this page, information on all the Cisco Unity subscribers within the scope defined is sent to the Bridge server. When performing a synchronization, consider doing it at a time when the system is less busy, such as after business hours of operation.

8 After you set the Bridge options, the next step is to create a delivery location for each remote Octel system to which subscribers will be sending messages.

9 You may choose to change the standard messaging menu conversation or default display name-parsing rule.

10 As an option, Bridge subscribers can be created for those that would like to be found on the corporate directory on a permanent basis.

11 The final step on a new installation of a Bridge is to configure the Octel systems so that they are aware of the new Node ID on the Octel network.

Understanding the UOmni Mailbox

The UOmni mailbox is an Exchange mailbox that is used to receive administrative messages from the Bridge server to Cisco Unity. Messages sent to this mailbox include notification of automatic creation, modification, and deletion of Bridge subscribers as a result of Octel NameNet emulation. Octel's NameNet is the feature that allows nodes to obtain new entries from directories on other nodes. When a message is sent from a new subscriber, the node requests the display name and recorded name. It then adds this information to the directory.

Cisco Unity Bridge works in the same way. However, it sends that information to the UOmni mailbox on the Cisco Unity system.

The UOmni mailbox is created on the Exchange server that is linked to the Cisco Unity system that is licensed for Unity Bridge. When it is first created, it has the default storage limitation put in place by the Exchange administrator. This limitation may be acceptable, because most of the messages it will receive are notification messages that subscriber change events have occurred, such as the creation of a subscriber. If necessary, you can move the UOmni mailbox after it is created. However, this requires that you stop and restart the Cisco Unity system, so that Cisco Unity is aware of UOmni's new location. Messages may be held in the mailbox if this is not performed.

Translating Bridge Messages

The Cisco Unity Bridge delivers fax and voice-mail messages between Cisco Unity and Octel nodes by translating the different protocols involved, then delivering the messages in the format the intended server is expecting. The Bridge server maintains a table for each system involved, which it uses for the translation that it performs. The Cisco Unity table contains the Cisco Unity server name, assigned serial number, and domain name. The Octel tables contain the server name, unique Octel serial number, and telephone number of each Octel node it needs to communicate with. When the Bridge server receives a message, it can look up the address of the intended server, reformat the message in the way that the target server is expecting, and then send the message to its destination.

Understanding Location Objects and Bridge Networking

Just as in the other forms of networking with Cisco Unity, location objects play a very important role in Bridge networking. When you are configuring the primary location for Bridge networking, there are two key properties that are specific for bridge networking: the Bridge Node ID and the server address. The Bridge Node ID is Cisco Unity's identification on the Octel analog network. The server address is the FQDN of the Bridge server that Cisco Unity is associated with. As previously stated, creating a dial plan for your organization that will result in callers reaching subscribers correctly and efficiently is very important, so be sure that the Dial IDs that you create do not conflict with previously assigned IDs.

You must create a delivery location for each Octel system using Bridge networking that subscribers will be sending messages to. When you are creating a delivery location, select Bridge as the destination type, and then enter the Octel Node ID, which is the serial number of the Octel node. The Octel Node ID must match on both the Octel node and the Bridge Administrator.

Using IVC and Bridge Networking

Cisco Unity uses IVC to send and receive Bridge messages. When a subscriber addresses a message to a remote Bridge recipient, the message is passed to IVC as an OMNI message. Because IVC is registered with Exchange for these types of messages, IVC changes the message into the VPIM proprietary format and sends it to the Bridge via SMTP. Incoming messages are changed from the VPIM format into voice messages and sent to Exchange for delivery.

When using Bridge networking, the IVC for Exchange 2000 is the only supported version. If your organization has both Exchange 5.5 and 2000 servers, the Exchange 5.5 Administrator cannot be used to manage IVC for Exchange 2000. You can use the appropriate MMC snap-in.

Adding Bridge Subscribers

Like VPIM and Internet subscribers, Bridge subscribers have no mailbox storage in the Exchange mail store. They each represent a subscriber on an Octel system. When you are creating these subscribers, be sure to first create the Bridge delivery location of where that subscriber is located.

There are three ways a Bridge subscriber can be created. You can use Octel's NameNet emulation to automatically create them in Cisco Unity; you can create them permanently on the Cisco Unity Bridge; or you can manually create them by using the Cisco Unity Administrator. When a subscriber is created, modified, or deleted using NameNet, that information is sent from the Bridge server to Cisco Unity. The same thing occurs when changes occur on the Bridge server.

Figure 10-32 shows a new Bridge subscriber being added with its key components.

Figure 10-32 *Adding a New Bridge Subscriber*

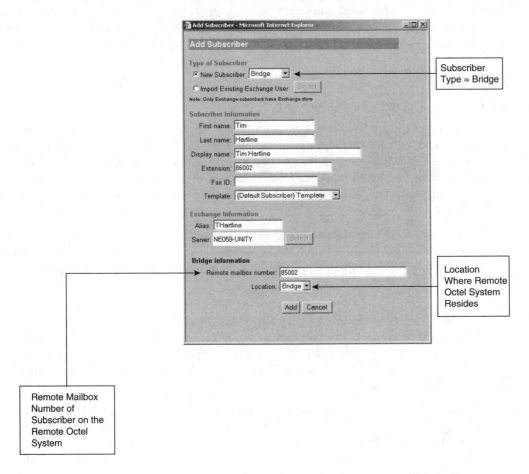

When you are creating Bridge subscribers manually, you specify the delivery location of the remote voice-mail system and the remote user mailbox number. A local extension for each Bridge subscriber is also required; however, it does not need to match the remote mailbox number. Bridge subscribers are also represented as contacts in AD. When Bridge subscribers are deleted, by either individually deleting them or deleting the delivery location associated with them, the contact information remains in AD. It needs to be manually deleted from there.

The message store options are not available to Bridge subscribers, because they do not have a local message store. Like Internet, AMIS, and VPIM subscribers, Bridge subscribers cannot log on to Cisco Unity via the telephone or use the Cisco Unity Assistant to receive message notifications, receive MWIs, and own private lists.

Chapter Summary

In this chapter, you learned different types of networking options with Cisco Unity. Knowing how messages are delivered and directories replicated is important in order to understand how Cisco networking works. You learned how SMTP, AMIS, VPIM, and the Cisco Unity Bridge are used to deliver messages, what Cisco Unity addressing options are available, which scenarios would appropriately use blind addressing in Cisco Unity, the advantages of Cisco Unity's networking capabilities, creating and using Internet, AMIS, VPIM, and Bridge subscribers. In particular, you learned how to do the following:

- Describe addressing options in Cisco Unity
- Describe the advantages of Cisco Unity's networking capabilities
- Describe Cisco Unity digital networking
- Configure the default location object correctly
- Determine whether it is appropriate to use a dialing domain
- Select the Cisco Unity software components that are used to implement digital networking
- Create and use location objects
- Select which search options are appropriate in the Cisco Unity System Administrator given a particular addressing and server configuration scenario
- Describe how Cisco Unity uses SMTP networking to deliver messages
- Create an SMTP delivery location
- Create and use Internet subscribers
- Describe how Cisco Unity uses VPIM networking to deliver messages
- Choose when a customer would appropriately use AMIS networking
- Choose when a customer would appropriately use the Unity Bridge

For additional information about Cisco Unity networking, refer to these resources:

- *Cisco Unity Bridge Networking Guide*
- *Networking in Cisco Unity Guide (with Lotus Domino)*
- *Networking in Cisco Unity Guide (with Microsoft Exchange)*

Chapter Review Questions

Use this section to test yourself on how well you learned the concepts discussed in this chapter. You can find the answers to the review questions for this chapter in Appendix A.

1 When implementing SMTP networking by itself between a Cisco Unity system and a non–Cisco Unity server, without IVC, in what format do recipients receive voice messages on the non–Cisco Unity server?

2 When using SMTP networking between two Cisco Unity servers that do not share the same global directory, are the voice attributes preserved when sending voice messages between the Cisco Unity systems and using IVC?

3 If you plan to use VPIM networking to communicate with a third-party messaging system, and you have several Cisco Unity servers networked together, how many Cisco Unity servers require the VPIM license?

4 What method of communication does AMIS networking use with Cisco Unity to transfer voice messages between voice-messaging systems?

5 What tool do you use to create the UAmis and UOmni accounts for AMIS networking and Bridge networking, respectively?

6 What types of voice-mail systems can Cisco Unity communicate with when using Bridge networking?

7 What types of messages can the UOmni mailbox receive when using Bridge networking?

8 When Cisco Unity synchronizes its Unity SQL database with the global directory, what type of information copies over onto the directory?

9 When determining the type of Cisco networking to use, what is the preferred choice when all the target servers are Cisco Unity servers and all use the same global directory?

10 You are the administrator of one Cisco Unity server in an organization that is using networking to communicate with other messaging systems. If you log in to your server using Cisco Unity Administrator, what location objects can you not delete from this server?

Upon completing this chapter, you will be able to perform the following tasks:

- Explain the recommended backup procedures for Cisco Unity
- Describe Cisco Unity administration tools
- Describe the Cisco Unity audio management tools
- Use Cisco Unity diagnostic tools
- Describe Cisco Unity reporting tools
- Understand the Cisco Unity switch integration tools
- Describe troubleshooting procedures for Cisco Unity and Cisco Personal Assistant (PA)

CHAPTER 11

Unified Communications Backup and Utilities

This chapter discusses the recommended backup procedures and various system utilities of a Cisco Unity server. In addition, it explores the general troubleshooting techniques to help find root causes for Cisco Unity and Cisco PA issues.

Backing Up Cisco Unity Systems

Cisco Unity, whether in a VoiceMail-only or Unified Messaging setup, requires regular maintenance to ensure an efficiently running system. Knowing the proper backup procedures for Cisco Unity is an important component of the maintenance.

To benefit fully from this section, it is recommended that you have the following prerequisite skills and knowledge. (If you need a quick review, see the designated chapter, where you can find more information on the topic.)

- General knowledge of backing up messaging systems (see Chapter 6, "Cisco Unified Communications System Maintenance")

- Knowledge of Cisco Unity UM and voice-mail configurations, and the message store you use for each (see Chapter 8, "Cisco Unified Communications System Software")

Here is a quick list of guidelines to follow when you are backing up a Cisco Unity system:

- **Server preparation**—See the *Cisco Unity System Administration Guide*
  - Turn off Circular Logging
  - Schedule backups during off-peak hours
- **Cisco Unity Standard Backup**—Use Backup Exec to back up the following items:
  - Cisco Unity
  - Operating system (OS)
  - Exchange (Domino) information store and Directory
  - Exchange (Domino) mailboxes
  - Structured Query Language (SQL)
  - System state

Having a good backup strategy in place that provides a schedule for performing full backups is important for the restoration of a Cisco Unity system, if the server requires it. If your organization does not have a strategy already in place as part of its disaster recovery plan for Microsoft Exchange, then you need to develop one; refer to the documentation provided by the backup software that is used by the organization and to the appropriate documentation available at http://www.microsoft.com.

If your organization does not already have a software package for performing scheduled backups, then consider the following data management programs, which have been qualified by Cisco to use with Cisco Unity 4.0(x) for backups:

- VERITAS Backup Exec for Microsoft Windows NT and Microsoft Windows 2000, version 8.5 and later
- VERITAS NetBackup version 4.5 and later

For technical assistance with Backup Exec or NetBackup, contact the VERITAS Software Corporation through its website at http://www.veritas.com.

When you are preparing your system for backups, one of the recommended steps is to turn off circular logging in Exchange. When new messages arrive on the Exchange server, the server writes them into a transaction log. The transaction logs can later assist you in restoring a message store if it becomes corrupted. When circular logging is on, the newest messages can potentially overwrite the oldest messages in the transaction log. When the system starts to overwrite log entries, you should not use the transaction logs to restore a message store.

NOTE   By default, Microsoft Exchange 2000 has circular logging turned off, but it is on by default on Microsoft Exchange 5.5.

The best time to perform backups on the Cisco Unity server is when the system is the least busy. This means when the system is not processing calls, such as after regular business hours or when no other tasks are running. This may include when the system is not generating system reports or you have some reports in queue to generate.

Understanding Administration Tools and Utilities

The administration tools, which are located in the Tools Depot of Cisco Unity, enable you to import different types of users into the system, upgrade the system, perform disaster recovery, and change certain registry settings.

Understanding the administration tools that are available in a Cisco Unity system will help you to maintain and possibly troubleshoot the system. Knowledge of and experience with these tools will make maintenance of Cisco Unity much easier.

To benefit fully from this section, it is recommended that you have the following prerequisite skills and knowledge. (If you need a quick review, see the designated chapter, where you can find more information on the topic.)

- Knowledge of Cisco Unity UM and voice-mail configurations, including the role of subscribers and call handlers. (see Chapter 3, "Setting Up Cisco Unified Communications")
- Knowledge of how calls are handled in Cisco Unity (see Chapter 2, "Using Your Cisco Unified Communications System")
- Knowledge of the Cisco Unity software components (see Chapter 8)

Using Audio Text Manager

The Audio Text Manager application provides a fast, graphical view of the flow patterns of call handlers configured in the Cisco Unity database and allows you to modify the flow patterns quickly and easily. This is particularly useful for systems with complicated audio text applications with many call handlers. It can be especially useful for troubleshooting an audio text application. To run Audio Text Manager, you must have Cisco Unity 3.1(3) or later installed, and it can run only on the local Cisco Unity system. Remotely using the application through Terminal Services is possible. It also requires that the user have read and write access to the Cisco Unity database SQL table, which by default the local Administrator group has.

You can view information in Audio Text Manager in either Tree View or Grid View. Figure 11-1 shows the application opened in Tree View. It shows the Opening Greeting with the option 0 highlighted. On the right side of the application, the tabs allow you to view most of the information that is normally available to an administrator through the System Administrator (SA). You can use the SA to view information about call handlers (such as Interviewer Directory call handlers). In the example shown in Figure 11-1, you can see and make changes to the settings of the Operator handler.

Figure 11-1 *Audio Text Manager*

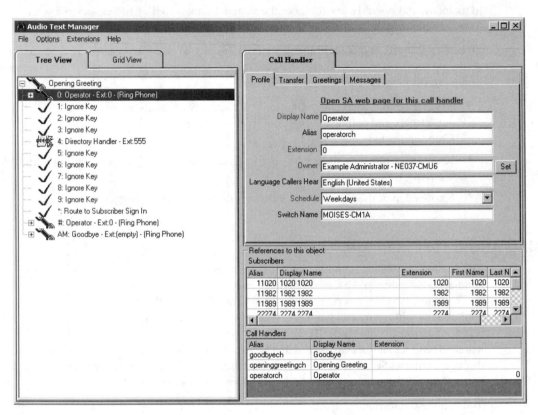

Using Bulk Edit

The Cisco Unity Bulk Edit utility enables you to make changes to a large number of call handlers or subscribers simultaneously. Almost every parameter that you can change via the system administrator is also available to change in volume using Bulk Edit, as well as some items that are not visible in the System Administrator. However, Bulk Edit has no undo method after you perform a change. This means that, for example, if you change a field incorrectly for a large number of subscribers while using this utility, you will need to run Bulk Edit again or individually correct the field using the System Administrator.

Figure 11-2 illustrates Bulk Edit being used to enable transfers to all the subscribers on a Cisco Unity system.

Figure 11-2 *Bulk Edit Utility*

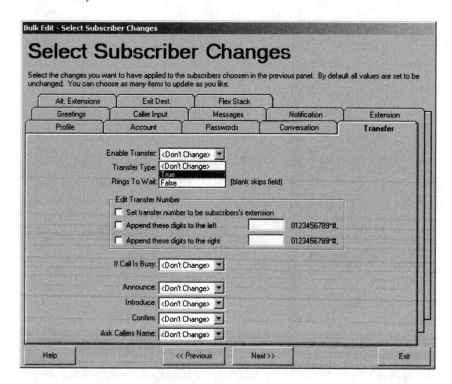

Bulk Edit also allows you to view a list of all the subscribers on Cisco Unity, or just a few of them. The tool also has the following capabilities: edit a range of subscribers with any specified starting and stopping extension; edit all subscribers on a particular distribution list or class of service (CoS); edit all subscribers attached to a particular telephone switch (in a dual-switch integration); or edit all subscribers referenced in a supplied comma-separated values (CSV) file.

Using Disaster Recovery Backup and Restore Tools

The Cisco Unity Disaster Recovery Backup tool, shown in Figure 11-3, captures all the Cisco Unity–specific data from a server so that it can be restored using the Disaster Restore tool. This is useful both for disaster recovery purposes using regularly scheduled backups and for migration purposes. It works if you are using Exchange 5.5 and Exchange 2000 as the message store and Cisco Unity 3.1(1) or later.

Figure 11-3 *Disaster Recovery Backup Tool*

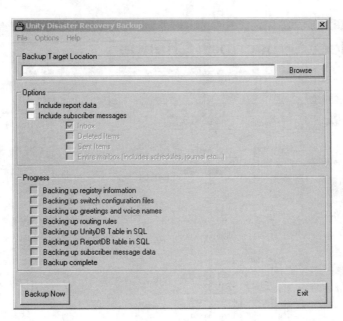

The Disaster Recovery Tools (DiRT) Backup provides a mechanism to back up all Cisco Unity–specific data from a server and store it on an off-box network drive. If the server suffers a catastrophic failure, the customer must rebuild it up to the point where Cisco Unity is running as a clean, freshly installed system. At that point, the customer can run the Disaster Restore utility to bring its server back up to the point at which the last backup took place.

The Restore utility will work on a newly built system with a different server name, on a different domain, or if Cisco Unity was originally installed on a different drive or folder. The restore utility will also work when the back-end connection is different. In other words, if the backup performed was on a Cisco Unity system that is running Exchange 5.5, it is also possible to restore it on a clean installation that is running the same version of Cisco Unity, but with Exchange 2000 now installed. However, in all of these cases, you must install the same version of Cisco Unity that existed when the original backup took place. The new Cisco Unity system must also be up and running.

If you are connecting to Cisco CallManager, you also need to configure your Telephony Application Programming Interface (TAPI) service provider (AvCiscoTSP) to integrate with the Cisco CallManager voice-mail ports. Once you have the system working as a new, clean install, you can perform the restore operation.

The information that is preserved includes all Cisco Unity objects and data such as greetings, voice names, routing rules, passwords, call handlers, interviewers, subscriber data, and switch configuration. Disaster Recovery Backup also gives you the option to back up report data and subscriber messages.

NOTE   DiRT should not be used to replace normal tape backups of your Exchange message store.

The Disaster Recovery tools are ideal for sites that install Cisco Unity in a UM configuration and whose users are homed off-box. Typically, sites already have Exchange backup procedures in place and want a way to quickly and easily back up and restore the Cisco Unity–specific configuration information, without having to back up the entire Cisco Unity server. This is also useful for sites that want to upgrade the server that Cisco Unity is running on, or would like to change the disk partition configuration or location of where you installed Cisco Unity. The Disaster Restore tool handles that on the fly.

DiRT does, however, have some caveats that are important to remember. Disaster Recovery Backup works only in an Exchange environment, not Domino. Restoration is possible to a system with the same version of Cisco Unity that the backup gathered. In other words, taking a Cisco Unity 3.1(1) database backup and trying to restore it to a Cisco Unity 3.1(5) or 4.0 system will not work.

NOTE   Once the restore is in progress, there is no undo feature. The Restore utility replaces the entire SQL database named UnityDb. Read the help files carefully before you use these Disaster Recovery tools in a production environment.

Using Failover Monitor

Cisco Unity has an optional feature called Failover Monitor that provides simple redundancy, maintaining voice-mail message functions for users if the Cisco Unity server becomes unreachable or when you want to perform maintenance. For Cisco Unity failover, you can install Cisco Unity on two servers, one being the primary and the other the secondary (or partner).

Figure 11-4 illustrates the Failover Monitor application where the Local Cisco Unity server is the active one.

Figure 11-4 *Failover Monitor Application*

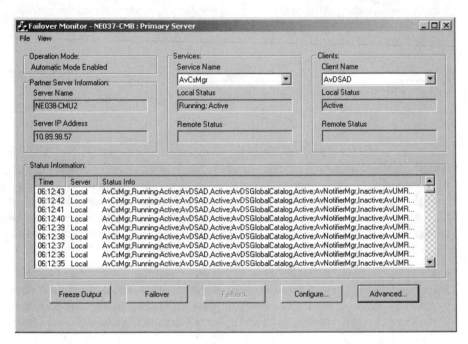

Failover Monitor enables you to view real-time status information, such as the state of your primary and partner failover Cisco Unity servers. You can see which one is active and ready to process voice-mail functions and which one is inactive. You can also perform a force failover condition between the two Cisco Unity servers to perform maintenance. For more information on Cisco Unity failover, visit:

http://www.cisco.com/en/US/products/sw/voicesw/ps2237/
products_installation_and_configuration_guide_book09186a00801b9241.html.

Using Migrate Subscriber Data Tool

Migrate Subscriber Data Tool, shown in Figure 11-5, enables you to move subscriber settings from a Cisco Unity subscriber account to a regular mail user account. This tool allows you to preserve all the subscriber settings, such as voice name, greetings, and private distribution lists, because it adds these Cisco Unity–specific attributes to the mail user account attributes. The mail user becomes the new Cisco Unity subscriber. The tool is useful for moving from a VoiceMail-only installation to UM, or for migrating users from another voice-mail system to Cisco Unity (for example, migrating Octel users who have been set up as Bridge subscribers).

Figure 11-5 *Migrate Subscriber Data Tool*

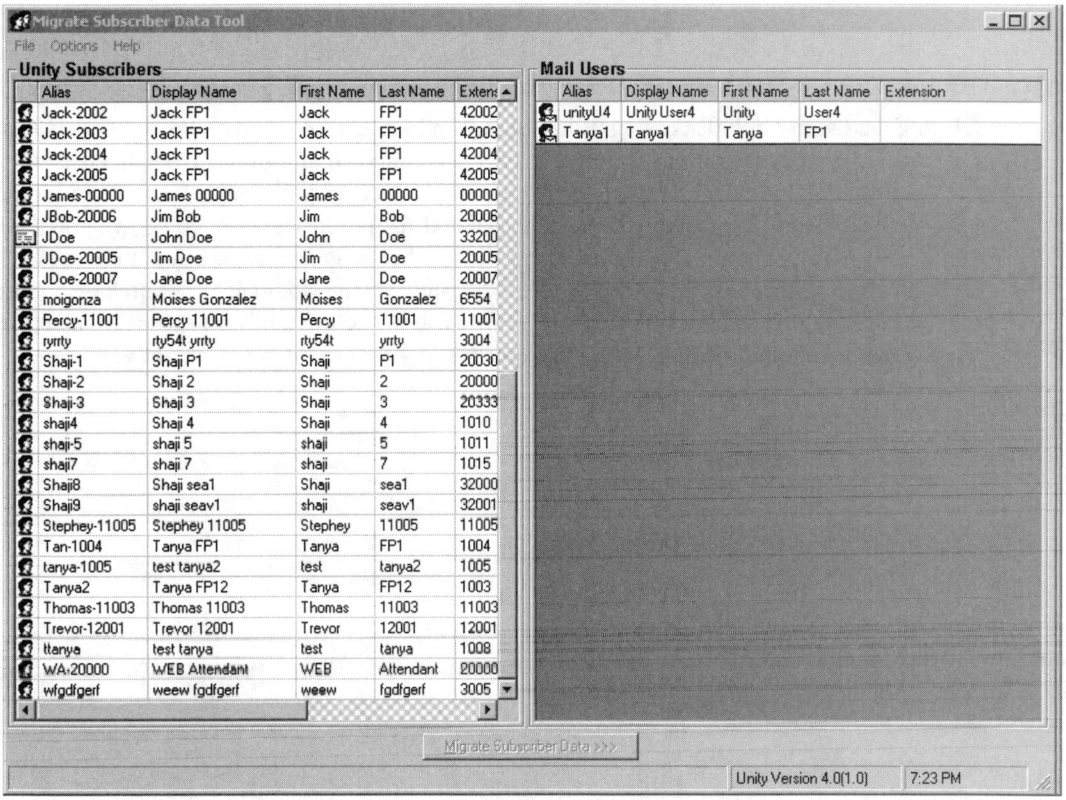

Here is an example of a scenario in which you would use Migrate Subscriber Data Tool: John Smith has two directory accounts. He uses one for voice-mail messages only (vJSmith) and the other for e-mail only (Jsmith). You (as the administrator) would like to move John's voice-mail account into his e-mail account because you want to consolidate them so that he has only one account. You open Migrate Subscriber Data Tool and select John's Cisco Unity subscriber account and his e-mail account, and then click the Migrate Subscriber Data button. The result is that John's subscriber record changes. His e-mail account directory ID overwrites his voice-mail directory ID.

His alias, display name, and first and last name transfer over from his e-mail account to his subscriber record. His primary call handler alias changes to match his e-mail account alias. These modifications take place first within the Cisco Unity database, not the directory. The Migrate Subscriber tool removes the subscriber-specific settings from his previous subscriber directory account, but it does not delete the account. When you exit the tool, the Cisco Unity database then synchronizes itself with the directory. When the directory synchronization is complete, any new voice-mail messages that John receives arrive at his e-mail account, which is now his subscriber account as well.

Using the Cisco Unity Licensing Utility

Using the Cisco Unity Licensing utility, shown in Figure 11-6, is an easy way to view Cisco Unity licensing information. The Cisco Unity server shown in Figure 11-6 is licensed for 72 voice ports. The FlexLM licensing controls many aspects of your Cisco Unity configuration, such as how many languages, voice ports, and text-to-speech sessions are allowed on the system. If you try to install a new feature or add another language and the system does not allow you to do so, it may be because the license is not present. You would need to purchase additional licenses. When you receive the new license file, you would run the License Wizard and then, as a check, look at the License Viewer to confirm that your new licenses are active.

Figure 11-6 *License Viewer Utility*

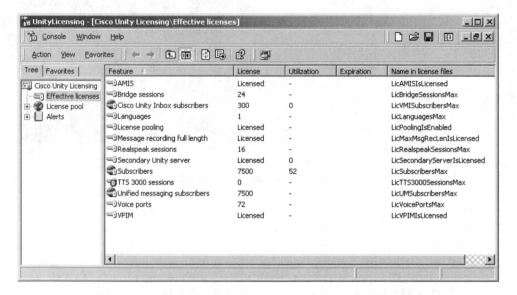

Using Global Subscriber Manager

Global Subscriber Manager (GSM), shown in Figure 11-7, shows your entire Cisco Unity network broken down by dialing domains (DDs) and servers. GSM enables you to locate individual subscribers quickly and, by double-clicking the subscriber, launch the system administrator console page for that subscriber, regardless of which server their message store resides on. You can select any scope to see all the subscribers at that level. Searching can be done by DD, by server, or globally across the entire Cisco Unity network.

Figure 11-7 *GSM Tool*

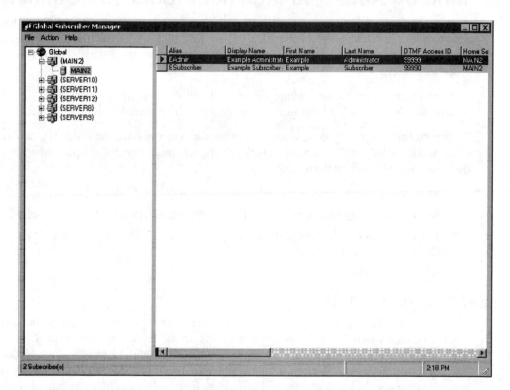

GSM displays your Cisco Unity network in a tree, organized by DDs and servers. The top of the Cisco Unity network is the Global directory. Under the Global directory is a node for each DD. Under each DD is a node for each server within that DD. If a Cisco Unity server does not belong to a DD, it shows up at the DD level with its name in curly brackets, {}.

Clicking any node in the tree shows all subscribers at that level. For example, clicking a DD shows all subscribers homed on any server that is a member of that DD. Clicking the Global node shows you all subscribers in your entire Cisco Unity network.

Once you have located the subscriber you want to view in more detail or edit, you just double-click that specific subscriber and the GSM will launch the system administrator console on the subscriber's home server and bring you right to their profile page.

GSM is also capable of importing users into Cisco Unity.

Understanding Audio Management Tools and Utilities

Audio management tools are accessible through the Cisco Unity Tools Depot. These tools are used to adjust audio levels and the quality of Cisco Unity prompts and greetings. You can also change the compression/decompression (codec) or audio formats in which Cisco Unity stores voice messages.

An organization may need to change the codec it uses on an existing Cisco Unity implementation. Modifying the audio levels may also be required after an upgrade.

To benefit fully from this section, it is recommended that you have the following prerequisite skills and knowledge. (If you need a quick review, see the designated chapter, where you can find more information on the topic.)

- Knowledge of how calls are handled in Cisco Unity (see Chapter 2)
- Knowledge of how to change the different greeting in Cisco Unity (see Chapter 3)
- Knowledge of corporate voice-messaging needs (see Chapter 9, "Cisco Unified Communications Integrations")

Using Set Record Format

The Set Record Format utility, shown in Figure 11-8, allows you to choose any sound codec installed on the Cisco Unity server and make it the default recording format that Cisco Unity uses for all new recordings. By default, the record format is set to 8Kbps Mu-Law (codec 711). You can select any codec and adjust the sample rates. Existing recordings and greetings do not convert to the new codec. It is not possible to select specific formats for items such as individual users, ports, and WAV file types. After you make a change, you need to restart Cisco Unity for the recording format changes to take effect.

Figure 11-8 *Set Record Format Utility*

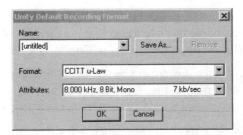

Be sure to select a codec that all clients are compatible with or else some users may encounter voice-quality issues. The audio quality of the G.711 and G.729 codecs is noticeably different. If you send a voice mail to a user who will be accessing that message via their desktop messaging client, they will need the same codec installed on their local system to play it. This utility will not run using Terminal Services.

Using Set WAV Format

The Set WAV Format tool, shown in Figure 11-9, allows you to convert all the existing greetings and voice names on a Cisco Unity server to a selected WAV codec. You can choose from G.711 Mu-Law, G.711 aLaw, or G.729a.

Figure 11-9 *Set WAV Format Tool*

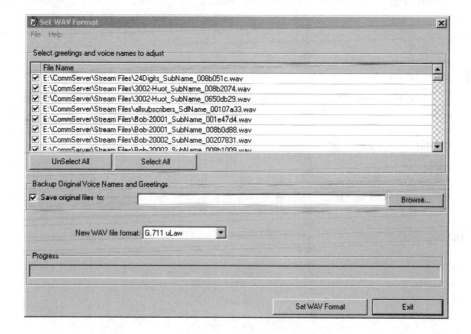

If a site has selected to change recording formats from G.711 (default) to G.729a, for instance, you may want to use this tool to convert all standard greetings and voice names into G.729a. Although Cisco Unity will convert from G.711 to G.729a (and vice versa) on the fly using software, this conversion does require some CPU cycles, so it is often desirable to have all WAV files in the same format to prevent this.

Cisco strongly recommends that you back up your greetings and voice names before changing their format. If the conversion damages the WAV files or the sound quality is poor, you can then recover some or all of them. The Set WAV Format tool has a built-in backup-and-restore mechanism for all greetings and voice names. You would simply check the Save Original Files To check box and then click Browse and select a directory to copy greetings to. Before modifying the WAV files, the tool copies all greetings and voice names to the target directory.

To restore these greetings, you would select the Restore Backed Up Greetings and Voice Names option from the File menu.

Set WAV Format does not convert standard messages in subscribers' mailboxes. Converting WAV files from G.711 to G.729 and back to G.711 degrades their sound quality, because the compression process of each format is different and you lose a certain amount of information during the conversion. After you convert messages, you do not need to reboot the Cisco Unity system for the changes to take effect.

NOTE   Setting a file to the same codec does not have any negative effect on the WAV files. The Set WAV Format tool will identify these instances and not modify the file.

Using WaveGain

The WaveGain utility, shown in Figure 11-10, allows you to adjust the overall volume for all new recordings or for all playbacks when using Cisco CallManager. The volume values used are in decibels, where a positive number increases the volume and a negative number decreases it. The changes take place immediately while Cisco Unity is running so that you can quickly adjust the playback/record levels until you are happy with them. Once you have found the values you want, you need to write them into the registry either manually or by using the Advanced Settings tool. In either case, you must edit the registry for the values to take effect the next time you restart your system.

Figure 11-10   *WaveGain Utility*

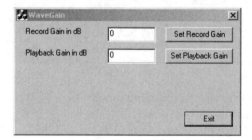

Understanding Diagnostic Tools and Utilities

Diagnostic tools are available with Cisco Unity. These tools help you to configure traces and capture information to resolve Cisco Unity issues.

The Cisco Unity diagnostic tools assist you to maintain a properly running Cisco Unity system. For example, the dbWalker utility checks the integrity of your database, and the Diagnostic Traces utility logs further information for Cisco TACACS to help troubleshoot any issues with your system.

To benefit fully from this section, it is recommended that you have the following prerequisite skills and knowledge. (If you need a quick review, see the designated chapter, where you can find more information on the topic.)

- Knowledge of the different networking features available for Cisco Unity, especially SMTP networking (see Chapter 10, "Unified Communications Networking")
- Knowledge of the Cisco Unity installation process (see Chapter 8)
- Understand the different Cisco Unity architectures (see Chapter 8)

Using Cisco Unity Data Link Explorer

One of the main features of the Cisco Unity Data Link Explorer (CUDLE) tool, shown in Figure 11-11 with the Subscriber table highlighted, is that it helps you quickly explore the Cisco Unity database in Microsoft SQL in a read-only view. It is safe to use because no updates can be made to the database, and you can run it off-box to connect to other Cisco Unity servers. The CUDLE tool also has the option to view the Cisco Unity local registry tree, and it comes with its own Query Builder, SQL Query Analyzer, that is similar to the one that comes with SQL 2000 Enterprise. The CUDLE tool is useful for learning more about Cisco Unity SQL tables.

Using Database Walker (dbWalker)

The dbWalker utility, shown in Figure 11-12, examines the Cisco Unity database and makes a series of checks on all objects in the database, including call handler, subscriber, subscriber template, Interview handler, location, and Directory handler objects. If dbWalker encounters an issue, the string "(error)" appears in red in the output HTML. Warning strings show up in yellow and start with "(warning)". They indicate items that you should check on, but they may not be actual problems. If an item is automatically fixed, a string that starts with "(fixed)" is logged in green directly under the error to indicate what was done.

Figure 11-11 *CUDLE Tool*

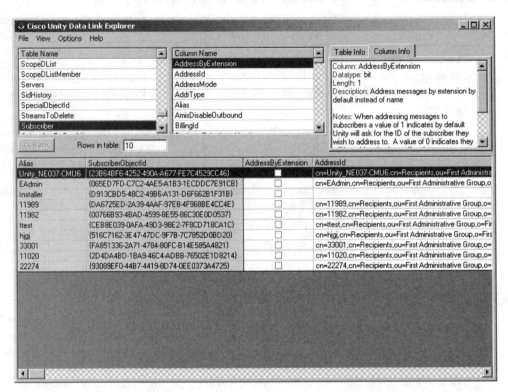

When dbWalker is complete, a dialog box pops up to let you know that it is finished and to tell you how many errors and warnings, if any, the utility found during the process. It gives you the opportunity to view the output file. By searching the output file for the string "(error)" or "(warning)", you can go right to each problem in the log. Brief explanations of the problems encountered usually appear on the following line in the log. Be sure to read them in their entirety to determine what you should do about them, if anything.

NOTE   The first time that you run dbWalker, it is strongly recommended that you run it with no options selected for it to automatically fix any issues that it finds. Instead, run dbWalker and check the results to see what errors or warnings it has found first. Once you understand the changes that the tool will make, choose the options that specify what you prefer it to fix automatically and then run dbWalker again.

Figure 11-12   *DbWalker Utility*

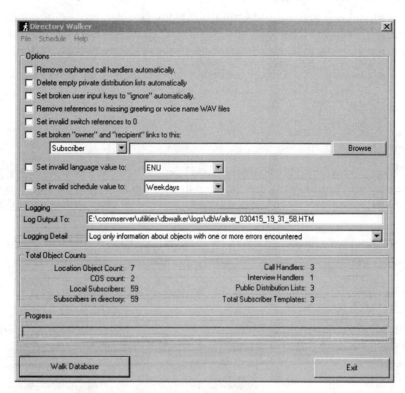

Some problems are logged as errors and fixed automatically (that is, if dbWalker finds the standard contact rule or greeting rule disabled, it re-enables it on the fly). The utility can optionally fix some problems if you indicate that it should do so (for example, it removes orphaned call handlers if you check the option for it to do so at the top of the form).

Other problems require manual intervention to clear up the issue. You can set the Logging Detail drop-down list box to show information about all objects checked during the database walk or you can choose to limit the output to only those objects that encounter one or more errors (default). Each time you click the Walk Database button, the utility generates a new output file and stores it under the \logs\ directory where you installed dbWalker. To view the logs directory quickly, select File > View Log Directory and File Explorer will open to that directory automatically. Whenever dbWalker runs, it automatically deletes any logs in this directory that are older than 10 days.

Using Event Monitoring Service

Event Monitoring Service (EMS) for Cisco Unity provides basic notification options when particular events are recorded in the event logs. You can choose which events will trigger a notification, who will be notified, and how they will receive the notification.

You can choose to send a voice mail or e-mail notification to either a subscriber or distribution list, or send an e-mail to one or more SMTP addresses that you define when an event arrives in the event log.

You can set up a notification for when a specific event ID is written to the event log or for any event IDs.

In Figure 11-13, the highlighted Monitored Event is for the source CiscoUnity_TSP, with event ID 114. If this error is written to the event log, a notification will be sent to the associated recipient, John Davis. John Davis will be sent an SMTP e-mail to the defined SMTP address.

Figure 11-13 *EMS Tool*

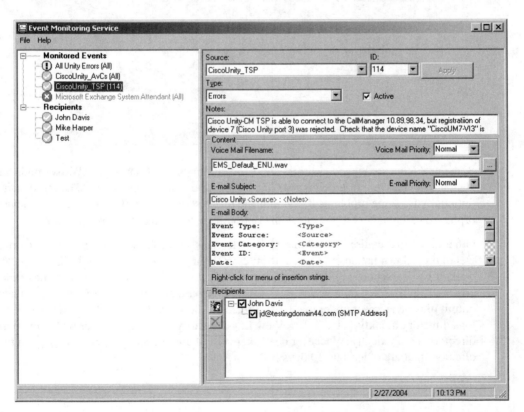

TIP	If you would like more information about Cisco Unity–specific errors that appear in the Application Event log, go to the following link and perform a search based on the event ID: http://www.ciscounitysupport.com.

Using Cisco Unity Diagnostic Tool

The Cisco Unity Diagnostic Tool enables you to create and view diagnostic log files to troubleshoot issues with Cisco Unity. Figure 11-14 illustrates Diagnostic Traces at the Macro Traces level.

Figure 11-14   *Diagnostic Traces Tool, Macro Traces*

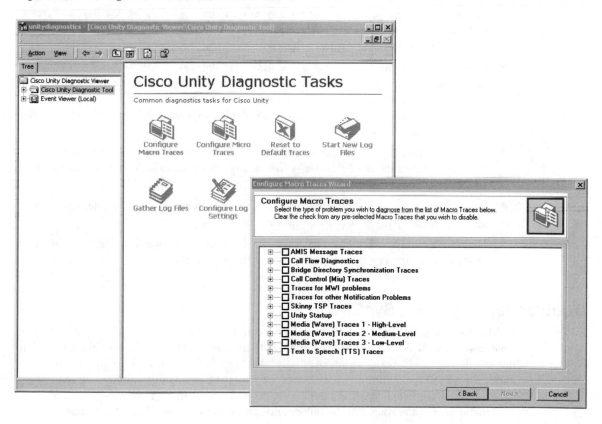

The wizard replaces the diagnostic log functionality in Maestro Tools and allows you or the Cisco TAC staff to select which of the diagnostic traces to run at either of two levels:

- Macro traces—These are component traces that are grouped together to help diagnose particular issues. Some examples of problems are message waiting indicators (MWI) problems and system problems.

- Micro traces—These are the individual component traces. Each component has up to 32 traces that you can choose from, and they normally provide more detail of the actual component or service that you want to monitor.

The Cisco Unity Diagnostic Tool also allows you or the Cisco TAC staff to perform the following tasks:

- Create new log files on demand—This makes troubleshooting a particular problem easier. When an issue can be reproduced reliably, you can close all existing log files and create new files prior to reproducing the problem. This eliminates many unnecessary and unrelated items from appearing in the logs.

- Configure log settings—You can adjust the maximum disk space allowed for all diagnostic log files. The default setting is 400 MB. The Logging Properties window also allows you to disable all diagnostic output by clearing the Diagnostic Output check box. You can also change the path of where to write the trace files. By default, they are located within the Commserver directory in the logs folder.

- Gather standard logs—This option enables you to gather all or selected Microsoft Windows event logs and Cisco Unity logs in a quick manner. This includes the System and Application Event logs.

- Disable all traces—This is a quick way to return diagnostic logs to their default settings after troubleshooting efforts are completed.

- View the event log—You can view or export the event logs for either the local computer or another computer within the Cisco Unity Diagnostic Tool.

Troubleshooting Using SysCheck

The Check Unity Configuration Wizard (SysCheck) tool, shown in Figure 11-15, is useful in troubleshooting difficulties when the Cisco Unity installation program is not able to complete due to missing rights, permissions, or applications. This is the same tool used by the setup application itself to determine if the account running the Cisco Unity setup has all the rights necessary to complete the task. Running SysCheck directly will give you more detailed information about the source of the failure and can assist you in resolving the problem.

Figure 11-15 *SysCheck Utility*

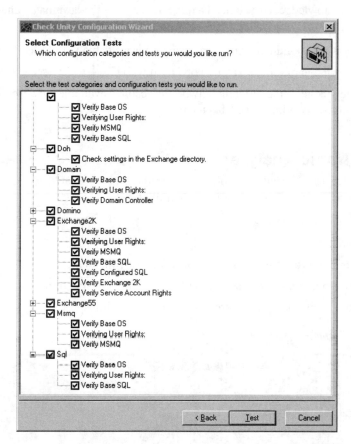

You can run SysCheck prior to installation, directly from the Cisco Unity installation CDs, or post installation to check if rights/permissions were removed from the Cisco Unity service account. You can also use this utility to check for basic database configuration issues, to check for database inconsistencies, and to see if the proper service packs and versions of applications are present. Although it has the ability to check for database inconsistencies, use the dbWalker tool for this purpose instead. SysCheck is primarily a rights-checking application.

Understanding Reporting Tools and Utilities

There are additional reporting tools that are part of the Tools Depot in Cisco Unity. These reporting tools gather important information about your Cisco Unity system. Some are useful particularly for monitoring or troubleshooting the Cisco Unity Bridge. Running them can assist you to keep a Cisco Unity system running efficiently and to isolate issues.

To benefit fully from this section, it is recommended that you have the following prerequisite skills and knowledge. (If you need a quick review, see the designated chapter, where you can find more information on the topic.)

- Knowledge of the historical reporting tools available with Cisco Unity (see Chapter 6)
- Knowledge of the messaging ports used with Cisco Unity (see Chapter 9)
- Knowledge of the different networking features available for Cisco Unity, especially Bridge networking (see Chapter 10)

Using Bridge Traffic Analyzer

The Bridge Traffic Analyzer tool, shown in Figure 11-16, enables you to obtain traffic data on your Cisco Bridge units to determine the following:

- Total size of messages sent
- Number of messages sent
- Which servers messages have come from or gone to
- How long it takes for messages to arrive at their destinations
- How many analog ports are in use for message transport

Figure 11-16 *Bridge Traffic Analyzer Tool*

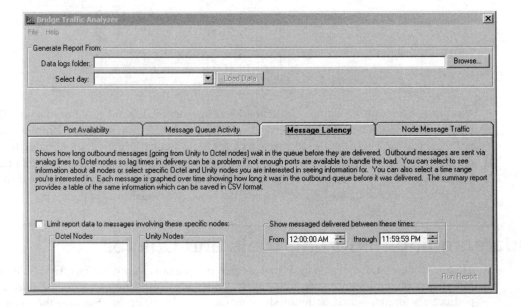

The Bridge Traffic Analyzer tool can generate four types of reports: Port Availability, Message Queue Activity, Message Latency, and Node Message Traffic.

The Port Availability report does not take any parameters; instead, it processes analog port activity on the log for the entire day. The purpose of this report is to show how many analog ports the Cisco Bridge uses to communicate to Octel nodes at any given time of the day. The report shows a bar for each minute of the day, indicating how many ports are in use and how many ports are available to take calls. You can choose to show busy ports, ports available to take calls, or both, by using the check boxes at the top of the report form.

The Message Queue Activity report shows how many messages and how much data are passing through the inbound and outbound message queues on the Bridge server. Inbound messages are those traveling from Octel nodes to the Bridge via analog lines and then to the Cisco Unity servers via IP. Outbound messages are those traveling from Cisco Unity to the Bridge via IP and then to the Octel node.

The Message Latency report enables you to see how long messages sit in the outbound queue before they are delivered to the Octel nodes via the analog lines on the Bridge. This report shows only the outbound messages because inbound messages that arrive at the Bridge server from Octel use the IP network to deliver the message, and, therefore, the total time in the queue is very short. Outbound messages, on the other hand, arrive from Cisco Unity via IP, enter the queue, and then the Bridge uses the analog lines to deliver the messages to the target Octel node. If port resources are limited on the Bridge unit, messages can wait in queue for delivery for a long time and thus create a bottleneck at the analog lines.

The Node Message Traffic report shows how many messages and how much data are passing between different Cisco Unity and Octel nodes. For example, this report can show which Octel nodes a specific Cisco Unity server exchanges messages with most heavily. As with the Message Latency report, you can run a report for a time range by selecting one or more Cisco Unity nodes.

NOTE   You can run Bridge Traffic Analyzer on or off the Cisco Unity server. The only necessity is access to the logging directory on the Bridge server. However, if possible, do not run the tool on the Cisco Unity server, to avoid adding additional overhead.

Using Port Usage Analyzer

Port Usage Analyzer, shown in Figure 11-17, can assist you to determine whether an implementation of Cisco Unity requires more ports. Having an insufficient number of ports could cause callers to receive a busy signal when they dial Cisco Unity, cause delay dialouts for message notification, or cause delayed MWIs, resulting in complaints of delayed messages.

Figure 11-17 *Port Usage Analyzer Tool*

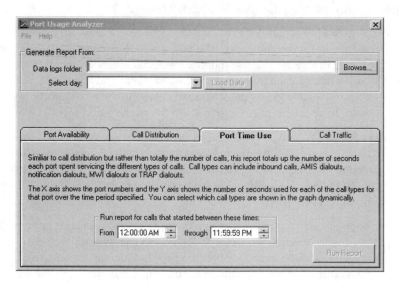

Port Usage Analyzer is a suite of four reports that is designed to give administrators a better idea of the call-traffic loads that their Cisco Unity servers are experiencing. The reports generate a graphical chart for easy analysis, which you can save in simple CSV files if you want to do more post-processing. The suite of reports includes the following, each of which has its own corresponding tab:

- **Port Availability**—This report does not have parameters to configure. Instead, it records port activity information on the log for the entire day. The purpose of this report is to show how many ports the system is using and how many are available to process incoming calls at any given time of the day. The report shows a bar for each minute of the day, indicating how many ports are in use and how many ports are available to take calls. You can choose to show busy ports, ports that are available to take calls, or both, by using the check boxes at the top of the report form.

- **Call Distribution**—This report shows what types of calls are coming in or going out of each port over the time range specified. By default, the report runs for the entire day and shows totals of call types for each port. However, you can select a custom time range to run against.

- **Port Time Use**—This report shows the same type of information that the Call Distribution report shows. However, it shows how many seconds each port was busy with each type of call. By default, the report also runs over the entire day.

- **Call Traffic**—This report shows how many of each of the five types of calls went into a port or originated from a port for each minute of the day. As with the other reports, the Call Traffic report runs over the course of the entire day, but you can zoom in from a full

24 hours to as close as 1 hour of data shown at a time using the Zoom menu. The Call Traffic report can be useful in gauging how many calls are being processed by the system during different times of the day, in particular, if Cisco Unity is acting as a call redirector to internal extensions or similar extension. In conjunction with the Port Availability report, it should give you a good idea of the traffic-load patterns that your system is experiencing over the course of a day.

Using Gather Unity System Information

The Gather Unity System Information (GUSI) utility, shown in Figure 11-18, gathers basic information about the local Cisco Unity server installation and the last 5 days' worth of Application Event and System Event log data.

Figure 11-18 *GUSI Utility*

GUSI is an easy to understand tool. When you run it, the basic system information appears in the window, as Figure 11-18 demonstrates. You can copy this information to the clipboard by selecting Paste to Clipboard from the File menu. To gather the additional Application Event log data that Cisco TAC needs for troubleshooting, you would click the Write To File button. This writes the Application Event and System Event log messages for the last 5 days, including the system information shown in the window, and bundles it all into a single cabinet file (Windows file with a .cab extension), in the directory indicated. In most cases, the default directory, under \Commserver\SystemInfo, should be fine. However, if for whatever reason you want to use a different directory, use the Browse button to select an existing directory or create a new one. You can also run this tool in silent mode and schedule it to run at a given time using the Windows Scheduler.

Understanding Unity Switch Integration Tools and Utilities

The switch integration tools, located in the Tools Depot, are a very important part of Cisco Unity's suite of tools. They are a great aid in troubleshooting the integration between Cisco Unity and a telephone system. If the integration is not set up correctly, Cisco Unity may not function properly, in which case callers may not be able to leave messages or users may not be able to retrieve their messages. At other times, technicians may spend a great deal of time troubleshooting Cisco Unity when in fact the issue is occurring on the telephone system. These switch integration tools can help in isolating these issues.

To benefit fully from this section, it is recommended that you have the following prerequisite skills and knowledge. (If you need a quick review, see the designated chapter, where you can find more information on the topic.)

- Knowledge of the different telephone switch integrations supported with Cisco Unity 4.0 (see Chapter 1, "Cisco Unified Communications System Fundamentals," and Chapter 9)

- Knowledge of Cisco Unity call flow (see Chapters 2 and 3)

Using Call Viewer

The Call Viewer application, shown in Figure 11-19, displays call information for incoming calls on an IP integration. It displays all incoming call information, which is sometimes used to create call routing rules in Cisco Unity. If any information for a call is not displayed by this application, then the switch integration did not send that information. You can use Call Viewer to initially troubleshoot calls that are not going to the proper mailbox, to view call duration, and to view the port numbers used for incoming calls.

Figure 11-19 *Call Viewer Application*

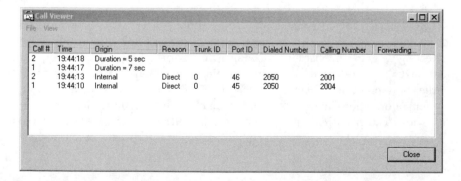

The Always on Top option on the View menu is useful when you are editing and testing new call routing rules in the System Administrator. You can have the Call Viewer open in the corner while you are testing your new rule values.

The Cisco TAC team may want to review call data on your system. Call Viewer has an option that allows you to save this information to a log file. It can log up to 1000 calls before clearing the log.

Call Viewer works only with IP integrations, such as Cisco CallManager. It does not work on circuit-switched PBXs. For circuit-switched PBXs, you would use Integration Monitor, discussed later in the chapter in the section "Using Integration Monitor."

Using the Switch Configuration Utility

The Switch Configuration utility allows you to edit specific integration information for a switch on the Cisco Unity server. You can set data such as MWI ON/OFF codes, the number of rings before Cisco Unity answers an incoming call, delays or access codes needed for out-dialing to a telephone switch, as well as tone definition settings, call supervision settings, and integration settings.

Figure 11-20 illustrates the Switch Configuration utility in Editor mode showing the Incoming Calls tab settings.

A field technician or a support person with knowledge of the switch integration features would most likely use this tool if they were applying it to an integration. The system may need to be restarted if changes are made using Switch Configuration. Use this tool carefully, because your switch integration with the phone system can possibly stop working if this tool is used incorrectly. The tool can modify Registry settings or change the protocol (language) used for the switch integration. Do not use this tool when making switch-related changes to a Cisco CallManager integration. Instead, select **Start > Settings > Control Panel > Phone and Modem Options** and click the **Advanced** tab, on which you can gain access to the TSP used by Cisco Unity and Cisco CallManager. You can also use the Cisco Unity Telephony Integration Manager tool for this purpose.

Figure 11-20 *Switch Configuration Utility*

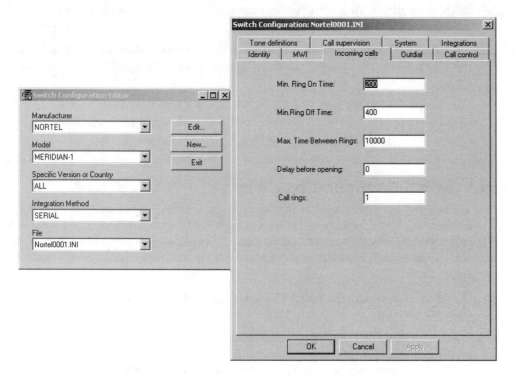

Using Integration Monitor

The Integration Monitor utility, shown in Figure 11-21, displays detailed call information that is coming from a circuit-switched phone system. This utility shows much of the same information that Call Viewer shows, but it also includes raw packet information. It also has the ability to monitor outbound call information.

Integration Monitor does not function when the integration is between Cisco Unity and Cisco CallManager. Use this tool for DTMF and Simplified Message Desk Interface (SMDI) integrations only.

Figure 11-21 *Integration Monitor Utility*

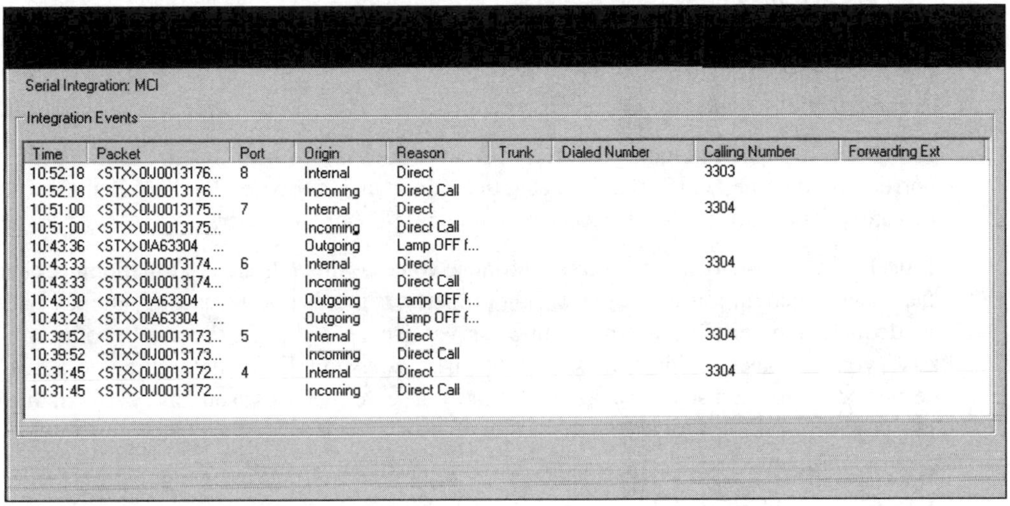

Serial Integration: MCI

Integration Events

Time	Packet	Port	Origin	Reason	Trunk	Dialed Number	Calling Number	Forwarding Ext
10:52:18	<STX>0IJ0013176...	8	Internal	Direct			3303	
10:52:18	<STX>0IJ0013176...		Incoming	Direct Call				
10:51:00	<STX>0IJ0013175...	7	Internal	Direct			3304	
10:51:00	<STX>0IJ0013175...		Incoming	Direct Call				
10:43:36	<STX>0IA63304 ...		Outgoing	Lamp OFF f...				
10:43:33	<STX>0IJ0013174...	6	Internal	Direct			3304	
10:43:33	<STX>0IJ0013174...		Incoming	Direct Call				
10:43:30	<STX>0IA63304 ...		Outgoing	Lamp OFF f...				
10:43:24	<STX>0IA63304 ...		Outgoing	Lamp OFF f...				
10:39:52	<STX>0IJ0013173...	5	Internal	Direct			3304	
10:39:52	<STX>0IJ0013173...		Incoming	Direct Call				
10:31:45	<STX>0IJ0013172...	4	Internal	Direct			3304	
10:31:45	<STX>0IJ0013172...		Incoming	Direct Call				

Troubleshooting and Monitoring Cisco PA

Issues can arise with the Cisco PA installation; however, you can use specific tools to monitor Cisco PA performance, to help you to detect any system problems, and then use other tools to troubleshoot any problems that you detect.

An efficiently running Cisco PA system greatly increases the customer's satisfaction with the product. Knowledge of how to troubleshoot Cisco PA will help you to find a resolution to a problem quicker.

To benefit fully from this section, it is recommended that you have the following prerequisite skills and knowledge. (If you need a quick review, see the designated chapter, where you can find more information on the topic.)

- Knowledge of the Cisco PA architecture (see Chapter 8)
- Knowledge of the Cisco PA call flow (see Chapter 1)

Resolving Issues Encountered when Using PA

You may encounter many common issues with Cisco PA. Here is a quick list:

- Users are unable to access the user interface
- Users are unable to use speech commands
- Users are offered too many dial-by-name options

- Dial rules are not working properly
- Users cannot browse voice mail

If you encounter other issues that are not listed here, a good place to look for a resolution is in the "Troubleshooting Cisco Personal Assistant" chapter of the *Cisco Personal Assistant Administration Guide* available at Cisco.com.

If a user is not able to log in to the Cisco PA user interface, verify that the user is using the correct login name, which should match the unique user attribute identified in the corporate directory. This may be the user's e-mail name or telephone number.

If users have to use touch-tone dialing because voice commands are not functioning, check that the speech-recognition server is working properly. If that is not the cause, you may have an inadequate number of speech-recognition server licenses to handle the number of users. In that case, you may need to add more speech licenses. You should also make sure you refresh the servers after you add any new speech-recognition server licenses. You must perform this before those servers can support users.

Users may report that too many matches are offered when they are using dial-by-name. Lowering the Max Disambiguate parameter located within the speech-recognition settings on the Cisco PA server will reduce the number of matches.

When searching for options on how to configure dial rules, it is possible to configure them in Cisco PA through the Cisco PA administration interface or through the user interface. Those that are set through the administration interface take priority. Therefore, if a user configures a dial rule that conflicts with one configured by the administrator, the system uses the administrator's dial rule.

If all users are unable to browse their voice-mail messages in Cisco Unity through Cisco PA, then select **System > Messaging** and check the messaging configuration. Cisco PA requires the use of unqualified DNS names to identify the voice-mail servers; in other words, Unity1 must be used rather than Unity1.domain.com. The IP address of the voice-mail server will also not work if it is used in place of the unqualified DNS name.

If only one user cannot browse their voice-mail messages, you should check to see that the user's voice mailbox number matches the user's extension in Cisco CallManager, and that the user's ID is the same in both as well.

Monitoring Performance of PA

Here is a list of performance monitor counters that are common when troubleshooting Cisco PA:

- Calls Answered
- Dial-by-Name: Disambiguations
- Dial-by-Name: Reconfirmations

- Dial-by-Name: Speech System Error
- Voice Mail
- Voice Mail Login Failure
- Voice Mail Reconfirmation

Cisco PA monitoring counters use Microsoft Windows Performance Monitor. These counters are helpful in determining issues that occur. For example, if there are many Dial-by-Name: Disambiguations, this may indicate issues related with speech recognition. Other counters may be helpful in determining whether the system requires additional resources for more speech-recognition sessions or overall Cisco PA sessions.

The "Troubleshooting" section of the *Cisco Personal Assistant Administration Guide,* available at Cisco.com, includes an explanation of all the counters.

Collecting Call History, Trace, and Debug Information

A customer may ask you to investigate telephone toll fraud on its system. The Call History logs can help you to track this information. The first line in the log file tells you how to read the call history records.

Cisco PA writes call history records to a series of files named PACallHistory*xx*.log while *xx* represents the range 00 to 99. These are stored on the Cisco PA server under the \logs folder. Each log is limited to 2 MB; when the logs are full, they start to write over existing log information.

Here is a list of some of the characteristics of call history information:

- Used to identify toll fraud
- PACallHistory*xx*.log in \logs folder
- Each log limited to 2 MB
- 100 files
- Overwrites when full

Cisco PA can also use the CiscoWorks 2000 Syslog facility, in which case syslog receives the call history information.

Cisco TAC may request traces from the Cisco PA server if you contact it for assistance on an issue. Collecting traces can have a performance impact on the system. Therefore, you should capture traces only when requested by Cisco TAC. Once the traces are captured, you can turn the traces off. Traces are set under the System Configuration menu in Cisco PA. When you go to the Traces page, you can select which traces to collect, and then click Save. After you do this, the traces start to be captured immediately. When you are finished collecting the traces, turn off the trace and then debug by clicking Clear All for each of the options you selected before and then clicking Save.

The following are the trace packages available, in which the packages trace:

- **PASRV**—Main PA server system
- **SS_PA_TEL**—Telephony system
- **SS_PA**—PA subsystem for LDAP access
- **SS_PA_MAIL**—Subsystem that interacts with the voice mail and paging
- **PASCCP**—Skinny protocol subsystem (SPS)
- **PARULES**—Rules-based call routing subsystem
- **PASpeech**—Speech-recognition subsystem
- **PADtmf**—DTMF interface
- **PAVmail**—Speech-enabled voice-mail package
- **PADbn**—Dial-by-name subsystem
- **DialRules**—System-wide dialing rules subsystem
- **GRMR**—Speech grammar generation
- **PASpokenName**—Subsystem that records the user's spoken name
- **Perfmon**—Performance monitoring subsystem

The collected trace information is stored in the \logs folder of the Cisco PA directory.

If you install CiscoWorks 2000 Syslog, the system will also write the collected trace information to syslog.

Example 11-1 shows a sample of the type of information that is found in the Cisco PA log files.

Example 11-1 *Cisco PA Log Files Sample Text*

```
21122: Sep 06 12:00:14.229 PDT %PA-PASpeech-7-DEBUG:4006: nresult = 0
21123: Sep 06 12:00:14.229 PDT %PA-PASpeech-7-DEBUG:4006: pauser is null for
disambiguation
21124: Sep 06 12:00:14.229 PDT %PA-PASpeech-7-DEBUG:4006: Nothing to disambiguate ..
21125: Sep 06 12:00:14.229 PDT %PA-PASpeech-7-DEBUG:4006: cmd = exit confidence=45
21126: Sep 06 12:00:14.229 PDT %PA-PASpeech-7-DEBUG:4006: MainMenu: isCmdexit:
condition check is true
21127: Sep 06 12:00:14.229 PDT %PA-PASpeech-6-INFO:PAVmailDialog: Entering the onExit
method
21128: Sep 06 12:00:14.229 PDT %PA-PASpeech-6-INFO:PAVmailDialog: Entering the
prepareEndResult method
21129: Sep 06 12:00:14.292 PDT %PA-PASpeech-6-INFO:4006: PAVmailDialog: play
VMAIL_PA_TRANSFER
21130: Sep 06 12:00:14.292 PDT %PA-PASpeech-6-INFO:4006: PAVmailDialog: exceptions,
return to PA
21131: Sep 06 12:00:14.292 PDT %PA-PASpeech-6-INFO:PAVmailDialog: Exiting the
prepareEndResult method
```

Chapter Summary

In this chapter, you learned about the guidelines for backing up Cisco Unity, about the different selected Cisco Unity utilities and tools, and about the troubleshooting approaches for Cisco Unity and Cisco PA.

Specifically, you learned about the function of the following utilities and tools:

- Selected Cisco Unity Administration tools
- Set Record Format
- Set WAV Format
- WaveGain
- Database Walker
- Diagnostic Traces
- SysCheck
- Bridge Traffic Analyzer
- Port Usage Analyzer
- Gather Unity System Information (GUSI)
- Call Viewer
- Switch Configuration
- Integration Monitor

You also learned how to do the following:

- Resolve selected PA issues
- Collect call history information
- Monitor PA performance
- Set and collect trace and debug information

For additional information on the topics presented in this chapter, refer to these resources:

- Cisco Unity white papers
  - Backing Up and Restoring a Cisco Unity Server
  - Security Best Practices for Cisco Unity
- *Cisco Unity Troubleshooting Guide*
- *Cisco Unity System Administration Guide*
- *Cisco Unity Bridge Networking Guide*
- Various Cisco Unity Integration guides
- *Cisco Personal Assistant Administration Guide*

These references can be found by going to Cisco.com and searching for the exact reference names.

Chapter Review Questions

Use this section to test yourself on how well you learned the concepts discussed in this chapter. You can find the answers to the review question for this chapter in Appendix A.

1 A Standard Cisco Unity Backup should include what components?

2 When is the best time to perform backups of a Cisco Unity system?

3 Which utility can you use to view the flow patterns of call handlers that are configured in the Cisco Unity database?

4 Suppose that you have ten subscribers in Cisco Unity and you would like to require them to change their phone password the next time they log in. Which Cisco utility best helps you to set this up quickly?

5 John Smith has two accounts in Exchange, one for voice mail only and the other for e-mail. He would like to have only one account for both functions. Which Cisco Unity utility can help you to consolidate these into one account for John?

6 Which Cisco Unity tool can you use to change the codec of all standard greetings and voice names from G.711 to G.729?

7 Which Cisco Unity utility can examine the Cisco Unity database by performing a series of checks on all call handler, subscriber, subscriber template, interview handler, location and directory handler objects in the database?

8 When using Bridge networking with Cisco Unity, which reporting tool can show you the amount of message traffic on your Bridge server?

9 If your organization has a Cisco Unity system integrated with a Cisco CallManager system, and some calls are not going to the proper mailbox, which Cisco Unity tool can you use to see call information that is received from CallManager?

10 If users are reporting that too many matches show up when they are using the dial-by-name feature in Cisco PA, what can you do to reduce the number of matches?

Chapter Review Questions

Chapter 1

1 *Name three of the standard features new to Cisco Unity 4.0.*

   Answer: The following are new standard features introduced in Cisco Unity 4.0:

   - Cisco PCA
   - CUGA
   - FlexLM software security
   - Live Reply
   - Flex Stack
   - 12- to 24-hour clock support
   - CUSPA
   - CUICA
   - DVD installation
   - Multiple directory handlers
   - SIP
   - Additional EMEA voice board support:
       - D/120JCT-LS and D/120JCT-Euro revision II cards
       - D/41JCT-LS and D/41JCT-Euro cards

2 *Name an optional networking feature that is new in Unity 4.0.*

   Answer: The following is the new networking feature introduced in Cisco Unity 4.0:

   - VPIM. Cisco Unity voice-mail only (VM) and Cisco Unity unified messaging (UM) for Exchange support VPIM with the Meridian Net Gateway for Meridian Mail, Mitel/Baypoint NuPoint Messenger, and Nortel CallPilot

3 *What new feature enables Cisco Unity to transfer a user immediately to the subscriber who left a message that the user is currently listening to?*

   Answer: Live Reply.

4 *True/False: Cisco Unity 4.0 now supports multiple directory handlers.*

Answer: True. This is a new feature in Cisco Unity 4.0.

5 *Which IETF standard does Cisco Unity now support in version 4.0?*

Answer: SIP.

6 *What client software package allows Unified Messaging on Lotus Notes client desktops with Cisco Unity?*

Answer: DUCS, which IBM Lotus developed.

7 *Name three of the qualified third-party fax solutions for Cisco Unity Integrated Faxing.*

Answer:

- Biscom FAXCOM for Microsoft Exchange, Version 6.19 or later
- Captaris RightFax Version 6 or later
- Esker FaxGate Version 7 or later
- Fenestrae FAXination Version 4 or later
- Interstar LightningFAX Version 5.5 or later
- Omtool Fax Sr. Version 3 or later
- Optus FACSys Version 4.5 or later
- TOPCALL, all versions

8 *What text-to-speech engine does Cisco Unity 4.0 support?*

Answer: The RealSpeak engine.

9 *What new networking feature in Cisco Unity 4.0 uses a standard that is based on the SMTP and MIME protocols?*

Answer: VPIM networking.

10 *When using Cisco PA, what feature enables you to be transferred to a person by saying that person's name?*

Answer: Name dialing, in PA.

11 *What Cisco PA feature can provide users with notification of upcoming appointments on the phone display?*

Answer: IP Phone Productivity Services, which is an optional feature of Cisco PA.

Chapter 2

1 *Explain briefly the process that occurs when a Cisco Unity subscriber logs in to the system for the first time.*

Answer: When a subscriber accesses the system for the first time and presses * (if the system does not recognize the calling party number) and then enters their extension number, they typically are presented with a special first-time subscriber conversation that is meant to enroll them in the system. If the system recognizes the calling party number as a subscriber, it logs in the subscriber with the default password. The system prompts the subscriber to record a voice name and a personal greeting. It then provides the opportunity to set a password.

2 *List four typical voice-mail subscriber options when using the TUI.*

Answer: Check messages, send messages, review messages, change message options.

3 *List at least two items that can be customized in the VMO settings.*

Answer: Modify sound notifications, change the saving of outbound messages in the Sent Items folder, configure automatic playback of messages, enable download prior to playback.

4 *When a user is prompted for a PIN by Cisco PA, what is the result when the PIN cannot be verified due to an incorrect entry?*

Answer: If Cisco PA cannot verify the entered PIN, the subscriber is transferred to the Cisco Unity voice-mail system and prompted to enter the password established with it.

5 *Which interface allows a subscriber to configure Rule-Sets to enable call forwarding based on personal preferences for PA?*

Answer: The Cisco PA User Administration web interface.

6 *Each subscriber must set a password as mandated by the subscriber template in effect at login. If a subscriber loses or forgets the password set, what course of action should be taken?*

Answer: Only a Cisco Unity administrator can delete the existing password and set a new temporary password for the subscriber. The subscriber should change the temporary password at first login.

7 *Describe the circumstance that will cause the MWI on the subscriber phone to be turned off.*

Answer: The last unheard message in the voice mailbox must be heard in its entirety.

8 *To configure call hold and screening features, which utility, discussed in this chapter, should be used?*

Answer: The Cisco Unity Assistant inside the Cisco Unity PCA.

9 *For Cisco PA to be fully used by a subscriber, it must be able to retrieve subscriber information from an LDAP directory. Under what circumstance does this feature properly function?*

Answer: Only with a CCM integration.

10 *Cisco PA's voice-recognition capabilities allow voice message access using voice commands. List at least two tasks that are possible using voice commands.*

Answer: List or read messages, skip messages, delete messages, and call back the sender of the message (if the message was left by a subscriber in the corporate directory).

Chapter 3

1 *List the three basic sections of the Cisco Unity System Administrator page.*

Answer: Title bar, navigation bar, and page body.

2 *List the two basic methods of authentication that are available for Cisco Unity subscribers.*

Answer: Integrated Windows authentication and Anonymous authentication.

3 *Which of the two authentication types is more easily configured? Why?*

Answer: Integrated Windows authentication is more easily configured because it is the default method in IIS. No configuration is necessary to implement it.

4 *How many system administrator accounts can be logged in to the Cisco Unity System Administrator tool concurrently?*

Answer: Five.

5 *List at least three options available on the Configuration Settings page and their functions.*

Answer: Refer to Table 3-2.

6 *On a date for which the Cisco Unity server has been configured as a holiday, which greeting will callers hear upon calling in?*

Answer: Callers will hear the Closed greeting as configured by the administrator for such days.

7 *Instead of using a hardware key for Cisco Unity licensing, what is used in Cisco Unity 4.x?*

Answer: FlexLM licensing and license files stored on the Cisco Unity server.

8 *Which tool can be used to retrieve near real-time port statistics?*

Answer: The port monitor in Status Monitor (web-based).

9 *List two methods that can be used to alter greetings.*

Answer: Phone or multimedia device.

10 *List two predefined call handlers.*

Answer: Operator handler and Opening Greeting.

Chapter 4

1   *If Account Lockout is enabled, how many logon failures are required, by default, to lock a subscriber account?*

Answer: After six failed logon attempts within any 30-minute period, an account is locked out. This is the default setting. The account is reinstated after 60 minutes.

2   *When does a change made in the Account Policy page take effect?*

Answer: Account policy changes take effect immediately for all subscribers. Subscribers are subject to the settings at next logon.

3   *A group of subscribers defined in the Cisco Unity system as sharing a common collection of system features and privileges is known as what?*

Answer: A COS.

4   *Where do you specify a CoS to place it into production to govern subscribers?*

Answer: A COS is specified in the subscriber template.

5   *Cisco Unity provides three default distribution lists to provide the ability to send messages to multiple users simultaneously. List each of these three distribution lists and its purpose.*

Answer: The following are the three public distribution lists that are created by default:

All Subscribers—All subscribers are automatically added to this list upon creation.

Unaddressed Messages—Subscribers assigned to this list receive messages left in the Operator call handler mailbox. This is typically a repository for messages received when the operator is not available. Any message that is deemed undeliverable is also forwarded to this list (for example, when a subscriber mailbox is full).

System Event Messages—Subscribers added to this list receive messages from the Event Notification utility. This could include error messages, problem notifications, or warnings about potential problems with the Cisco Unity server.

Initially, the Example Administrator account is the sole member of both the Unaddressed Messages and System Event Messages distribution lists.

6   *What information can be specified by a subscriber template?*

Answer: The following information can be specified by a subscriber template:

- Account
- Passwords
- Conversation
- Call Transfer
- Greetings

- Caller Input
- Messages
- Distribution Lists
- Messages Notification

7 *Subscriber templates provide a powerful tool for setting user options. What should be configured prior to the creation of any subscriber templates?*

Answer: One of the first settings in a subscriber template configuration is the CoS. Before you create any subscriber template, you must define a CoS so that it can be applied to the subscriber template.

8 *A Cisco Unity subscriber can create private distribution lists. How many lists may be created by subscribers and administrators in Cisco Unity 4.0(2) or later? Where are they created?*

Answer: There is no defined limit. Private lists are defined in the Cisco Unity Assistant or via the subscriber telephone.

9 *Cisco Unity has the capability to place a call to any subscriber to notify them of new messages. What means of notification are available to subscribers when new messages arrive?*

Answer: Telephone, pager, or e-mail.

10 *List the Cisco Unity accounts created by the Cisco Unity installation process.*

Answer: Installer, Example Administrator, and Example Subscriber. There is also an account named the Unity server name messaging account. This account is hidden and does not take up a user license (unlike the other default accounts).

Chapter 5

1 *List the three predefined call handlers.*

Answer: Opening Greeting, Operator Greeting, and Goodbye Greeting.

2 *Which default call handler is used to allow callers to search for subscribers in a Cisco Unity system?*

Answer: The Directory handler.

3 *Which call handler page provides detailed information about ownership, ownership type, and name of a call handler?*

Answer: The Profile page.

4 *If a voice message is less than 1 second in length, how does the Cisco Unity system handle it?*

Answer: Calls lasting less than 1 second are deleted and the Cisco Unity system generates an event in the application log.

5 *If a call is compared to all rules in the call routing table, and it matches none of the defined rules, how will the call be routed?*

Answer: The last rule in any call routing table is the Default Call Handler. This rule exists to catch calls that do not match any other rules in the table.

6 *In call routing rules, a call can be forwarded to a number of potential destinations. Among these are destinations known as Attempt Sign-In and Sign-In. What is the difference between these two call destinations?*

Answer: Attempt Sign-In attempts to match the calling number to that of the subscriber. If a match is found, the call is sent to the subscriber logon conversation. If not, the next rule in the table is applied to the call.

Sign-In sends the call to the subscriber logon conversation, causing the system to prompt for the subscriber extension rather than checking the calling number. This allows a sign-in from any phone or extension.

7 *What page can be used to set up one-key dialing on a call handler?*

Answer: The Caller Input page.

8 *The Cisco Unity system provides two default routing tables. List them along with a brief description of each.*

Answer:

Direct Calls—Handles calls from subscribers and unidentified callers that are directly dialed to the Cisco Unity system; for example, a subscriber who is calling to check their voice mail and retrieve messages.

Forwarded Calls—Handles calls that are forwarded to Cisco Unity from a subscriber extension or an extension that is not associated with a subscriber account; for example, an external call that is forwarded to the Cisco Unity system because the subscriber has set the Call Forward No Answer option. The subscriber extension does not ring. Instead, the call is automatically redirected to the subscriber's configured greeting.

9 *List the five greetings you can use on a call handler.*

Answer: Alternate, Busy, Closed, Internal, and Standard greetings.

10 *Which call handler is typically used at the end of a call cycle within the Cisco Unity system?*

Answer: The Goodbye greeting.

Chapter 6

1 *What are Cisco Unity real-time monitoring tools?*

Answer: Cisco real-time monitoring tools capture and display system functions as they occur. These tools are the HTML Status Monitor, Status Monitor program, and Port Status Monitor program.

2 *What information does the HTML-based Status Monitor application provide?*

Answer: The HTML-based Status Monitor application provides information about the status of the Cisco Unity system. It can tell you whether Cisco Unity is running, provide status information for ports, the status on reports that are in queue, and display disk statistics.

3 *List the items to consider when maintaining a Cisco Unity server.*

Answer: These are tasks to consider when maintaining a Cisco Unity server:

- Forward unaddressed messages to the appropriate recipients.
- Scan for viruses.
- Keep virus-scanning definitions up to date.
- Run Exchange Optimizer on Exchange 5.5 when more than 100 subscribers are added.
- Keep up to date with Cisco Unity qualified service packs and hot fixes.
- Run the Exchange Eseutil utility twice a year.
- Verify that the backup medium used has enough available space to back up the Cisco Unity server.
- Back up Cisco Unity and message stores regularly.
- Include Cisco Unity servers in the schedule if you are restarting other network servers.
- Run the DBWalker utility.
- Check that messages left in the UMR are delivered to subscriber mailboxes.
- Check whether Cisco Unity Administrator sessions are not being released and whether any are not being used.
- If using Exchange, check for mailboxes that are over their storage limit.
- If using Exchange, schedule mailbox maintenance tasks using the Message Store Manager.
- Update the system clock.
- Monitor forums that are available for Cisco Unity.

4 *When generating a Cisco Unity report, which two file formats can you choose from to have Cisco Unity generate the report?*

Answer: Cisco Unity can generate the report in either web page (HTML) or CSV format.

5 *When running a Cisco Unity report, if you suspect that it will be larger than 220 MB, which file format should you use?*

Answer: At present, web browsers are limited to opening files of no more than 220 MB. Try using the comma-delimited format.

6 *If there are some Cisco Unity reports in queue and the an administrator stops Cisco Unity, what happens to the reports?*

Answer: Cisco Unity deletes the reports in queue.

7 *A user is stating that their MWI does not turn on immediately after they receive a message on their Cisco Unity voice mailbox. Which Cisco Unity Subscriber report can you run to help troubleshoot this issue?*

Answer: The Subscriber Message Activity report will help to troubleshoot this issue.

8 *When you want to track which system administrator changed values in Cisco Unity and what values they changed, which System report will help you track these changes?*

Answer: The Administrative Access Activity report will assist in finding this information.

9 *Which Cisco Unity report will help you determine how many times callers simply hung up from the opening greeting?*

Answer: The Call Handler Traffic report can help in finding out this information.

10 *What are some of the PA statistics you can monitor by using Performance Monitor counters?*

Answer: You can use Performance Monitor counters to keep track of the following information:

- Total number of calls made to Cisco PA
- Number of errors in the speech system while callers were trying to dial a party by name
- Total number of times callers were asked to access voice mail

Chapter 7

1 *List two hardware manufacturers that are certified to provide Cisco Unity server and PA server functionality.*

Answer: IBM and HP.

2 *Which overlay template supports quad-processor capabilities, but does not require it?*

Answer: Platform Overlay 4.

3 *Which voice card provides the highest density of ports available for a Cisco Unity server?*

Answer: Intel/Dialogic D/240PCI-T1 provides 24 digital ports.

4 *Which voice card(s) provides four-port connectivity?*

Answer: Intel/Dialogic D/41EPCI, D/41JCT-LS, D/41JCT-Euro, and Brooktrout Technology TR114+P4L.

5 *List three types of optional hardware that are supported by the Cisco TAC.*

Answer: External modem, tape drive, UPS, mass storage array, and multiple NICs.

6 *List two types of unsupported hardware configurations that are not supported by the Cisco TAC.*

Answer: SAN solutions, and multiple IP addresses on load-balancing NICs.

7 *What codecs can you use when integrating Cisco CallManager with Cisco Unity?*

Answer: Cisco Unity accepts only G.729 and G.711 calls from a Cisco CallManager.

8 *List three unsupported hardware configurations for Cisco Unity.*

Answer: Multiple NICs for load balancing, remote data storage connectivity through frame or packet switch fabrics or networks, such as Fibre Channel, InfiniBand, or IP packetization, and multiple IP addresses for two or more load-balanced NICs.

9 *What type of modem is typically recommended for use with the Cisco Unity system?*

Answer: A v.34 external modem, which is provided by the customer.

10 *How many voice ports does the Intel/Dialogic D/240PCI-T1 card provide?*

Answer: The Intel/Dialogic D/240PCI-T1 voice card provides 24 ports.

Chapter 8

1 *Name the different message stores that you can choose when installing Cisco Unity 4.0.*

Answer: Exchange 5.5, Exchange 2000, Exchange 2003 (with Cisco Unity 4.0(3) and later), and Lotus Domino are the message stores supported for Cisco Unity 4.0.

2 *When is the Microsoft SQL Server 2000 software required for a Cisco Unity installation, as opposed to the MSDE?*

Answer: For Cisco Unity systems that require UM or more than 32 ports, SQL Server 2000 is required. If the system will be a VoiceMail-only setup with 32 ports or less, then MSDE can be used. It is also required for all Cisco Unity Failover configurations.

3 *Which component developed by IBM Lotus can be used to integrate Cisco Unity 4.0 with Domino R5/R6?*

Answer: You can use the DUCS component provided by IBM Lotus.

4 *Name the three major components Cisco PA consists of.*

Answer: The three major components Cisco PA software consists of are Cisco PA Server, PA Web Administration, and PA Speech Recognition Server.

5 *When is Windows 2000 Advanced Server required for Cisco Unity 4.0?*

Answer: Windows 2000 Advanced Server is required for Cisco Unity Platform Overlay 4 and 5 servers when performing a new installation, replacing an existing system, or purchasing an additional Cisco Unity Platform 4 or 5 server.

6 *What configuration setup is supported with Cisco Unity for Domino?*

Answer: Cisco Unity for Domino currently is supported in a UM configuration with Domino installed off-box.

7 *When installing Cisco PA 1.4, where can the Cisco PA Speech Recognition Server software be installed?*

Answer: The Cisco PA Speech Recognition Server software can be installed on the PA server or on its own server.

8 *When preparing to install VMO on a client machine, where is this software found?*

Answer: VMO software can be found on the Cisco Unity Installation CD 1 in the ViewMail folder.

9 *What does the CUSPA tool do?*

Answer: The CUSPA tool helps you to prepare your Cisco Unity system for a Cisco Unity installation. It checks the Cisco Unity server for the required software and service packs.

10 *Which version of PA must your system be on to upgrade to PA 1.4?*

Answer: The PA system must be on Version 1.3(3) before you upgrade to PA 1.4.

Chapter 9

1 *Name the three main integration features present when integration between Cisco Unity and a PBX takes place.*

Answer: The following are the three main features present when integration between Cisco Unity and a PBX takes place:

- Call forward to a personal greeting
- Easy message access
- Message waiting indicators

2 *What communications protocol does Cisco Unity use to communicate with Cisco CallManager?*

Answer: Cisco Unity uses SCCP to communicate with Cisco CallManager systems.

3 *When using PA, what type of ports must you configure in CCM?*

Answer: You must configure CTI route points in CCM for PA to work.

4 *List at least three types of integration that Cisco Unity 4.0 uses to integrate with telephone systems.*

Answer: The following are the types of integration that Cisco Unity 4.0 uses to integrate with various telephone systems:

- IP integration
- DTMF integration
- SMDI integration
- PBXLink integration
- SIP integration

5 *When using DTMF integration, what mechanism does Cisco Unity use to turn on a lamp on a phone?*

Answer: Cisco Unity sends DTMF tones to the telephone system to tell it to turn MWI on or off on a particular phone.

6 *What type of cable does the SMDI integration usually use to send information about a call?*

Answer: An SMDI integration usually uses an RS-232 cable to connect the voice-mail system and telephone system to send call information.

7 *When using PBXLink integration, you attach the PBXLink box to the PBX using what type of lines?*

Answer: You attach the PBXLink to the PBX via digital lines.

8 *In Cisco Unity, what is another name for a messaging port?*

Answer: Session is another term for messaging port in Cisco Unity.

9 *What is the TRAP Connection setting used for on the Cisco Unity messaging ports?*

Answer: TRAP Connection is used during telephone recording and playback of greetings through the Media Master Control in Cisco Unity.

10 *List at least three telephone systems that Cisco Unity 4.0 currently supports.*

Answer: The following are the currently supported telephone systems for Cisco Unity 4.0:

- Alcatel 4400 (DTMF)
- Avaya Definity G3 (DTMF)
- Avaya Definity Gx (PBXLink)
- Avaya Definity ProLogix (DTMF)
- CCM (IP)
- Cisco SIP Proxy Server (SIP)

- Centrex (SMDI)
- ECI Coral III (Serial)
- Ericsson MD-110 (Serial)
- Fujitsu 9600 (Serial)
- Intecom E14 Millenium (Serial)
- Matra 6500 (DTMF)
- Mitel SX-200, SX-2000 (DTMF) ONS
- NEC NEAX 2000, 2400 (Serial) MCI
- Nortel Meridian 1 (PBXLink)
- Siemens 9751 9006i (DTMF)
- Siemens Hicom 300 (DTMF)
- Syntegra ITS (SMDI)
- Syntegra ITS (SMDI)

Chapter 10

1 *When implementing SMTP networking by itself between a Cisco Unity system and a non–Cisco Unity server, without IVC, in what format do recipients receive voice messages on the non–Cisco Unity server?*

Answer: Voice messages appear as e-mails with WAV attachments because the voice attributes do not arrive at the non[nd]Cisco Unity servers when using only SMTP networking.

2 *When using SMTP networking between two Cisco Unity servers that do not share the same global directory, are the voice attributes preserved when sending voice messages between the Cisco Unity systems and using IVC?*

Answer: Yes. Voice-mail messages between these two Cisco Unity systems have the ability to retain their voice attributes because of IVC. Not installing IVC would result in a message arriving at its destination as an e-mail with a WAV attachment.

3 *If you plan to use VPIM networking to communicate with a third-party messaging system, and you have several Cisco Unity servers networked together, how many Cisco Unity servers require the VPIM license?*

Answer: Only one requires the VPIM license and VPIM configuration.

4 *What method of communication does AMIS networking use with Cisco Unity to transfer voice messages between voice-messaging systems?*

Answer: AMIS networking uses the PSTN to place calls to transfer the voice messages. It uses standard analog telephone lines to exchange voice-mail messages with other systems.

5 *What tool do you use to create the UAmis and UOmni accounts for AMIS networking and Bridge networking, respectively?*

Answer: You use the ConfigMgr tool, located in the \Commserver folder of the Cisco Unity server.

6 *What types of voice-mail systems can Cisco Unity communicate with when using Bridge networking?*

Answer: Cisco Unity uses Bridge networking to communicate with supported Octel voice-mail systems. You can find a list of supported Octel systems in the *Cisco Unity Pre-Installation Guide* found at Cisco.com.

7 *What types of messages can the UOmni mailbox receive when using Bridge networking?*

Answer: The UOmni mailbox can receive messages that provide notification of automatic creation, modification, and deletion of Bridge subscribers as a result of Octel NameNet emulation.

8 *When Cisco Unity synchronizes its Unity SQL database with the global directory, what type of information copies over onto the directory?*

Answer: Only information that is needed to address messages to subscribers, find them, and transfer a call to their phone is stored in the global directory. The type of information copied to the directory includes:

- First name
- Last name
- Display name
- Recorded voice name
- E-mail alias
- Fax ID
- Primary ID
- Up to nine alternate IDs
- Location object assignment
- System ID
- Transfer string

9 *When determining the type of Cisco networking to use, what is the preferred choice when all the target servers are Cisco Unity servers and all use the same global directory?*

Answer: Digital networking is the best choice.

10 *You are the administrator of one Cisco Unity server in an organization that is using networking to communicate with other messaging systems. If you log in to your server using Cisco Unity Administrator, what location objects can you not delete from this server?*

Answer: You cannot delete the primary location, or any other delivery locations that were created on remote Cisco Unity servers that other administrators configured. Delivery locations created on a remote Cisco Unity server appear as read-only on the local system. You can, however, delete delivery locations created locally on that Cisco Unity server.

Chapter 11

1 *A Standard Cisco Unity Backup should include what components?*

Answer: A Cisco Unity standard backup should include the following components when backing up your Cisco Unity system:

- Cisco Unity
- Operating system (OS)
- Exchange (Domino) information store and Directory
- Exchange (Domino) mailboxes
- Structured Query Language (SQL)
- System state

2 *When is the best time to perform backups of a Cisco Unity system?*

Answer: The best time to perform backups of a Cisco Unity system is when the system is the least busy—when the system is not processing many calls, such as after regular business hours or when there are no other tasks running. This may also include a time when the system is not generating system reports.

3 *Which utility can you use to view the flow patterns of call handlers that are configured in the Cisco Unity database?*

Answer: Audio Text Manager allows you to view the following settings: Call Handlers, Subscriber information, Interviewer Handler, as well as Directory handler information.

4 *Suppose that you have ten subscribers in Cisco Unity and you would like to require them to change their phone password the next time they log in. Which Cisco utility best helps you to set this up quickly?*

Answer: The Bulk Edit utility allows you to set this for all ten subscribers at one time.

5 *John Smith has two accounts in Exchange, one for voice mail only and the other for e-mail. He would like to have only one account for both functions. Which Cisco Unity utility can help you to consolidate these into one account for John?*

Answer: Migrate Subscriber Data Tool allows you to move subscriber settings from a Cisco Unity subscriber account to a regular mail user account.

6 *Which Cisco Unity tool can you use to change the codec of all standard greetings and voice names from G.711 to G.729?*

Answer: You can use the Set Wave Format tool to convert existing standard greetings and voice names from G.711 to G.729.

7 *Which Cisco Unity utility can examine the Cisco Unity database by performing a series of checks on all call handler, subscriber, subscriber template, interview handler, locations, and directory handler objects in the database?*

Answer: The Database Walker utility examines the Cisco Unity database for these things.

8 *When using Bridge networking with Cisco Unity, which reporting tool can show you the amount of message traffic on your Bridge server?*

Answer: Bridge Traffic Analyzer can show you message traffic on your Bridge server.

9 *If your organization has a Cisco Unity system integrated with a Cisco CallManager system, and some calls are not going to the proper mailbox, which Cisco Unity tool can you use to see call information that is received from CallManager?*

Answer: Call Viewer helps you to troubleshoot this situation. Call Viewer can be used to troubleshoot Cisco Unity with an IP integration.

10 *If users are reporting that too many matches show up when they are using the dial-by-name feature in Cisco PA, what can you do to reduce the number of matches?*

Answer: Lower the value of the Max Disambiguate parameter located within the speech-recognition settings on the Cisco PA server.

INDEX

Symbols

E

DISCUSS
NETWORKING PRODUCTS AND TECHNOLOGIES WITH CISCO EXPERTS AND NETWORKING PROFESSIONALS WORLDWIDE

VISIT NETWORKING PROFESSIONALS A CISCO ONLINE COMMUNITY WWW.CISCO.COM/GO/DISCUSS

CISCO SYSTEMS

THIS IS THE POWER OF THE NETWORK. now.